MARTYN'S NOTES ON JAFFNA

PURCHASED MARTYN'S NOTES ON JAFFNA

CHRONOLOGICAL, HISTORICAL, BIOGRAPHICAL

JOHN. H. MARTYN

WITH AN APPENDIX

GYAN

Published by

Gyan Publishing House
5, Ansari Road
Daryaganj, New Delhi-110002
Phone: 011-47034999, 9811692060
E-mail: books@gyanbooks.com

Distribution Network
gyanbooks.com
India, USA, Canada, UK, Australia, France

ISBN : 978-81-212-3763-5 (PB)
First Published, 1923

2nd Impression 2020

Printed at: Gyan Press, Delhi.

Purchased Martyn's Notes on Jaffna
Author: John. H. Martyn

NOTES ON JAFFNA

Chronological, Historical, Biographical

etc.

With an Appendix

BY

JOHN H. MARTYN

American Ceylon Mission Press
Tellippalai Ceylon
1923

To

The memory of

Henry Martyn Esquire,

One of the first Graduates of the far-famed
" Batticotta Seminary ",

who rose to the singular distinction of being the
first Journalist and first Photographer
among the Ceylonese

and who was well and widely known as a sound
English and Tamil Scholar, Scientist, Poet,
Artist and Mathematician,

This book is affectionately

Dedicated

By (his son)

The Compiler

PREFACE

To my countrymen, the Jaffnese, to whom Jaffna should ever be dear, this compilation, I trust, can not fail to be of interest. For them it is chiefly intended, and of them and their country it treats. Whatever may be the defects or short-comings of the work, it will at least be found to be a faithful record of what has taken place in Jaffna, since it came under European away.

The Chronological Table of Events has been compiled from reliable sources. Special care has been taken to render the same accurate and useful; but considering the length of the period, covering over four countries, the kind and indulgent reader will, it is hoped, pass over any errors that may have crept in. A few events relating to the introduction and propagation of the Catholic faith in this country have been taken from the Chronological Notes published by the late illustrious Arch-Bishop Bonjean, while he was in charge of the Jaffna Vicariate, and a few others from the Chronological Table of Events connected with Ceylon given in Ferguson's Hand-Book and Directory.

In the Notes is brought together from various sources, information-which the young reader will find interesting and useful-regarding the advent and establishment of the different missions working in the North, the rise and growth of Educational, Religious, and other Public Institutions, and noteworthy incidents and details in the lives of the sons of the soil who have risen to prominence and public recognition. The Notes should be read along with the Table of Events, on which they are intended to give additional information. The authorities bearing on these notes have been quoted in every case.

Omissions there are, and of some of these I am not unaware. But I regret very much that the information and assistance earnestly sought for in regard to them have unfortunately not been furnished.

The paper on "a Disputed Point of Local History," intended for separate publication, was prepared on the appearance of the second edition of Mr. Mootootamby Pillay's "Jaffna History," and though ready for the press in 1916, its publication was put off owing to war conditions and the consequent abnormal price of paper. It is now given as an appendix to the pres- ent sent work.

The note on the "Yalpana Vaipava Kuvmuthy" was subsequently added.

J.H.M

Jaffna
3rd December 1922.

CONTENTS

ERRATA

PAGE	LINE	FOR	READ
1	8	firs.	first
8	13	Bibilical	Biblical
15	38	Gallee	Galle
16	17	Feb. 30	Feb. 3
39	3	Pope Pins	Pope Pius
73	29	Young Men's Hindu	Hindu Young Men's
78	3	Sir	Sri
92	13	Complied	Compiled
107	30	1916, Sept.	1915, Decr. 10
160	38	8 tons under	8 tons and
232	32	Mine	Music
288	37	[illegible]	[illegible]
296	23	Ammal	Annual
297	16	Salay	Salary
305	35	4 inch guns	Ten 4-inch guns
310	21	399	299

A
Chronological Table
OF
Events Connected with Jaffna
From 1505 Downwards

PORTUGUESE PERIOD
1505—1658

1505—April. - The Portuguese under Don Lorenzo de Almeida firs visit Ceylon, and are permitted to trade. See Note 1.

1518—Lopez Suaar Alverenga arrives in Ceylon with a fleet of nineteen ships, and after some ineffectual opposition from the Singhalese, erects a fort at Colombo.

1536—Death at Colombo of Joao Monteiro, the first Bishop of Ceylon.

1544—The Roman Catholic Religion first preached at Mannar by Missionaries sent by St. Francis Xavier, at the request of the inhabitants; 600 of the converts are massacred by the King of Jaffnapattam. See Notes 2, 3, 9.

1544—The eldest son of the King of Jaffnapattam embraces the Catholic Faith. He is put to death. The second son flies to Goa. See Notes 3, 9.

1544—By an agreement, the King of Jaffnapattam pays an yearly tribute to the Portuguese. See Note 9.

1545—A Portuguese fleet attempts to wrest Mannar from the King of Jaffnapattam. See Note 2.

1545—April. - Voyage of St, Francis Xavier to Mannar. An epidemic which made 100 victims daily, stayed by him. See Notes 2, 24.

1548—St Francis Xavier visits Mannar and comes over to Jaffna. He has an interview with the King, whom he persuades to form an alliance with the Portuguese. See Note 24

1548—St. Francis Xavier visits Galle, Kandy and other places. See Note 24.

1552- Dec. 2 - Death of St. Francis Xavier in the Island of Sancian.

1554—Mar. 15 - Translation of St. Francis Xavier's body to Goa.

1560—Mannar ceded to Portugal.

1575—In digging the foundations of St. John's Church, Mannar, Joan Mellus discovers brass and gold coins with the effigy of the Emperor Claudius. See Note 4.

1580—Dharma Paala bequeathes the whole Island to the Crown of Portugal.

1580—The Portuguese are permitted by the King of Jaffna to build a Franciscan Church in his Capital.

1588—The Portuguese obtain possession of Kandy, where they raise Don Philip to the throne in violation of their engagement to Konaapoo Bandar.

1591—Andre Furtado de Mendonca, a famous Portuguese General, subdues Jaffnapattam; several of the inhabitants embrace the Catholic Religion. See Note 6.

1592—Dec. 3 - First English ship, the "Edward Bonaventure," arrives at Galle.

1592—Rajasingha I dies, aged 120 years, and Konaapoo Bandar proclaims himself King in his stead, under the title of Wimala Dharma.

1593—Don Pedro de Sousa is sent from Goa in command of a strong force. He makes himself master of Kandy; and, in order to favour the desire of the Singhalese, proclaims as Queen, Dona Catherina, daughter of a former King of Kandy, who had been placed under the guardianship of the Portuguese at Mannar, and educated as a Christian. See Note 2.

1593—Wimala Dharma defeats De Sousa and captures Dona Catherina, whom he afterwards marries.

1602—May. - The Dutch visit Ceylon. Admiral Joris Spilbergen offers to the King the friendship and alliance of the Prince of Orange and the States General of Holland, which are accepted. See Note 5.

1613—July. 20 - The Queen Dona Catherina dies. See Note 2.

1614—May. 8 - The foundation of the Portuguese Church in Jaffna laid. See Note 6.

1615—Para Raa Sekara Pandara dies, leaving as his heir a child of three years. See Note 6.

1617—The Portuguese flag hoisted in Jaffna. De Oliveira becomes first Governor. See Notes 6, 9.

1621—A battle between the Portuguese and Tamils at Valvedditurai, which ends in the defeat of the latter. See Note 6.

1622—March. 12 - Canonization of St. Francis Xavier.

1624—The Portuguese commence erecting a fort at Jaffnapattam. See Notes 6, 7, 45.

1627—Feb. 20 - A violent storm accompanied by a tidal wave causes great loss of life and property in Jaffna. See Note 6.

1627—March. 22 - Death of De Oliveira, first Portuguese Governor of Jaffnapattam. See Note 6.

1628—Revd. Frs. Antonio Pecci and Mathew Fernandez of the order of Jesus suffer martyrdom at Jaffna.

1632—The fort at Jaffna completed. See Notes 6, 7, 45.

1638—Fr. Robert De Nobili, who founded the famous Jesuit Mission of Madura in 1606, gets blind and comes to reside in Jaffna. See Note 22.

1644—A report of the work of the Jesuit Missionaries in Ceylon made to the Superior General of the Society. There were then 12 residences in Jaffna. See Note 8.

1646—A temporary pacification ensues between the Dutch and the Portuguese.

1651—April. 21 - Birth in Goa of Father Joseph Vaz. See Notes 16,17.

1655—Hostilities resumed between the Dutch and Portuguese.

1655—Dec. 10 - Antonio Admiral de Menezes, Governor of Jaffnapattam, taken prisoner by the Dutch at Mutwal on his way from Mannar to Colombo.

1658—Feb. 22 - Mannar taken by the Dutch. See Note 2.

1658—Mar. The Dutch lay siege to the fort of Jaffnapattam. See Note 10.

1658—April. 10 - Fort Hammanheil at Kayts taken by the Dutch.

1658—June. 22 - Jaffna surrendered to the Dutch. See Notes 6, 9, 10.

Portuguese Period
of
Settlement of Jaffna
1617—1658

DUTCH PERIOD

1658—1795

1658—June. 23 - The Hollanders reduced and occupied the fort of Jaffna, the last stronghold of the Portuguese in Ceylon. There were then in the Jaffna Peninsula about fifty priests, a College belonging to the Society of Jesus, a Franciscan Convent, a Dominican Monastery, 14 Churches in Valigamam, 5 in Thenmaradchy, 3 in Patchilaipally and one in each of the adjacent Islands. There was also within the fort of Jaffna a Church built in the shape of a cross. See Notes 6, 11

1658—Aug. 29 - The Reformed Religion first introduced into Jaffna by the Revd. Dr. Baldaeus.

1658—Sept. - A conspiracy, formed against the Dutch at Jaffna by Don Louis Pooda-Tamby and some Portuguese, discovered by Don Manuel de Andrado Mudaliyar, and the conspirators executed. See Notes 12, 23.

1658—Sept. - The Revd. Fr. Caldeiro of the Society of Jesus beheaded on a charge of having concealed his knowledge of the treasonable correspondence Don Louis Pooda-Tamby had with the Portuguese. See Note 23.

1658—Catholic Priests were banished. See Note 13.

1658—Sept. 19 - Proclamation issued forbidding the harbouring or concealing of the Roman Catholic Priests under pain of death. See Note 13.

1658—Nov. 20 - The Dutch set apart this day as a day of thanksgiving for their victory over the Portuguese.

1659—Captain Robert Knox, his son and several of the crew of the "Ann Frigate," taken prisoners at Batticaloa and removed to Kandy.

1661—Dr. Baldaeus, the Dutch Protestant Minister and Historian, visits Point Pedro. A handsome Church was built here by the Dutch and also a fort. See Note 14.

1661—April. - A Pearl-Fishery.

1663—A Pearl-Fishery.

1676—The ordination to the priesthood of Joseph Vaz. See Notes 16, 17.

1678—The building of the Dutch Church at Batticotta completed, This Church is now used by the American Missionaries to whom it was made over by Governor Brownrigg on their first arrival in Jaffna in 1816. See Note 15.

1679—Oct. 18 - Knox effects his escape from Kandy and reaches Aripu. See Note 15.

1682—The Oratory of St. Philip Neri at Goa founded.

1682—Governor Lourens Van Pyl imposes penalties on devil-worship and similar idolatrous ceremonies.

1685—Father Vaz joins the Oratory of St. Philip Neri at Goa. See Notes 16, 17.

1687—The Venerable Joseph Vaz of the Oratory of St. Philip Neri comes to Jaffna, disguised as a beggar, and goes about preaching at Chilalai and the neighbouring villages. See Note 16.

1688—Baldaeus reports 180,000 baptised Christians in the Kingdom of Jaffnapattam.

1689—Floris Blom appointed Commandeur of Jaffnapattam. See Note 25.

1690—Dec. 24 - A large number of Catholics assembled for celebrating Christmas midnight Mass arrested and flogged by order of Van Rheede. See Note 16.

1691—Fr. Vaz visits Wanny and Puttalam.

1692—Fr. Vaz penetrates into Kandy and endeavours to re-establish the Roman Catholic Religion in that City. Imprisoned there, he exercises his ministry in jail for two years. See Note 17.

1694—Fr. Vaz visits Mantotte, Poonaryn, Jaffna and other places. See Notes 16, 17.

1694—July. 3 - Death at Jaffna of Floris Blom, Commandeur of Jaffnapattam. See Note 25.

1694—Hendrick Zwaadecroon appointed Commandeur of Jaffnapattam. His memoirs are regarded as a standard authority on matters relating to the Northern possessions of the Dutch East India Company in Ceylon.. See Note 27.

1696—Fr. Joseph Vaz appointed Vicar-General of Ceylon. See Note 16.

1697—Governor Gerret de Heere visits Jaffna.

1700—Fr. Joseph Beschi arrives in India. See Notes 22, 29.

1703—Arrival in Ceylon of Fr. Jacome Gonsalvez. See Note 21.

1704—Governor Cornelis Joan Simons visits Jaffna. See Note 38.

1705—A Seminary established in Colombo by the Dutch Government in which the Hebrew, Greek, Latin, Dutch, Portuguese, Singhalese and Tamil languages were taught. See Note 31.

1707—June. 4 - The Thesawalame sanctioned by the Dutch Government, and the Civil Courts directed to be guided by it. See Note 18.

1711—Jan. 7 - The Venerable Fr. Joseph Vaz dies at Kandy. See Note 17.

1711—June. 6- A law enacted by the Dutch Government prohibiting Hindu Ceremonies under severe penalties. See Note 13.

1715—The Catholic Clergy prohibited from administering Baptism. See Note 13.

1715—Public assemblies or private conventicles of Roman Catholics forbidden. See Note 13.

1719—Governor Rumpf visits Jaffna.

1722—Jacob de Jong (Senior) appointed Commandeur of Jaffnapattam. See Note 30.

1726—Heavy rain in Jaffna, flooding the country and causing starvation and sickness.

1732—Aug. 25 - Gaulterus Wouterez appointed Commandeur of Jaffnapattam.

1732—A Pearl Fishery.

1736—A printing office for printing books in the native languages established by the Dutch Government and brought into active operation. See Note 31.

1739—Governor Van Imhoff visits Jaffna and Mannar.

1740—A new set of "Thombus" commenced to be compiled. See Note 28.

1742—Death at Manaparai of Fr. Joseph Beschi, better known as Veeramamuniver. See Notes 22, 29.

1746—Governor Stein Van Golleness visits Jaffna.

1746—A Pearl-Fishery yielded £4,766-13-4. See Note 36.

1747—A Pearl-Fishery yielded £21,400. See Note 36.

1748—Feb. 26-Jacob de Jong (Junior) appointed Commandeur of Jaffnapattam. See Note 30.

1748—A Pearl Fishery yielded £38,580. See Note 36.

1748—Proclamation issued forbidding the education of a Roman Catholic for the ministry. See Note 13.

1749—A Pearl-Fishery yielded £68,375.

1749—The New Testament, translated from the Greek into Tamil by the Revd. Philip Melho, Clergyman at Jaffna, published by the Dutch Government. See Note 31.

1751—The Catholic Clergy prohibited from celebrating Mass. See Note 13.

1753—A Pearl-Fishery yielded £6,360.

1754—The last revision of the "Thombus" of Jaffna. See Note 28.

1754—A Pearl-Fishery yielded £1,469.

1756—Sept. 29 - Poelogisinghe Mudaliyar Philippoe Comarawelen of Tellippalai appointed the Company's first native physician for the Commandements of Jaffnapattam. See Note 32.

1758—Tax laid on Catholic Marriages.

1758—June. 26 - Don Philippoe Chitambela Mudaliyar of Wannarponne appointed the Company's broker. See Note 33.

1759—March. Punkas come into use among the Dutch grandees of Jaffna.

1759—The Revd. Christian Fredrick Schwartz visits Ceylon, landing at Jaffna and preaching all over the Island. See Note 26.

1761—Aug. 10 - Retirement of Don Manuel Rajakarie Mana Mudaliyar as Shroff or Cashier of Mannar and the appointment to his place of his son-in-law Walayren Joan Ramanaden of Manipay. See Note 34.

1765—May. 13 - Anthony Mooyaart appointed Commandeur of Jaffnapattam. See Note 35.

1768—April - The last Pearl-Fishery under the Dutch.

1776—Marriages of Catholics ordered to be solemnized before the Reformed Ministers or the Civil Officer. See Note 13.

1782—Jan. 11 - A British Squadron under the Command of Sir Edward Hughes, and some land forces, under Sir Hector Munro, take possession of Trincomalee.

1782—Feb. 10 - Exposition of the body of St. Francis Xavier at Goa.

1784—Silver Coins issued by the Dutch Government from its own mint in Colombo. See Note 37.

1784—Death of Kanapathy Ayer of Batticotta. He is the Author of several "Nadagams." See Note 39.

1785—Plakaat interdicting Catholic Schools. See Note 13.

1785—Death at Colombo of Governor Falck, after an able administration of twenty years.

1785—Aug. 15 - St. Michael's Church, Klaly, built.

1785—Paper currency first introduced into Ceylon by Governor Vander Graaf.

1789—An enumeration made by order of Governor Vander Graaf, of all the inhabitants in the maritime districts subject to the Dutch East India Company and that reckoning gave 817,000 inhabitants of both sexes and all ages.

1789—The foundation of St. Mary's Church, the premier Church of Jaffna, laid. See Note 40.

1790—Jan. - Don Nicholas Tisseveerasinghe Mudaliyar appointed a volunteer in the Jaffna Kachcheri. See Note 41.

1790—The Pentateuch, translated into Tamil from the Hebrew by the Revd. P. de Melho, published by the Government. See Note 31.

1790—Aug. 10—Death in his 67th year of Philip de Melho, celebrated as a Dutch Divine, Tamil Bibilical translator and poet. He was the first Ceylonese who was admitted to the Christian Ministry by the Dutch Government. He was also the Dutch Chaplain of Jaffna for some years. See Note 31.

1793—Steps taken to develop cotton cultivation in Jaffna.

1794—Building of St. Mary's' Church (now the Jaffna Cathedral) completed. Revd. Fr. Leonard Rebeiro, a Goanese priest, was the first Parish Priest; and Tomaipillai Anthonipillai, Ordnance Store-keeper, during the latter days of the Dutch Government and a munificient contributor in land and money to the building of the Church, was the first President Moopu. See Note 40.

1795—Aug - Death in his 97th year of Kulangkai Thampiran, an Indian poet, domiciled in Jaffna. In his latter days he lived at Chiviateru. He wrote an excellent commentary on the Nanool of Pavunanthy besides several other Tamil works. See Note 42.

1795—Sept - A British force under Captain Stewart lands at PointPedro and advances on Jaffnapattam.

1795—Sept. 28- Jaffna surrendered to the British forces under General Stewart. See Note 7.

BRITISH PERIOD

1795—1920

1795—Sept. - The British occupy Jaffnapattam.

—Dec. 3 - John Jarvis appointed Collector of Jaffna.

1796—Feb. 16 - Surrender of Colombo. The English become masters of the Island. Ceylon governed from Madras.

1796—Feb. 26 - The first Pearl-Fishery under the English yielded £60,000.

1796—The Wanny formed into a separate Collectorate.

1797—A Pearl-Fishery yielded £ 110,000.

—Burton Gage Barbet appointed Collector of Jaffna.

1798—Oct. 12 - Ceylon made a King's Colony; and the Hon. Fredrick North (afterwards Earl of Guildford) appointed Governor.

1798—Don Nicholas Tisseveerasinghe Mudaliyar appointed Thombu-Holder of the Jaffna Kachcheri. See Notes 41, 43.

1799—A Pearl-Fishery yielded £ 30,000.

1799—Jan. 15 - The importation of slaves into Ceylon prohibited.

1799—Sept. 23- Torture and other barbarous modes of punishment abolished.

1799—Sept. 23 - Liberty of conscience and the free exercise of religious worship allowed to all His Majesty's subjects in Ceylon.

1799—Dec. 15 - The first English Seminary for natives founded at Colombo.

1800—June - A murrain carried off four-fifths of the cattle in the Northern Province.

1800—June. A tumult at Mannar—Mantotte, on account of the jewel tax, in which KumaraSinghe Mudaliyar, a poet and physician of Mantotte, was implicated. See Note 46.

1801—The Revd. Christian David appointed Government Colonial Chaplain of Jaffna. Two of his predecessors here were William Franciscus and Manuel Morgappa. See Notes 47, 106.

1801—Sept. 3 - Rent or tax on paddy and fine grain levied. Under the Dutch a large area of rice land was held in return for personal services under the little of "accommodesans."

1802—March, 15 - The publication of the Ceylon Government Gazette commenced.

1802—March. 27 - Treaty of Amiens, all Dutch possessions in Ceylon pass into the hands of the English. See Note 48.

--The Supreme Court of Judicature instituted.

1802—Aug. 11 - Vaccine innoculation commenced at Trincomalie.

1802—The Protestant Christians among the Tamils of Jaffna are reckoned at 136,000. See Note 49.

1803—A Pearl-Fishery at Chilaw yielded £ 15,000.

—Pandara Wanniya, the rebel chief of the Wanny, assisted by the Kandyans, raises an insurrection.

1803—Aug. 25 - The Kandyans attack Mullaitivu.

—Pandara Wanniya, the rebel chief, attempts to plunder the village of Vidattaltivu, but is prevented by Major Vincent at the head of the Mannar Independent company.

1803—Sept. - KoomaraSegara Mudaliyar of Mullaitivu and several others executed on a charge of treason.

—The Ceylon civil fund established.

1803—Oct. 31 - Captain Drieberg attacks Pandara Wanniya's troops, many of whom are killed.

1804—A Pearl-Fishery yielded about £ 75,000.

1804—Three London missionaries arrive in Ceylon and are stationed at Galle, Matara and Jaffna, but they soon after leave the Island again save Revd. Mr. Palm, who eventually becomes minister of Wolfendhal Church.

1805—47 schools in Jaffna suddenly closed for want of funds.

1806—A Pearl-Fishery yielded £ 35,000.

1806—April. 2 - The Hon'ble Alexander Johnston appointed Provincial Chief Justice.

1806—June. 4 - Roman Catholics relieved of the restrictions imposed upon them by the Dutch.

1806—July- Police Vidhans first appointed.

1806—Aug. 5 - Mahomedan laws relating to inheritance and marriage sanctioned by the Council.

1807—Jan. - The Bazaar tax first established.

1808—A Pearl-Fishery yielded £90,000

—Dec. 16 - The foundation laid of the stone-house called the Maddam in the land lying in close proximity to the front gate of the Jaffna Cathedral.

1809—March. - A Pearl-Fishery yielded £ 25,000.

—March. 1—The Hon'ble William Coke appointed Provincial Chief Justice.

1811—Feb. 1- Erroomaravooyanda Mana Mudaliyar appointed Parpathiagara of Calapoomi in Karativu. See Note 19.

1811—Nov. 8 - A new Charter of Justice read and promulgated, by which the Supreme Court became divided into two divisions, the first consisting of the Chief Justice to sit at Colombo, and the second consisting of the Puisne Justice to sit at Jaffnapattam, the benefit of trial by Jury in Criminal cases extended to all His Majesty's subjects in Ceylon.

—Edward Nolan takes charge of Delft being appointed Superintendent of that Island—See Note 50.

1812—March. 10 - His Excellency Lieutenant-General Robert Brownrigg appointed Governor and Commander-in-Chief of the British Settlements in Ceylon arrives at Colombo. See Note 106.

1812—March. - A Pearl-Fishery yielded £ 90,000.

—March. 16 - A new Charter of Justice granting Trial by Jury, read and promulgated.

—Aug. 1 - Auxiliary Bible Society instituted.

—Aug. 11 - A Royal Botanic Garden established in Ceylon.

—Potatoes first successfully cultivated in Ceylon.

—Missionaries first sent to India by the American Board of Foreign Missions. See Note 51.

1813—Feb. 10 - Death of Mrs. Ault, wife of the Revd. Ault, Wesleyan Missionary. See Note 53.

—Feb. - Revd. Mr. Newell, an American Missionary, lands in Colombo.—See Note 52.

Aug. 10— Bazaar tax abolished.

1814—A Pearl-Fishery yielded £ 64,000.

—May. 2 - Death at sea of Dr. Coke, a very learned and philanthropic Wesleyan Missionary, on his way to Ceylon. See Note 53.

1814—June. 29 - Arrival at Galle of six Wesleyan Missionaries viz. Rev. Messrs James Lynch, Thomas H. Squance, Ault, Erskine, Clough and Harvard. See Note 53.

—Nov. 5 - Dreadful hurricane in the North and North-West coast of Ceylon, which occasioned great devastation in Jaffna, Vidattaltivu and Mannar.

1815—Ethirveerasinghe Nitsinghe Talaivasinghe Mudaliyar, a distinguished Jaffna gentleman, assists Colonel Hardy in the subjugation of the Kandyan Kingdom.

—March - W. H. Hooper appointed collector of Jaffna.

—April 15 - The Dutch Copper Coins called Challies put into circulation. Challies to pass current at the rate of 12 for one fanam.

1815—Aug. - Revd. Messrs Edward Warren, Richard, Bardwell, Poor and Meigs of the American Mission, leave Boston with their families for Ceylon.

1815—John Wilkins, a merchant, farms the exclusive privilege of exporting Beche-de-mer for five years.

1816—March. 23 - Arrival in Colombo of the American Missionaries. See Note 360.

—April. 21 - The American Missionaries organise themselves into a congregational Church.

—July. 11 - Revd. E. Warren of the American Mission arrives in Jaffna. Revd. Benjamin C. Meigs, Revd. Daniel Poor, D. D. and others follow soon after. See Note 54.

1816—Aug. 12 - The proprietors of slaves in the Maritime Provinces, 763 in number, declared that all children born of their slaves after this date should be thenceforward free.

—Oct. 15 - Messrs Warren and Poor take up their residence at Tellipallai. Hastings and Meigs settle down at Batticotta.

--Rev. E. Warren and James Richard of the American Mission commence to practise European Medicine among the native population. See Note 55.

1817—Revd. E. Warren of the American Mission establishes a small hospital at Tellipalai. See Note 55.

—Sept. At the request of Sir Alexander Johnston, Chief Justice of Ceylon, the Church Mission consents to send missionaries to preach the Gospel in the Island. See Note 56.

—Dec. 20 - Four Missionaries, Samuel Lambrick, Benjamin Ward, Robert Major, and Joseph Knight sail for Ceylon. See Note 56.

1818—First cargo of cocoanut oil taken from Ceylon to the United Kingdom.

—June. 17 - Arrival in Colombo of four Missionaries of the Church Mission. See Note 56.

—July. Establishment of the C. M. S. in Jaffna. The Rev. Joseph Knight arrives in Jaffna and takes up his residence at Nallur. See Note 56.

—Aug. - Death at Cape Town of the Revd. E. Warren of the American Mission.

1819—Dr. Scudder of the American Mission arrives as Medical Missionary and commences the training of a few native young men to practise medicine in the country on European principles. See Note 55.

1820—The Madhu pilgrimage commences to become popular after its repression by the Dutch.

—The Association of the Holy Family Nuns established at Bordeaux, France. See Note 126.

—Revds. Miron Winslow, and Henry Woodward and Miss Lydia Woodward, and Miss Harriet Scudder arrive and join the American Mission of Jaffna.

—Feb. 1 - Lieutenant-General Sir Robert Brownrigg leaves for England and Sir Edward Barnes assumes office as Lieut-Governor.

1821—Dead chanks first discovered in the Jaffna lagoon. See Note 57.

1822—Feb. 2 - Lieutenant-General Sir Edward Paget, K. C. B., assumes the Government of the Colony.

—Feb. 6- Charles Scott appointed Collector of Jaffna.

—April 23 - Jordon Lodge, Nathaniel Niles, Charles Hodge, Onesimus, and Ebenezer Porter examined and admitted as members of the American Church. They were the first native American Pastors.

1822—July. - Major General Sir James Campbell, K. C. B., appointed to the staff of the Army in Ceylon, arrives at Trincomalie.

—Nov. 6 - Lieutenant-General Sir Edward Paget, K. C. B., leaves Colombo for Calcutta and Major General Sir James Campbell, K. C. B., takes his seat in Council as Lieutenant-Governor.

The Revd. Joseph Knight establishes an English School at Nallur known as the Nallur English School. See Notes 56,93.

1823—The New Chapel of the Wesleyan Mission, Jaffna, opened See Note 53.

—July, 22 - The Batticotta Seminary opened and placed in charge of Dr. Daniel Warren Poor. See Notes 58, 112.

—July- Mr. Moyce builds a small Chapel at Madhu.

—The Revd. Mr. Adley of the Church Mission comes to Jaffna and joins the Revd. Mr. Knight. See Note 68.

1824—Jan. 18 - Lieutenant-General Sir Edward Barnes, K. C. B, appointed Governor and Commander-in-Chief of Ceylon.

1824—The opening at Uduville of a Central School for girls under the charge of Mr. and Mrs. Winslow of the American Mission. See Note 59.

1824—Feb. - .The Revd. Mr. Squance of the Wesleyan Mission engaged in the work among the Portuguese and Dutch descendants of Jaffna, leaves for Galle on account of ill-health. The Revd. Mr. Carver succeeds him.

—March. 1 - Percival Ackland Dyke appointed assistant to the Collector of Jaffna. See Note 131.

—Experiments commenced with powerful engines to raise the water from the tidal well at Putoor with a view to irrigation. See Note 60.

—July. 23 - A Silver Sword and buckler presented to St. James at Klaly in fulfilment of a vow by one Samuel. He was employed as a horse-keeper under the Revd. Mr. Adley, the Church Missionary in charge of the English School at Nallur. See Note 61.

1825—Feb. 1 - P. A. Dyke appointed Fiscal and sitting Magistrate of Jaffna. See Note 131.

1825—July. 1 - Pounds, Shillings, Pence and Farthings, the currency of the United Kingdom of Great Britain and Ireland, declared the legal and established currency of the Island. All Government accounts commence to be kept, entered and adjusted in that currency.

—Death in his 92nd year of Don Deigo Warnasuriya Arasunilayitta Mudaliyar, Respadore under the Dutch Government. See Note 62.

—Mathew Philips engaged as a pundit to the American Missionaries becomes a catechist under the Rev. Mr. Knight of the Church Mission. See Note 63.

—Dec. 30- C. Brownrigg appointed Collector of Jaffna.

—The Jaffna Religious Tract Society instituted.

—S. Wala Supramanier Ayer commences to practise as a Proctor in Jaffna.

1826—A printing office established at Nallur by the Revd. Joseph Knight. மோக்ஷவழி (The way to Paradise) was the Tamil work first printed in Jaffna in this press. This press was lent to him by the American Mission of Jaffna. See Note 64.

1827—Death at Araly of Muttucumara Pulavar, a well-known poet of his day, who established a School at Kayts. He is the author of Devasagaya Nadagam and other poetical works. See Note 65.

—Death in his 50th year of Mappana Mudaliyar, Maniagar of Tenmaradchy. He is the author of some well-known Tamil works. See Note 66.

1827—May. 17 - William Gisborn appointed Collector of Jaffna.

1828—March. 28 - A Lunar Eclipse. An interesting controversy took place between Dr. Poor of the Batticotta Seminary and the famous Visuvanatha Saahtriar of Araly, about the extent of obscuration and the time of duration of this eclipse. Dr. Poor's calculations thoroughly tested and agreeing with the Nautical Almanac proved exactly in accord with the movements of the heavenly bodies, greatly to the discomfiture of the Sashtriar. See Note 67.

—April. A Pearl-Fishery yielded £ 29,072-5-3¾

1828—July. 12- Joseph Price appointed Collector of Jaffna.

—Commencement of operations for opening the Paumban Channel.

—July- The N. M. Gem and Jewel shop started by Nagalinga Paththar at Kannathiddy. The present proprietor is N. Muttukistna Paththar of Wannarponne.

—The Nayanmar Kadu hospital started. See Note 69.

—Revd. Mr. Adley of the Church Mission takes a few Jaffna boys to Colombo to be educated at the Cotta Christian Institution. See Note 68.

1829—March. 18 - Mana Mudaliyar Ehamparam appointed Parpathiagar of Calapoomi in Karative. See Note 20.

—Oct. 1 - P. A. Dyke appointed Collector of Jaffna. See Note 131.

—A Pearl-Fishery yielded £ 37,307-13-4.

1830—A Pearl-Fishery yielded £ 21,529-19-0.

—The Monopoly of the chaya root abolished.

1831—Population of the Jaffna Peninsula 146,528.

—March - A Pearl-Fishery yielded £ 28,332-0-8¼.

—March. 30 - The American Mission buildings at Manepay consumed by fire.

—June. 1 - Charles Peter Layard appointed Fiscal and sitting Magistrate of Jaffna.

—Oct. 23- The Right Hon. Sir Robert Wilmot Horton, appointed Governor and Commander-in-Chief of Ceylon, arrives and takes his seat in Council.

1832—Feb. 1- The Kandy Mail-Coach, the first Mail-Coach in Asia, started.

—Feb. 18- An extraordinary metor appeared at Colombo, Gallee, Jaffna, Trincomalie and other parts of the Island.

—April. 12- Order of the King in Council abolishing the Rajakaria or compulsory service to Government received.

—April- Revd. John Hensman (Murugesar) gets admission into

the C. M. S. Seminary at Cotta through the influence of the Revd. Mr. W. Adley. See Note 70.

1832—A Pearl-Fishery at Calpentyn Mutwal, yielded £3,887-5-3.

—Aug. 6- Ceylon Savings Bank opened.

—Sep. 8- First Cricket Club established in Colombo.

—Sep. 28 - The order of the King in Council abolishing c ompulsory labour in the Colony proclaimed.

—Nov. - Sir Robert Wilmot Horton, Governor, visits Jaffna and presides at a public examination in the Batticotta Seminary. See Note 72.

—Dec. 1- Mr. Henry Martyn appointed teacher in the Batticotta Seminary. See Note 71.

1833—The Island divided into five provinces.

—Jan. 7- Mr. Henry Martyn receives an autograph reply from Sir R. W. Horton. See Note 72.

—Feb. - A Pearl-Fishery at Arippo yielded £25,043-10-0.

—Feb. 30- The first attempt at watch-repairing successfully made by a Jaffna gentleman. See Note 73.

—Oct. 1- Percival Ackland Dyke appointed Government Agent, Fiscal and Collector of Customs of the Northern Province, inaugrates his memorable administration, the most unique among provincial administrations, which lasted nearly forty years, and by which he earned the title of the "Raja of the North". See Notes 68, 131.

1833—The Department of Public Works installed in Jaffna. See Note 68.

—Dr. Nathan Ward M. D. of the American Mission, arrives and joins the Batticotta Seminary as a professor. See Note 58.

—The establishment of the Executive and Legislative Councils.

—Removal of the restrictions imposed by Government on the American Mission. See Note 74.

—An Infant School started at Pandeterippo by Mrs. Eckard of the American Mission. This was the first "Infant School" in Ceylon. See Note 74.

1834—May. 19 - The School Commission constituted.

—May. 22 - The first Meeting of the Legislative Council held at Colombo.

1834—Ceylon, for purposes of ecclesiastical administration, detached from the Diocese of Cochin and erected into a separate Vicariate Apostolic. The Revd. Fr. Francis Xavier appointed first Vicar Apostolic of Ceylon. See Note 76.

1834—The printing establishment at Nallur transferred to the American Mission and removed to Manipay. See Note 64.

—The Jaffna Temperance Society started by the American Mission. See Note 97.

—Henry Richard Hoisington D. D. arrives and joins the American Mission of Jaffna. See Note 58, 74.

1834—The Jaffna Central School started by the Rev. Peter Percival. He was then the General Superintendent of the Wesleyan Mission in the Northern and Eastern Provinces, and Financial Secretary. A Boarding Institution divided into separate Departments for boys and girls was also established. This institution was intended for the benefit not only of the youths of Jaffna but also of the children of parents residing in other parts of the Island. Mr. Percival had also under him two girls' English Schools, six boys' Tamil Schools and two girls' Tamil Schools in Jaffna. The course of study adopted in the day and boarding schools included in addition to the ordinary branches of a plain education, Ancient and Modern History, Algebra, Geometry, Mensuration, Natural Philosophy and the elements of Mental and Moral Science. English and Tamil Schools were also opened in the course of time at Puttur, Kaddevely and Point Pedro. Mr. Percival was succeeded in the Management of these Institutions by the Revds. Gillings, Williams, Robinson, Barber, Talbot, Mitchel, Hornby and Rhodes. See Note 53, 75.

1834—Messrs G. W. Colette, G. Koch, C. Ollegesegerampulle and A. Soosaipillai commence to practise as Proctors in Jaffna.

1835—New stations at Varany and Chavakachcheri opened by the American Mission.

—Death of the Revd. Fr. Francis Xavier, first Vicar Apostolic of Ceylon. See Note 76.

—July, 18 - Receipt by the Royal Society of Great Britain and Ireland of two Terrestrial Globes sent by Mr. Henry Martyn of Jaffna. See Note 79.

1835—Messrs C. Speldwinde, A. H. Bultjens and P. E. Toussaint begin to practise as Proctors in Jaffna.

1836—Feb. 6 - The Ceylon Temperance Society formed.

—A Pearl-Fishery yielded £25,816-3-11.

1836—Revd. Fr. Vincent De Rosario appointed Vicar Apostolic of Ceylon in succession to Revd. Fr. Francis Xavier with the title of Bishop of Tamacene. See Note 76.

—Revd. Poor resigns his connection with the Batticotta Seminary and proceeds to Madura. See Note 58.

—The building of the Puthankuli bridge, the best in the North undertaken. See Note 78.

—Taxes upon imports and exports first imposed in Ceylon.

1837—Jan. 5 - Mr. Henry Martyn appointed Professor of Mathematics and Natural Philosophy in the Batticotta Seminary. See Note 71.

—Jan. - Mr. George Dashiel appointed tutor of Hindu Astronomy, Sanskrit and Native Arithmetic in the Batticotta Seminary.

—A society called the Tirupanichangam formed for the purpose of carrying out all works in connection with St. Mary's Church, Jaffna. See Note 80.

—A Pearl-Fishery yielded £10,631-4-9¾

—April. 5 - Ordination of the Revd. John Philips Sanmugam, the first Wesleyan Tamil Minister of Jaffna. See Note 53.

1837—The Jaffna Wesleyan Girls' boarding school started. See Note 53.

—Nov. 7 - The Right Hon. J. A. Stewart Mackenzie appointed Governor and Commander-in-Chief of Ceylon arrives and takes his seat in Council.

1838—Mr. Henry Martyn constructed a Perambulator for the purpose of determining the mile posts on the public roads and presented the same to Mr. P. A. Dyke, G. A., N. P.

1839—Mr. W. Volk appointed Professor of Geography, Chronology and History, and Mr. E. Rockwood of Mathematics, in the Batticotta Seminary. See Note 269.

—Sandrasegara Mudaliyar Saverimuttu Mudaliyar appointed to succeed Philip Muttukistna Mudaliyar as chief Kachcheri Mudaliyar of Jaffna. See Note 77.

—Crown lands sold at five shillings an acre as upset price.

1839—July - An appeal made to the Propaganda for European Catholic Missionaries to work in Ceylon. See Note 76.

—Dec. 18 - An ordinance for regulating the publication of News-papers.

1839—A census of Jaffna: Jaffna 62,137; Mallagam 45,305; Tenmaradchy 43,927; Vadamaradchy 35,747; Islands 25,292; Total 212,408.

—Mr. W. Maartensz commences to practise as a Proctor in Jaffna.

1840—Death in his 60th year of Chenathiraya Mudaliyar, a renowned Tamil scholar and poet. See Note 81.

—Jan. 4 - The abolition of the fish tax.

—Mar. 1 - H. E. O'Grady appointed acting Assistant Government Agent at Jaffna.

—June - Mr. P. A. Dyke, G. A., N. P. donates a piece of land at Copay, 75 lms. in extent, to the C. M. S.

—Sep. 24 - Bank of Ceylon incorporated by Royal Charter.

—Graduation from the Batticotta Seminary, then under the Revd. Dr. Hoisington, of Messrs J. R. Arnold, Nevins, Caroll, Evarts, Rogers, Stickney and other distinguished students.

—Oct. 19 - Death from hydrophobia of Mappaner Mudaliyar, Manager of the Kandaswamy Temple at Nallur.

—The Revd. Robert Bren takes charge of the C. M. S. work at Copay.

1841—Jan. 7 - The publication of the Morning Star commenced, the first editors being Messrs. Henry Martyn and Seth Payson. This is the first attempt at journalism in Jaffna. See note 82.

1841—Jane. 15 - The first brig built in Jaffna by Arumugam Chetty, a wealthy Native Merchant, launched from the beach near the Customs House at Jaffna.

—The Girls' boarding school at Nallur started by the Church Mission. See Note 56.

—Feb. - Mr. Hardy, an enterprising merchant from the West Indies, arrives in Jaffna and buys 2000 acres of crown land in the Thenmaradchy District for the cultivation of tobacco and other plantations.

—Feb. 28 - Arrival from Trincomalie of Captain Cochrane as Commandent at Jaffna.

—March. 5 - Arrival from England of Miss Tweedle, connected with the "Society for promoting Female Education in the East," to assist the Revd. P. Percival in the "Young

1841—"Ladies School" under the Jaffna Wesleyan Mission. See Note 53.

—March, 9 - At a public meeting of English, Burgher, and Tamil gentlemen held at the local Court House, and presided over by Captain Cochrane, "A Friend-in-Need Society" for Jaffna was formally organised. See Note 83.

1841—March. - Revd. Mr. Johnston of the C. M. S. and Mrs. Johnston arrive in Jaffna and take up their residence at Nallur to work for the benefit of the native population.

—March. - Mr. Thomas Mortimer, then a catechist connected with the C. M. S, who accompanied the Revd. W. Adley to England, returns to Jaffna. He was the first Jaffna man who visited Europe.

—April. - The Nallur English School removed to Chundicully. See Note 93.

—April, 5 - His Excellency Lieutenant-General Sir Collin Campbell, K. C. B. appointed Governor and Commander-in-Chief of Ceylon, arrives and takes his seat in Council.

—April. - Tappal communication between Jaffna and Kayts established.

—April. - A Tamil Dictionary, the first attempt at a complete Dictionary of the Tamil language in alphabetical order, printed at the American Mission Press, Manipay.

—June. - The Ceylon Bank opened.

1842—Death of Bishop Vincent De Rosario. See Note 76.

1842—April. - Two planters from England, Messrs Baynes and Clarke come to Jaffna with a view to carry on agricultural operations in the Northern Province.

—May. 13 - Mr. Henry Martyn commences at Manipay and Uduvil, a course of lectures on astronomy illustrating the principles by means of an improved Phantasmagoria lantern designed for the purpose.

—June. 2 - Death in his 76th year of P. Kandapillai, familiarly known as Aradchy Kanther, poet and physician. He is the father of a more talented son, the late Arumuga Navalar, and is said to have composed over twenty poetical works. See Note 84,

—Aug. 22 - The Colombo Observer of this date states that an English gentleman, engaged in the cultivation of tobacco in Jaffna, has raised a superior description of cotton from Pernambuco seeds and this has been valued

1842—by brokers in England at one shilling a pound.

—Oct. - The first Reading Room in Jaffna opened by Mr. F. C. Grenier, Secretary, Courts, Jaffna. This is now the present Jaffna Public Library.

—Oct. 22 - Opening at Vannarponne of a Sivite Tamil School See Note 85.

1842—Nov. & Dec. - Cholera at Mannar; 700 cases and 500 deaths reported.

—Dec. 5 - Death of John Rodrigo Muttiah, District Judge of the Islands.

1843—Arrival in Jaffna of the Revd. Fr. Oratio Bettachini, an Italian Missionary, who became the first Vicar apostolic of Jaffna. See Note 76.

—Feb. 8 - Mr. Dyke, who was, for 15 years, Government Agent of the Northern Province, leaves Jaffna for Colombo to take up his new appointment of "Acting Auditor and Accountant-General and Controller of Revenue."

—April. 1. - Mannar Government School opened. It was first held in a room at the Kachcheri of that Town.

—April. 1 - Supramania Ambalawanar, Proctor and Deputy to the Queen's Advocate of the District Court of Valigamam, appointed Acting District Judge of the Islands. See Note 86.

—June. - Mr. Henry Martyn severs connection with the Batticotta Seminary, where he was employed for 11 years. See Note 87.

1843—July. - Crown lands in the Northern Province sold to European planters at 5 shillings per acre.

—Aug. - Breaking out of small-pox in Jaffna. Patients removed to Sirutivu for treatment.

—Aug. 11 - The Jaffna Native Improvement Society established.

—Nov. 1. - Return of Mr. Dyke as Government Agent of the Northern Province.

—Nov. 12 - The Catholic Press established in Colombo.

—Nov. 13 - The Spire of the Dutch Church in the Fort of Jaffna struck by lightning.

—Dec. 2 - A Severe gale at Jaffna.

—Henry Martyn appointed Government Storekeeper. See Note 88.

1843—Dec. - 15,877 acres of crown land in the Northern Province advertised for sale. Five hundred acres sold at upwards of 20 shillings per acre.

—Discovery at Mannar of a gold ring marked Ann P. L. O. C.

1844—Death of Swampillai, a poet of Vilan in the village of Tellippalai. He was the author of some Tamil works. He also made a collection of Tamil poems for the use of Catholic Schools.

1844—Death in his 40th year of Kadirasa Pulavar of Achchuveli. He wrote the Pathuma Poorany Nadagam and some fragmentary pieces. See Note 89.

—June. - No less than 150 elephants reported to have been killed in the Wanny, Government having offered a reward of fifteen shillings for every elephant destroyed. A certain number was also reported to have been killed in the Mannar and Pachchillapally districts. The tails of the elephants as proof of the animals having been killed were sent to the Jaffna Kachcheri, where they were cut in pieces and buried.

—July. 13 - Police Courts established.

—July. - During the criminal sessions at Jaffna, Chief Justice Sir Anthony Oliphant announced that all the District Courts in the Northern Circuit, except those at Jaffna, Mannar, Mullaitivu, Trincomalie, Batticaloa and Chilaw, were soon to be abolished and Courts of Requests substituted.

—Aug. 14 A gang of robbers supposed to number between 300 & 400 armed with cudgels and knives, make a night attack on the salt-pans at Vellaparavai in Puttur. Two of the ring-leaders arrested, tried and committed to jail.

1844—Aug. - The Church of St. Mary at Illavalai completely burnt down with all its fixtures.

—Sept. 20 - Death at Mannar of John Podmore, an Indo Briton of Fort St. George, Madras, aged 84 years and 3 months. He was the first Interpreter under Colonel Barbet soon after Jaffna surrendered to the British in 1795.

—Sept. 24 - Nomination as Vicar Apostolic of Ceylon of the Right Revd. Dr. Francis.

—Oct. - A New Province called the North-Western Province created.

—Oct. 30 - Death at Tanjore of the Revd. Gnanapragasam David, brother of the Revd. Christian David of Jaffna, at the advanced age of 96 years.

1844—Nov. - Small-pox breaks out in Jaffna, Nallur and other places.

—Nov. - Robert John Dunlop arrives in Jaffna and engages in coconut planting. See Note 173.

—Nov. 18 - 800 acres of Crown-land situated in the Pachchilapally District purchased by European planters at cne pound per acre.

1844—Dec. 20 - An ordinance passed for the total abolition of slavery in Ceylon.

—Mr. Byrne of the P. W. D. takes steps to improve the system of drainage in Jaffna,

1845—Jan. 1 - Courts of Requests established.

—Jan. 1 - A new division of Circuits and Judicial Districts established. S. Ambalawanan appointed Commissioner of Requests and Police Magistrate of Kayts. See Note 86.

—Feb. 1 - Civil Servants interdicted from engaging in agricultural or commercial pursuits.

—Feb. 7 - The Ceylon Branch of the Royal Asiatic Society formed. See Note 90.

—Messrs J. Smith and S. Edirmannasinghe sworn in as unofficial members of the Legislative Council in the room of Mr. Armitage resigned and Mr. Casie Chetty. See Note 91.

—Death of Saravanamuttu Pulavar. He is the author of a well-known Tamil work and translator of another from the Sanskrit. See Note 92.

1845—Death of Inasitamby, a Catholic Tamil poet.

—May. 6 - Ceylon divided into the two Vicariates Apostolic of Colombo and Jaffna, Rev. Fr. Bettachini elected Coadjutor to the Bishop of Usula. See Note 95.

—Oct. 5 - Installation of the Right Revd. Oratio Bettachini as Bishop of Torona, and Coadjutor to the Vicar Apostolic of Ceylon.

—Serious out-break of small-pox in Jaffna.

—Death in his 78th year of Philip Chinnavar, Land owner and model farmer. See Note 94.

1846—Feb. 8 - Dr. Bettachini consecrated Bishop of Torona at St Lucia's Cathedral, Colombo.

—March - Cholera which had been raging throughout several Districts of the Island especially at Kandy and Jaffna,

1846—began to abate. About 10,000 deaths had occurred in the Northern Province. See Note 95.

—April 1 - J. L. Flanderka appointed writer attached to the office of the Government Agent at Jaffna.

1846—April - The first Ceylon Railway Scrip received in the Colony.

—Death of Edirweerasinghe Nitsinghe Talaivasinghe Mudaliyar, Maniagar of Valligamam West and the adjoining Islands.

—June 15 - Publication of the first number of the journal of the Royal Asiatic Society of Ceylon.

—June 16 - Election of His Holiness Pope Pius IX-21st June His coronation.

July - Dr. Chapman, the first Protestant Bishop of Colombo, comes to Jaffna and visits the Revd. Christian David.

—Nov. 16 - The Ceylon Widow's and Orphan's Pension Fund established.

—Dec. - Arrival in Jaffna of the Revd. Wm. W. Howland of the American Mission. See Note 186.

—The boarding school for girls at Uduvil under the American Mission placed in charge of Miss Eliza Agnew and Miss Capell.

1847—April. 19 - The Hon'ble Sir J. E. Tennent sworn in as Lieutenant-Governor.

1847—May. 29 - Lord Torrington arrives from Galle and takes his oaths as Governor of Ceylon.

—Sep. 17 - Bishop Bettachini appointed Pro-Vicar of Jaffna.

—Oct. 19 - Ordinance passed for the Registration of marriages.

—Nov. 28 - Arrival in Jaffna of Father Semeria of the Oblates of Mary Immaculate. See Note 95.

—First establishment in Jaffna of the congregation of the oblates of Mary Immaculate founded in 1815 by the Right Revd. Dr. De Mazenod, Bishop of Marseilles;—Revd. Fr. Semeria, the Revd. Fr. Keating and Brother Stephen Gaspard, being the first members. See Note 95.

—Dec. 31 - Arumuga Navalar, Tamil Scholar and Sivite reformer, commences a series of lectures or sermons at the Sivan Temple of Vannarponne, in defence of Hinduism. See Note 96.

—Dr. Ward of the American Mission leaves for America, Dr. Samuel Fisk Green of the American Mission comes to Jaffna and takes charge of its medical establishment. See Note 98.

1848—March - An Oppary (The Lamentations of the Blessed Virgin Mary at the foot of the cross) composed and completed by Henry Martyn. See Note 99.

—April. 11 - First importation of Ice into Ceylon.

—Aug. - The Catholic Boys' English School known as the Jaffna Boys' Seminary started by the Right Rev. Dr. Bettachini. See Note 103.

—Oct. 1 - W. C. Twynam Esqr. (now Sir William Twynam) appointed Assistant Government Agent of Jaffna. See Note 199.

—The Road Ordinance comes into operation.

—Dec. 24 - Commotion at the Jaffna Cathedral, Bishop Bettachini at the Church of Adaikkalamatha. Mr. Robert William Langslow D. Q. A. seriously injured in the melee. See Note 100.

—Dec. 31 - Henry Pole appointed Commissioner of Requests and Police Magistrate of Jaffna.

1849—Jan. 6 - Death in his 55th year of Channmukach Chaddambiyar, a well-known scholar and Tamil professor in the Batticotta Seminary. See Note 101.

1849—The translation by Dr. Hoisington into English of the three treatises on Sivasidanta Philosophy completed.

—July. 15 - Death of Robert Wm. Langslow D. Q. A. Jaffna, See Note 100.

—Aug. - Revolt in Mantotte of the Goanese priest Miguel Philip Mascarenhas against Bishop Bettachini. Commencement of the schism in Mannar and Mantotte.

Sep. - Stewart's Garden in the Main Street, Jaffna, purchased for the purpose of a residence for Bishop Bettachini. See Note 102.

1850—Jan. - The Jaffna Boys Seminary placed in charge of Mr. Patrick Foy, an Irishman. See Note 103.

—March. - Mrs. Flannagan, widow of an Irishman, and mother of the Rev. Father P. O'Flannagan O. M. I. takes charge of the English School for the Catholic girls of Jaffna under the R. C. Mission. See Notes 104, 223.

—The Rev. Fr. Cassinelli's first report on the Vicariate Apostolic of Jaffna issued.

—July. 4 - T. Mudaliyar Abraham appointed Notary Public of Jaffna by Mr. P. A. Dyke, G. A., N. P. See Note 231.

1850—Aug. - Arrival in Jaffna of Fathers Mauroit and Vivier.

—Mr. Nicholas Puvirajasinghe acts as Store-keeper to the P. R. C. and continues to work in that capacity till 1866.

—Nov. 27 - Sir George Anderson arrives as Governor.

—A piece of land purchased for the new Catholic Cemetery at Jaffna.

—The Jaffna Friend-in-Need Society's Hospital building completed.

—The first upstair house built in Jaffna. See Note 43.

1851—June. 4 - Father Semeria appointed Vicar General of Jaffna. See Note 95.

—The Dedication of the C. M. S. Church at Copay.

1852—Jan. - Rev. Mr. Percival of the Wesleyan Mission commences the translation of the Bible into Tamil. See Note 105.

—May. 8 - Death at the age of 81 of the Rev. Christian David. He was styled "The Patriarch of the Church in Ceylon" by Dr. Wardsworth, Bishop of Lincoln. See Note 106.

—A Silver Medal Granted to Mr. Vencatachellum, who was a private in the Military stationed in the Jaffna Fort, for long service and good conduct. He was the grandfather of K. Kandasamy, No. 356 of the Jaffna Police Force. See Note 350.

—Dec. - Out break of Cholera at Point Pedro.

—Report of the American Mission of Jaffna published.

—The Tirupanai Changam, in which laymen administered the temporalities of St. Mary's Church, the premier church of Jaffna, collapses. See Note 80.

1853—Jan. - St. Peter's School (now Kilner College) in Chetty Street, Vannarponne, opened as a branch school by the Rev. Mr. Percival. It is an off-shoot from the Central College.

—May. 6 - 'The Literary Mirror' a monthly Magazine, started by Mr. Wyman Katiravetpillai. See Notes 107, 127.

—A High Tamil school at Copay started by the C. M. S. See Note 108.

—June - The American Missionaries introduce the photographic art into Jaffna. See Note 109.

—Nov. - Cholera breaks out in Jaffna.

—The ordinary monthly expenses of a European gentleman in Jaffna at this time seldom exceeded £ 4.

o

1854—Mar. 13 - Ordination of the Revd. Richard Watson Vairamuttu, one of the first Tamil Wesleyan Ministers of Jaffna.

—Mar. 21 - Mr. Hardy, a European planter, donates a piece of land at Chavakachcheri for the use of the Catholic Mission of Jaffna.

—May. 1 - Bishop Bonnand arrives at Kankesanturai as Visitor Apostolic to settle certain matters in connection with the Vicariates of Colombo and Jaffna.

—Dec. 8 - Definition of the Immaculate Conception of the B V. M. See Note 95.

—Death of Kasinatha Pulavar, a Poet and Astrologer of Achuvely. He wrote a poem called Thalapuranam and some fragmentary Pieces. See Note 110.

—The case instituted by Father Laureant in connection with the Kayts cemetery decided. The cemetery is declared common.

—Publication of the work entitled Siva-dhusana-parikaram, by Arumuga Navalar. It excites some sensation in Jaffna. See Note 111.

1855—Feb. 3 - Death at Manipay of the Rev. Daniel Poor, D. D., aged 65 years and 7 months. See Notes 58, 112.

—Feb. 7 - Cholera which had been raging throughout the peninsula ceases on the termination of a Tridium in the Jaffna Cathedral in honour of the Immaculate Conception of the B. V. M. See Notes 95, 98.

—May. 11 - Sir Henry Ward arrives and assumes the reins of Government.

—May. 22 - First meeting held by Dr. Rufus Anderson, and the Rev. A. R. Thompson. who were sent to Jaffna as the Deputation of the Prudential Committee of the American Board of Commissioners for Foreign Missions, to inquire into the working of the American Ceylon Mission of Jaffna. See Note 55.

—Nov. 15 - Death at Jaffna of Asseervatha Mudaliyar of the Jaffna Kachcheri. See Notes 43, 102.

1856—Cholera breaks out in Jaffna and rages to an alarming extent.

—June. 24 - The Photographic art first introduced into Ceylon by Mr. Parting. See Note 109.

1856—Aug. 20 - Revd. Fr. Semeria consecrated Bishop of Olympia and elected co-adjutor to Bishop Bettachini. See Note 95.

—Sept. A sum of fifteen thousand pounds is proposed to be devoted to complete a telegraph line of 300 miles from Mannar to Kandy, from Kandy to Colombo and from Colombo to Galle.

—Nov. 27 - Fr. Bonjean, a missionary of the Foreign Missions at Coimbatore, having obtained from Bishop Bonnand leave to join the Oblates and having been accepted by the Vicar Apostolic of Jaffna, lands at Kayts. See Note 95.

1857—April. - A. Pearl-Fishery yielded £ 20,000.

—May. 1 - Opening at the Pettah, Jaffna, of a Private Tamil School. See Note 113.

—June. 1 - Mr. J. R. Arnold succeeds Mr. Caroll alias D. C. Visuvanathapillai, B. A. as Tamil Editor of the "Morning Star." He continues in this post till the end of his life. See Notes 114, 115.

—July. 26 - Bishop Bettachini dies at Bollawatta ; Bishop Semeria succeeds him. See Note 103.

—Aug. - Henry Martyn's Poetical work entitled Esther Vilasam commenced. See Note 99.

1858—Jan. 1 - The first Telegraph line opened in Ceylon between Colombo and Galle.

—April. - A Pearl-Fishery at Arippo yielded £ 24, 129.

—May. 5 - Coomaraswamy Mudaliyar Wyman Katiravetpillai enrolled as an advocate, begins to practise in Jaffna.

—July. 22 - Arrival of Steamer "Pearl."

Aug. 3 - Inauguration of the Ceylon Railway by Sir Henry Ward.

—Sept. 17 - The Submarine Cable connecting Ceylon with India laid between Thanaikai Pt. and Talaimannar.

—Oct. - Opening of Telegraphic communication from Kandy to Mannar via Mihintale.

—The tax on spirits reaches £ 75,000.

—Oct. - Establishment of through Telegraphic communication between Ceylon and India.

1859—Feb. - A Catholic Library, the first of its kind, opened in Jaffna by Bishop Semeria.

—April. - A Pearl-Fishery at Arippo yielded £ 48, 215.

—Population of the town of Jaffna 28,500.

1859—Nov. - The "Paliar Nasan," a small newspaper for children, issued under the direction of Messrs. Sanders and Hitchcock of the American Mission.

—The old church of St. John's, Chundikully, C. M. S., replaced by the present building.

—Death of Nicholas Tisseveerasinghe Mudaliyar. See Note 41.

1860—Feb. - Death of S. Davidupillai, a clerk in the Paddy Department of the Jaffna Kachcheri. See Note 116.

—March - A Pearl-Fishery yielded £ 36, 681.

—May - Mr. Francis Muttiah Armstrong promoted to the rank of Commanding officer in the P. W. D. See Note 117.

—June. 30 - Sir Henry Ward appointed Governor of Madras. General Lockyer appointed Lieut. Governor of Ceylon.

—July. 15 - Sir E. S. Creasy appointed Chief Justice of Ceylon. He was a historical writer of great eminence.

—Aug. 2 - Death at Madras from an attack of cholera of Sir Henry Ward, late Governor of Ceylon.

—Chapel of St. Alphonsus Liguori established at Chavakachcheri.

—Aug. 4 - Sir Charles Mac'Carthy appointed Governor of Ceylon.

—Sept. - The controversial dialogues at the Jaffna Cathedral commenced by Henry Martyn. See Note 118.

—Oct. - Death at Chilaw of Simon Casie Chetty, the author of some learned works on Ceylon.

—Dec. 21 - Father Pelissier commences the erection of St. Thomas' Church at Pt. Pedro.

- Dec. - Indian University examinations begin to be held in Jaffna.

1861—March - Mr. Pennefather appointed Auditor General of the Colony. See Note 125.

—March. 31 - Death of Henry Martyn, the talented Government Store-keeper. He was Teacher, Preacher, Editor, Scholar, Poet and Artist. See Note 119.

—May. 21 - Death of Mgr. Mazenod, founder of the Society of the Oblates of Mary Immaculate.

—St. Joseph's orphanage established in Jaffna for the benefit of orphan children of heathen parentage. See Note 120.

—July. - Mr. Muttu Coomara Swamy (afterwards Sir) appointed Tamil member of the Legislative Council. See Note 121.

—July. 25 - Rev. Fr. Mauriot lays the foundation of St. James' Church Karaiyoor, Jaffna. See Note 122.

1861—Dec. 14 - Death of the Prince consort.

—Dec. 16 - By a decree of the S. C. the Parapankandal Church is made over to the Goanese schismatics.

1862—March. 9 - A sacrilegious theft committed in the Jaffna Cathedral.

—April - Re-appearance of cholera since 1855.

—June. 15 - Governor Mac. Carthy visits Jaffna.

—June. 16 - Proctor Bastiampillai presents an address to His Excellency on behalf of the Catholics of Jaffna.

—Cholera rages at Passaioor.

—Aug. 15 - St. Thomas' Church at Pt. Pedro opened for Divine worship.

—Sept. - Bronze money first introduced into Ceylon.

—Sept. - The "Jaffna Freeman" started by N. G. Gould. See Note 127.

—Sept. 29 - Death at the age of 39 of the Revd. Richard Watson Vairamuttu, the younger of the first two Wesleyan Tamil Ministers of Jaffna.

—Oct. - Death at Jaffna of Proctor Bastiampillai immediately after his nomination as acting M. L. C. See Note 124.

—Nov. 2 - The Sisters of the Holy Family from Bordeaux arrive in Jaffna. See Note 126.

—Dec. - Martyn's Road opened by Mr. Dyke, as a lasting compliment to a distinguished Jaffna man. See Note 125.

1863—The Jaffna Catholic Girls' School delivered over to the charge of the Sisters of the Holy Family by Mrs. O. Flannagam. See Note 126.

—Feb. 6 - The Ceylon Patriot started by Mr. W. C. Katiravetpillai. See Note 127.

—Feb. - Mr. Coomaraswamy, the first Tamil Barrister, called to the bar at Lincoln's Inn. See Note 121.

—April. 14 - Consecration of the Episcopal Chapel of the Immaculate Conception, Jaffna.

—June. 27 - Colombogam, the property of Mr. Joseph Price, purchased for St. Joseph's Orphanage. See Note 128.

—Dec. 20 - Sensational meetings and memorials by Catholics against the New Marriage Bill. The Bill however passes as Ordinance No. 13 of 1863.

—The Tamil seat in the Legislative Council becomes vacant by Mr. (afterwards Sir) M. Coomaraswamy going away on leave. Mr. J. H. Eaton is appointed to the vacancy. See Note 121.

1863—Dec. - Sir Charles Mac. Carthy leaves for Europe owing to ill-health. Major General O'Brien assumes the Government.

1864—Jan. - The first Locomotive Engine landed in Colombo.

—March. 2 - First telegraph message received by the Indo-European line.

—April - Launching on the Jaffna Lagoon of the steam tug, "Comet," the first steam boat built in Ceylon.

—April. 17 - The Society of the Brothers of St. Joseph established at Colombogam. Its object is to train teachers for Vernacular Schools; and catechists to assist the Oblate Missionaries of Jaffna.

—April. 22 - Death in his sixty-fifth year of the Rev. John Philips Sanmogam, the elder of the two first Wesleyan Tamil Ministers of Jaffna. See Note 53.

—May 24 - The ceremony of laying the foundation of the convent of the Holy Family of Jaffna performed by Bishop Semeria. See Note 129.

—Death of Joseph, Thombo-holder of the Jaffna Kachcheri, popularly known as Vandy Soosaipillaiar.

—Sept. - Serious out-break of cholera at Adaikalamada, Painter's Street.

—A branch of the Oriental Bank Corporation opened in Jaffna, See Note 130.

—Oct. - Government offices to be closed at 2 P. M. on every Saturday.

—Dec. 27 - First special train runs on Ceylon Railway.

1865—Jan. 24 - Congregation of the Native Sisters of St. Peter founded in Jaffna.

—Mr. Solomon Johnpulle becomes proprietor of the "Ceylon Patriot." See Note 170.

—Feb. 7 - Apostasy of Mola.

—March. - Sir Hercules Robinson assumes the Government of Ceylon as Lieutenant-Governer.

—May. 16 - Sir Hercules Robinson sworn in as Governor.

—June. 13 - The Jaffna Premier Bakery started by Mr. Saverimuttu Pedurupillai, a well-known townsman of Jaffna. See Note 278.

1865—Aug. 11 - Fr. Bonjean commences the famous Boake controversy on Jesuit's oath in the columns of the "Ceylon Examiner." See Note 440.

—Mr. John Hensman ordained at the Nallur Church by Bishop Piers Claughton. See Note 157.

—Aug. 21 - Death at Jaffna of Br. Dowling from consumption. See Note 103.

—Sept. 27 - Death of the Hon. R. T. Pennefather, Auditor-General.

1866—Jan. 1 - The establishment of a Police Force at Jaffna.

—The Revd. John Kilner, the head of the North Ceylon Wesleyan Mission, leaves for Europe. The Revd. W. William Walton, who succeeds him, dies shortly after. See Note 53.

—Feb. 27 - The Oblate Fathers withdraw from the Colombo Vicariate and join the Jaffna Vicariate.

—Oct. - Violent out-break of Cholera in Jaffna. The epidemic rages furiously up to March 1867. See Note 98.

1867—Jan. - Telegraph Cable laid between India and Ceylon.

—March. - Cholera Commission sent to Jaffna. The Commission carries on its enquiry till April.

—March. - Great distress at Delft. People starving, relief sent by the Catholic Mission. A large sum of money placed at the disposal of the Catholic Mission by the Friend-in-Need Society for the relief of distress.

—April. 20 - Cholera Commissioners report 16,298 attacks and 10,210 deaths from October 1866 to April 1867.

—June. - Major Skinner "The Great Ceylon Road-maker," retires from the public service of Ceylon after 40 years residence in the Island. See Note 143.

—July - An association founded at Marseilles by Bishop Semeria for providing dowries for the Jaffna orphan girls.

—Oct. 9 - Death at Copay of Mr. Percival Ackland Dyke, G. A. for the Northern Province and the oldest Ceylon Civil Servant. See Note 131.

1868—Jan. - The School Commission superseded by the Department of Public Instruction. See Note 58.

—Jan. 23 - Death at Marseilles of Bishop Semeria from Pleurisy. See Note 95.

—Death of P. Thambapillai, a patient and painstaking teacher. See Note 104.

1868—April. 30 - Death at Hongkong of Karli Appar employed as a Private at Jaffna, Trincomalie, Colombo and Kandy. He was the father of K. Kandasamy, No. 356, Senior Sergeant of the Jaffna Police Force, who is well-known as a keen and clever detective. See Note 350.

—July. - The Registration of Births and Deaths Ordinance comes into force.

—Aug. 24 - Episcopal consecration of Bishop Bonjean at St. Martins' of Tours. See Note 95.

—Aug. - Gift by the French Government of a press for the Jaffna Catholic Mission. See Note 175.

—Oct. 25 - Arrival of Bishop Bonjean in Jaffna. He is accorded a cordial reception.

—Nov. - The *Via Crucis* canonically erected at Chillalai.

—Dec. 21 - Bishop Bonjean lays the foundation stone of the Church of St. Thomas at Mathagal.

1869—March. 6 - Death of Sir J. Emerson Tennent, the eminent writer and Colonial Secretary.

—Mr. Laurie, the first Director of Public Instruction in Ceylon, visits Jaffna.

—March. - Society of the "St. Anns' Ladies of Charity," Jaffna, established. See Note 215.

—May. 20 - Completion of the Telegraph line to Jaffna.

—July. 13 - An English School opened at Vannarponne by Arumuga Navalar for the Education of Hindu children. See Note 132.

—Sept. 15 - Sir William Crofton Twynam appointed Government Agent, Northern Province. See Note 199.

—Nov. 19 - Opening of the Suez Canal.

—Solemn inauguration of the new Convent, Jaffna.

—The Confraternity of the Sacred Heart of Jesus, Jaffna, formed. See Note 133.

—Nov. The Ecclesiastical Seminary (St. Martin's) established in Jaffna. See Note 348.

—Dec. 8 - Mr. J. Rowley Smythe of the Ceylon Civil Service received into the Catholic Church by the Revd. Father Salaun. See Note 103.

—Dec. - Mr. T. C. Changarapillai, Crown Proctor, takes up the editorial management of the "Ceylon Patriot." See Note 127

1870--Jan. - Export duties abolished.

—Jan. - The first steamer from India passes through the Suez Canal.

—Jan. 22 - The Sisters of the Holy Family installed in the new Convent at Jaffna. See Note 129.

—Feb. 22 - Death at Jaffna from paralysis of Brother Conway. See Note 103.

—Feb. - Mr. Samuel Nevinspillai admitted to the degree of Bachelor of Laws, Madras. See Note 173.

—Mar. 9 - Purchase of new ground for the house of the Oblate Missionaries at Jaffna.

—Mar. 29 - Arrival in Colombo of H. R. H. the Duke of Edinburgh.

—July. 19 - Announcement received of the commencement of the Franco-Prussian War.

—Sept. 11 - Ordination at the Nallur Church by the Bishop of Colombo of Messrs E. Hoole, P. Henry and G. Champion of the Church Mission.

1871- "The Jaffna News" started by Mr. Hughes. See Note 127.

—March - £ 1,056 collected in Ceylon for the French and Prussian Sick and Wounded.

—Mar. 26 - First General Census of Ceylon. Population of the Island 2,405,287.

—Aug. 2 - Arrival in Colombo of the new Colonial Government Steamer "Serendib."

—Aug. 9 - Death of Mr. C. A. Lorenz, a leading Lawyer, Journalist and Legislator. See Note 107.

—Aug. - Mannar Government School made over to the Catholic Mission.

– Nov. 7 - The famous Will Case of Jaffna No. 10,099, (in which Nicholas Goutier Gould of Jaffna, Suppar of Nallur. Ramalingam of Anaicottai, and others were implicated,) tried in Colombo. The accused found guilty and sentenced to six years imprisonment. See Note 135.

—Dec. 12 - Total Eclipse of the sun. An expedition under Norman Lockyer arrives to take observations at Jaffna and Trincomalie. Mr. Lockyer delivers an address on the Eclipse at the D. C. House, Jaffna.

—Dec. 19 - Imposing ordination at the Jaffna Cathedral of Farthers P. O. Flanagan, A. Roux, and O. Vedrenne by Bishop Bonjean. This is the first ordination of Catholic Priests held in Jaffna. See Note 103.

1872—Jan. 1 - Inauguration of the rupees and cents currency of Ceylon.

—Jan. 1 - First Indian Mail passes through Mount Cenis Tunnel.

—Jan. - Revd. Fr. J. Boisseau, who was director of the Colombogam Orphanage for five years, transferred to Kayts as Parish Priest. The Revd. Fr. G. Salaun, O. M. I. succeeds him.

—Jan. 4 - Sir Hercules Robinson leaves Ceylon. Hon. Henry Turnour Irving sworn in as Lieutenant Governor.

—Mar. 4 - Rt. Hon. Mr. W. H. Gregory assumes the administration of Ceylon.

—Mar. - An elderly Indian Lady named Gnanathepam, a daughter of the late Vethanayagasastriar, the celebrated Tamil Poet of South India, comes to Jaffna and inaugurates a system of public and religious instruction called "Lyrical preaching."

—April. 4 - His Excellency Sir William Gregory visits Jaffna.

—May. 21 - His Excellency Sir William Gregory confers on Mr. Wyman Katiravetpillai, the appointment of Police Magistrate of Kayts.

—July. 3 - Inauguration of the Jaffna College, Revd. E. P. Hastings being the first Principal. See Note 136.

—Aug. 8 - Foundation Stone of the Church of our Lady of the Rosary at Madhu laid by Bishop Bonjean. See Note 227.

—Aug. 8 - The building of St. Charles' Mission House in Jaffna commenced.

—Aug. 24 - Death from diabetes of John Ollegasagaram Mudaliyar, Government General Store-keeper, Jaffna.

—Sept. - The Jaffna Catholic Young-men's Society started.

—The Jaffna College Miscellany started. See Note 127.

1873—Jan. 9 - Death of Kanagasabaipillai Alias Evarts, a distinguished Native Physician and Tamil poet. He was the author of the Thiruvakupuranam (Scripture History in verse.) His son Jeremiah Evarts was the well-known Head-master of the Chundikuli Seminary. See Note 137.

—Feb. - The Jaffna Catholic Printing Press established. See Note 175.

—April. 28 - Mr. Daniel Earnest de Saram assumes duties as District Judge of Jaffna.

1873—June. 18 - Death at the age of 83 of the Revd. Levi Spaulding of the American Mission, who was in charge of the Uduvil Parish. He was a good Tamil scholar and the author of an English-Tamil Dictionary and other works. He served in Jaffna for 54 years. See Note 138.

—Sept. 6 - The erection of the North-Central Province, making in all seven Provinces. Mr. J. E. Dickson appointed Govt. Agent.

—David's Road opened by Sir William C. Twynam. See Note 116.

1874—Jan. 22 - Death at Colombo of the Revd. Matthews Caetano, the last of the Goanese Missionaries.

—Mr. Mac Mahon of St. Peter's College, Agra, takes charge of the Jaffna Boys' Seminary. See Note 103.

—Feb. 8 - Sir W. Gregory pays his second visit to Jaffna. He is accompanied by his Private Secretary Mr. Cockburn Stewart, Major Clay, the Hon. the Colonial Secretary and Dr. Charlesly. See Note 139.

—Feb. 11 - S. Mudaliyar Saverimuttu Mudaliyar presented with a gold medal and chain by Governor Gregory. In the after-noon of the same day the Mudaliyar had the honor of entertaining His Excellency and party at his house. See Note 139.

—March. 10 - A Pearl-Fishery at Mannar yielded £10,000.

—April. 14 - Death at Jaffna from consumption of the Revd. Fr. Salaun O. M. I. See Note 103.

—July. 23 - The honour of Knight-hood conferred on Mr. Muttu Cumaraswamy, Representative of the Tamils in the Legislative Council.

—The Gnananantha Puranam printed at Madras. See Note 393.

—Aug. - Death of Nicholaspillai Sinnatamby, a well-known officer of the Jaffna Kachcheri. See Note 140.

—Sept. 21 - A new school at Chernia Street opened by the Revd. J. Kilner of the Wesleyan Mission.

—Oct. 7 - Telegraph line extended to Anuradhapura.

—Oct. 28 - Death at Batticotta of Mrs. Mary C. Spaulding. She is interred at the American Mission burial ground at Tellippalai.

Nov. 2 - Blessing of the Catholic Cemetery at Jaffna.

Dec. 30 - Death in his 83rd year of Coomaraswamy Mudaliyar father of Wyman Katiravetpillai. P. M. of Kayts. He wrote a drama called "Indra Kumara Nadagam" and a poem called "Arulampala Kovai." See Note 141.

1875—April. - Death of Suppiar, a noted scholar and astrologer of Manipay.

—May. 25 - Grand celebration of the 25th anniversary of the ordination to the Priest-hood of the Revd. Fr. Mauroit. He was presented with a costly chalice.

—Death in his 53rd year of D. Joseph, Udaiyar of Jaffna Town.

—July. - Out-break of Cholera among immigrant coolies on the North Road, 500 deaths reported.

—Aug. 11 - Grand meeting at Colombo to make arrangements for the reception of the Prince of Wales.

—Oct. - An address, gold plate and chain presented by the Colombo Tamils to Sir M. Coomaraswamy on the occasion of his Knight-hood. See Note 121.

—The Jaffna Prince of Wales reception Fund reaches Rs. 10,000. Casket and jewels prepared for presentation. See Note 142.

—Nov. - Cholera breaks out in Jaffna.

—Dec. 1 - H. R. H. The Prince of Wales (afterwards King Edward VII) lands in Colombo. Mr. Solomon Johnpulle (nominated by Sir William Twynam, Chief of the Deputation from the North that waited on His Royal Highness) reads the address to the august Visitor as the Representative of the Tamil population of the Island. Casket and jewels prepared at Jaffna presented by K. Kanagaratna Mudaliyar of the Jaffna Kachcheri. See Note 170.

—Dec. 8 - The foundation stone of the Colombo Break-water laid by the Prince of Wales, who leaves the same day. Official expenditure on account of the Prince of Wales' visit Rs. 110,000 besides private subscriptions to the amount of Rs. 50,000.

1876—Jan. 9 - Blessing of the Catholic Cemetery at Kayts. Half the cost of building the walls paid by Government.

—Jan. 27 - Death of Sir R. F. Morgan, Queen's Advocate. He acted as Chief Justice of the Island for some time and was one of the most distinguished and prominent Ceylonese of his time.

—Feb. 19 - Publication of the "Jaffna Catholic Guardian" commenced. Mr. P. E. Morgappa placed on the editorial staff. See Notes 127, 175, 176.

1876—Mr. Armstrong at the request of Government transports to Colombo the Stone Lion which was discovered by him at Pollenaruwa on the Habarana-Tammankaduwa Road, where it had remained buried for many years. It is now placed inside the Colombo Museum where it is now seen to great advantage and occupies a prominent site in the outer Gallery.

—April - The marble tabernacle brought from England placed on the Central altar of the Jaffna Cathedral. It cost Rs. 1,000. See Note 351.

—April. 28 - Proclamation of Queen Victoria as Empress of India made in the London Gazette.

—Oct. 21 - Cholera breaks out in Jaffna.

—Oct. 26 - A proposal to connect Ceylon and India by railway, made by the Duke of Buckingham.

—Nov. 26 - Violent recrudescence of Cholera at Karaiyoor. People oppose the removal of patients to the Hospital. The Police insist. Disturbance arises. The Police are assaulted.

—Dec. 23 - Ordination to the priest-hood of Bros. Xavier N. Sandresegara and Michael A. Murphy.

—Dec. - Death of Velupillai Mudaliyar, a well-known Jaffna gentleman and a distinguished officer of the P. W. D. He constructed the Katugastotta bridge, considered a master-piece of Engineering. See Note 143.

—The photographic business of Messrs S. K. Lawton & Co. established in Jaffna and Colombo.

1877—Jan. 1 - Queen Victoria proclaimed Empress of India at a great assemblage in Delhi of all the Native Kings, Chiefs and Nobles of India under the Presidency of the Viceroy Lord Lytton.

—Jan. - Cholera continues to prevail in Jaffna.

—Jan. 8 - Mr. P. E. Morgappa gives up all connection with the Catholic Guardian and joins the teaching staff of the J. B. Seminary. Mr. James H. Martyn appointed to the editorial staff of the Guardian. See Note 127.

—Jan. 10 - Cholera breaks out at Passayoor, Kayts, Navaly and other places.

—March. 9 - Lieut-Governor A. N. Birch visits Jaffna.

—April - Cholera rages at Allaipitty.

—May. 7 - Death of Gabriel Solomon Puvirajasinghe (Proctor.) See Note 144.

1877—May - The title of Mudaliyar of the Governor's Gate conferred on Mr. Francis Muttayah Armstrong.

—June. 3 - The Jubilee of His Holiness Pope Pins IX celebrated with great rejoicing in Jaffna, Mannar and other places.

—June. 13 - The Jaffna Cholera Commissioners appointed, consisting of Lieut. Col. Fyers, Dr. Kynsey and G. W. R. Campbell Esq.

—July. 16 - Report of the Jaffna Cholera Commssioners published. The report was characterised as unfair. There were according to the report 541 cases and 224 deaths in 1875; 1,700 cases and 826 deaths in 1876; 10,972 cases and 5,481 deaths up to June 1877. In all throughout the Jaffna Peninsula and the Islands there were 13,213 cases and 6,891 deaths.

—July. 24 - Death of Major Thomas Skinner the great Roadmaker of Ceylon. See Note 143.

—Sept. 2 - Governor Sir James R. Longden arrives at Galle.

—Sept. 22 - Arulappa Mudaliyar, a Tamil scholar of South India, appointed to the editorial staff of the Jaffna Tamil Catholic Guardian.

—Oct. - A recrudescence of Cholera in Jaffna.

—Oct. - A form of famine diarrhoea succeeds the real epidemic of Cholera and carries off large numbers. 20,000 deaths reported in the Northern Province.

—Oct. 24 - 1,175 francs received from France by the Catholic Mission for the relief of the distressed in Jaffna.

—Oct. 26 - The promoters of "The Jaffna and Batticaloa Commercial and Agricuitural Co. Ltd." get the promise from Governor Longden of the first offer of 20,000 acres of Kanthalai Tank land for their enterprise.

—Oct. 27 - Death of N. Ekamparam, a scholar and poet. He was the only Jaffna man who was recognised as an Addavathany, (one who can remember many things simultaneously.)

—Nov. 30 - Publication of the report on the grain taxes. The commissioners recommend the abolition of the renting system, and the introduction of compulsory commutation.

—Dec. 1 - Great distress in Jaffna among the poor classes.

—Dec. 19 - Cholera and small-pox prevail in Delft. The people suffer from want of food and clothing. Several die of starvation. Relief sent by the Catholic Mission. Sum expended Rs. 1,454.

1877—Dec. 27 - Cholera breaks out at Chillalai.

—The Karaiyoor Reclamation scheme started as a relief work by Sir William Gregory.

1878—Mar. 5 - Death of Mr. T. Sinnatamby of Udupiddy, a Tamil scholar and poet. He wrote the "Rama Vilasam" and other works. See Note 145.

—May - Armstrong Mudaliyar transferred to Jaffna as District Engineer and Superintending officer. See Note 146.

—Oct. - Mr. L. Gasparpillai (popularly known as seeni adigar) appointed adigar of Mannar Island. See Note 189.

1879—Feb. - Very Revd. Fr. Soulier, Visitor-General of the Oblates of Mary Immaculate, comes to Jaffna on a visit.

– Feb. 30 - A large and representative meeting held at the J. B. Seminary for the purpose of establishing a Catholic College for higher education in Jaffna. See Note 103.

—March. - A Pearl-Fishery at Mannar yielded Rs. 52,430.

—May. 3 - The Hindu Temple at Karavetty takes fire during one of the festival nights. About 50 persons burnt to death.

—May. 4 - Death of the Hon. Sir. M. Coomaraswamy, Tamil M. L. C. According to the "Ceylon Observer," he was "the foremost man among the 30 millions or more of the Dravidian Race." See Note 121.

—July. 18 - Revd Fr. T. A. Melizan elected Bishop of Adrana and Co-adjutor to the Vicar Apostolic of Jaffna. See Note 95.

–Oct. 26 - Death of Sandrasagra Pandithar, a reputed Tamil Scholar. He was of assistance to the Protestant Missionaries in the translation of the scriptures and other religious tracts and books. See Note 147.

–Dec. 5 - Death at Vanarponne at the age of 56 of Arumuga Navalar, the well-known Tamil Scholar and Sivite Reformer. See Note 148.

1880—Jan. 14 - Arrival at Udupiddy of Mary and Margaret W. Leitch of the American Mission. See Note 206.

—Jan. 24 - Consecration of Dr. Theophilus Andrew Melizan O. M. I. as co-adjutor to the Bishop of Jaffna at Marseilles by Bishop Bonjean.

—Jan. 28 - Sir James Longden pays his second visit to Jaffna accompanied by Lady Longden, this being the first occasion in which a Lady of the Governor of Ceylon comes to the Peninsula. See Note 263.

1880—Feb. 1 - Mail coach between Jaffna and Point-Pedro started by Mr. V. Ynanamuttu, an enterprising Jaffna man. See Note 149.

—Feb. 3 - Mr. Twynam (Now Sir William) swears an affidavit before Mr. De Saram, District Judge of Jaffna, against Mr. Ludovici, Editor of the "Ceylon Examiner," for defamation contained in an article criticising Mr. Twynam's administration. Case subsequently committed to the Supreme Court and Mr. Ludovici fined Rs. 1,000 by Chief Justice Sir Richard Cayley.

—April. 1 - Central Road Mail coach started. See Note 347.

—April. - A Pearl-Fishery at Mannar yielded Rs. 130,000.

—April. 22 - Death in his 78th year of Changarapillai Mudaliyar Cherubim, father-in-law of Mr. G. S. Arianayagampillai, Puisne Judge of the High Court of Travancore.

—June. - The Jaffna Trading Company started. See Note 151.

—June. - S. Mudaliyar Saverimuttu Mudaliyar, Chief Mudaliyar of the Jaffna Kachcheri and Mudaliyar of the Governor's Gate, named a Chevalier of the Order of St. Gregory the Great on the recommendation of Bishop Bonjean. See Note 152.

—July. 1 - Meeting held at the Jaffna Kachcherri to consider the best way of disposing of the balance remaining from the Prince of Wales' Reception Fund. The erection of a Clock Tower on the Esplanade decided on. See Note 211.

—July. - First Electric Telephone established in Ceylon.

—Sept. 10 - Death in Colombo from dysentery and liver complaint of Mr. David Todd, Cocoanut planter, Jaffna. He acted as Police Magistrate and was for a time Consul for the United States and a Justice of the Peace for the Island.

—Sept. - A Dharma Chattiram (a charity house for Hindu pilgrims, mendicants and others) established in Colombo at a cost of Rs. 30,000 by Thambyah Mudaliyar, a Jaffna Tamil resident in that city.

—Oct. 1 - Money Order system with India commenced.

—Nov. - Mr. S. Mervin, Clerk, Jaffna Kachcherri and a distinguished student of the Batticotta Seminary, retires on pension after thirty five years' service. See Note 87.

—Dec. 1 - Death from apoplexy at his residence in Jaffna of Mr. P. S. Sandrasegara, the Jaffna Agent of the British India Steam Navigation Company. See Note 130.

1880—Dec. 5 - Return to Jaffna from Europe of Bishop Melizan accompanied by Fathers Thiery, Joulain and Lafarge.

—Dec. 18 - Imposing Ordination Service in St. Mary's Cathedral, Jaffna. Bishop Bonjean, assisted by his two Vicars-General and twenty Priests, ordains the Revd. Brothers Iserbyt, John Aloysius and Charles Collin as priests, the Revd. Brothers Jeandel and Jules Collin as Deacons, and Revd. Brother Smythe as Sub-Deacon. Brothers Stouter and Murphy received the order of Porter; and Brothers Royer and Kirby, the clerical Tonsure.

—Dec. - Publication of an interesting report on the Irrigation System of the Mannar District by Mr. Henry Parker.

—Dec. 31 - The Church at Columbuturai, the first Church in Ceylon dedicated to St. Patrick and built by Fr. O'Flannagan, mainly with the aid of contributions from Irishmen, is blessed by Bishop Bonjean. This church collapsed and on it was built the present St. Mary's Church.

1881—Jan. - Receipt by Governor Longden of a Semi-official despatch from the Secretary of State intimating that the Anglican Church in Ceylon will be dis-established and that henceforth no Colonial Chaplain or Bishop will be appointed. The Ministers, however, to continue to draw their salaries for 5 years.

—Jan. 10 - St. Patrick's College opened by Bishop Bonjean, assisted by his Co-adjutor, Dr. Melizan, and his Vicars-General, the Very Revd. Fathers Pulicani and Boisseau. Bishop Bonjean delivers an impressive inaugural address. See Note 103.

—Jan. 25 - Anniversary of Dr. Melizan's Consecration as Bishop. Saverimuttu Mudaliyar in the name of the Catholics of the Northern and Eastern Provinces, presents the Bishop with a chalice of antique design richly wrought.

—Feb. 6 - Ceremony of investing S. Mudaliyar Saverimuttu Mudaliyar with the insignia of the order of St. Gregory the Great performed in St. Mary's Cathedral by Bishop Bonjean. The brief of His Holiness Pope Leo xiii to the Mudaliyar, dated 22nd February 1880, is read in the Church in the presence of a crowded congregation.

—Feb. 17 - Second general Census taken in Ceylon. Total population of the Island, 2,759.738. Northern Povince, 302,500. Town of Jaffna 40,057.

1881—Mr. J. R. Arnold appointed Tamil Professor at the Jaffna College. See Note 115.

—March. 1 - A Pearl-Fishery at Arippo yielded Rs. 599,533.

—Dec. 3 - The foundation stone of the large hall of St. Patrick's College laid by Dr. Bonjean in the presence of a large and representative gathering. See note 103.

—Dec. 31 - A severe shock of Earth-quake felt throughout Ceylon.

1882—Jan. 25 - Arrival in Colombo of Their Royal Highnesses Princes Albert Victor and George of Wales.

—Feb. - Publication of the report on the Giant's Tank and its ancient history by Mr. H. Parker.

—Feb. - Revd. E. W. Griffith takes charge of the Jaffna Mission of the C. M. S.

—June. - The Northern Districts of Ceylon attract attention as a field for farming, planting and hunting.

—July. 31 - Death of T. Mudaliyar Joseph, head accountant, Paddy Department, Jaffna Kachcherri.

—Sep. 25 - The S. S. "Lady Longden" built in London for Mr. S. Thambyah Mudaliyar, a Jaffna Tamil Resident in Colombo, and intended to run between Ceylon and India, arrives in Colombo.

—Sept. 26 - Death of Mr. Nathaniel Niles, popularly known as "Prasangiar", one of the earliest converts of the American Mission.

—Oct. 4 - Death of Sandrasagara Mudaliyar Saverimuttu Mudaliyar, Chief Mudaliyar of the Jaffna Kachcheri and Chevalier of the order of St. Gregory the Great. See Note 152.

—Dec. 1 - A. Paul Mudaliyar appointed Chief Mudaliyar of the Jaffna Kachcheri. See Note 188.

—Dec. 26 - Violent storm accompanied by rain and thunder in Jaffna, Mannar and throughout Ceylon.

1883—April. 10 - Bishop Bonjean transferred to Colombo as Bishop there, Bishop Melizan succeeding him in Jaffna. See Note 103.

—April. 11 - The S. S. "Lady Longden" sold by the proprietor for Rs. 69,000 to a Singapore Company.

—May. - Importation of the first Jin Rickshaw into Ceylon by Messrs Whittall & Co.

—June. 14 - Death at Manipay at the age of 77 years of Miss Agnew of the Jaffna American Mission. She served in Jaffna for 43 years. See Notes 59, 153.

1883—July. 10 - Sir John Douglas, K. C. M. G., sworn in as acting Governor.

—Aug. 2 - Formation of the C. M. S. Native Missionary Association. Its object is to raise funds for assisting the C. M. S. in the Evangelization of the Pallai and Vanni Districts.

—Aug. 14 - Death of Bar Kumarakulasinghe Mudaliyar, Secretary and Interpreter of the Mallagam and Jaffna Courts. See Note 87.

—Aug. - Sub-division of the Island into three Bishoprics.

—Aug. - Mr. M. M. Edirmannasingham, Assistant Forester, completes the boundary walls of St. Mary's Cathedral premises, left unfinished. See Note 351.

—Dec. 3 - The Hon. Sir Arthur Hamilton Gordon arrives and assumes the Government of Ceylon.

—Death at Jaffna of Nicholas Puvirajasinghe Mudaliyar, popularly known as "Store Tamber." See Note 68.

1884—March. - Death of Naganathapillai, a well-known scholar and poet, and at one time Interpreter Mudaliyar of the Mullativu Courts. See Note 155.

—March. - Mr. M. M. Edirmannasingham, Assistant Forester, presents a splendid cross for the celebration of the Pascal Representation in connection with the Jaffna Cathedral.

—March. - A Pearl-Fishery at Chilavaturai yielded Rs. 15,686.

- The Right Revd. E. A. Coplestone, afterwards Metropolitan of India, visits Jaffna.

-April. 26 - The first Young Men's Christian Association in Jaffna started by Professor Frank Sanders in connection with the Jaffna College.

-May. 3 - Collapse of the Oriental Bank Corporation. See Note 130.

—May. 5 - Governor Gordon guarantees the O. B. C. notes. A new Bank and Company proposed to be started. See Note 130.

-May. 28 - Announcement received of the death in America of Dr. Green, who was connected with the American Medical Mission of Jaffna, for several years. Great regret felt throughout Jaffna at the news. See Note 98.

—July. - Death of C. Sapapathy Mudaliyar, of the Jaffna Fiscal's Office, brother of Wyman Katiravetpillai, P. M. of Kayts. See Note 141.

—July. - Sir A. Gordon visits Jaffna.

1884—Death of G. P. Savundranayagampillai, B. A. B. L., Madras High Court Pleader. See Note 156.

—July. 21 - Mr. W. C. Twynam G. A., N. P., invested with the order of "C. M. G."

—Mr. C. W. Katiravetpillai, on the recommendation of Governor Gordon, is confirmed in his appointment as a Member of the Ceylon Civil Service by the Secretary of State.

—Aug. - Death in Colombo of S. Thambiah Mudaliyar, who got the S. S. "Lady Longden" built. He is said to have left over half a million rupees.

—Sept. 5 - Death in his 68th year of the Revd. John Hensman, the first ordained Tamil clergyman of the Church Mission. See Note 157.

—Sept. - The Jaffna St. Joseph's Catholic Library started. See Note 291.

—Oct. - Owing to the falling off of revenue, fresh taxation is resorted to. Postal rates and customs duties increased.

—Oct. 16 - A cyclone in Jaffna which causes great and extensive damage. Wind and rain striving for the mastery, fields and dwellings were flooded, trees uprooted, plantain gardens demolished, tiles blown off, boats and brigs wrenched from their moorings and sent adrift, and postal and telegraphic communication interrupted. See Note 158.

—Dec. 14 - A violent cyclonic storm throughout Ceylon, Jaffna suffers great loss of life and property. See Note 158.

—Dec. 27 - Death in his 90th year of Mr. Matthew Philips. See Note 63.

—First Christian Endeavour Society started at Uduvil.

1885—Jan. 31 - The new Ceylon Government Currency notes received and issued.

—Feb. 16 - Death of V. Ramalingam, a well-known Tamil Scholar and Poet. He wrote the "Thamayanthy Vilasam," "Manikavasagar Vilasam," and other works. His ancestors for three generations held the post of Udaiyars under Government. See Note 159.

—Mar. 29 - Death of the Revd. Br. J. J. Brown, who was connected with the J. B. Seminary for 27 years. See Note 103.

—Mar. 31 - Government allows the observance of the Tamil, Singhalese and Mohammedan New Year days as public holidays.

—April. 16 - Establishment of the Post-office Savings Bank.

1885—May. 20 - General meeting of the Confraternity of the Sacred heart held at St. Patrick's College. Mr. James H. Martyn delivers a lecture on "Duty." See Note 160.

—June. 18 - Sir Arthur Gordon leaves for England.

—June. 20 - Sir John Mac Leod sworn in as officer administering the Government.

—July. 1 - A serious epidemic of fever in some districts during the first quarter of 1885. 1,868 Cases reported in the Jaffna Peninsula.

—July. 18 - A meeting held at the Jaffna Kachcherri to aid the Head Committee at Colombo, towards a satisfactory and efficient representation of Ceylon at the Indian and Colonial Exhibition.

—July. 21 - Mr. Watson, the American entertainer, opens his performances in Jaffna.

—July. - Mr. J. H. Marsh, Inspector of Schools, Jaffna, transferred to Kandy. See Note 103.

—Aug. - A branch of the new O. B. C. opened in Jaffna.

—Aug. - St. James' Church at Klaly repaired by Mr. James Nicholas, Proctor.

—Sept. 18 - Miss Leitch of the American Mission of Jaffna visits Colombo and collects Rs. 5,000 for the Uduvil Girls' Boarding School.

—Nov. 14 - A large and influential public meeting held in the local District Court House to advocate Railway extension to the North. See Note 161.

—Nov. - Death of Ambalavaner Mudaliyar, Maniagar of Valigamam North. See Note 162.

—Nov. - Death of Mr. A. Eliathamby, Head Clerk of the Jaffna Kachcheri. See Note 163.

—Dec. - Death of Mr. C. A. Patterson, one of the oldest planters of Jaffna. He came as a Superintendent under Mr. Dunlop, who was the first to open the Pachchillipalli District for the systematic cultivation of the cocoanut.

—Dec. - T. Kathiritamby appointed Maniagar of Valigamam.

1886—Feb. - Passing of the Mohammedan Marriage-Registration Bill in the Legislative Council.

—Publication of the Galaxy of Tamil Poets or "Pavalar Charitra Theepakam" by J. R. Arnold. See Note 164.

—March. - Filling in the ground and forming a roadway round the Reclamation wall, Jaffna.

1886—March. - Building a grain shed at Kayts.

—April. - A collection in Ola-Books of all the Tamil Classics, with a brief account in English of each book prepared by Mr. C. W. Katiravetpillai, is sent to the Colonial and Indian Exhibition to be held in London.

—June. 5 - General meeting of the Confraternity of the Sacred Heart at St. Patrick's College. Dr. A. C. Evarts, then on the Tutorial Staff of St. Patrick's College, reads a paper on the "Immortality of the Soul," See Note 210.

—July. - Death of the Revd. W. Oakley, the Father of the Church Mission in Ceylon. He was connected with the Church Missionary Society for more than half a century.

—Aug. 7 - Death at Colombo from heart failure of Father Joseph Boisseau, Vicar-General of the diocese. He was formerly connected with the Jaffna diocese and was very popular here. He was a Missionary of great intellect, superior administrative qualities and gentle manners. See Note 103.

—Sept. 1 - The constitution "Humanae Salutis Auctor" by which Ceylon is erected into an ecclesiastical province with the Arch-bishop of Colombo as Metropolitan and the Bishops of Jaffna and Kandy as suffragans, promulgated.

1887—Jan. 6 - The Arch-bishop of Colombo and the Bishops of Jaffna and Kandy installed by Dr. Agliardi at St. Lucia's Cathedral.

—Jan. 19 - Death under painful circumstances of the Revd. Fr. M. A. Murphy at Kankesanturai. See Note 103.

—Feb. 1 - Establishment of the Catholic Hierachy in the Island.

—March. - Great scarcity of silver in Jaffna. Much difficulty experienced in changing notes. Ten per cent charged for changing ten rupee notes.

—March. 28 - Death of Mr. Bastiampillai, father of Mr. M. B. Swampillai; and of Philip Bastiampillai, Proctor, son of Bastiampillai Velichorupillai.

—April. 2 - A Pearl-Fishery at Chilavaturai. 800 divers at work daily.

—April. 12 - A large water-spout seen at about 5.30 p. m, in the Jaffna Lagoon between Arialai and Chavakachcheri. The phenomenon collapsed within six minutes.

—May. - The Pearl-Fishery at Chilavaturai realises Rs. 396,095-57.

—June. 14 - Lady Gordon leaves for England with Rs. 17,000, a Jubilee offering to the Queen from the women of Ceylon.

1887—June. 28 - The Queen's Jubilee celebrated with great rejoicing in all the towns of the Island. In Jaffna a large concourse assembled at the Esplanade. A record of the Queen's reign was read in English by the Government Agent, Mr. (now Sir) W. C. Twynam. The following programme was gone through in Jaffna. 9 a. m. Church of England Service at Christ Church, Pettah. 11 a. m. Feeding of and distribution of rice to the poor. 4 p. m. Reading of the Record at the Esplanade Pandal. 7.30 p. m. Tamil Play "Varthaga Nadagam," native music, fiddlers & c.—June. 29 - 4 p. m. Laying the Foundation stone of the Victoria Lying-in-Home for women. See Note 431. 7.30 p. m. Fireworks, Native Music, Fiddlers. 9 p. m. Tamil Play "Arichandra Vilasam."

—July. 28 - His Excellency Sir Arthur Hamilton Gordon K. C. M. G., visits Jaffna.

—July, 28 - Death at Trivandram of Mr. Gabriel Simon Arianayagampillai, B. A., B. L., Puisne Justice of the High Court of Travancore. See Note 165.

—July. - Artesian well borings at Mannar commenced.

—Aug. - The inhabitants of Jaffna send a memorial to the Governor for securing Railway extension to the North.

—Nov. 8 - Death of Mr. Breckenridge, retired Sub-Inspector of Schools. See Note 115.

—Nov. - The salt rent for 1887—1888 purchased by Mr. S. Manuelpillai for Rs. 50,000.

—Dec. 27 - A dramatic and musical entertainment held in St. Patrick's College Hall in aid of the Jaffna Catholic Library.

—The Native Town High school started by Mr. William Nevins. See Note 166.

1888—Jan. 29 - The Victoria Reading Hall at Vannarponne started.

—Feb. 12 - Mr. C. P. Ponniahpillai, the Jaffna Agent of the British India Steam Navigation Company, celebrates the 25th Anniversary of his marriage. He took the initiative in the starting of the "J. C. Guardian" Newspaper.

—A Pearl-fishery at Mannar yielded Rs. 80,000.

—March. - Mr. James H. Martyn takes up the Editorial management of the "Ceylon Patriot." See Note 127.

—April. 19 - The Jaffna Arrack rent for 1888—1889 bought by Mr. Sathupathy Soosaipillai for Rs. 37,000.

1888—April. 30 - Foundation stone of the New Church of St. John, Piravukalkudi Irruppu, laid by His Lordship the Bishop of Jaffna. The new church is to be built in place of the old one, which had been knocked down.

—May. 2 - A meeting held under the Presidency of Mr. Ch. Morrison, Agent of the Local Branch of the new O. B. C., to consider the advisability of forming a company to take up cotton cultivation in Jaffna.

—May. 4 - Death of Revd. Fr. John Rowley Smythe, O. M. I. See Note 103.

—May. 4 - Death by sun-stroke of Joseph Gabriel Cherubim of the Govt. Firewood Depot. He was an amiable young-man. See Note 167.

—May. - Rinderpest among cattle, known as Maddu-Noi, breaks out at Koddady and spreads, committing sad havoc.

—May. 4 - Death of St. John Puvirajasinghe Mudaliyar, retired Interpreter of the District Court of Jaffna. He was made a Mudaliyar of the Governor's Gate in 1871 by Governor Sir Hercules Robinson.

—May. 24 - Death from apoplexy of S. M. Moyadeen, Shroff of the Jaffna Kachcheri.

—Death from dropsy of Jacob Abraham Tisseveerasinghe, Notary Public of Jaffna. See Note 104.

—June. 12 - At a public meeting held at Jaffna, resolutions were passed, asking for Railway extension to the North.

—June. - Survey of the Kanagarayankulam Tank commenced.

—June. 23 - The right of patronage exercised by the King of Portugal declared extinct in Ceylon.

—June. 24 - Death at Furres, Elgin, Scotland, of Mr. J. Maclean, late P. M. of Jaffna.

—June. 29 - A lecture on "The Third National Congress of India," delivered at the Victoria Reading Hall, by Mr. Nevins Selvaduraipillai, B. A.

—July. - The Jaffna cotton cultivation company, issues its Prospectus.

—July. 24 - Death of Mr. Fredrick Mortimer, once Assistant Collector of the Jaffna Customs, and latterly a cocoanut planter. See Note 168.

—Aug. - Mr. W. M. S. Twynam appointed Consular Agent at Jaffna for the United States of America. See Note 208.

1888—Sept. 5 - A cocoanut breaking match in aid of the Jaffna Catholic Library in which Messrs. Manuelpillai and Pedropillai took part as leaders of the respective sides. The profit to the Library amounted to Rs. 500.

—Sept. - Arrival of the Goanese Priest Alvares in Colombo.

—Sept. 29 - "The S. S. Lady Gordon", which is to take the place of the old "Serendib," in doing the Island's Postal Service, arrives in Colombo Harbour.

—Oct. - "S. S. Lady Gordon" makes its first trip round the Island.

—Nov. - A portion of Tenmaradchi, lying to the East of Vadamaradchi, made into a new Maniagarship and Veeragatty Mudaliyar of Karavetty appointed its chief Head-man.

—Nov. - The salt rent of Jaffna for 1888—1889 purchased by Mr. S. Manuelpillai for Rs. 52,800.

—Dec. 7 - Arrival in Colombo of six "Little Sisters of the Poor."

—Dec. 13 - A cyclone in Jaffna which causes some damage.

—Dec. 18 - Death at Jaffna of Mariapillai, widow of the late Mr. Henry Martyn, the well-known Scholar, Poet and Scientist.

1889—Jan. 4 - Sir E. N. Walker, Lieut-Governor, erects a new Province and names it the Sabaragamuwa Province.

—Jan. 19 - His Excellency, Sir Edward Noel Walker, officer administering the Government of Ceylon, visits Jaffna.

—Jan. 24 - Messrs V. Casipillai and A. Cathiravelu commence to carry on business as Proctors in partnership. See Note 259.

—Jan. 28 - Death of the Rev. Fr. P. O.'Flannagan, an able, zealous and accomplished Missionary of Jaffna, and an eloquent and impressive preacher among the Oblate Missionaries of Jaffna. See Note 169.

—Jan. - A tobacco company with a capital Rs. 500,000 formed in Ceylon.

—Feb. 4 - A Fancy Bazaar held at the Queen's House, Jaffna, in aid of the funds for the erection of the Victoria Lying-in-home for women. See Note 431.

—Feb. 8 - Death at Colombo of Solomon Johnpulle, Editor and Proprietor of the "Ceylon Patriot", and a versatile writer of English. See Note 170.

—Feb. 17 - Revd. Fr. J. B. Meary succeeds Revd. Fr. O'Flannagan as Director of the Colombogam Orphanage.

—Feb. 21. - Death at Chillalai of Innasithamby, the well-known Native Physician. See Note 171.

1889-Mar. 13 - Death at Nallur, Jaffna, from dysentery, of the Rev. Edward Moule Griffithe of the Jaffna Church Mission. The Rev. J. I. Pickford of the Colombo Tamil Station succeeds him.

—Mar. 16. - An imposing ordination at the Jaffna Cathedral, when four natives of Ceylon, all alumni of St. Martins Ecclesiastical Seminary—Revd. Brs. A. L. Poologasingham, M. Joseph, D. Chrysostom and John Pahamunay—were raised to the Priest-hood. See Note 172.

—March. - Publication of the "Annai Allungal Oppari," a small poem composed by Mr. C. Andrew, the head-printer of the Jaffna St Joseph's Catholic Press. See Note 175.

—March. 18 - Death of Mr. William Nevins, for many years Headmaster of the Jaffna Wesleyan Central School, and a sound English and Tamil Scholar. See Note 173.

—March. 19 - The blessing of the new buildings of St. Martin's Ecclesiastical Seminary. See Note 348.

—April. - The arrack rent of the Jaffna and Mannar Districts for 1889—1890 bought for Rs. 41,000 and Rs. 15,000 respectively by Don Henrick Appuhamy, the Sinhalese renter.

—April - A Pearl-Fishery at Mannar. It was suddenly brought to a close owing to the out-break of Cholera. Sum realised Rs. 497,975.

—May. 5 - Death at Tellipalai of Proctor Arulampalam. See Note 174.

—May. 7 - Death of the Revd. Fr. John Ovidius Vedrenne, O. M. I. He had served in the Crimean and Italian wars and won three medals.

—May. 15 - The second Centenary of the Sacred Heart of Jesus celebrated in Jaffna. There was a grand procession through the town.

—May. 24 - The following Jaffna gentlemen receive distinctions at the Durbar held in Kandy on the occasion of the 70th birth-day of Her Majesty Queen Victoria.

—To be Gate Mudaliyar-Arumugam Idantalawasinghe Iragunather. To be Mudaliyars—Levi Samuel Strong Kulatunka Arasakone; George Henry Hallock Charavanamuttu Murugasapillai and Parinpanayaka Mudaliyar Illankanayagar.

—June. - A lady elected as a member of the Ceylon Branch of the R. A. Society.

—June. 2 - Death in England of Mr. W. J. S. Boake. See Note 440.

1889—June. 3 - General meeting of the Confraternity of the Sacred Heart at St. Patrick's College. Revd. Fr. P. Dunne delivers a lecture on "The Importance of Religious Training in the Education of Youth."

—July - The total number of cases of Cholera in the District 376. Deaths 247.

—July. 24 - Death of Mr. Mailvaganam, the Government General Store-keeper, Jaffna.

—Aug. 5 - A large public meeting at Colombo for advocating Railway Extension to the North.

—Sept. - A Whale 57 feet long drifts ashore between Pesalai and Talaimannar.

—Sept. 11 - The "Hindu-Organ" the organ of the Hindu community of Jaffna, started by Mr. T. P. Chellappapillai, retired Chief Justice of Travancore. See Note 177.

1890—May. - The Jaffna F. N. S. Hospital gets a vote of Rs. 2000.00 in addition to the sum of Rs. 4000.00 already allowed.

—May. 11 - Death of S. Francispillai, a well-known Native physician of Tellipalai.

—May. - Out of 12 candidates who went in for the F. R. C. S. examination, two of Ceylon, namely Dr. M. Sinnatamby and Dr. Alfred Santiago, pass with credit. Dr. Sinnatamby obtained distinctions. He is the son-in-law of conductor Ramanathan in the employ of Sir G. H. D. Elphinstone. See Notes 279, 413.

—May. 21 - Sir Arthur Elibank Havelock sworn in as Governor and Commander-in-Chief of Ceylon.

—June. 2 - General meeting of the Confraternity of the Sacred Heart of Jesus. Mr. D. A. Philips reads a paper on "Temperance."

—June. 5 - Death at Galle from Carbuncle of Mr. Crozier, who was formerly Secretary of the District Court of Jaffna.

—July. - Mr. Proctor Alwis of Colombo appointed to act as P. M. of Jaffna.

—July. 14 - His Excellency Sir Arthur Elibank Havelock visits Jaffna.

—July. 23 - Death of Anthonypillai Rajakariar, Merchant, father of Mr. Benjamin Rajakariar, Udaiyar of Jaffna Town. See Note 178.

—July. 13 - Death at Batticotta of the Revd. E. P. Hastings of the American Mission. He was for a long time Principal of the Jaffna College. See Note 237.

1890—Aug. - His Lordship the Bishop of Jaffna permits the exposition of the Blessed Sacrament during Special Mass of the First Friday of every month.

—Aug. 11 - Death of His Eminence Candinal John Henry Newman, one of the leaders of the Oxford Movement.

—Aug. 18 - Death of Sandrasagra Mudaliyar Nicholaspillai Mudaliar. See Note 179.

—Sept. 13 - Arrival in Jaffna of the Railway Commissioners—Hon. Messrs: F. R. Saunders, G. S. Williams, P. Ramanathan C. M. G., T. N. Christie, H. Bois and Bowden Smith.

—Sept. 28 - Death of the Ceylon millionaire, Mr. C. H. De Lloysa.

—Oct. 6 - Sudden collapse of one of the stalls in the Small Bazaar, Jaffna. Some killed and several wounded.

—Oct. 18 - Death of C. P. Ponniahpillai, Agent of the B. I. S. N. Company. See Note 180.

—Nov. 28 - The Draft of an Ordinance to abolish the tax on dry grains published in the Government Gazette of this date.

—Nov. - Drs. Murugasu Sinnatamby and Alfred B. Santiago made Fellows of the Royal College of Surgeons, Edinburgh. They were the first Asiatics to be admitted to this honour. See Notes 279, 413.

—Dec. 19 - Death at Allavetty of Dr. Evarts Arulampalam, well-known as a Medical man and a Tamil Poet. See Notes 108, 137.

—Dec. - Publication of the Interim Report of the Jaffna Railway Commissioners, recommending the survey of the proposed line.

1891—Jan. 10 - A cocoanut breaking match in aid of the Jaffna Catholic Library. 40,000 nuts collected and a good profit realised.

—Jan. - Introduction of the Palmyrah Fibre Industry into Jaffna. See Note 181.

—Jan. 24 - Death of Francis Muttiah Armstrong Mudaliyar, District Engineer, Jaffna.

—Feb. - Small-pox breaks out at Karaiyoor.

—Feb. - Dr. Marston of the American Mission, who was doing very good work here, leaves Jaffna. Deep regret felt by the people at his departure.

—March. - A Pearl-Fishery yielded Rs. 959,801.38, considered the most successful Pearl-Fishery of the century. Black pearls were found at this fishery.

1891—April. 4 - Death at Vannarponne from apoplexy of Candappa Mudaliyar Tambippillai.

—May - Construction of the Telegraph line connecting Kankesanturai, Valvettiturai and Pt. Pedro with Jaffna.

—June - Mr. John Rudd, assistant Superintendent of Police, transferred to Galle. Mr. Van Houten succeeds him.

—June. 5 - Death of Mr. Mailvaganam, sub-collector of Valvettiturai.

—June. - Death at Batticaloa of Dr. Covington, a distinguished Jaffna-man. See Note 182.

—June. 19 - Death from Carbuncle at Chunnagam of Mr. Harward, a well-known Medical Practitioner.

—July. - The big black pearl found at the last Pearl-Fishery by Mr. Don Carolis of Colpitty sold for Rs. 5,000.

—July. - 16 Delft horses sold at the General Stores, Jaffna, and fetched Rs. 1,020.

—Aug. - The beacon at Mullaitivu completed.

—Aug. Apparatus for boring an artesian well at Karandai received from Madras. Fr. Lytton took the initiative in the matter. The boring operations commenced in right good earnest but fell through as a similar attempt at Mannar undertaken by Government.

—Sept. 7 - Death at Jaffna of J. H. Toussaint, a well-known and wealthy Dutch gentleman long resident in Jaffna. He built Christ Church, Pettah, at his own expense. See Note 183.

—Nov. 6 - Arrival in Colombo of the "Lady Havelock," the new steamer of the Ceylon Steamship Co., Ltd.

—Dec. 28 - A daring burglary at Vannarponne when the locks of the strong Store-room of the Sivan Temple were broken and jewellery of the Temple to the value of Rs. 30,000 removed.

—St. John's Seminary, Chundicully, converted into St. John's College. See Note 93.

—Dec. 28 - A grand dramatic and musical entertainment in St. Patrick's College Hall. Two dramas were acted, St. Sebastian or the Roman Martyr" and a comedy entitled "Cox and Box."

1892—Jan. 1 - Publication of the Supreme Court Circular suspended.

—Jan. - Mr. C. Kanagasuriam, C. E., B. C. E., appointed Chief Irrigation Inspector for the North Central Province, on a salary of Rs. 3000 and allowances, to succeed Mr. A. D. Renganathan, who goes back to the P. W. D. as District Engineer.

1892—Jan. 15 - Announcement received of the death of H. R. H. the Duke of Clarence and Avondale, who succumbed to a severe attack of Influenza and Pneumonia. The Governor orders all Public Offices to be closed and flags on public buildings and vessels half-masted.

—Jan. - Father S. J. Muller, S. J., who has under his care 40 lepers at Jeppoo Hospital, Mangalore, is on a short visit to Jaffna for the benefit of his health.

—Jan. - Cholera shows itself at Mannar.

—Jan. 14 - Death of His Eminence Cardinal Manning, Archbishop of Westminster and Primate of England, an illustrious convert.

—Jan. 19 - Revd. Fr. C. H. Lytton leaves for Colombo being transferred to that diocese in connection with the erection of St. Joseph's College.

—Jan. - The vacancy caused in the Public Instruction Department by the death of Mr. D. Alwis, Inspector of Schools, filled up by the appointment of Mr. Arthur Van Cuylenburg, Inspector of Schools, Northern Province. Mr. R. H. Leembruggen, Head Clerk of the Secretarlate, succeeds Mr. Van Cuylenburg as Inspector of Schools, Northern Province.

—Feb. 19 - Mr. R. H. Leembruggen, Inspector of Schools, for the Northern and Eastern Provinces, arrives in Jaffna. See Note 236.

—Feb. 29 - The new upstair house of Mr. S. Manuelpillai Rajakariar blessed by the Very Revd. Fr. Mauroit, Vicar-General.

—March. 7 - Death is announced of Sir William H. Gregory, a former Governor of Ceylon.

—March. 18 - The brig Annalachchemy, belonging to Tirumani Periathamby, a wealthy merchant of Valvettiturai, capsized off Mandaitivu in the offing.

—March. 19 - Death of Mrs. Magdalene Bastiampillai, wife of S. Bastiampillai Mudaliyar, and second daughter of Sandrasagara Mudaliyar Saverimuttu Mudaliyar, K. C. S. G. See Note 184.

—March. 30 - A lecture on "Decision of Character" delivered in the Victoria Reading Hall by Mr. Nevins Selvaduraipillai, B. A., Headmaster of the Hindu High School. He laid particular stress on the point that the first thing that should be instilled into the minds of youth is the existence of God and the reverence to be paid to Him.

1892—April. 1 - Death at the age of 33 of James Bastiampillai, second son of the late Proctor Bastiampillai.

—April. - The Old Dutch Church, Jaffna, bought by Government for Rs. 6000.

—April. - The building of the Kankesanturai Beacon reaches completion. Height already reached is 70 feet. It is built in the form of a regular octagon. An iron ladder runs to the very top. The estimate is Rs. 5260.

—April. - Some half a dozen strong benches firmly fixed in the ground along the sea-beach road from the left arm of the jetty on towards Passaioour. The work was done by the P. W. D.

—April. - The draft of an ordinance to abolish the Paddy tax published in the Government Gazette. It is to come into operation from July 1st following.

—May. 18 - Mr. Advocate J. Homer Vanniasingham receives baptism at the hands of the Very Revd. Fr. E. Vorlander, O. M. I., at St. Joseph's Chapel, Colombogam. The sponsors were Mr. A. Paul Mudaliyar and Mrs. Paul.

—June. 9 - The new O. B. C. suspends payment.

—June. 13 - At a general meeting of the Committee of the Jaffna Friend-in-Need Society, it was decided to appoint Dr. Grenier as the visiting surgeon of the Hospital.

—July. - A shipment of 200 logs of the best satin, yavaranai, ebony and other timber for the Ceylon Court and Tea Kiosk at the Chicago Exhibition made by the local Forest Department.

—July. - A new Dispensary opened at Nedunkeney.

—July. - The Draft of the small Towns Sanitary Ordinance published in the Government Gazette.

—Aug. 2 - Death in Colombo of His Grace Dr. Bonjean, the first Arch-bishop of Colombo. The zeal, energy and devotion with which he built up the work of the Northern Vicariate are well-known. To his endeavours mainly are due the enviable position of the Roman Catholics of Jaffna and the flourishing condition of its various educational and religious institutions. He commanded great influence by his writings. See Notes 185, 440.

—Aug. - 70 cases of new coins from London received in Colombo. One of these contained the new 10 cent pieces to the value of a lakh of rupees.

1892—Aug. 26 - Death at Batticotta, after a long lingering illness, of the Revd. Mr. W. W. Howland, the oldest member of the American Ceylon Mission. See Note 186.

—Sept. 18 - Death of Dr. Chapman at Uduvil. See Note 187.

—Oct. 1 - The Indian two anna piece ceases to be legal tender in Ceylon. The new subsidiary silver coins become current.

—Oct. - A complete repair of the Church of St. James the Greater at Kilaly, undertaken by Proctor James Nicholas.

—Oct. - Messrs Cathiraveluppillai, Tisseveerasinghe and Thambiah come off successful in the Proctor's Final Examination.

—Oct. - A movement to form a volunteer corps for Jaffna set on foot by Mr. Bellamy, D. E., Jaffna.

—Oct. 4 - Death at Jaffna of Mr. Philip Tamber. See Note 75.

—Nov. - Mr. J. Cherubim, Agent of the B. I. S. N. Company, appointed the Jaffna Agent of the Standard Life Insurance Company. See Note 104.

—Dec. 4 - His Lordship Dr. Melizan starts for Europe from Colombo.

—Dec. 13 - Death of Mrs. Patterson, relict of the late Mr. Patterson, Cocoanut Planter.

—Dec. 16 - In the Parapankandal Church Case, Mr. Jackson, the District Judge of Mannar, delivers judgment in favour of Fr. Sandrasagara.

1893—Jan. 14 - Death at Jaffna of A. Paul Mudaliyar, Chief Mudaliyar of the Jaffna Kachcheri. See Note 188.

—Jan. 15 - Death at Mannar of L. Gasparpillai Mudaliyar, Adigar of Mannar. See Note 189.

—Jan. 22 - Death at Jaffna from pneumonia of Mrs Casipillai, wife of Mr. V. Casipillai, one of the leading and most popular proctors of Jaffna. The deceased was noted for her private charity.

—Jan. 24 - H. E. Sir Arthur Havelock accompanied by Captain Mac Neal, A. D. C., and Mr. Gerald Browne, P. S., arrives in Jaffna. He is received at a large and tastefully decorated Pandal put up in front of the Jaffna Customs. Mr. T. M. Tampoe, Crown Proctor and J. P., reads the address.

—Jan. - The Paddy Tax abolished.

—Feb. 1 - Mr. P. Coomaraswamy, brother of Mr. Ramanathan, appointed Tamil Representative of the Legislative Council, See Note 277.

1893—Feb. - The Central Road Mail Coach service by horses from Jaffna to Elephant Pass, extended to Kanagarayankulam. (68 miles.)

—Feb. 18 - Death at Jaffna of the Revd. Fr. J. Roux, O. M. I. He came to Jaffna in 1884, and was ordained Priest by Dr. Melizan on the 19th December 1885. He was Parish Priest of Trincomalee, Batticaloa and Point Pedro and was for some time Director of St. Joseph's Orphanage, Colombogam.

—Feb. - Mr. Vallipuram, Udaiyar of Mannar West, appointed acting Adigar of Mannar.

—Feb. 19 - The Papal Jubilee celebrations commence at the Jaffna Cathedral.

—Feb. 28 - The Railway Survey between Jaffna and Kangasantural completed. The work was supervised by Mr. Maine.

—Mar. 5 - By Apostolic Brief of this date, the Ecclesiastical administration of the Arch-diocese of Colombo entrusted to Dr. Theophilus Andrew Melizan, O. M. I.

—Mar. - Death at Mannar of Mr. S. Anthonypillai, otherwise called Ponniah Kanakkar. He was an overseer in the P. W. D. and a brother of Mr. S. Saverimuttu, a teacher in the Jaffna Boy's Seminary.

—March. - Copra sells at Rs. 50 a candy.

—April. - Mr. B. Constantine gazetted to act as Police Magistrate and Commissioner of Requests of Jaffna and Mallagam.

—April - The arrack rent of the Jaffna District for the year 1893--1894 purchased for Rs. 47,000 by Don Henrick Appuhamy.

—May. 1 - Death at Colombo of the Very Revd. Fr. D. Pulicani, O. M. I. He was for many years Vicar-General of Jaffna.

—May. - Publication of the "Ceylon Review" commenced.

—May. 17 - Vettukadu gets to be known as a new and attractive field for Cocoanut planting.

—May. 17 - Marriage at Colpetty, Colombo, of Mr. B. Constantine, Police Magistrate of Jaffna, with Miss Pattie Emsley.

1893—May. 22 - General meeting of the Confraternity of the Sacred Heart of Jesus. Mr. Homer Vanniasinkam delivers a lecture on the "Aims of Life."

—May. 31 - The Jaffna upstair building of the new Oriential Bank Corporation put up for sale by Mr. Alex. Toussaint, Merchant, and bought by Mr. Melville Geddes, Planter, for Rs. 14.000. See Note 130.

—June. 6 - Mr. Charles Morrison, local agent of the defunct new O. B. C., leaves for Colombo. While in Jaffna, he identified himself with every movement having for its object the material advancement of the people of this Province. See Note 130.

—July. - The Jaffna Railway Survey reaches Elephant Pass—a distance of about 46 miles.

—July. - A large model of the Royal Mail Cart running between Elephant Pass and Anuradhapura, placed in the Ceylon Court at the Chicago Exhibition. It was forwarded by Mr. Skinner, the Post Master General, and made for him at Jaffna by the Central Road Mail Coach Contractor, Mr. S. Asaipillai.

—July, 19 - The Rupee of Portuguese India having been demonetized by order of Her Majesty in Council, ceases to be legal tender.

—Aug. 4 - His Lordship the Right Revd. Dr. Henry Joulain., O. M. I., elected Bishop of Jaffna, in succession to Dr. Melizan transferred to the Arch-diocese of Colombo.

—Aug. 9 - Death at Jaffna at the age 80 of Mr. B. Deogupillai, Sworn Translator of the District Court of Jaffna. See Note 190.

—Aug. 24 - Episcopal Consecration of His Lordship Dr. Henry Joulain, O. M. I., Bishop of Jaffna.

—Sept. 3 - Draft of an ordinance relating to pawn-brokers published in the Government Gazette.

—Sept. - Death at Vannarponne of Mr. C. Arunasalam, Sub-collector. See Note 191.

—Sept. 9 - Death at Mannar, at the age of 45, of Seemampillai Mudaliyar, Adigar of Musali Nanaddan. See Note 192.

—Sept. 11 - Death at Kayts of Mr. V. Visuvanathapillai, Chief Clerk of the Minor Courts of that station.

Sept. 29 - Death at Point-Pedro as the result of an accident of the Rev. J. Newham, a young Wesleyan Missionary.

1893—Oct. - Mr. John Rodrigo, Post Master, Pallai, severs his connection with the Postal Depeartment and engages in Cocoanut planting.

—Dec. 15 - Arrival of His Lordship Dr. Joulain as Bishop of Jaffna.

1894—Jan. - Abolition of the system of Port-Headmen or Adappans in the Northern Province and the appointment of a number of Boatswains in their places.

—Jan. 2 - Death at Jaffna of Mr. G. Bastian, Teacher. See Note 103.

—Feb. 3 - A shock of Earth-quake felt in several parts of Jaffna.

—Feb. 4 - Death of Mr. Frederick Johnpulle, retired Sub-collector. See Note 193.

—Feb. 13 - Death at Manipay of Mr. Nathan Strong. See Note 194.

—Feb. 24 - Death at Chavakachcheri of Mr. Naranar Varithamby, Udaiyar, and a large land owner. See Note 195.

—April 1 - Mr. Wm. Mather, long employed in the firm of Walker & Sons, Colombo, returns to Jaffna and assumes duties as the local agent of the Ceylon Steamship Company. See Note 407.

—April. 1- Laying the corner-stone of the Mortuary Chapel at St. Mary's Cathedral Burial Grounds.

—April. 6 - Death at Mannar of Saverimuttu Philippupillai Supprumania Mudaliyar, Adigar of Mantotte. See Note 212.

—May. 19 - General meeting of the Confraternity of the Sacred Heart. S. Bastiampillai Mudaliyar delivers a very practical lecture on "Our duties as Laymen."

—Aug. - A donation of Rs. 1,000 given to the Jaffna Friend-in-need Society by N. Swaminathan, Broker of Messrs Delmege Forsyth &. Co., and son of Navaratnasingam of the P. R. C., Jaffna.

—Aug. - Several cases of Cholera reported to have occured at Puloly and Alvay.

—Sept. 15 - Celebration of the Silver Jubilee of Mr. S. Abraham, the veteran Headmaster of St. Patrick's College.

—Oct. - The Arialai Estate, the property of the late Mr. Price and subsequently owned by Mr. Geddes, purchased by Mr. Proctor Casipillai for Rs. 47,000.

—Nov. 10 - Death at Vannarponne of Mr. Ranganathan, District Engineer of Pallai.

—Nov. 27 - Death at Jaffna of Vivveendapillai, widow of Saverimuttu Suprumania Mudaliyar.

1894—Systematic training of Tamil nurses commenced at the Manipay Hospital by Mrs. Scott. The work is followed at Inuvil shortly after. See Note 418.

—Dec. 6 - Death at Mannar of T. Swampillai Mudaliyar.

—Dec. - The Postal Department introduces reply letter-cards.

—Dec. 25 - The Centenary of St. Mary's Cathedral, Jaffna, celebrated with great grandeur. A sketch of the chief events connected with the Cathedral, in which the story of its erection and completion, and of the introduction and propagation of the Catholic Faith in these parts is briefly told, was read on the occasion by Mr. John. H. Martyn, who composed it from reliable sources with the approbation of the Ecclesiastical Authorities. See Note 213.

1895—Jan. The Post-Master-General visits Jaffna. A deputation waits on him with a petition praying that a Post-office may be opened at Vannarponne on the Jaffna-Kankesanturai Road.

—Feb. 26 - The trial of the Guardian Libel Case before the Supreme Court at Jaffna. See Note 197.

—Mar. 17 - Laying of the new Indo-Ceylon cable.

—Mar. 19 - Death at Colombo of the Very Revd. Fr. J. Vistarini.

—June. 1 - Burials in the Dutch Burial Ground, Pettah, Jaffna, discontinued.

—June. 12 - General meeting of the Confraternity of the Sacred Heart of Jesus. Mr. John H. Martyn reads a paper on "The Advantages of Association."

—Aug. 1 - Death of Mr. Chelliahpillai, B. A., B. L., in Cudappah, India. See Note 198.

—Aug. 19 - G .P. O., Colombo, opened.

—Aug. 24 - Death of D. W. N. Senathirajah, Proctor. He was a brother of Advocate Senathirajah of Colombo and he edited the "Ceylon Patriot" for some time. See Note 127.

—Sept. - Sir A. E. Havelock appointed Governor of Madras.

—Sept. 5 - Death of Mr. A. Joseph, Teacher, and a prominent figure in Jaffna. See Note 281.

—Sept. The inauguration of the Hindu High School in the new upstair building, under the presidency of the Hon. P. Coomaraswamy. See Note 166.

- Sept. - The Jaffna Maniagar's division sub-divided into three registration divisions for purposes of registering Births and Deaths, viz. (1) Vannarponne West, with a Mohammedan Registrar, (2) Vannarponne East and Nallur with a Protestant Registrar, and (3) Chundikully with a Roman Catholic Registrar.

1895—Oct. 30 - Death at Vannarponne at the age of 22 of C. Muttutamby, brother of Mr. Sundram of the Colombo Customs, after passing very creditably the Proctor's Examination. His sister died the previous day. Both succumbed to typhoid fever.

—Nov. 6. - Death at Jaffna of Mr. Ignatius Saverimuttu of the Jaffna Fiscal's Office, a son of the late Supramania Mudaliyar.

—Nov. 9 - The golden Jubilee of Mr. (now Sir) William Twynam's official career celebrated with great eclat in Jaffna. See Note 199.

—Nov. - The question raised regarding the appointment of a Maha Mudaliyar for the Tamils of the Island causes great interest and excitement.

—Nov. 11 - Death at Jaffna of Mr. Arthur Fletcher, retired Teacher of St Patrick's College and Moopu of St. Mary's Cathedral. See Note 103.

—Nov. - The Victoria Lying-in-Home at Jaffna opened.

—Dec. - Mr. S. Duraisamy appointed Maniagar of Valikamam East. See Note 239.

1896—Jan. 1 - The honour of Knight-hood conferred on Mr. William C. Twynam, Government Agent of the Northern Province.

—Jan. 4 - Death at Tellipalai from heart disease of Mr. Advocate Muttiah. He was a rising lawyer and had a fairly good practice in the Chavakachcheri and Pt. Pedro Courts.

—Jan. 16 - Sir William Twynam, K. C. M. G., granted three months full pay leave prior to his retirement on the 16th April. Mr. R. W. Ievers succeeds him as Government Agent, N. P. Sir William quits the old Park and moves into Marine Villa. See Note 363.

—Feb. 20th - Death at Manipay of Mr. J. R. Arnold, Professor, Author, Editor, Poet and Tamil Scholar. See Note 115.

—Feb. 22 - Sir William Twynam entertained at a grand dinner at the Queen's House. Fort, Jaffna.

—Feb. 24 - Mr Tampoe, Crown Proctor, assumes duties as acting Police Magistrate of Jaffna.

—March. 2 - St. Joseph's College, Colombo, opened.

—Mar. 6 - Death at Jaffna of Arasunilayitta Mudaliyar Santiagopillai, retired Maniagar.

1896—Mar. - A strike among cigar makers to obtain an increase of wages.

—Mr. C. M. Chellappa, Manager of the Chulipuram English School, secures the services of an able Headmaster in the person of Mr. Small, a lecturer in the Tinnevely College. See Note 316.

—April. 17 - The Jaffna Commercial Corporation started. See Note 200.

—May. 1 - The arrack rent of the Jaffna District for the year 1896—97, put up for sale at the Kachcheri and purchased by Mr. R. Valupillai of Kandermadam for Rs. 82,000.

—May. - Death at Trincomalee of Sattanathapillai. He was a native of Vadamaradchy who, having settled in Trincomalee, amassed a large fortune.

—June. 15 - Mr. Advocate Nagalingam assumes duties as acting Police Magistrate of the Point Pedro and Chavakachcherri Courts. See Note 166.

—July. 2 - The Kumbapishakam ceremony of the new Sivan Temple at Keerimalai.

—July. 4 - Mr. Tomalin, Provincial Engineer, with Mr. Cameron, D. J., visits the Puttur well, with the object of carrying on experimental pumping and testing its water supplying capacity. See Note 60.

—July. 12 - Death at Colombo at the age of 39 of Mr. J. B. Sathupathy, Barrister-at-law. See Note 201.

—July. 24 - An "At Home" function, the first of its kind in Jaffna, held in the Old Park, Jaffna Kachcheri, by Mrs. Ievers.

—Sept. - A Board of Education appointed by Government. See Note 440.

—"Tiruchelvarkaviam," a well-known Tamil epic by Poologasingha Mudaliyar, printed at the Gnanapiragasa Press, Achuvely. See Note 202.

—Oct. 6 - Death at Jaffna of the Very Revd. Fr. L. Mauroit, O. M. I., the veteran Missionary of Jaffna. See Note 103.

—Oct. 30 - Death of Proctor J. E. Nicholas, eldest son of Nicholaspillai Sinnathamby. He was an intelligent and distinguished Proctor. See Note 337.

1897—Jan. 15 - Sir Joseph West Ridgeway, Governor, with Captain Ward Jackson, P. S, Sir W. Kinsey, P. C. M. O., Hon. W. Taylor, Auditor General, and Captain Graeme, lands at Jaffna at 6.30 p. m. and proceeds to Queen's House.

1897—Jan. 16 - H. E. the Governor lunched at the Residency at 2.30 p. m. Garden Party at 4.30 p. m. Public reception at the Esplanade pandal at 6 p. m. Public address, the Governor's reply. Fireworks. Illumination of the Fort.

—Jan. 17 - The Governor visits the Puttoor well and Kankesanturai.

—Jan. 18 - The Governor inspects the Public offices, interviews about 150 Headmen, holds a Levee at Queen's House, Fort Jaffna. A Tamil Drama (Damayandi) acted later on for the entertainment of the Governor.

—Jan. 19 - The Governor visits Jaffna College, Batticotta, under Dr. Hastings, goes to Kayts where he is most loyally received by Father Sandrasagara and others.

—Jan. 20 - The Governor visit. St. Patrick's College, St. Charle's Mission House, St. Martin's Seminary, St. John's College, Jaffna Convent School, Wesleyan Central College, and Girl's Boarding School, and leaves for Elephant Pass at 3 p. m.

—Jan. 24 - Swami Vivekananda (Norendra Nath Dutt. B. A. Calcutta) who was at the Parliament of Religions, Chicago, arrives in Jaffna and receives an enthusiastic reception at the Hindu College, Vannarponne.

—Jan. 29 - The Very Revd. Fr. Cassian Augier, Assistant to the Superior General of the Oblates of Mary Immaculate, arrives in Jaffna at 10-30 a. m. No public reception given as was done in the case of the Very Revd. Fr. Soullier's visit in 1878.

—Jan. 29 - Mr. A Mylvaganam of Copay appointed a Justice of the Peace for the District of Jaffna and unofficial Police Magistrate for the Judicial Division of Jaffna. See Note 299.

—April. 17 - Death of Lady Twynam at Belle-View Villa, Jaffna.

—April. 19 - Funeral of Lady Twynam. Sir William, who was in Colombo, reached Jaffna the previous evening. Interment at St. John's Chundikully. A very large concourse present.

—May. 11 - Meeting at the District Court House, Mr. Fisher, G. A. in the chair, for determining local celebration of the Queen's Diamond Jubilee.

—May. 16 - Death of Mr. Van Houten, Deputy Fiscal, and of Mr. Vytilingam, commonly called "Singapore Vytilingam", both from diabetes.

1897—June. 20 - The Diamond Jubilee celebrations. Rejoicings universal and enthusiastic.

—English School at Uduville under the American Mission opened by K. H. E. Myers.

—Aug. 4 - Death of advocate S. Nagalingam, a highly popular and philanthropic gentleman. See Note 166.

—Dec. 28 - Death at Jaffna of Revd. Fr. Boniface Gourdon.

—Dec. 31. Telegram received from the Secretary of State sanctioning construction of the Northern Railway.

1898—Jan. 13 - Mr. P. A. Manners assumes duties as 5th Clerk of the Jaffna Kachcheri. See Note 104.

—Jan. 15 - The Jaffna Catholic Guardian enters upon the 23rd year of its existence. See Note 176.

—Jan. 27 - Death at Jaffna of Mr. Brown Sinnatamby, the senior member of the local Bar. See Note 203.

—Feb. - Mr. J. Gregory, late of St. Patrick's College, appointed a field surveyor, after receiving a course of training at the Surveyor General's office and passing the prescribed examination. See Note 103.

—Feb. - Publication by the Revd. Fr. Dunne, O. M. I., Principal of St. Patrick's College, of a system of Short-hand he had invented for the Tamil language. See Note 205.

—Feb. 14 - Death at Alutmawatta, from dropsy, in the 66th year of his age, of Mr. J. L. Bertus. He was Head Clerk of the Mannar Kachcheri and retired after 35 years' service.

—Mar. 5 - Death at Jaffna, of Catherine, wife of Mr. Manuelpillai Rajakariar. The deceased was well-known by her good qualities and good deeds.

—Mar. 14 - Dr. William Gabriel Rockwood appointed Tamil Representative in the Legislative Council. See Note 297.

—Mar. 14 - His Lordship Dr. Joulain, Bishop of Jaffna, leaves *en route* to Europe.

—April. - Announcement received of the death, in England, at the ripe old age of 85, of Mr. John Capper, well known in Ceylon as an old Colonist and the Editor and Proprietor of the "Ceylon Times". See Note 107.

—May. 11 - Death at Achuvely, at the age of 84, of Thilliampalam Santiapillai, Udaiyar.

1898—May. 27 - Death at the age of 75, of Hannah Hensman, a daughter of Matthew Philips and the wife of the Revd. John Hensman.

—May. 28 - Death at Manipay of Dr. Strong Arasakone Mudaliyar.

—June. 26 - Death at Jaffna of Mr. Sathupathy Soosaipillai, a well-known and wealthy merchant. See Note 201.

—July. 15 - The O. B. C. building in Jaffna, owned by the heirs of the late Mr. Geddis, put up for sale and purchased by R. M. M. S. T. Raman Chetty for Rs. 15,500. See Note 130.

—July. 30 - Arrival in Jaffna of Mr. Hopman, Sub-Inspector of Telegraphs, in connection with the Telegraph line to Manipay.

—Aug. 6 - The inauguration of the Manipay Hospital at the New Building under the management of Dr. Scott. See Note 418.

—Aug. 12 - Death at Jaffna of Edward Sattrukalsinghe. See Note 204.

—Aug. 29 - Arrival in Jaffna of His Excellency Sir Noel Walker.

—Aug. - Death at Jaffna of Mr. John Nicholas, Head Clerk of the District Court of Jaffna and the son-in-law of the late Dr. Abraham, the popular native physician of Jaffna. See Note 285.

—Sept. 1 - Government takes possession of the O. B. C. building, purchased from its last owner, R. M. M. S. T. Raman Chetty, for Rs. 16,500. See Note 130.

—Sept. 1 - Death at Mihintale, of Cecelia, youngest daughter of the late Henry Martyn and the wife of Mr. M. M. Puvirayasinghe, Superintendent of Immigration Stations, Anuradhapura.

—Sept. 24 - Formal opening of the McLeod Hospital at Inuvil for women and children with Dr. Isabella Curr in charge. See Note 206.

—Oct. 17 - Death at Jaffna of Mr. Kandavanam of the Jaffna F. N. S. Hospital.

—Oct. 23 - Death at Jaffna, in her 27th year, of Cecil Ponnammah, daughter of the late Mr. Samuel Nevinspillai, B. A., B. L., of the Madras Presidency College and latterly of the Madras High Court Bar, and wife of Mr. Muttoocoomaru, Post-Master of Lunugalla.

1898—Nov. 1 - Mr. B. Francis of the Registrar General's Office, Colombo, appointed Registrar of Lands, Batticaloa, vice Mr. Karalasingham, who takes charge of the Jaffna Office. See Note 372.

—Nov. - The district of Vavuniya parcelled and merged into the Jaffna, Mannar and Mullaitivu divisions.

—Nov. - Mr. James De Niese, the well-known artist of Jaffna, presents to the Parish Priest of St. James, Karayoor, a beautiful life-size oil painting of the late Very Revd. Fr. Mauroit. See Note 287.

—Nov. - Retirement of Mr. C. W. Kathirvetpillai from the C. C. S. See Note 244.

—Nov. 22 - Death at Point Pedro, at the age of 89, of the Revd. Mr. Asbury of the American Mission of Jaffna. See Note 207.

—Nov. 27 - Death at Jaffna of Mr. W. M. S. Twynam. See Note 208.

—Dec. 25 - Rate of Postage between Ceylon and the United Kingdom fixed at 6 cts. for half ounce.

—Dec. - Death at Jaffna from fever of Jaccova Thangamuttu, relict of Mr. Santiogupillai, brother of the late A. Paul Mudaliyar of the Jaffna Kachcheri, and eldest daughter of the late Nicholas Sandrasagara Mudaliyar. Revd. Fr. Sandrasagara and Mr. J. N. Sandrasagara, Superintendent of Minor Roads, Jaffna, are her brothers.

1899—Jan. 23 - Death at Cantherodai from diabetes of Mr. Coomaravelupillai, eldest son of the late Weluppillai Mudaliyar, the well-known District Engineer.

—Jan. 29 - Revd. Fr. Norbert Perera of the Jaffna Diocese ordained priest by His Grace the Archbishop of Colombo in the Borella Chapel.

—Feb. 6 - Death at Colombo of Mr. Navaratnasinghe, for many years the Scavenging Superintendent of the Jaffna Board of Health.

—Feb. 10 - Death at Mannar from fever of Mr. Nicholas Puvirajasingham, Second Clerk, Mannar Kachcheri. See Note 209.

—Feb. 14 - Death at Jaffna of D. Christian, employed as a clerk in the Guardian Office under the Catholic Mission for 20 years. He was a brother of the late Revd. Fr. Chrysostom.

—Feb. 18 - An "At Home" held at the "Old Park," Jaffna Kachcheri, by Mr. and Mrs. Ievers.

1899—Feb. 25 - A public meeting held under the Presidency of Mr. Ievers, Government Agent, to provide the people of Jaffna with a Town Hall.

—Mar. 1 - The Ceylon Penal Code comes into operation.

—April. 9 - Death at Jaffna of Isabella, relict of S. Mudaliyar Cherubim.

—April. 11 - A native schooner wrecked off the coast of Mullaitivu.

—April. - Dr. Alfred C. Evarts comes off successful in the M. B. C. M. examination of the Madras University. See Note 210.

—May. 4 - Death at Manipay of Mr. Alfred Hensman, a gentleman of long standing at the Jaffna Bar. See Note 70.

—May. 15 - Death at Jaffna of Mr. J. I. Pieris, well and widely known as a merchant. See Note 214.

—June. 1 - Death at Jaffna of Miss Mary Saverimuttu, eldest daughter of the late Chevalier Saverimuttu Mudaliyar. See Note 215.

—June. 8 - Death at Jaffna, from puerperal fever, of Mary, wife of Revd. John Carter, Principal, St. John's College, Chundicully.

—June. 11 - A meeting held in the Hall of St. Patrick's College, under the presidency of the Very Revd. Fr. Collin, Vicar-General, for the purpose of raising funds for the repair of St. Mary's Cathedral, Jaffna. See Note 351.

—July. 28 - Death at Trincomalie of Simon Cherubim Mudaliyar, Secretary of the Trincomalie Courts.

—July. 29 - Death at Jaffna of Mr. John Karalasingham, Shroff of the Jaffna Customs.

—July. 29 - A Girls' School at Jaffna, in memory of the Revd. Hastings, formally opened.

—Aug. 10 - Death at Nallur of Mr. C. Thiagar, a well-known Tamil Scholar and Pundit. See Note 216.

—Aug. 11 - Death at Jaffna of Victoriapillai, eldest daughter of Nicholas Puvirajasinghe Mudaliyar and wife of Mr. V. Yanamuttu, Merchant.

—Aug. 11 - Death at Loretto (Italy) of the Right. Revd. Fr. Abbot Cingolani, Sylvestrine monk of the O. S. B., for a long time Missionary Apostolic in Ceylon and late Lord Abbot of St. Antony's Abbey, Kandy.

1899—Aug - Mr. T. M. Tampoe confirmed by Government in his appointment of Police Magistrate of Jaffna and Mallagam.

—Sept. 11 - Death at Nallur of Mrs. Kailasapillai, wife of C. Kailasapillai Mudaliyar, Tamil Interpreter of the Supreme Court, and a daughter of the late Overseer Thambipillai.

--Sept. - Mr. A. Canagaratnam, brother of Mr. Proctor Cathiravelu and a nephew of Mr. Proctor V. Casipillai, comes off successful in the Proctor's final examination. See Note 127.

—Sept - The arrack rents for the Mullaitivu and Vavuniya Districts bought by Mr. M. Asaipillai for Rs. 14,500 and 8,160 respectively.

—Oct. 1 - The Jaffna Premier Restaurant opened under the management of Mr. J. Don. Manuel.

—Oct. 4 - Death at Jaffna of Mr. A. Philippiah, Post-Master of the Jaffna Kachcheri. See Note 217.

—Oct. 4 - Announcement made in the Legislative Council that the Secretary of State had authorized the construction of the whole line of Railway connecting the North of the Island with Colombo. See Note 232.

—Oct. 5 - Death at Trevandram of Angelina, wife of Mr. C. R. Arasaretnam and the eldest daughter of Justice Arianayagampillai.

—Oct. 8 - Death at Vannarponne of S. Ramupillai, a distinguished and successful native physician. See Note 218.

—Oct. 12 - Death in Colombo of the Revd. Fr. A. Trouchat. He was first stationed in Jaffna and laboured in the Missions of Jafina, Mullaitivu, Kayts and other parts. He died in his 52nd year and served as a missionary for 27 years.

—Oct. 12 - Messrs L. Shipton, C. Speldewinde, N. Kelenberg, E. H. Kock and J. Gregory of the Survey Department, commence the acquisition surveys in connection with the Northern Railway.

—Oct. - Government sanctions Rs. 5,000 for a site and Rs. 15,000 for the building of a new Hospital at Point Pedro.

—Oct. - Arrival in Colombo of Mr. Oliver, Chief Construction Engineer, to take charge of the Northern and Kelany Valley Railway extension. See Note. 232.

—Oct. - Death from Cancer of Mr. Suntharam, Udaiyar of Chundicully and brother-in-law of Pundit Thiagar.

—Oct. - Materials received in Colombo for the Jaffna Railway.

1899—Oct. 17 - Mr. Louis Herb, the Y. M. C. A. Secretary for Ceylon, who has been spending a fortnight in Jaffna, returns to Colombo.

—Nov. 27 - Death at Bopeitya, Pamunugama, of Mr. Don, Hendrick Appuhamy. See Note 219.

—Dec. - Death in his 54th year of Mr. Lionel F. Lee, the Treasurer of the Colony. See Note 107.

—Dec. 14 - At a general meeting of the subscribers to the F. N. S. Hospital held at the Jaffna Kachcheri, it was decided to hand over the Jaffna F. N. S. Hospital to the Government. See Note 431.

1900—Jan. 1 - The General Cemeteries and Burials Ordinance comes into operation.

—Jan. 1 - Point Pedro brought under the operation of the Small Towns Sanitary Ordinance of 1892.

—Jan. 4 - The Crown Agents call for tenders for the construction of a Railway from Kurunegalla to Kangasanturai. See Note 232.

—Jan. 5 - Death at the age of 92 of Tisseveerasinghe Mudaliyar Abraham, Notary Public, Jaffna. See Note 231.

—Feb. 9 - A shock of earth-quake felt in Ceylon and India.

—Mar. 21 - Death of Dr. William Paul, Resident Surgeon, F. N. S. Hospital, Jaffna. See Note 250.

—May. - A historical report on the Pearl-Fishery of Ceylon by Sir. W. C. Twynam, submitted to the Government.

—Oct. 27 - Death at Jaffna from snake-bite of Mr. L. F. White, Railway Engineer.

—Dec. 26 - The Golden Jubilee of St. Patrick's College celebrated on a grand scale. See Note 426.

—"Central"—the Magazine of the Jaffna Wesleyan Central College, started. See Note 127.

1901—Jan. 22 - Death of Her Majesty Queen Victoria, the Good.

—Jan. 23 - His Majesty Edward VII proclaimed King and Emperor.

—Jan. 29 - Death at Colombo of Venus S. Mariampillai, a young and enterprising merchant. See Note 233.

—Feb. 2 - Public ceremonies all over the Island connected with the funeral of Her Majesty Queen Victoria.

—Feb. 2 - Winding up of the Batticaloa Trading Co. Ltd.

—Feb. - The newly built Hall of St. John's College, Chundicully, opened by the Metropolitan Bishop of Colombo. See Note 93.

1901—March. 1 - The fourth decennial census of Ceylon taken. Population 3,565,954 ; Northern Province 340,936, Jaffna 33,879; males 1,896,212, females 1,669,742. See Note 222.

—May. 28 - Mr. W. Romaine Cooke arrives as the new Vice-Principal of the Central College. This is the first time when the institution had two Europeans in its staff.

—June. - Ping-Pong introduced into Ceylon.

—June. 3 - General Oliver visits the Jaffna Wesleyan Central College.

—June. 6 - Death of S. Bastiampillai Mudaliyar, Chief Mudaliyar of the Jaffna Kachcheri. See Note 140.

—July. 14 - The wife of Mr. R. W. Ievers, G. A., Jaffna, encounters a bear at Vavuniya. The servant who accompanied her accidentally shot in the scuffle that ensued.

—Oct. - The Jaffna Agricultural Association formed.

—Oct. 25 - The gold coin called the sovereign made legal tender in Ceylon at Rs. 15.

1902—Jan. 20 - Professor W. A. Herdman with his assistant, Mr. Hornell, arrives in Colombo, to report on the Pearl Oyster beds off Mannar. See Note 234.

—Jan. - New rules and regulations published in the Government Gazette regarding land sales as well as pensions to Public Servants.

—Feb. 8 - Public Meeting at Point Pedro presided over by Mr. R. W. Allagakone, P. M., to consider steps for a memorial to Sir West Ridgeway, in connection with Railway extension to Jaffna.

—Feb. - Movement set on foot by the people of Jaffna to collect funds for a permanent memorial to H. E. Sir West Ridgeway for the introduction of the Railway to the North.

—Mar. 10 - H. E. Sir West Ridgeway visits Jaffna.

—Mar. 11 - Opening of the first section of 21 miles of Railway from Kāngasanturai to Chavākachcheri through Jaffna by Sir West Ridgeway. See Note 232.

—May. - Death at Vannarponne of Mr. T. P. Chellappapillai, retired Chief Justice of Travancore. See Note 177.

—June. 20 - Publication of the rules framed under the provisions of the Village Committee's Ordinance, 1889 and adopted by the Committee appointed by the inhabitants of Delft.

1902—June. 25 - Announcement received of the serious illness of His Majesty the King. Universal regret felt. arrangements made for his Coronation cancelled.

—July. 25 - An agricultural show held in Jaffna.

—Aug. 9 - The Roman Catholic Church and School at Tinnevaly wantonly destroyed in broad day light by a gang of fanatic Hindus.

—Sept. 5 - Opening of the section of the Northern Railway from Chavakachcheri to Pallai, a distance of 14 miles. See Note 232.

—Sept. 5 - An Agricultural Company formed in Jaffna. See Note 266.

—Oct. 9 - The inauguration of the Catholic Union of Ceylon.

—Dec. 21 - The Boer prisoners finally leave Ceylon for South Africa.

—Dec. - A statue of Buddah, cut out of white lime-stone, dug up at Chunnagam and removed to the Jaffna Kachcheri Park.

1903—Jan. 20 - Opening of the Training College at Colombo for teachers.

—Jan. - Motor-Cycle first imported into the Island.

—Jan. - Hon. P. Ramanathan appointed King's Counsel for Ceylon.

—Mar. 1 - A Pearl-Fishery at Marichikaddy.

—Mar. 25 - The Governor visits the Pearl Fishery.

—April. 1 - Celebration by the Roman Catholics of Ceylon of the Jubilee of His Holiness Pope Leo XIII.

—June. 9 - Serious riots at Anuradhapura, the Buddhist pilgrims destroying the Catholic Church, assaulting the priest and doing other damages. Some forty of the rioters were tried, convicted by the Supreme Court and sentenced to terms of imprisonment varying from one to seven years with fines. See Note 246.

—June. 13 - The Reform of the Legislative Council of Ceylon introduced by the Hon. Mr. J. Ferguson, the General European Member, discussed in Council.

—June. - Mr. Chit. Kailasapillai, Chief Mudaliyar of the Batticaloa Kachcheri, appointed Chief Tamil Translator and Interpreter to His Excellency the Governor. See Note 346.

—June. - The Paumben Railway and Canal Scheme proposed with a view to connect Ceylon with India by a Broad Gauge Railway.

1903—July, 9 - The Jaffna Hindu Young Men's Association started.

—Aug. - The Hon. Dr. William Gabriel Rockwood re-appointed Tamil Member of the Legislative Council. See Note 297.

—Oct. 2 - The "S. S. Jaffna", belonging to the Jaffna Steam Navigation Company, makes its trial trip.

—Oct. 14 - The "S. S. Jaffna" goes on a pleasure trip to Delft.

—Oct. 15 - The salt rent of the Jaffna District for 1904 sold to Raman Chetty for Rs. 63,521.

—Oct. 17 - A meeting held in the Jaffna District Court House under the presidency of Mr. J. P. Lewis, Acting Government Agent, when it was unanimously resolved to build a hall in the esplanade to be called the "Ridgeway Memorial Hall," as the permanent memorial to Sir West Ridgeway for the great boon of the Railway which he has given to the people of Jaffna.

—Oct. 27 - At a meeting held in the Jaffna Library, Mr. Advocate Tirunavukarasu elected to represent the people of Jaffna at the farewell function to be given at Colombo to H. E. Sir West Ridgeway on the eve of his departure from Ceylon.

—Nov. 18 - 40,000 cwts. of salt for Jaffna brought by the B. I. Steamer Chilka from India.

—Nov. 18 - Sir West Ridgeway and family leave Ceylon.

—Nov. - Mr. T. C. Changarapillai appointed Crown Proctor of Jaffna. See Note 341.

—Dec. 1 - A lecture on "Social Tyrannies." delivered by Mr. A. Canagaratnam, Proctor, at the Hindu College under the auspices of the Jaffna Young Men's Hindu Association. See Note 127.

—Dec. 3 - His Excellency Sir Henry Blake arrives in Colombo as Governor of Ceylon.

—Dec. 4 - Heavy rain and stormy weather.

—Dec. 31 - Mr. R. H. Leembruggen, Inspector of Schools, N. P., retires. See Note 236.

1904—Jan. 1 - The Vannarponne Post-office removed to the house built for the purpose by Dr. Sivapragasam.

—Jan. 5 - Mr. T. B. Russel appointed Police Magistrate of Jaffna in succession to Mr. T. M. Tampoe.

1904—Jan. 26 - Death at Mallakam of Mr. R. Mailvaganam, Proctor. He was a true type of a Tamil gentleman and took a keen interest in public affairs.

—Jan. - A new road opened from Pallai 4th mile post to Chempianpattu, a distance of about three miles.

—Jan. - Mr. J. P. Lewis recommends a Local Board for Jaffna.

—Feb. 1 - Mr. John Rudd leaves Jaffna. The officers of the Police and Fiscal's offices present him with a farewell address on the eve of his departure. Mr. Rudd was long in Jaffna. He was an able, energetic and impartial officer.

—Feb. 22 - Death at Udupiddy of S. Duraisamy, Maniagar of Valigamam East. See Note 239.

—Feb. - Retirement of Dr. Pararasasinghe, the Port Medical Officer of Kangasanturai, after a long and faithful service of 32 years spent in various parts of the Island. See Note 265.

—Feb. - Fever of a malignant malarial type prevails in all parts of the peninsula in an epidemic form.

—March. - Receiving Post Office opened at Delft.

—March - The operations in connection with the water supply of Jaffna carried on for some weeks past, at Tinnevely, completed. The well tested is said to be capable of supplying the town of Jaffna with the required quantity of water. See Note 242.

—March. 31 - Death at Nallur of Dr. M. Kandiah. See Note 240.

—April. 6 - Mr. Advocate Armstrong Talaivasingham appointed to act as Police Magistrate and Commissioner of Requests of Point Pedro and Chavakachcherri.

—April. 14 - Death at Nallur at the age of 80 of Mr. C. W. Kathiravetpillai, senior Advocate of the Ceylon Bar and the retired Police Magistrate of Kayts. See Note 244.

—April. 19 - The Hon. Dr. Rockwood, the Tamil member of the Legislative Council, leaves for England. Mr. W. N. Aserappa, Advocate, appointed to act for him. See Note 243.

—April. - Messrs AbdulCader, W. D. Niles and Culanthaivelu, come off successful in the Advocates' final Examination. See Note 241.

—April - Mr. M. Vaitilingam, a. son-in-law of Rai Bahadur Murugesampillai, retired Deputy Collector of Tanjore, commences to practise as a Proctor in Jaffna, where there are already forty Proctors and eight Advocates. See Note 385.

1904—May. 10 - Death at Vannarponne of Mr. N. Ponniahpillai, the retired Maniagar of Poonakari. See Note 245.

—May. 14 - Serious riots in Vannarponne in front of the Sivan Temple.

—May. - Mr. H. R. Freeman arrives and assumes duties as District Judge of Jaffna.

—May. - A gun commenced to be fired daily in the Jaffna Fort at 12 o'clock in the noon.

—June. 14 - Death at Kaithady of Saravanamuttu Mudaliyar, Maniagar of Tenmaradchy. See Note 247.

—June. - Commencement of the Law-Suit between the Jaffna Steam Navigation Company and Walker Sons & Co., touching the "S. S. Jaffna."

—July. 1 - The Dogs Ordinance comes into force in Jaffna.

—July. 13 - Announcement received of the death in England at the age of 73 of James Laurie, first Director of Public Instruction in Ceylon.

—July. 15 - Death at Kandy from an abscess in the liver, at the age of 63, of S. T. R. Kanagasundra Mudaliyar.

—July. 27 - Death at Nallur of Mr. S. Canter, father of Mr. C. Sundram of the Colombo Customs. See Note 249.

—July. - Mr. A. Kanagasabai Mudaliyar of Puttur appointed Maniagar of Valigamam East.

—July. - Mr. James Hensman of Kumbakonum College retires. He was in receipt of Rs. 12,000 a year. See Note 267.

—Aug. - Dr. A. J. Chalmers sent by Government to Jaffna to inquire into the causes of the malarial fever prevailing in Jaffna during rainy and dewy seasons.

—Aug. - Mr. Lewis, G. A., recommends an increase of salary to the Maniagars of the Jaffna District.

— Aug. - Dr. S. C. Paul, F. R. C. S. (England), obtains the M. D. degree of the Madras University.

—Aug. 8 - Death at Batticaloa of the Rev. Jos. Benjamin, Pastor. See Note 429.

—Sept. 21 - Pillar Letter Boxes erected on the Main Street, Jaffna, and also at the Grand Bazaar.

—Sept. - Death at Matale of Mrs. Gould, wife of Mr. N. G. Gould, who at one time was in extensive practice as an advocate in Jaffna.

1904—Sept. - The social and material condition of Jaffna as contrasted with that of 1873 shows vast changes. See Note 251.

—Sept. - Mr. Muttukumarasamy appointed Maniagar of Tenmaradchy in succession to the late Saravanamuttu Mudaliyar.

—Oct. - Announcement received of the death in England of Mr. William Digby, C. I. E., who at one time was connected with the "Ceylon Observer." See Note 253.

—Oct. 8 - Death in Colombo from pneumonia at the age of 31 of Mr. A. Naganather. See Note 252.

—Oct. 15 - Road tax in Jaffna raised from Rs. 1 to Rs. 1.25.

—Oct. 21 - Death at Batticotta of J. Velupillai, Surveyor. See Note 254.

—Oct. 30 - Death at Vannarponne of S. Sapapathypillai. See Note 255.

—Nov. 1 - The Northern Railway opened for traffic as far as Anuradhapura.

—Nov. 5 - Death at Batticaloa, at the age of 71, of Mrs. Covington, widow of the late Dr. M. Covington, Senior Medical Officer, Eastern Province. See Note 268.

—Nov. 9 - Mr. Sabaretnam, Chief Mudaliyar of the Jaffna Kachcheri, invested with the rank of Mudaliyar. See Note 435.

—Nov. 29 - Death at Arali of Iampillai Vytialingampillai alias N. Ford. See Note 256.

—Nov. - Death at Nallur of Mr. S. Kantapasekarar, retired Notary Public. See Note 257.

—Dec. 23 - Death at Arali of Wiseborn Volk, who was connected with the Batticotta Seminary as Teacher of Chronology, History and Geography. See Note 269.

—Dec. - Mr.M. B. Swampillai, the well-known merchant of Jaffna receives a gold medal for the cigars and tobacco he sent to the St. Louis Exhibition. See Note 258.

1905—Jan. 5 - The "Morning Star" commences to be published weekly with size enlarged. See Note 82.

—Jan. 9 - A meeting of the old boys of the Hindu College held in the College Hall to consider the desirability of forming an Old Boys' Association and of starting a College Magazine.

—Jan. 13 - The Noria or Bucket Pump fixed to the well of the Church garden at Vasavilan and worked in the presence of Mr. Lewis, G. A., and Mrs. Lewis, Frs. Collin, Alosyus and Baron, Messrs B. Santiagopillai, Proctor, J. A. Tisse-

1905— veerasinghe, retired Sub-collector, James H. Martyn, Editor "J. C. Guardian" and many others. Mr. Thomas, the importer, was congratulated by all. See Note 270.

—Jan. 24 - The celebration in Colombo of Dr. Melizan's Episcopal Silver Jubilee. Delegate Apostolic and five Bishops present. Jaffna Catholics presented address accompanied by pectoral chain and cross.

—Jan. 25 - Hon'ble Sir Charles P. Layard and Lady Layard entertained at a native musical and miscellaneous entertainment at Sangara Villa, Nallur.

—Jan. 26 - Death of Mr. S. Ponnampalam, 2nd son of Hardy Sinnatamy and brother in-law of Overseer Murukasu. See Note 259.

- Jan. - Temperance movements started in various centres throughout Jaffna with some spirit and enthusiasm.

—Feb. 9 - Death at Manipay, at the age of 63, from heart disease, of Mr. T. A. Thambypillai, father of Advocate Isaac Thambyah.

—Feb. 10 - Announcement received of the death at Worthing, Sussex, of Mr. R. W. Ievers, C. M. G., Government Agent of the Northern Province. See Note 271.

—Feb. - Death at Colombo of Mrs. Senathirajah, wife of Adv. E. S. W. Senathirajah and the eldest daughter of Adv. C. Brito, the well-known Lawyer and Scholar. See Note 260.

—Feb. 18 - Return to Colombo of Mr. and Mrs. P. Arunachalam from a visit to England. During their stay there, they had the honour of a private audience with her Majesty the Queen (at Buckingham Palace) who was pleased to present her portrait and autograph to Mrs. Arunachalam with a Message to Ceylon.

—Mar. 11 - The linking of the whole line of the Northern Railway at Madawachi completed, Assistant Foreman Wothand Taip doing the work. See Note 261.

—April. 23 - Arrival in Jaffna of the first Motor Car. Mrs. Scover and Mr. and Mrs. D. Dyer and Messrs G. Brooks and S. H. Dyer come in the car from Newara-Eliya.

—May. 8 - The Jaffna agricultural company wound up, the Government not having entertained favourably some of the terms offered for the purchase of land. Mr. W. Mather appointed liquidator. See Note 266.

—May. 20 - Sudden appearance of Sea water at a field in Navaly about 1½ miles from the Manipay Post Office.

1905— It gradually extended to a circular pool of 90 feet in circumference and 36 feet in depth.

—May. - Sir N. Cathiravetpillai, a learned scholar in Tamil and a member of the Madura Tamil Sangam, delivers a series of lectures in Jaffna and Point Pedro on subjects relating to Hinduism.

—May. 30 - The Buddhist High Priest Jayawaranara from A'pura visits Dr. Joulain with letters of introduction from H. E. the Governor and gives a cheque for Rs. 1000 as a donation from the Buddhists as compensation for the distruction of Church property at A'pura.

—June. 12 - Sampurokshanam (dedication ceremony) of the Temple known as the Kailasa Pillayar Koil at Nallur, performed.

—June. - A standard time fixed owing to a decision being made to have the same time all over India and Ceylon, adopting in time 5 hours and 30 minutes ahead of Greenwich. Hitherto Ceylon followed the Madras time.

—June. 27 - Death at Toulouse of Dr. Theophilus Andrew Melizan, O. M. I., Archbishop of Colombo. See Note 95.

—Aug. 1 - The formal opening of the Northern Railway, 198 miles in length. See Note 261.

—Aug. 11 - Publication of the Ordinance providing for the registration of medical practitioners.

—Aug. 11 - Death at Tellippalai of Visuvanatha Sinnappa Mudaliyar, the retired Maniagar of Valigamam North. See Note 262.

—Aug. 19 - His Excellency the Governor and Lady Blake arrive by special train from A'pura. They are received at the Jaffna Railway Station and conducted in procession by Martyn's Road and the Main Street to the reception pandal at the Esplanade, where the public address of welcome was read by Mr. Advocate Kanagasabai. See Note 263.

—Aug. 19 - Representatives of the Colombo Press come to Jaffna in connection with the gubernatorial visit. See Note 264.

—Aug. 22 - H. E. Sir Henry Blake visits the Central College.

—Aug. 24 - H. E. Sir and Lady Blake preside at the prize-giving at the Victoria College, Chulipuram, and the opening of the newly built Ridgeway Hall in connection with that College.

1905—Aug. - Dr. Thompson arrives and takes charge of the Manipay Hospital. See Note 275.

—Aug. - Government Officials, whose inspection duties extend through different parts of the Island, are allowed the privilege of using Motor Cars.

—Sept. - The claim made by the officiating Brahmins of the Nallainatha Swami Temple, commonly called Saddanather Temple, to the possession of the Temple and its properties, dismissed in appeal and Dr. Sivapragasampillai, father of Proctor S. Thambyahpillai, declared entitled to the possession of the Temple and all its properties, moveable and immovable.

—Sept. - Dr. Joshua, L. R. C. P. & S. (Edinburgh), returns to Ceylon and receives an appointment under Government.

—Sept. - By a Government Proclamation, the Division of Delft extended so as to include the island of Kakerativu which is uninhabited but from which some revenue is derived. Delft was brought under the operation of the Village Communities Ordinance of 1889 in 1901 on the recommendtion of the late Mr. R. W. Ievers. See Note 50.

—Sept. - Mr. T. W. Crosette of Uduvil, a teacher at Indore, comes off successful in the Calcutta M. A. Examination in the first class and as first in the Presidency taking honours in English. See Note 93.

—Sept. - Government sanctions the establishment of a Local Board in Jaffna.

—Sept. 24 - Construction of a Telephone line from the Police Station to the Jaffna Kachcheri commenced. Mr. Van Langenburg, Asst. Inspector of Telephones, superintends the work.

—Oct. 12 - At a meeting of the Jaffna Y. M. C. A., the question of the disposal of the F. N. S. Hospital was discussed, with the result that it was not good for the Hospital to be handed over to Government.

—Nov. - The Secretary of State sanctions the offer of £20,000 per annum made by a Syndicate formed in England to take the Ceylon Pearl-Fishery on lease, provided that the Ceylon Government will accept it.

—Nov. 7 A reception at St. John's College, Chundicully, to Dr. H. B. Mylvaganam on his returm from Europe after obtaining the degree of F. R. C. S. (England).

1905—Nov. 9 - Mr. Paul Sinnadurai Nicholas, Head Clerk, Trincomalee Kachcheri, invested with the title of Mudaliyar. See Note 434.

—Nov. 10 - A Proclamation in the Government Gazette establishing a Local Board for Jaffna.

—Nov. 17 - Death at Chandilipay of Dr. A. A. Pararasasinghe Mudaliyar. See Note 265.

—Nov. 29 - Return to Ceylon, after a distinguished career in England, of Mr. A. C. Tampoe. See Note 272.

—Dec. 5 - A meeting held in the Central College Hall with the object of giving a public reception to Mr. A. C. Tampoe—the talented son of Mr. T. M. Tampoe, the retired Police Magistrate of Jaffna—who had risen to the unique position of being the first Ceylonese to enter the Indian Civil Service. See Note 272.

—Dec. 11 - Death at Pannalai of Mrs. A. Kanagasabai, wife of Advocate (now Sir) A. Kanagasabai, the leader of the Jaffna Bar. The deceased lady was noted for her admirable and esteemable qualities of head and heart and had the reputation of being a charitably disposed lady.

—Dec, 11 - In the "S. S. Jaffna" Case (Messrs Walker Sons & Co. versus the Jaffna Steam Navigation Company) judgment was given by the Additional District Judge of Colombo in favour of the Plaintiffs for Rs. 13,000 as claimed.

—Dec. 29 - Death of Cathiripillai, the retired Udaiyar of Thaiyiddy. He was more than 100 years old at the time of his death.

—St. Patrick's College Annual started. See Note 127.

1906– Jan. 1 - The system of renting salt in the Jaffna District ceases and that of retail by licence commences. The price of salt is raised from Rs. 2.25 to 3.50 per cwt. See Note 273.

—Jan. 6 - A large and representative meeting held in the Central College Hall in which an Association called the Jaffna Association was formed, 54 gentlemen being enrolled members and Mr. James Hensman elected President.

—Jan. 7 - Death at Nallur of Mr. Sabapathy Mudaliyar, Interpreter of the Police Court of Jaffna. See Note 249.

—Jan. 7 - Death at Jaffna of Mr. S. Visuvalingam of the P. W. D. Office, Jaffna. He erected temples and sunk wells for public use.

1906—Jan. - The Tamil Seat in the Legislative Council falls vacant by the resignation of the Hon. Dr. W. G. Rockwood owing to failing health.

—Jan. 8 - At a meeting of the Ceylon Agricultural Board held in Colombo, it was resolved to appoint a tobacco expert with a view to the improvement of tobacco cultivation in the Northern Province.

—Jan. 10 - At a meeting of the Jaffna Agricultural Society, Mr. J. P. Lewis, Government Agent, read a paper on Manioc, which, he said, was introduced into the Island by the Dutch.

—Jan. 16 - A Social gathering of Jaffna Tamil Ladies, the first of its kind, held in Vannarponne at the residence of Mr. and Mrs. Masillamany.

—Jan. 20 - Arrival in Jaffna of Warren's Circus, the first Circus ever seen in Jaffna. The first performance took place on the 22nd instant. Crowds of people from all parts of the peninsula were present.

—Feb. 4 - Mr. A. Kanagasabai, Advocate, appointed Tamil member of the Legislative Council in succession to Dr. Rockwood. See Note 427.

—Feb. - Mr. M. Karalasingham, Registrar of ands, Jaffna, transferred to Colombo. Mr. B. Francis, Registrar of lands, Batticaloa, succeeds him in Jaffna.

—Feb. 19 - The corner stone of the Memorial Hall to the late Mr. Charles Wadsworth of the Copay Training School, laid by the Lord Bishop of Colombo. See Note 359.

—Feb. - The Government Officer's Salaries Scheme sanctioned by the Secretary of State.

—Feb. 23 - Death of S. Nicholas Edirveerasinghe, Post Master, Vannarponne. He was an intelligent and honest officer. See Note 274.

—Feb. 27 - Dr. Thompson, who was in charge of the Manipay Hospital, leaves for Madras. See Note 275.

—March. 9 - Death at Vannarponne of Mr. S. T. M. Pasupathy Chettiar, President of the Saiva Pari Palana Sabhai. See Note 166.

—Mar. 9 - The Hon. Mr. A. Kanagasabai appointed a member of the Board of Education. See Note 427.

1906—Mar. 12-19 - The Great Eastern Abell's Circus Company are in Jaffna giving performances.

—March. - The death is announced of the Revd. Edmund Rigg, retired Superintendent of the North-Ceylon Wesleyan Mission. See Note 53.

—April. - R. Kantyah Mudaliyar, the well-known and popular Secretary of the District Court of Jaffna, promoted to the first class of the Clerical Service. He is one of the ablest and most intelligent officers to be found in any Department. He is the first Tamil to be appointed Secretary of the District Court of Jaffna.

—April. - Death at Manipay of Dr. C. T. Mills. See Note 276.

—May. - Miss Nallamma Murugasan, daughter of the late Mr. G. Murugasu of the P. W. D., and sister of Advocate Arulanandam, comes off successful in the Preliminary Scientific L. M. S. Examination of the Madras University. She went to Paris to represent the Christian Community of S. India at the conference of Y. W. C. A. held on the 10th May 1906 in that city.

—June. 7 - Death in Colombo of Ponnampalam Coomaraswamy, Tamil M. L. C. See Note 277.

—June. 23 - Arrival in Jaffna by the evening train of Swami Abhedananda and party.

—July. 10 - Announcement received from Manipay of the death of the Revd. W. C. Tacker.

—Aug. 4 - Death of Mr. S. Pedropillai, a well-known and popular townsman of Jaffna. See Note 278.

—Oct. 13 - A large and influential meeting held in the Central College Hall with the object of forming a North-Ceylon Educational Association.

—Dec. 22 - Death at the General Hospital, Colombo, of Dr. A. B. Santiago, L. R. C. P. & S. and F. R. C. S. See Note 279.

—Dec. 28 - A meeting held for starting an Old Boys' Association in connection with the Central College.

—Dec. - Calcutta Entrance Examination held in Jaffna for the last time.

1907—Jan. 1 - Revd. Greegon and A. Hitchcock, Secretaries of the American Board, respectively of New York City and Chicago, arrive in Colombo to visit the American Mission of Jaffna.

—Jan. - Death in his 97th year of Seth Payson, better known as Arunachalam Seth Payson, Udaiyar of Sandilipay. See Note 82.

1907—Feb. 1 - The Students' Home for Hindus started in connection with St. Patrick's| College.

—Feb. 16 - Death at Jaffna of Mr. V. Yanamuttu, a well-known and enterprising merchant. He was the pioneer of the Coach Service in Jaffna. See Note 149.

—Feb. 21 - A concert held in the Jaffna Central College Hall in aid of the New College building fund.

—Feb. - Mr. S. Chinniah appointed Maniagar of Jaffna.

—June. 1 - Mr. C. Sundram appointed Chief Appraiser of the Customs— an office newly created—on a salary of Rs. 3,000 per annum together with a personal allowance of Rs. 500.

—June. 30 - Death at Kuala-Lumpur of K. Thananayagam, who belonged to a very respectable family of Delft. He was a leading contractor in the Straits for nearly 20 years.

—July. - Mr. R. R. Williams, son of Mr. L. C. Williamspillai, Inspector of Schools, South India, obtains the Edinburgh Triple qualification of L. R. C. P. & S. and L. P. S. Glasgow. See Note 323.

—July. 6 - Reception accorded at the Jaffna Railway Station to Thambapillai Mudaliyar on his return from Colombo after receiving from His Excellency the Governor a gold medal for long and faithful service. See Note 392.

—July. 10 - Their Excellencies Sir Henry and Lady Blake leave for England by the P & O. S. S. Sardinia.

—July. - Mr. Advocate K. Balasingham appointed Acting District Judge of Ratnapura. See Note 280.

—July. 17 - Arrival in Jaffna from Colombo by train of Mr. R. R. T. R. M. M. S. T. Chidamparam Chettiar. He is one of the richest Chetty Merchants and head of the Firms bearing his initials in various parts of India, Ceylon and the Straits. He was given an enthusiastic reception by the local chetties.

—Aug. - The gateway at Nallur with the site on which it stands acquired by Government. This gateway stands on the former palace of the Jaffna Tamil Kings.

—Aug. 3 - Swami Dayaram arrives in Jaffna and delivers lectures at Erlalai, Columbuturai, Vannarponne and other places. The Swami belongs to the Ramachandra Mutt at Coimbatore, S. India. He left here on the 13th instant.

1907—Aug. 9 - The draft of an Ordinance to incorporate the American Ceylon Mission published in the Government Gazette.

—Aug. 17 - Arrival in Jaffna of Sir Hugh Clifford, Officer administering the Government. He stayed at the Old Park as the guest of Mr. F. H. Price, G. A., N. P.

—Aug. - Mr. S. Katirasu, Proctor, Supreme Court, appointed Notary Public to practise in the English Language in Jaffna. He is a member of the Jaffna District Road Committee. See Note 244.

—Aug. 24 - H. E. Sir Henry Edward McCallum arrives and assumes the Government of the Island.

—Sept. 2 - Death at Devacotai from fever of Chidamparam Chettiar—the Chetty millionaire who lately visited Jaffna.

—Sept. - Sir William Twynam assumes dutes as acting G. A. of Jaffna. His activity, energy and endurance at the age of 80 are wonderful.

—Sept. 6 - The draft of an Ordinance providing for the registration of copyright in Literary and Artistic works published in the Government Gazette.

—Sept. - Announcement received of the death in Colombo of Mr. J. S. Drieberg, Commissioner of Requests, Colombo. He was for some years Police Magistrate of Point-Pedro and Chavakacherri.

—Sept. 11 - The Chetty Street Improvement Society started.

—Sept. - The Secretary of State sanctions the Survey of the line for the proposed Mannar Railway which will not only connect Mannar with the Northern Railway but also India with Ceylon.

—Sept. 27 - Death at Jaffna of Mr. James H. Martyn, Editor of the "Jaffna Catholic Guardian" See Note 281.

—Oct. - Mr. J. P. Lewis, G. A., N. P. obtains from Paris an enlarged portrait of Mr. P. A.' Dyke, Rajah of the North. See Note 131.

—Oct. 6 - Death at Narantanai of Mr. S. Abraham, Head Master and Teacher of Mathematics, St. Patrick's College. See Note 103.

—Oct. 27 - Death at Colombo of Mr. Tirunavakarasu, Advocate. See Note 282.

—Oct. 28 - Death at Manipay of Mr, A. Visuvalingam, Proctor.

1907—Nov. 6 - Death at Mantota, Mannar, of Dr. V. Chinniahpillai, Medical Officer. He was a brother of Mr. Valauthampillai, Manager, Hindu High School, Point-Pedro and a cousin of Mr. Coomaraswamipillai, Tamil Scholar, Point-Pedro.

—Nov. 8 - Death of Mr. M. P. Samarasinghe Mudaliyar, Postmaster and Superintendent of Post offices, Jaffna. See Note 283.

—Nov. 8 - The Government Gazette notifies the appointment of Mr. T. C. Changarapillai, Proctor, and Mr. S. Sabapathy, to be visitors to the Jaffna Civil Hospital. See Note 431.

—Nov. 21 - Arrival in Jaffna of Takur Khan Chandra Varma, the famous Punjabee Orator. He delivers a series of lectures at different centres in Jaffna.

—Dec. 1 - A Receiving Post office opened at Tellippalai.

—Dec. 14 - The biennial election of the Jaffna Local Board, in which Messrs S. Thambiahpillai, A. Cathiravelu and A. Sabapathy were elected as unofficial members for the years 1908 and 1909.

—Dec. - News received from England of the success of Mr. Alfred N. Santiago, son of Dr. A. B. Santiago, F. R. C. S., in the first examination in Law, obtaining the distinction of second class honours in Roman Law. See Note 366.

—Dec. 20 - The Ceylon dinner in England held in the Oak Rooms, Trocadero Restaurant, London. See Note 284.

—Dec. 23 - The unveiling of the portrait of Mr. R. W. Ievers, C. M. G., in the Hall of the Jaffna Kachcheri by Mr. F. H. Price, G. A., N. P. The portrait was got out of subscriptions from friends and admirers in Jaffna of Mr. Ievers.

1908—Jan. - At a meeting of the Jaffna Local Board the rates and taxes for the year were fixed. The assessment tax was raised from 2 to 3 per cent and a tax of Rs. 1·50 imposed on Rickshaws.

—Jan. 6 - Mr. Isaac Thambiah, Advocate, leaves for Colombo to practise his profession there. See Note 349.

—Jan. 7 - Death at the General Hospital, Colombo, of Mr. Taylor, District Superintendent, Northern Railway. He was a popular officer.

—Jan. 15 - The Karativu Ferry opened for traffic and the horse-boat commenced to ply.

—Jan. - The Survey of the Mannar Railway commenced.

1908—Jan. 21 - Death at Jaffna of B. Manuelpillai, Teacher, St. Patrick's College, the brother of Mr. B. Benjamin of the Jaffna Government Firewood Depot.

—Jan. - Cigar makers go on strike, demanding increased pay.

—Jan. - Dr. H. B. Mailvaganam, F. R. C. S., England, 3rd Surgeon, General Hospital, Colombo, appointed Assistant Surgeon and Superintendent in ear, nose and throat diseases, Victoria Hospital, Mysore, India.

—Feb. 1 - Death at Jaffna from pneumonia of Avirampillai Joseph, a well-known blacksmith, who distinguished himself by skilful and ingenious work in iron and secured the patronage of the European residents of Jaffna. See Note 287.

—Feb. 2 - The Atthothayam of the Hindus, which occurs once in 60 years. Very large crowds of people from all parts of Ceylon and India went to Keerimalai to bathe on this occasion sacred to the Hindus. See Note 288.

—Feb. - The establishment of a Post-office at Chunnakam sanctioned.

—Feb. - The work of building the Ridgeway Memorial Hall in the Jaffna Esplanade commenced by the contractor, Mr. Chinnappa of Moolai.

—Feb. 15 - Death at Singapore from pneumonia of Mr. A. C. Rudra, Barrister-at-Law. He appeared as the defending counsel in certain cases in the Jaffna Courts and took the local public by storm.

—Feb. 30 - Opening of a new market in Copay North.

—March. - Death at the age of 88 of the Rev. G. W. Pope, a distinguished Tamil Scholar.

—March. - The Inspector and Superintendent of Works, Local Board, Jaffna, prepare a statement of all cess-pits in the Town with a view to introducing the dry-earth system into the Pettah.

—Mar. 3 - Rev. H. Highfield, Principal, Wesley College, Colombo, delivers a lecture in the Wesleyan Chapel, Jaffna, on the "External Evidences of Christianity." The following evening, he gave another on the "Internal Evidences" at the Jaffna Central College.

—Mar. 6 - A public meeting held in the Jaffna Kachcheri Bungalow to consider a proposal to conduct experimental cul-

1908— tivation of tobacco, and introduce new and modern or improved methods of curing.

—Mar. 6 - Death at Anaicottai from pneumonia of Mr. C. M. Sinnatamby, brother of Mr. C. M. Sinnyah . Mudaliyar, Shroff, Jaffna Kachcheri.

—Mar. 9 - Muthali Sadayan, the accused in the Pandivirichan murder case, underwent the extreme penalty of the law within the Jaffna Fort Jail.

—Mar. 11 - Rev. M. P. Wilkes, Principal, Central College, is given a farewell on his leaving the College to take charge of his new work at Point Pedro.

—Mar. 11 - Death at Mallagam from paralysis of Dr. S. Sinnappoo. See Note 289.

—Mar. 18 - Mr. J. H. Vanniasinkam acts as District Judge of Jaffna.

—Mar. 19 - Death at Vannarponne of Mr. S. Sidamparapillai. See Note 290.

—Mar. - Death at Vannarponne of Mrs. Kandiah, a grand daughter of the late Mr. A. Eliatamby, Head Clerk, Jaffna Kachcheri.

—April. - News received of the appointment of Mr. C. A. M. Tampoe, as Assistant Collector, Bangalore.

—April. - Small-pox very bad at Valigamam West; patients removed to Changanai for isolation and kept at the Old Dutch-Church for treatment. Dr. S. Arumugam in attendance. The disease breaks out at the Chetty quarters at Vannarponne and also at Suthumalai.

—April. 1 - Cremation in the cremation grounds situated at Uduvil discontinued by order of Government.

—April. 3 - Death at Narantanai of Mr. S. Ponniah, retired officer of the Fiscal's Department, Jaffna. His wife died on the same afternoon while preparations were being made for her husband's funeral.

—April. - Small-pox continues to prevail at Chankanai, Thavady and Vannarponne.

—April. 11 - At a meeting of the Jaffna Local Board, the scheme for the water supply of the town was considered.

—April. 16 - Death at DevaCotkai from dropsy of R. M. M. S. T. Raman Chettiar. He was the chief agent of the well-known and leading Firm of R. M. M. S. T. and was not only the most prominent figure among the Chetties

1908— of Jaffna but very popular among all classes of the local community.

—April. 16 - Death at Mallagam of Appucutty Kingsbury, Professor of Mathematics, in the Jaffna College. See Note 292.

—April. 30 - Small-pox shows a decrease.

—May. 1 - Death at the age of 82 of Vairamuttu Udaiyar Kartigasa Udaiyar of Mattuvil.

—May. - Six Tamils of Jaffna (three of whom head the list) come off successful in the Advocate's Final Examination.

—May. - News received of the success of a number of Jaffna students of the Madras Medical College in the Medical Examination of that University.

—May. 24 - Death of Rev. C. C. Handy, B. A., who was Headmaster of St. John's College, Chundikully, for about 20 years. See Note 93.

—May. 25 - Death at Vannarponne of Mr. C. Sundaram, brother of Advocate Tirunavukarasu. He was employed as a Clerk in the Colombo Customs and was married to a niece of Mr. T. Kailasapillai, Manager, Sivapragasa Vithiasalai, Vannarponne.

—June. 1 - The Port of Kayts closed owing to the out-break of plague.

—June. 2 - H. E. Sir Henry Edward McCallum arrives in Jaffna by train accompanied by Mr. A. J. Hedgeland, Private Secretary, and Captain Curling, A. D. C. From the Railway Station H. E. is driven in a torch-light procession to King's House, Fort. At 10 a. m. the next day the address of welcome is read by Mr. J. M. Hensman at the pandal in the esplanade. At 11 a. m. H. E. received the Deputation on the question of the closing of the Port of Kayts.

—June. 4 - Death at Mannar of C. Coomariah Mudaliyar, retired Registrar of Lands, Jaffna. See Note 293.

—June. 5 - H. E. Sir Henry McCallum visits the different colleges of Jaffna.

—June. 8 - At a meeting of the Jaffna Local Board, the question of introducing the dry earth system into the Pettah is considered.

—Aug. 7 - Death at Jaffna of Mr. Benjamin Santiapillai, one of the veteran Lawyers of Jaffna. See Note 294.

1908—Aug. 16 - Hon. P. Ramanathan comes to Jaffna for the purpose of selecting a site for the proposed college for Hindu girls.

—Aug. - Mr. R. R. Nalliah, second son of Mr. Nalliah, the well-known Surveyor, comes off successful in the Proctor's Final Examination. See Note 298.

—Sept. 25 - The foundation stone of the new Jaffna Wesleyan Central College buildings laid on the site of the old St. Pauls' Wesleyan Church.

—Oct. 13 - Death at Jaffna of Mr. S. Manuelpillai Rajakariar, the widely known merchant, planter and renter. See Note 295.

—Dec. 31 - One of the newly built markets at Pandaterrippu collapses during the heavy storm and rain.

1909—Feb. - The "Ceylon Patriot" changes hands. Mr. A. Canagaretnam, Proctor, purchasing the whole concern. See Note 127.

—Feb. - The Finance Committee of the Agricultural Society votes a sum of Rs. 250 annually for an experimental garden at Jaffna.

—March. - Mr. Thurairetnam Nalliah, son of Mr. M. Nalliah, Surveyor and Merchant, and brother of Proctor R. R. Nalliah, takes his oath as an Advocate of the Supreme Court. See Note 298.

—March. 15 - A lecture delivered in the Ridgeway Hall of the Victoria College, Chulipuram, by Mr. A. Hoisington, B. A., Cambridge, a native of Jaffna, on his "Experiences of Life in London and New York." See Note 296.

—Mar. 19 - Death of Mr. John Philips, Teacher.

—Mar. 27 - Death at Colombo of Dr. W. G. Rockwood. He is a Jaffna man and an eminent Surgeon with a European reputation. See Note 297.

—April. 2 Death at Jaffna of Mr. M. Nalliah, the well-known Merchant and Surveyor, Jaffna. See Note 298.

—April. 12 - The foundation stone of the Thirunavukarasu Memorial out-door dispensary laid by Sir Allen Perry, Kt., P. C. M. O., in connection with the Civil Hospital Jaffna. See Note 282.

—April. 30 - Mr. M. Stephenson, the energetic A. G. A. of Mannar, opens the Agricultural Show at Mannar. Eight classes of exhibits thrown open for competition in 8 respective stalls.

1909—May. 1 - The unveiling in the Kayts Courts, of the portrait of the late Mr. C. W. Kathiravetpillai, Police Magistrate, Kayts.

—May. 4 - Death at Batticaloa of Mr. N. Subraman. retired Head Clerk of the Jaffna Kachcheri.

—May, - Mr. M.S. Ramalingam, Second Tamil Interpreter, Supreme Court, appointed Chief Mudaliyar of the Jaffna Kachcheri. See Note 347.

—May. 9 - Death at Vaddukoddai at the age of 34 of Dr. W. A. Joshua, L. R. C. P. & S., medical officer, Kangesanturai, son-in-law of Mr. Chelliah Cooke of the Jaffna College. See Note 400.

—June. 1 - At the Durbar of Tamil Chiefs held at Queens House, Colombo, His Excellency Sir Henry MacCallum, presiding at the meeting, it was decided to revive the rank of Adigar to be conferred as a mark of pre-eminence among the Tamils.

—June. 10 The 41st Annual General Meeting of the confraternity of the Sacred Heart of Jesus held at St. Patrick's College Hall, Jaffna. Revd. Fr. J. T. A. Lortie reads a paper on "Lay Catholic Action." At this meeting the first formal proceedings towards the formation of the Jaffna Catholic Club commenced. See Note 291.

—July - The Secretary of State sanctions the construction of the Mannar Railway.

—Aug. 8 - Death of the Rev. R. W. Ryde, sometime Principal of St. John's College, Chundicully, and President of the Old Boys' Association of that College. See Note 98,

—Aug. 16 - The Shield Competition Match, played in the Esplanade between St. Patrick's and Central Colleges, results in a victory for the former.

—Sept. 4 - Death at Copay of Mr. A. Mailvaganam, J. P., U. P. M. He was one of the best and noblest sons of Jaffna. See Note 299.

—Sept. 8 - Inauguration of the Jaffna Club and the 25th Anniversary of St. Joseph's Catholic Library. See Note 291

—Sept. Death of Mr. Supramania Chinniah, Maniagar of Jaffna. See Note 300.

—Sept. 8 - Death of Mr. C. Strantenburgh one of the veteran Lawyers of Jaffna. See Note 301.

—Sept. 24 - Death of the Rev. Fr. M. Joseph, O. M. I.

1909—Oct. - The building of the Ridgeway Memorial Hall completed and the keys of the building handed over to the Committee by Mr. Chinnappah of Moolai, the Contractor.

—Oct. 8 - Death of the Very Rev. Fr. John Aloysius, Parish Priest, St. James, Jaffna. See Note 123.

—Oct. 23 - Death at Chunnagam of Mr. Kadirithamby Mudaliyar Sivasamboo. See Note 302.

—Nov. 26 - Mr. Nevins Selvadurai, B. A. Principal, Hindu College, leaves Jaffna for Kandy to take up his new appointment at Trinity College Kandy. See Note 166.

—Nov. - A vote of Rs. 40,000 sanctioned towards a scheme for supplying water to the Town of Mannar.

—Nov. 26 - Death at Point Pedro of Taivar Nagalinga Mudaliyar. See Note 303.

—Nov. - A coir yarn manufactory opened at Kalvalavu Estate, Pallai, by Mr. A. Pararasasinghe, a nephew of Mr. E. S. W Senathirajah.

—Dec. - The Mavilankai (Cocoanut) Estate, one of the biggest in the Pachchilaipali District and the property of Sir William Twynam, bought by Dr. S. C. Paul of Colombo for Rs. 60,000.

—Dec. 4 - The biennial election of the members of the Jaffna Local Board. See Note 304.

—Dec. 25 - Death of M. Philips of Messrs Walker Sons & Co., the esteemed Mupoo of the Jaffna Catholics resident at Colombo.

1910—Feb. 6 - Death at Jaffna of Mr. Lopez Manuel shortly after his retirement from the Public Instruction Department. See Note 306.

—Mar. 5 - A branch of the Brother-hood of St. Joseph of Colombogam established at Ilavalai.

—Mar. 28 - Death at Mandativu of Charles Hensman who was employed in the Government Educational Department of Madras for over ten years. See Note 157.

—Mar. 30 - Mr. H. R. Freeman appointed Government Agent, Jaffna. See Note 441.

—May. 6 - Death of His Majesty, King Edward VII. The funeral took place on the 20th instant following.

—May. 14 - The Shield Cricket Match played between the Central and St. Patrick's Colleges results in a victory for the former by a large margin.

1910—June. 5 - Death at Karampan, Kayts, at the age of 70, of Saverimuttu Bastiampillai, popularly known as Sevaliyar. See Note 307.

—June. 24 - Death at Jaffna of Mr. Gabriel Robert Puviraja-singhe of the Irrigation Department, Anuradhapura. See Note 308.

—June. 31 - The copper five cent coins cease to be legal tender. The concession of exchanging them in the Trea-sury and Kachcheries extended to the 31st December 1910.

—July. 4 - Foundation Stone of the Manipay Hindu College, laid by Chief Justice Sir Joseph Hutchinson.

—July. - Publication of the first volume of the Tamil Diction-ary, complied by Mr. C. W. Kathiravetpillai, Police Mag-istrate of Kayts. Advocate Balasingham, son of the learn-ed author, gives in a Tamil Preface to the work, the history of its compilation, and the circumstances under which he handed over the manuscripts to Sri Panditor, Thevar of Madura, at whose instance, it was edited and published by the Pundits of the Madura Tamil Changam. See Note 244.

—July. - Tamil included as a second language in the list of subjects for the Senior, Junior and Preliminary Examina-tions of the London College of Preceptors.

—Aug. 4 - The second consignment of the new nickel coin to the value of Rs. 100,000, received at the General Treasury, Colombo.

—Aug. 9 - Mr. V. Casippillai, Crown Proctor, appointed to act as District Judge, and additional Commissioner of Re-quests and Police Magistrate of Jaffna. See Note 166.

—Aug. 13 - The import duty on Jaffna Tobacco to Travan-core reduced from Rs. 900 to the old rate of Rs. 90. See Note 309.

—Aug. 16 - Second visit of His Excellency, Sir Henry MacCa-lum to Jaffna. He is accorded a cordial and enthusiastic reception; and presented with a golden casket of exquisite workmanship. See Note 309.

—Aug. 17 - The Durbar of Tamil Chiefs held in Jaffna under the presidency of His Excellency the Governor. The sub-jects discussed were Tobacco Industry, Colonization of the Wanny, Hindu Temporalities, Cattle Breeding and Pasture Lands, Crime, Malarial Fever, Experimental Gardens, Rin-derpest and Measures against straying cattle.

1910—Sept. - Publication of the Franchise Bill relating to the Elective Franchise and Provincial Representation in the Island.

—Sept. 9 - Arrack rents sold: Jaffna for Rs. 182,995; Mannar for Rs. 69,500; and Mullaitivu for Rs. 28,601.

—Sept. 13 - The Copay Siva Girls' School opened by Mr. P. Ramanathan, K. C., C. M. G.

—Sept. 16 - Opening of the elective campaign in connection with the educated Ceylonese seat in the Reform Legislative Council.

—Sept. 30 - Death at the Manipay Hospital, from fever, of Mr. F. N. Johnpulle, Inspector of Vaccination, Jaffna.

—Oct. 13 - Death at Chiviateru of Mr. V. Arumugam, brother of Mr. V. Casippillai, Supreme Court Proctor. See Note 310.

—Oct. 14 - Death at Jaffna at the age of 80 of Mr. J. N. Sandresegara, retired superintendent of minor works, Jaffna. See Note 311.

—Oct. 14 - The second trial of the S. S. "Jaffna" case, before Mr. Schineider, specially gazetted as acting District Judge of Colombo, who delivers judgment extending to over forty pages of foolscap.

—Oct. 15 - A receiving Post Office opened at Analativu.

—Oct. Dr. M. Kailasapillai, Medical Officer, retires on pension. See Note 312.

—Nov. 8 - Death at Anaicottai, at the age of 58, from heart-failure, of Dr. V. Muttucoomaru. See Note 313.

—Nov. 12 - A public meeting at the Jaffna Ridgeway Memorial Hall to protest against the abolition of the Minor Courts of Mallagam.

—Nov. 20 - Arrival in Colombo of the Crown Prince and Princess of Germany.

—Nov. - Completion of the Rail-Road between Mannar and Talaimannar.

—Dec. - News received of the success of Dr. M. Coomaraswamy, only son of Rao Bahadur Murugasampillai, in the final F. R. C. S. Examination of London. See Note 385.

—Dec. 7 - Inauguration of the Manipay Hindu College in its new building.

—Dec. 21 - Tolls in Ceylon abolished and additional taxes imposed instead.

—Dec. 26 - Death at Trivandrum of Mr. C. Brito, the well-known Scholar and Advocate. See Note 314.

1910—Dec. 27 - Death at Colomboturai of Mr. K. Arumugam, retired sub-collector. He was a well-informed officer.

1911—Jan. 4 - Mr. Maurice Selvador Shresta appointed acting District Judge of Jaffna.

—Jan. 23 - Death of Mr. J. M. Varunakulasinghe, Adigar of Mantai. See Note 315.

—Jan. 25 - The newly-built Hall of the Chetty Street high school opened by the Revd. J. M. Brown, General Secretary of the Wesleyan Mission, and the Ladies Gallery by Mrs. Brown. Revd. J. T. Garret, Revd. H. Highfield and Revd. Appapillai were present and gave addresses.

—Jan. - News received of the success in the L. R. C. P. and S. Examination of the Edinburgh University of Miss. Dr. Nallammah Murugasan, daughter of the late Mr. Murugasu of the P. W. D. and sister of Mr. M. A. Arulanandan, B. A., Advocate. She is the first Jaffna Tamil Lady to obtain this distinction. See Note 317.

—Feb. 9 - Death at Batticotta of M. N. Sinnappa, commonly known as Moolai Sinnappa. See Note 316.

—Feb. - Mr. S. K. Lawton, the well-known Photographer of Manipay granted an English patent for 14 years, on a preparation for preventing injury to paper. See Note 390.

—Mar. 3 - The Hippodrome circus opens its show in the Jaffna Esplanade.

—Mar. 10 - The fifth Decennial census of Ceylon taken. Population 4,092,973, an increase of 527,019 over that of 1901. Total population including military and shipping 4,096,021. Northern Province 369,651. Jaffna 40,441.

—April. 20 - The Dog Registration Ordinance comes into operation in the Northern Province.

—April. 21 - A meeting held at the Jaffna Ridgeway Memorial Hall to make arrangements for the due celebration of the coronation of His Majesty King George V. At this meeting Mr. K. Vytilingam, renter, makes an offer to feed the poor on the occasion of the celebration. See Note 320.

—April. 24 - Inauguration at Gold-smith street, Vannarponne, of Nagalinga Swamy Vidyasalai, under the management of Mr. K. Sivakolundu, Proctor, S. C. See Note 381.

—April. 30 - Death at the age of eighty-five of Sri Sumangala, the famous Buddhist High Priest and Oriental Scholar.

1911—May. 29 Death at Mallagam of Mr. Hemphill Thambo, Proctor. He was Crown Proctor at Mannar and retired some years ago.

—May. 31 - Arrival in Jaffna of Miss Dr. Nallamma Murugasan, L. R. C. P. & S., (Edinburgh) L. F. P. & S. (Glas) and L. M. (Dublin). See Note 317.

—June. 10 - Celebration at Batticaloa by Dr. and Mrs. A. Chinniah of the Silver Jubilee of their marriage.

—June. 17 - Death at Pannalai of Mr. S. Ponnampalam, Proctor. See Note 318.

—June. 22 - The Coronation celebrations in Jaffna of His most Gracious Majesty, King George V. See Note 320.

—June. 22- The Freeman Tanneer Pandal opened at Batticaloa.

—July. 3 - Death at Jaffna of Rasiah William Allagacoon, Police Magistrate of Point Pedro and Chavakachcherri, from an abscess in the index finger of the right-hand. See Note 319.

—July. 3 - A cricket match, Advocates vs. Proctors, played in the Jaffna Esplanade, ends in a win for the Advocates by 35 runs.

—July. 9 - Death at the age of 85 of Mr. Ramanather Murugasu of Tirunelvely, an influential and leading tobacco merchant. Mr. S. Ehamparam, Surveyor, Tirunelvely, is his grandson.

—July. 17 - The Jaffna Matrimonial Rights and Inheritance Ordinance, superceding the Thesawalamai, comes into operation. See Note. 18.

—Aug. 11 - A lecture at the District Court, Jaffna, on Anti-Tuberculosis, by Sir Allen Perry, P. C. M. O.

—Aug. 21 - Mr. P. E. Pieris, M. A L. L. M., (of the Ceylon Civil Service) delivers a lecture in the Hindu College Hall, on "Jaffna in Portuguese Times."

—Sept. 2 - Death at Jaffna of Victoria, widow of the late Gabriel. S. Puvirajasinghe, a distinguished Proctor, and the eldest daughter of Mr. Henry Martyn, the well-known and talented Government Store-keeper. See Note 104.

—Sept. 16 - Death of Mr. A. N. Tiruchelvam, President Moopu of the Church of our Lady of Refuge. (Adaikalamatha.) See Note 321.

—Sept. 18 - Death at Vannarponne of Mr. Vallipuram, who rose to eminence by his industry and philanthropy. He

1911—was the first to start Tea and Confectionary shops in Jaffna. See Note 322.

—Sept. - Death of Mr. V. Kanagasabai, a well-known native physician of Tirunelvely. See Note 324.

—Oct. 21 - Arrival in Jaffna of His Excellency Sir Hugh Clifford, Acting Governor.

—Nov. - Cigar makers go on strike. This strike creates a serious situation, there being no work in any of the cigar manufactories for several days.

—Nov. 19 - Death at Vaddukoddai of Rao Bahadur L. C. Williamspillai. See Note ·323.

—Dec. 2 - Death at the age of forty-five of Sriman Panditori Thevar, a great Scholar, Author, Patron and Leader of movements for the advancement of Tamil Literature.

—Dec. 11 - Inauguration of the newly built Hindu English School at Urumpirai.

—Dec. 13 - The polling or voting for the Ceylonese Electorate

—Dec. 16 - The biennial election to the Jaffna Local Board. Messrs S. Katiresu, A. Cathiravelu and S. Thambiahpillai elected members.

—Dec. 18- The Hon. P. Ramanathan, K. C. C. M. G., elected Ceylonese Member of the Legislative Council.

—Dec. 25 - Death at Udupiddy of Mr. M. Coomarasuriar, an influential, much respected and extensive land-owner. See Note 325.

1912—Jan. 3 - Death at Colombo from cellulitis of Dr. V. Saravanamuttu, M. D. See Note 326.

—Feb. 6 - Death at Jaffna of Mr. M. B. Swampillai, a well-known merchant and planter. He was a most amiable gentleman of high principles, loved and respected by all. See Note 327.

—Feb. - Dr. S. C. Paul appointed a member of the Ceylon Medical College. See Note 250.

—Feb. - Announcement received of the success of Mr. W. G. S. Mather, son of Mr. W. Mather, the well-known Managing Director of the Jaffna Commercial Corporation, in the M. R. C. S. and L. R. C. P. examination in midwifery six months before the prescribed time. See Note 407:

—Feb. - Mr. Allen Abraham, Professor, Jaffna College, elected a fellow of the Royal Astronomical Society. See Note 328.

—Feb. 8 - Death of Revd. Fr. X. N. Sandrasegara, O. M. I. See Note 179.

1912--Mar. 9 - Death at Vannarponne at the age of 59 of Srimuth V. Sabapathy Iyer, a well-known scholar and astrologer.

—Mar. 31 - Death of the Revd. S. W. Howland of the American Mission. See Note 238.

—March. - Mr. G. C. Patrick appointed headmaster of St. Patrick's College, the leading Catholic Educational Institution of the North. See Note 391.

—April. 3 - A reception accorded at the Victoria Masonic Hall, Colombo, to Mr. J. N. Tisseverasinghe on his being appointed Additional Tamil Member of the Legislative Council.

—April. 10 - The Titanic, the largest liner (50,000 tons) sinks down in the Atlantic, on her maiden voyage to America. See Note 329.

—April. 16 - "The Rockwood Hall" opened by His Excellency the Governor.

—April. 22 - Mr. V. Casipillai, Crown Proctor, appointed to act as District Judge of Jaffna. See Note 166.

—May. - Mr. C. Kandiah, nephew of Mr. A. Cathiravelu, Proctor, S. C. and Member Local Board, Jaffna, comes off successful in the M. B. & C. M. examination of the Madras University.

—May 8 - A public reception accorded at the Victoria Masonic Hall, Colombo, to Dr. R. Saravanamuttu, M. B. C. M. (Madras) M. R. C. S. (England), L. R. C. P. (London), eldest son of Dr. V. Saravanamuttu, on his return to the Island, after completing his Medical Studies and obtaining British qualifications. See Note 326.

—May. 14 - Death of Master Retnavelu, eldest son of M. S Ramalinga Mudaliyar, Chief Mudaliyar of the Jaffna Kachcheri.

—May. 26 - Seven prisoners forming the first batch of prisoners from Ceylon sent to the Andamans.

—June. 3 - St. Patrick's College wins the Lawyers' Shield for the third time.

—June. 3 - Mr. R. C. Kailasapillai, Tamil Interpreter to H. E the Governor invested with the title of Mudaliyar of the Governor's Gate. See Note 346.

—June. 13 - Death at Tellipalai, at the age of 46 of Mr. T. S. Appadurai, third son of the late Mr. Sinnappah, Maniagar of Valigamam North. He was Head Clerk of the Jaffna Provincial Road Committee and discharged his duties with

1912—conspicuous ability and spotless integrity and introduced several important reforms into the Department.

—June. 20 - Death at Jaffna of Mrs. Mortimer, widow of Mr F. Mortimer, Planter, and eldest daughter of Sir William Twynam. See Note 168.

—June. 22 - Death at Batticotta, at the age of 82. of Mr. J. P. Cooke, a prominent figure among the Tamil Christian Community of Jaffna. See Note 330.

-June. 30 Consecration at St. Antony's Cathedral, Kandy, of the Rt. Revd. Bede Beckmeyer O. S. B. He is the first Ceylonese to be elevated to the position of a Bishop.

—July. 5 - Death at Anuradhapura of Mudaliyar M. Philips, Head Clerk, Anuradhapura Kachcheri. He was not only a capable officer, but one deserving of great regard as a public spirited citizen.

—July. 13 - Barowsky's Circus opens performance at the Jaffna Esplanade.

—July. 14 - Return to Jaffna of Mr. A. N. Santiago, Bar-at-law. See Note 366.

—Aug. - Arumugam, the arithmetical prodigy. comes to Jaffna and electrifies the town by the rapidity of his calculations and his wonderful memory.

—Sept. 6 - Death at Jaffna of Mr. Thomas Peter Ollegasegram Chief Clerk, Sub-Collector and Ware house keeper, Jaffna Customs.

—Oct. 6 - Mr. S. K. Nair of Travancore, member of the Indian National Congress, who is on a visit to Jaffna, delivers a lecture at the Court House on "Our Economic Problem." He also gives addresses at St. Patrick's and Central Colleges and other places.

—Oct. 19 - Death at Manipay from heart-failure of Mr. W. Sangarapillai, the veteran broker of Volkart Brothers, Colombo.

—Nov. - Mr. M. S. Pinto (Shresta), District Judge of Jaffna, contributes a long and interesting account of the arts and crafts of Jaffna, to Mr. Freeman's Report for 1911-1912, in which he deplores the causes that led to their decay.

—Dec. 3 - The Ceylon Bioscope Company arrives in Jaffna and gives exhibitions.

—Dec. 17 - Heavy rain commences and continues the following four days.

1912—Dec. 6 - Death at Point Pedro at the age of 36 of Mr. G. N. H. Tampoe, Proctor, S. C., son of Mr. T. M. Tampoe, J. P., retired Police Magistrate of Jaffna.

—Dec. 18 - Death at Jaffna of R. Murugasu, alias Paul, father of P. Nicholas Mudaliyar, then Head Clerk of the Jaffna Kachcheri.

1913—Jan. 17 - Arrival in Jaffna of His Grace Archbishop Dontenwill, O. M. I., Superior General. A grand reception accorded to him by the Catholics of Jaffna.

—Jan. 20 - Ramanathan's College for the Hindu Girls of Jaffna opened. See Note 331.

—Jan. 31 - Laying of the foundation stone of the Mount Carmal Hall, Karaiyoor, by his Grace Archbishop Dontenwill, O. M. I.

—Feb. 12 - Death at Jaffna of Dr. C. Dutton, who was long connected with the Jaffna Friend-in-need Society. See Note 332.

—Feb. 21 - The Jaffna Hostel opened.

—Feb. 24 - Departure from Jaffna of His Grace Archbishop Dontenwill, O. M. I.

—Feb. 24 - Death at Jaffna of Mr. B. Manuelpillai Satturukalsinghe, a well-known Proctor of the District Court of Jaffna. See Note 333.

—March. 3 - Death at Jaffna from dropsy of Mr. Simon C. Ollegasegaram, retired Head Clerk of the Provincial Road Committee, Jaffna.

—March. 26 - The toddy rents of Jaffna sold. 113 taverns realised Rs. 385,200.

—March. 31 - Death of A. Mudaliyar Sinnatamber, an extensive land owner of Alaveddy and father-in-law of W. Mudaliyar Muttuvelupillai of Kanderodai. See Note 334.

—April. - A syndicate started in Colombo with the object of establishing a factory in Jaffna for the extraction of palm sugar from sweet toddy.

—May. - Announcement received of the success of Dr. George S. Mather in the final examination for L. R. C. P. (London) and M. R. C. S. (England). See Note 407.

—May. - Two Co-operative Credit Societies, one at Copay, and the other at Tellippalai, formed.

1913—May. 24 - The Empire Day celebrated in the Schools. Its object is to encourage feelings of interest and devotion to the British Empire and Sovereign.

—July. 8 - A batch of 100 prisoners arrive in Jaffna in connection with the dredging and filling up of the Karaiyoor Reclamation grounds. See Note 340.

—Aug. 8 - Major J. S. F. James, the Yellow Fever Expert, arrives in Jaffna, with Mr. James Perera, Sanitary Inspector of the Colombo Municipality and some coolies, to investigate into the sanitary condition of Jaffna.

—Aug. 11 - The Hon. Mr. Charles Stewart Vaughan appointed Government Agent of the Northern Province, See Note 338.

—Aug. 22 - A meeting convened at the Jaffna Ridgeway Memorial Hall to consider steps to raise a memorial to Mr. H. R. Freeman, late Government Agent of Jaffna. It was agreed to establish a Maternity Ward. See Note 395.

—Aug. 27 - Reception accorded at the Ridgeway Hall to Mr. Isaac Tambiah on his return from England after qualifying himself as a Bar-at-Law. See Note 349.

—Sept. - From the annual report on the Inuvil Hospital for the year 1912 the following statistics are gathered:—Hospital in-patients 1878; Dispensary patients 3690; Dispensary treatments 7567; Operations (major and minor) 271; Maternity Cases 3141; visits to villages 297; No. of villages from which patients came 115; number of office consultations 83. Income—Sale of medicine etc. Rs. 7667-80; Fees from patients Rs. 5240; Rent of rooms Rs. 1342; Miscellaneous Rs. 1648-35; Total Rs. 15,898-15. See Note 418.

—Sept. - Mr. V. Francis Tampu, Editor of the Tamil Guardian newspaper, receives through the most Revd. Dr. A. Dontenwill, Superior General, O. M. I., a fine photo of His Holiness with an autograph blessing for himself and family.

—Oct. 1 - H. E. Sir R. E. Stubbs Acting Governor and Mrs. Stubbs arrive in Jaffna and are accorded a hearty welcome..

—October. - Death of S. T. Carthigasan, D. E., P. W. D., See Note 370.

—Nov, 12 - Death at Colombo of J. W. P. Senathirajah, J. P., U. P. M., Crown Proctor Puttalam.

—Nov. 12 - Death at Manipay of Dr. K. Mudaliyar Curtis Sup-

1913—piah, Assistant Physician of the Manipay Green Memorial Hospital.

—Nov. 29 - Death at Tellipalai of Mrs. Ambalavanar, mother of the Hon. Mr. A. Kanagasabai, M. L. C. (now Hon. Sir A. Kanagasabai.)

—Dec. - Death at Singapore of Mr. C. M. Chelliah.

—Dec. 13 - The biennial election of the unofficial Members of the Local Board, Jaffna. Messrs Cathiravelu, Kandiah and Katiresu elected.

1914—Jan. 5 - At a meeting held in the Ridgeway Hall and presided over by the Hon. Mr. A. Kanagasabai, it was decided that the Memorial to Mr. Freeman, late Government Agent of Jaffna, should take the form of a ward for the poor to be attached to the McLeod Hospital at Inuvil. See Note 395.

—Jan. - Fever, dysentery and other ailments prevail throughout the Peninsula.

—Feb. 3 - Death at Jaffna of Mr. James Nicholas Saverimuttu, correspondence clerk of the Jaffna Kachcheri. See Note 335.

—Feb. 3 - Death at Jaffna of Mr. A. Saverimuttu, Editor, "Jaffna Catholic Guardian." See Note 336.

—A few cases of plague reported to have taken place in Kandy and Colombo. There are three types, Bubonic, Pneumonic and Septicaemic. The latter is as dangerous as the Bubonic and proves fatal within 48 hours.

—Feb. 7 - Death at Jaffna of Mr. N. Saverimuttu, retired Subcollector, at the age of 65.

—Feb. 10 - Mr. Charles Russel Cumberland appointed Government Agent of Jaffna. See Note 441.

—Feb. 12 - Death at Old Park, Jaffna, of Master Boreland, son of Mr. C. S. Vaughan, G. A., N. P.

—Feb. 13 - The honour of Knight-hood conferred on Mr. Ponnampalam Arunachachlam, late Registrar General of Ceylon. The investiture took place at Buckingham Palace by His Majesty the King. See Note 277.

—Feb. 20 - Mr. C. R Cumberland arrives and assumes duties as Government Agent of Jaffna in succession to Mr. C. S. Vaughan. See Note 441.

—March. - An aerated water manufactory opened in the Pettah, Jaffna, by Mr. Joseph Machado, merchant. See Note 130.

1914—March. - Mr. A. Weigel and another gentleman arrive in Jaffna and visit Pt. Pedro as representatives of Mr. Walter de Soyza in connection with the opening of a Sugar manufactory in the north.

—April. 22 - Death at Manipay of Mr. Hallock Ponnusamy, retired Sub-collector of Customs. He was the son of Saravanamuttu Murugasu Mudaliyar of Manipay (head clerk of the Jaffna Customs) and father-in-law of S. Rasanayaga Mudaliyar, Secretary of the District Court of Jaffna. See Note 414.

—May. 13 - Mr. Ford Duraisamy appointed to act as District Judge of Jaffna. See Note 256.

—June. 17 - Mr. Bickmore arrives and assumes duties as Police Magistrate of Jaffna.

—June. - Mr. V. Chelliah, extra clerk of the Jaffna Kachcheri, who was acting as Maniagar of Karachi, appointed Maniagar of that Division on six months' probation. He is the son-in-law of Mr. V. Thambippillai, J. P., retired Deputy Fiscal, and nephew of Mr. M. S. Ramalingam, Chief Mudaliyar of the Jaffna Kachcheri.

—June. 28 - Assasination of the Archduke Francis Ferdinand, heir to the throne of Austria, when at Serajevo, with his wife. See Note 344.

—July. 4 - Death at Jaffna of Mr. F. X. Nicholas, proprietory planter. See Note 337.

—Aug. 1 - Establishment of a day service between Mannar and Madawatchy in connection with the Mannar Railway.

—Aug. 4 - Great Britain enters into the great European War. See Note 344.

—Aug. 17 - An enthusiastic reception accorded to Sir P. Arunachalam, on his arrival in Jaffna after being knighted.

—Aug. 20 - Death of His Holiness Pope Pius. X. He was 79 years old and was Pope 11 years.

—Sept. 5 - Cardinal Giacomo Della Chiesa, Archbishop of Bologna, elected Pope, under the title of Benedict XV.

—Sept. 19 - A public meeting held at the Jaffna District Court to make arrangements to collect subscriptions for the "Prince of Wales" fund to aid the widows and dependents of those engaged in the front.

—Sept. - The German Raider "Emden" commences to terrorise the waters of Ceylon. See Note 345.

1914—Sept. 25 - A variety entertainment held at the Jaffna Wesleyan Central College in aid of the Prince of Wales relief fund.

—Oct. 8 - Death at Colombo of the Hon. Mr. J. N Tisaveerasinghe, Tamil Representative of the Legislative Council of Ceylon and leader of the Batticaloa Bar.

—Oct. 18 - Death at Colombo of John O'Kane Murty, a senior member of the Ceylon Civil service and a Catholic. Mr. P. J. Rajah, who served under Mr. Murty at Mullaitivu, had a solemn Mass of Requiem celebrated at the Jaffna Cathedral for the repose of the soul of the deceased gentleman.

—Nov. - Mr. P. Rajagopal of the Fiscal's office, Jaffna, appointed to act as Maniagar of Poonaryn. He is the son of the late Ponniah, Maniagar of that division. See Note 245.

—Nov. 15 - Death of Lord Roberts.

—Dec. 11 - Death at Colombuturai of Mr. C. Arumugam, Maniagar of Jaffna.

—Dec. - Rise in the price of Food Stuffs. The paddy problem engages the attention of the public at large.

—Dec. 16 - Mr. K. Balasingham appointed first Tamil Member of the Legislative Council in the place of the late Hon. J. N. Tisseveerasinghe. Mr. Balasingham is a gentleman of great public spirit, disinterestedness and practical common sense. See Note 280.

1915—Jan. 1 - Mr. Benjamin Horsburgh appointed Government Agent of the Northern Province. Mr. C. S. Vaughan transferred to Kandy. See Note 338.

—Jan. - Mudaliyar Joseph N. Chandrasegara, Maniagar of Delft, appointed Maniagar of Valigamam West. See Note 368.

—Jan. - Fever in an epidemic form prevails throughout the Jaffna District and deaths are numerous.

—Jan. 22 - Death at Jaffna of the Revd. Fr. A. M. Roux, O. M. I.

—Feb. 2 - Blessing of the New Hall and Chapel at Karayoor built for the Confraternity of Mount Carmel for young men.

—Feb. 10 - The night train service resumed.

—Feb. - Mr. V. M. Muttukumaru, Secretary, Local Board, appointed Maniagar of Jaffna. See note 313.

—Feb. 11 - Death at Chilaw of the Revd. Arul. Veerasingham Teacher, Catechist, and Pastor. C. M. S.

1915—Feb. 14 - Death in his 75th year of the Revd. Father Alphonsus Delpech, O. M. I.

—Feb. 16 - Return to Jaffna of Mr. J. Homer Vanniasinkam from England, after qualifying himself as a Barrister-at-law. See Note 311.

—Feb. - Mr. K. Chinnatamby appointed Maniagar of Vadamaradchy West. See Note 339.

—March. 1 - His Excellency Sir Robert Chalmers visits Jaffna.

—March. 13 - An "at Home" held at the Ridgeway Hall by the Members of the Jaffna Bar to commemorate Mr. Proctor Changarapillai's fifty years' service in the legal profession. See Note 341.

—April. 2 - Death at Jaffna of Mr. F. J. Ponniah, Medical officer at Delft. He was a very popular and trusted officer of the Department.

—April 22 - Dr. Lyne, Director of Agriculture, Mr. Hew Kennedy, Chairman, C. P. A., and Mr. Jas. Ryan, Planter, arrive in Jaffna and visit the Tobacco Experimental Gardens at Tinnevely conducted by Mr. Scherffius.

—May. 7 - Death at Mannar of Mr. V. Vraspillai, retired adigar of Musali, who commanded extensive influence and acquired great wealth. Mr. V. Joseph, who is practising as an advocate in Jaffna, is his eldest son.

—May. 28 - Serious rioting and looting commence at Kandy and rapidly extend to Colombo and the surrounding villages.

—June. - The export duty on chanks raised from Rs. 2 to Rs. 10 per thousand.

—June. 8 - Death at Jaffna at the age of 78 of Mr. John J. Tisseveerasinghe, Licensed Surveyor.

—June. - Fourteen sheds each 100 ft. by 18 ft. with kitchens and lavatories, erected at the Karayoor Reclamation Grounds to accommodate 600 riot prisoners sent from Colombo in connection with the Reclamation works, Jaffna. See Note 340.

—Aug. 2 - A lecture on the Biology of the Catholic Church, delivered at the Jaffna Catholic Club by the Revd. Father Le Goc of St. Joseph's College, a great scientist.

—Aug. - Capsizing of a boat off Mandaitivu. Some sixty persons lost.

—Oct. 5 - A lecture on Tobacco read before the Jaffna Tobacco Committee by Mr. A. Sabapathy, Editor, Hindu Organ. See Note 177.

1915—Oct. 18 - Death at Jaffna at the age of 63 of Mr. Samuel Fredrick Toussaint, Planter.,

—Nov. - The title of Mudaliyar of the Governor's Gate conferred on Mr. C. M. Sinniah, Shroff of the Jaffna Kachcheri. See Note 313.

—Nov. 26 - A branch of the Queen Mary's Needlework Guild started at Jaffna.

—Nov. 19 - Death at the Jaffna Civil Hospital of Edmund Hewavitarne, head of the firm of Messrs Don Carolis and sons. He came to Jaffna as a riot prisoner.

—Nov. 20 - Celebration, at the Church of our Lady of Refuge, of the Sacerdotal Silver Jubilee of the Revd. Fr. Baron O. M. I.

—Dec. 3 - His Excellency Sir R. Chalmers leaves for England,

1916—Jan- 7 - A Total Abstinence League started among the members of St. Antony's Confraternity, Chundicully. This is the fifth Total Abstinence League, the four others being the Sacred Heart Confraternity, St. James', St. Joseph's Confraternity, Mount Carmel Confraternity, Karaiyoor, and St. Nicholas, Navanturai.

—Jan. 11 - Death in Colombo of W. Toussaint, at one time a leading Merchant and Planter of Jaffna.

—Feb. 11 - Death at Jaffna, at the age of 90, of Mr. C. Lawrencepillai.

—Feb. 14 - Death of Arumugam, the mathematical prodigy.

—March. - The building of the Factory in connection with the Sugar Refinery Works commenced at Valvettiturai.

—March. 14 - The cricket competition match commenced to be played at the Esplanade for Mr. R. Duraiswamy's cup. Four teams entered—Central, Jaffna College, St. John's and Hindu College. The Central won.

—March. 24 - A meeting held in the Hall of the Jaffna Wesleyan Central College to bid farewell to Mr. W. M. P. Wilkes, on his leaving for England. He was Principal of the College for 13 years. Mrs. Wilkes was presented with a pair of gold bangles of exquisite workmanship.

—April. - Announcement received of the appointment of Dr N. R. Nalliah, M. R. C. S., L. R. C. P. and S. (London) as Resident Surgeon, Western General Dispensary, London. See Note 298.

1916—April. 15 - Arrival in Colombo of the New Governor, Sir John Anderson, K. C. B., G. C. M. G. See Note 364.

—April. 17 - Three water spouts seen between Mandativu and Palaitivu.

—April. - Mr. C. Sittampalam, eldest son of Mr. A. Cathiravelu, Crown Proctor, comes off first in the Colonies in Mathematics in the Cambridge Examination. See Note 410.

—April. - Five tons of paper consigned to the Jaffna "Catholic Guardian" Press and forming part of the cargo of the B. I. S. S. "Chantala" goes to the deep in the Mediterranean.

—May. - The Kovilam Light-House completed. It is the highest in the Peninsula, being 115 feet.

—May. 12 - Death at Jaffna of the Revd. Joseph Beebee, Wesleyan Minister.

—May. 13 - Death at Point Pedro of Venayaga Mudaliyar, retired Post and Telegraph Master.

—May. 14 - Death at Achuvely of B. Soosaipillai, Udaiyar.

—May. 16 - The Wesak Festival celebrated for the first time in Jaffna by the Singhalese residents here. An image of Buddha was taken in a torch-light-procession with native music.

—May. 19 - Death at Vannarponne of Mr. C. Parinpanayagam, Wesleyan Minister.

—May. - Certain Hindus of Vannarponne, under a superstitious belief, that they could obtain a treasure-trove by offering human sacrifice, lead a fine able-bodied young man of 20 to the temple of the goddess Muttumareeamman, drug and stupify him and have his throat cut. Nine men including the officiating Brahmin of the temple are alleged to be the perpetrators of this horrible crime.

—May. 22 - Mr. E. B. Denham assumes duties as Director of Education.

—June. 2 - H. E. Sir John Anderson, with his daughter-in-law Mrs. Anderson, Mr. W. T. Stace, P. S., and Captain Livingston Learmouth A. D. C., arrives in Jaffna. The next day His Excellency visits the various Government Departments and the Tobacco Experimental Gardens, and leaves by train on the fourth.

—June. - Mr. A. Cathiravelu, Crown Proctor, appointed Justice of the Peace and unofficial Police Magistrate for the District of Jaffna. See Note 177.

1916—June. 7 - Death at Jaffna, at the age of 84, of Mr. T. C. Changarapillai, the oldest member of the Legal profession in Jaffna. See Note 341.

—June. - The newly built Saraswathy School at Copay opened.

—June. 15 - Mr. Samuel F. Johnpulle appointed Chief Clerk, Loan Board, Colombo. See Note 401.

—July. 18 - Severe gale at Jaffna interrupting telegraphic communication and breaking telephone wires. Trees uprooted., plantations damaged, tiles of houses blown off and several lives lost.

—Aug. 8 - The manufature of Sugar at the Ceylon Sugar Refinery Ltd. at Polikandy, commenced. The first flow of juice being started by Miss Cox, daughter of Mr. G. Lionel Cox, the Company's Chairman.

—Aug. 28 - A Co-operative Credit Society, called the Valigamam West Headmen's Co-operative Credit Society, started. Mudaliyar Jos. N. Sandrasegra elected President.

—August - News received of the success of T. C. Jayaretnam, Government Scholar, in the mathematical Tripos at Cambridge and the London B. Sc. Examination. See Note 400

—Sept. 9 - The inauguration of Our Lady of Refuge Catholic Youngmen's Association.

—Sept. - Mr. Vincent Mendis, Scout master of Richmond College, Galle, and four of his Scouts, come to Jaffna to start Scout troops in the local colleges.

—Sept. 20 - Revd. Mr. Bullough arrives in Jaffna as Principal of the Wesleyan Central College.

—Sept. - Death of the Revd. D. P. Niles, a distinguished teacher and preacher of the Jaffna Wesleyan mission. He was a good Tamil Scholar.

—Oct. 4 - Death at Copay of Mrs. Mailvaganam, widow of Mr Mailvaganam of Copay, J. P., U. P. M.

—Oct. 7 - Death at Nallur of Mr. V. Thambipillai, J. P., retired Deputy Fiscal of Jaffna.

—Oct. 10 - The first Centenary of the establishment in Jaffna of the North Ceylon American Mission, celebrated at Batticotta, the head quarters of the Mission. See Note 360.

1916—Oct. 12 - The first consignment of sugar manufactured by the Ceylon Sugar Refinery Company, sold at Colombo by public auction. 1510 bags sold at Rs. 18 a bag.

—Oct. 15 - Death at Puttur of Mr. Kanagasabai, Maniagar of Valigamam East.

—Oct. - The foot-ball competition match, played at the Jaffna Esplanade for Mr. V. M. Muttukumaru's cup, results in a victory for St. John's College, Chundicully.

—Dec. - Mr. Ratna Mailvaganam, Advocate, appointed Maniagar of Valigamam East. See Note 342.

—Dec. 12 - Death at Negombo of the Revd. Fr. Y. Lecan, O. M. I.

1917—Jan. 6 - Death at Jaffna of Mr. Joseph Abraham Tisseveerasinghe, retired Sub-Collector, at the age of 73. He was a gentleman of high principles and of great intergrity as a public officer. See Note 343.

—Jan. 9 - Mr. Arunachalam Sabapathy, Editor, "Hindu Organ", nominated Second Tamil Member of the Legislative Council. See Note 177.

—Jan. - The base of a Dagoba discovered at Chunnagam, on the south of the Railway Station, as the result of an excavation, carried out at the instance of Mr. Paul Pieris, District Judge of Jaffna.

—Feb. 1 - Mr. A. Cathiravelu, Proctor, appointed Additional Police Magistrate of Jaffna. See Note 177.

—Feb. Death at Uduville of Mary R. Page of the American Mission.

—Feb. 1 - The Hon. Mr. A. Kanagasabai appointed Justice of the Peace for the Island. See Note 427.

—Feb. 17 - Death at Colombo of R. C. Kailasapillai, Mudaliyar of the Governor's Gate, Chief Tamil Translator to Government. See Note 346.

—Feb. 19 - A lecture delivered at the Jaffna Ridgeway Hall on "Old Scot's Legal Life and Humour" by Sir A. Wood Renton. At the close of the lecture a silver collection was made in aid of Servia.

—April. 5 - A paper on "Nagadipa and Buddhist Remains in Jaffna" read by Mr. Paul Pieris, D. J., Jaffna, before the Ceylon Branch of the Royal Asiatic Society.

—April - The two Rupee currency notes received and put in circulation. The amount is five Lakhs.

1917—April. - Mr. A. Cathiravelu, J. P., U. P. M., who has been acting as Crown Proctor, confirmed in the appointment. See Note 177.

—April. - Arrival in Jaffna of Fillis' Circus.

—April. 30 - Death at Bopitiya, Pamunugama, of Mr. D. Don. Paul. He was renter at Jaffna for some years.

—May. - News received that the Cambridge University has conferred the Degree of Doctor of Letters on Mr. P. E. Pieris, the learned District Judge of Jaffna. He is the first Ceylonese to be admitted to this honour.

—June. 4 - Portrait of Hudson Paramaswami unveiled at Ottly Hall, Jaffna College. See Note 428.

—June. 6 - The title of J. P. for the Island conferred on Mr. Cathiravelu Namasivayam; of Mudaliyar of the Governor's Gate on Ambalavanar Naganathar Mudaliyar; of Mudaliyars on Soosaipillai Mudaliyar Philip Vanderkoon, Mangaperumal Sinnatamby Ramalingam and George W. Rasiah Vallipuram; of J. P. for the Western Province on John Douglas Philip and Vanniyanar on Sayampunathar Asaipillai. See Note 347.

—June. 10 - Death at Araly of A. Arunasalam, Head Overseer.

—June. 11 - Mr. Swampillai Benedict of the Salt-Store, Puttalam, assumes duties as Government General Store-keeper, Jaffna.

—June. 23 - At a meeting of Principals, Inspectors, and Headmasters of Secondary Schools, held in the Hall of the Jaffna Central College, under the Presidency of Mr. E. B. Denham, it was arranged to have a series of lectures for teachers.

—July. 5 - A meeting at the District Court of Jaffna to discuss measures for supporting the Premium War Loan, held under the Presidency of Mr. B. Horsburgh. G. A. N. P.

—July. 6 - Mr. Selvarajah Windham, late of the Middlesex Regiment, delivers a fascinating address in St. John's, Chundicully, on his experiences at the front.

—July. 6 - The letters patent conferring Knight-hood on the Hon. Mr. Ambalavanar Kanagasabai, handed over to him by Mr. B. Horsburgh, G. A., N. P., at the Jaffna Ridgeway Memorial Hall, in the presence of a large and representative gathering. See Note 427.

—July. 9 - Public reception at the Hindu College to the Hon.

Mr. A. Sabapathy in honour of his being nominated Second Tamil Member of the Legislative Council. See Note 177.

917—July. - Smuggling of about 300 bags of rice into Delft. An inquiry was held and some of the Head-men found guilty.

—July. 21 - A large and representative meeting of the educated Tamils held at the Siva Piragasa Vidiyasalai at Vannarponnai and presided over by Sir P. Arunachalam for the purpose of forming a Chen Tamil Paripalana Sabhai with a view to the revival of the study of the Tamil Language and Literature.

—Aug. 3 - Death at Colombo at the age of 29 of Mr. A. Paramanathan who is believed to be the first Jaffna Tamil to enlist in the Army. See Note 352.

—Aug. - P. Nicholas Mudaliyar, Head clerk of the Jaffna Kachcheri, appointed Extra Office Assistant to the Government Agent, Jaffna. See Note 434.

—Aug. - A woman residing near about the Jaffna Civil Hospital gives birth at one time to four children, two males and two females—all still born.

—Aug. 20 - One Rupee currency notes issued.

—Aug. 23 - A lecture delivered at the Jaffna Central College Hall by the Revd. Fr. Le Goc on the "Power of Organization."

—Aug. 31 - The Sugar Refineries Company dispenses with the services of Mr. Weigel and appoints Mr. Mac Glashan as Works Manager.

—Sep. 1 - Sir William Twynam presents the whole of his valuable collection of the products and industries of Jaffna to St. John's College, Chundicully. See Note 363.

—Sept. 13 - Mr. Mac Glashan assumes duties as the General Manager of the Ceylon Sugar Refineries Ltd.

—Sept. - Death at Slave Island, Colombo, of Dr. L. A. Valladares, L. M. & S. (Bombay). He was practising at Jaffna for some years and was very popular here.

—Sept. 29 - Death at Jaffna at the age of 80 of the Revd. Fr. Jacques Batayron, O. M. I. He was a good classical scholar.

—Oct. 13 - The Local Board area of Jaffna divided into three wards:— 1st Central Ward, consisting of Pettah, Karaiyoor, Chundicully and Passayoor; 2nd Western Ward, consisting of Vannarponne S. W. Moor Street, Navanthurai,

Vannarponne N. W., and Vannarponne N. E, and 3rd Eastern ward, consisting of Nallur, Tinnevely West Chiviateru W. & E. and Colombuturai West and East.

1917--Nov. 3 - Death at Vannarponne of Mr. A. Mootootambypillai, a good Tamil scholar and author of some popular Vernacular School Books. See Note 353.

—Nov. 12 - The first large size tyre turned out by the Garage and Taxicab Company's mills.

—Nov. 30 - Lance Corporal R. Aiyadurai, a Jaffna young man, killed in action in the great European War. See Note 430

—Dec. 1 - Mr. P. Vytilingam, Advocate, succeeds Mr. P. C. Coomaraswamy as Police Magistrate of Pt. Pedro and Chavakachcheri.

—Dec. 1 - Death at Velanai of V. Muttiahpillai, Maniagar of the Islands Division of Jaffna.

—Dec. 2 - Death at Punnalai Kadduvan of K. Sithamparapillai, Land-owner.

—Dec. - Mr. C. Sundralingam, a Jaffna young man and Science Scholar from St. Joseph's College, Colombo, wins the Lubbock Memorial Prize of the University of London.

—Dec. - A Memo on the Karachi Irrigation Scheme submitted to the Land Development Committee by Mr. Advocate Talaivasingham.

—Dec. 31 - The biennial election for the Jaffna Local Board. Mr. R. R. Nalliah for ward No, 1, Mr. C. Kanagasabai for ward No. 2, and Mr. C. Arulampalam for ward No. 3. See Note 354.

—Dec. 27 - A Lecture on the "Cult of the coming man" delivered at the Ridgeway Memorial Hall by Swamy Sharvananda.

1918—Jan. 4 - The Government Gazette notifies that December 28, 29, 30, 31, have been approved as public holidays in substitution for Ash-Wednesday, Ascension day, the Accesion day of his Majesty the King and the Prince of Wale's Birthday.

—Jan. 9 - Death at Keerimalai of Mr. S. Cathiravelpillai, for many years shroff of the Colombo Branch of the now defunct Oriental Bank Corporation. See Note 355.

—Jan. 11 - Death at Mathagal of Sabina Sandrasagara, mother of Mudaliyar Jos. N. Sandrasagra, Maniagar, Valigamam West.

1918—Jan. 15 - Reception accorded at the Ridgeway Memorial Hall to Mudaliyar A. Naganather, J. P. U. P. M. in honour of his being invested with the rank of Mudaliyar of the Governor's Gate. See Note 347.

—Jan. 22 - The Jaffna Police Sports come off at the Police Grounds, the full Band of the Ceylon Police being in attendance.

—Jan. 23 - Death at Jaffna of Charles Alfred Johnpulle, retired Station Master, C. G. R.

—Jan. 27 - Death at Jaffna of Mr. Bastiampillai Saverimuttu, Merchant, who traded chiefly on Beche-de-mer.

—Jan. 29 - A farewell demonstration at Kankesanturai to Dr. J. R. Jeremiah on the eve of his departure to Mullaitivu.

—Feb. 6 - Mr. P. J. Rajah, Salt-Storekeeper, Tondamannar, appointed Maniagar of Delft. See Note 356.

—Feb. 6 - Mr. Somasundaram, son of Maniagar Muttiahpillai, appointed Maniagar of the islands. See Note 357.

—Feb. 6 - Mr. S. M. Rasiah of the Jaffna Government Salt Store, appointed Salt-Storekeeper, Tondamannar. See Note 358.

—Feb. - Mr. C. Arulampalam, Advocate, appointed a member of the Excise Advisory Committee for the Jaffna Local Board area vice Mr. A. Cathiravelu resigned.

—Feb. 15 - The Government Gazette notifies that the Police Tax for the town of Jaffna has been fixed at five per cent on the annual value of houses, buildings, lands, etc.

—March. 1 - Mr. William Wadsworth assumes duties as Additional District Judge of Colombo. See Note 359.

—March. 1 - Dr. G. S. Mather appointed Registrar of Births and Deaths of Locality No. 2 of Jaffna Town vice Dr. M. Chellappa retired. See Note 407.

—March. - A commission appointed to report on the methods of improving the breeds of cattle and other live stock in the Island.

—March. - The money lending bill which was brought into council at the instance of the Hon. Mr. Balasingam, passed.

—March. 7 - Death at Jaffna of Mary Annamuttu, relict of Mr. S. Pedropillai. See Note 362.

—March 22 - The 91st Birthday of Sir William Twynam. On this day was laid by Miss Twynam, in the grounds of St. John's College, Chundicully, the foundation stone of the

1918—Museum for housing Sir William's unique collection of Jaffna products and industries, already presented by him to that College. See Note 363.

1918—March. 24 - Death at Queen's Cottage, NewaraEliya, of His Excellency Sir John Anderson. K. C. B. See Note 364.

—March. 25 - Death of Pedropillai, President Moopu of St. Sebastian's Church, Karampan.

—April - The Ceylon Safety Matches Manufacturing Company started.

—April. 10 - Death at Changuvely of Mr. Kasinather Vytilingam, Merchant, Planter and Renter. He was well and widely known and much respected for his philanthropy and munificence. See Note 320.

—April 17 - Mr. F. O. Hopman arrives and assumes duties as District Inspector of Telegraphs of the Northern Province in place of the late Mr. V. Muttucoomaru, who died suddenly at Trincomalie, when on official duty. Mr. Hopman is a son-in-law of Mr. James De Niese, the well-known artist of Jaffna.

—April 18 - Death at Jaffna of Mr. P. S. J. Chrysostom, Proctor, S. C. See Note 365.

—April. 24 - Karaiyoor Reclamation Prison closed,

—May. 2 - Two cases of plague reported from Pt. Pedro. Both removed to hospital and both proved fatal.

—May. 2 - Death at Jaffna from enteric fever of Mr. A. N. Santiago, Barrister-at-law. See Note 366.

—May. 3 - Death at Archbishop's House, Colombo, of the Rev. Fr. Ch. Massiet, O. M. I. He was 67 years old and spent 42 years in Ceylon.

—May. 3 - Death at Hambantotte of Dr. Vathacan, Medical Officer. He was connected with the Jaffna Civil Hospital for some time.

—May. - Unprecedented rise in the price of cloth. Horrocks and chintz rise from 25 cts to 75 cts. per yard.

—May. 7 - A party of twenty men who attended a cremation at Allavetty, and who took shelter under a huge banyan tree as it drizzled then, were struck by lightning. They were taken senseless to the hospital but recovered afterwards. Some had their hair singed and others bore scald marks in different parts of the body.

1918—May - Sadu Sunder Singh, a Christian Evangelist of India, arrives in Jaffna and preaches in different centres. His addresses are characterised by intense earnestness and simplicity of language with apt illustrations.

—May. 18 - The 25th anniversary of the foundation of the Papal Seminary at Kandy. See Note 367.

—May. 21 - The unveiling by His Excellency, the acting Governor, at the P. W. D. Office, Colombo, of the Portrait of the late Armstrong Mudaliyar, District Engineer.

—May. - The old reredos of St. Mary's Church, Kayts, burnt.

—May. 23 - The arrack rents of Jaffna and Mannar bought by Mr. Kathirasapillai for Rs. 232,500 and Rs. 65,555 respectively and that of Mullaitivu by Mr. Vallipuram for Rs. 27,555.

—June 2 - Death at Jaffna of C. Mudaliyar Muttiah. He was a public-spirited and independent gentleman and widely respected.

—June. 3 - Mudaliyar Jos. N. Sandrasagara, Maniagar of Valigamam West, appointed a J. P. for the Jaffna District. See Note 368.

—June. 7 - The shed put up at the Government Salt Store premises by the Jaffna Local Board declared a public slaughter house.

—June. 11 - Death of Sittampala Mudaliyar Malavarayer of Puttoor, well-known as the "Jaffna Millionaire."

—June. 12 - At a general meeting of the Colombuturai—Poonakarai Co-operative Credit Society held at the Colombuturai Sivite School and presided over by Mr. B. Horsburgh, G. A, Mr. V. M. Muttukumaru, Maniagar, and President of the Society, traced its origin and growth and described the benefits conferred by its working on the people of both localities.

—June. 14 - Mr. M. Kanagasabai appointed Additional Asst. Collector of Jaffna. See Note 249.

—June. - The contributions in Colombo to the Red-Triangle War Fund, reach half a lakh of rupees, the share allotted to Ceylon being one lakh.

—June. - Death of the Rev. George Daniel, retired incumbent of St. John's Church, Chundicully. He was a convert and throughout his long life of 85 years maintained his zeal for the cause to which he devoted himself. See Note 369.

1918—June. 30 - Hon. Mr. Sabapathy accorded a grand reception at Trincomalie on his way to Batticaloa.

—July. 6 - Public reception accorded to Mudaliyar Jos. N. Sandrasagara at the Jaffna College grounds in honour of his being invested with the title of Justice of the Peace. Mr. B. Horsburgh, G. A. presided. See Note 368.

—July. - Small-pox, which was prevailing at Mannar for some time past, subsides. 148 cases reported up to the end of June with 17 deaths.

—July. 11 - A meeting held in Colombo, presided over by the Hon. Mr. Balasingham, in which it was resolved to form a Benevolent Association for Ceylon Tamils.

—July. - The Pope grants the Medal, "Bene Merenti", to Mr. Jos. Abraham, Head Master, St. Michael's College, Baticaloa, for 35 years. He was an Old Boy and Teacher of the Jaffna Boy's Seminary.

—July. 12 - The little chapel and presbytery built at Navatkadu burnt.

—July. 15 - Mr. Alfred Hart of the International Bible Students Association, commences a series of lectures, illustrated by Magic Lantern slides at the Central and St. John's Colleges. The lectures are on Bible History.

—July. 17 - The inauguration of the Boarder's Union in connection with Hartley College, Point-Pedro.

—July. 20 - Old Boy's day celebration at the Jaffna College, when a portrait of the late Samuel Hensman was unveiled. See Note 157.

—July - A leopard strays into the peninsula, and causes great panic. It mauled two persons at Uduthurai and five at Chiviatheru. It was shot and the carcass removed to the Jaffna Kachcheri. The animal is a male one, full grown, measuring 6 feet 6 ins. A sensational incident of a similar sort occurred half a century ago.

—July - The Jubilee celebration of the Udupiddy Boarding School.

—Aug. 24 - The Episcopal Silver Jubilee of His Lordship the Right Rev. Dr. Henry Joulain, O. M. I., Bishop of Jaffna, celebrated with great eclat; His Excellency the Delegate Apostolic to the East Indies, His Grace the Archbishop of Colombo and the Bishops of Kandy and Trincomalie being present.

1918—Aug. 29 - Death at Pallai of Muttutamby, Maniagar of Pachilapaly.

—Sept. - An epidemic fever, said to be Bombay fever, breaks out, and spreads out all over the peninsula, causing many deaths.

—Sept. 7 - Shakespeare's Othello and Wilson Barrette's dramatised novel, 'The sign of the cross,' staged at St John's College, in aid of the Anderson Memorial. Mr. E. B. Denham, Director of Education, who witnessed the performance, expressed it, as his opinion that in all South India it would not be possible to come across a dramatic performance of such high order.

—Sept. 11 - Death at Colombuturai of Brother V. Michael, S. S. J. He was a convert from a heathen family of Trincomalie and was at the head of the Industrial Department of St. Joseph's Orphanage.

—Sept. - Rice, hitherto selling at 18 cents, rises to 30 cts a measure. The generality of the people are put to great straits.

—Sept. 14 - Through the munificence of Mr. Karalapillai, Broker, Colombo, cloth to the value of Rs. 10,000 begins to be distributed to the poor of Jaffna in different centres.

—Sept. 24 - Death at Uduvil of Ramanather Swaminather, Udaiyar.

—Sept. - Ceylon mails despatched between 7th and 11th instants reported lost.

—Sept. - Death of V. K. Rajanayagam of the Avissawela Bar, son of Proctor Kathiravelpillai of Jaffna and nephew of the late T. Chellappapillai, retired chief Justice of Travancore.

—Oct. 1 - Mr. C. N. Deva Raja elected an unofficial member of the Local Board area.

—Oct. 2 - M. S. Ramalinga Mudaliyar, Chief Mudaliyar of the Jaffna Kachcheri, holds an "At Home" in his new built house at Vannarponne. A large and distinguished attendance including the Government Agent, Mr. Horsburgh, grace the occasion with their presence.

—Oct. - The Influenzal Pandemic rages all over the island, causing great distress among people of all classes.

1918—Oct. 3 - Death of the Rev. Samuel Abraham.

—Oct. 8 - Death at Jaffna from pneumonia of Mudaliyar B. Francis, Registrar of Lands, Jaffna. He was an able, and talented officer, quite up to the mark. See Note 372.

—Oct. 11 - Death at Colombo from pneumonia of Mr. William Saverimuttu, Shroff of the General Post Office.

—Oct. 17 - Death of the Rev. Fr. S. M. Vas, Parish Priest of Delft.

—Nov. - The high rise in the price of the staple article of food entails great hardship on the poor. A bag of Muttu-samba goes up to Rs. 25.

—Nov. 2 - Death at Chillalai, at the age of 71, of Mr. Soosai-pillai Innasitamby, a reputed native physician of Valigamam West. See Note 373.

—Nov. 10 - Looting in Jaffna; continued the two following days at Chunnakam and Point Pedro. See Note 374.

Nov. 11 - Signing of the armistice at the eleventh hour (11 o'clock.) See Note 375.

—Nov. 17 - A storm of wind and rain, unprecedented in the annals of Jaffna, commences and continues. Houses and compounds flooded and hundreds of people rendered houseless and foodless. Relief Fund started. See Note 376.

—Nov. 23 - Mr. M. J. Pillainayagam, assessor of the Jaffna Local Board, appointed Maniagar of Karachi.

—Dec. 23 - Ordination of the Rev. J. S. Retnathicam of the C. M. S., Jaffna.

—Dec. 25 - A new ten-room building, erected in the McLeod Hospital Grounds, Inuvil, and known as the SommerVille Ward, opened by Miss Susan Howland. See Note 418.

—Dec. 28 - Advocate M. A. Arulanandam, and Dr. Nallamma Murugasan, take part in the All-India Social Conference.

1919—Jan. 11 - The C. M. S. Centenary celebrations at Jaffna commence and continue till the 13th. The Bishop of Dornakal is present and preaches in all the services.

—Jan. 14 - The foundation of the new church of St. Joseph at Anuradhapura laid by Rev. Fr. C. A. Boury O. M. I.

—Jan. 15 - H. E. Sir William Manning accompained by the Hon. Robert Trefusis., P. S. and Mrs. Trefusis, arrives in Jaffna. Addresses are read to him by the Jaffna Local Board and by the inhabitants of the District. H. E. visits

—Government Offices, Public Institutions and places of interest and leaves for Elephant Pass on the evening of the 19th instant.

1919—Jan. 15 - Mr. William Adam Clough of Karadivu presented with the I. S. O. medal for good and efficient service in the F. M. S. See Note 377.

—Jan. 20 - Reception accorded to Mr. T. C. Jayaratnam, I. C. S., Assistant Commissioner, Central Provinces, India, at the Jaffna Wesleyan Central College. See Note 400,

—Jan. - Rev. K. C. McPherson, B. A., Headmaster, Trinity College, Kandy, arrives in Jaffna to act for the Rev. Mr. Thompson, Principal. St. John's College, Chundicully, who leaves for England.

—Jan. 22 - Death at Naranthanai of Mariapillai, widow of Pedropillai, a distinguished physician of the Islands, and mother of Rev. Brother Ignatius, S. S. J.

—Jan. 27 - An "At Home" held at St. Patrick's College, by the staff and old boys of the college, to take leave of the Rev. Fr. Francis who was professor of the college for several years, and who has been appointed to take charge of the Jaffna Catholic Guardian.

—Feb. 3 - Dr. W. P. Morris, M. D. delivers at the Central College an interesting lecture on "Hook-Worm," illustrated by Magic Lantern slides.

—Feb. 4 - The members of the Jaffna Bar hold an "At Home," in the grounds of the Ridgeway Memorial Hall, in honour of Sir Anton Betram, Chief Justice.

—Feb. - Messrs K. Thambaiyá, S. Subramaniam and S. M. Coomarasoorier, appointed members of the Jaffna Dictrict Road Committee.

—Feb. - Mr. W. F. Ratnagopal, Superintendent of Works, Local Board, appointed Superintendent, Minor Roads, Jaffna.

—Feb. - The "Young Hindu"—a magazine intended for the young—converted into a monthly and enlarged in size, under the management of Mr. C. N. Deva Rajan of the staff of Ramanathan College, and the editorship of Mr. C. Arulampalam, Advocate, Jaffna.

Feb. 7 - Death at Jaffna of His Lordship Dr. Henry Joulain, O. M. I. The next morning the body, robed in full pontificals, was exposed in the hall of St. Charles and later removed to the Episcopal Chapel, where it lay in state till the following Monday evening, when it was placed in a superb coffin and taken in a long, solemn and impressive procession to the Cathedral and placed on the catafalque that stood in the centre. The next morning after High Mass at which His Grace, the Archbishop of Colombo officiated, the coffin was laid in the grave prepared in front of the main altar within the sanctuary. The Bishops of Kandy and Trincomalee took part in the service. The leading Europeans and other high officials in Jaffna were also present. See Note 378.

1919—Feb. 14 - Dr. P. E. Peiris, District Judge, Jaffna, pays a visit to the Nayanmarkadu Hospital. See Note 69.

—Feb. 26 - Death of the Rev. Samuel Veerakatty.

—Feb. 26 - The members of the Jaffna Bar meet at the District Court House to bid farewell to Dr. P. E. Peiris, who leaves Jaffna the same evening, having been appointed Additional District Judge of Colombo. Hon'ble A. Kanagasabai assumed work as District Judge the following day.

—Feb. 28 - Mr. A. E. Christofelsz, P. M., Jaffna, transferred to Badulla.

Mar. 1 - New paying wards opened in connection with the Jaffna Civil Hospital. See Note 431.

—Mar. 1 - Dr. A. Visuvalingam opens a dispensary in the town of Jaffna.

—March. - Mr. Denham, Director of Education, proposes to build a Technical School in the Jaffna Peninsula.

—Mar. 9 - Death at the ripe old age of 90 of Mrs. Parker, widow of the late Dr. Parker. See Note 382.

—Mar. - The toddy rents of Jaffna for 1919-1920 realize Rs. 377,535—an increase of Rs. 19,730 over that of the previous year.

—Mar. 20 - The Jaffna Police sports held at the esplanade and continued till the 22nd instant.

—Mar. - The Jaffna Tamil Residents of Battu Gaja make arrangements to offer five scholarships to the Director of Education, Ceylon, tenable in the Jaffna Technical School.

—April. 12 - Mr. W. Sinnatamby, son-in-law of P. Nicholas Mudaliyar, appointed Superintendent of Works, Jaffna Local Board. See Note 434.

—April. 12 - Mr. B. Horsburgh, G. A., leaves Jaffna, being appointed Controller of Revenue, Colombo. Mr. B. Constantine succeeds him in Jaffna.

1919—April. - Announcement received of the death of Capt. R. B. Constantine, son of Mr. B. Constantine, G. A., N. P. The deceased was 24 years of age and was born in Ceylon.

—April. - Rinderpest breaks out in Jaffna.

—April. 14 - Death at Colombo of Mr. M. M. Thurai Rajasingam, son of the late Mudlr. J. T. Muttiah, Chief Interpreter, Supreme Court. See Note 383.

April. 19 - Death at Vannarponne, of Mr. S. Thambiahpillai, Proctor, S. C. See Note 384.

—April. - Mr. Simcock, the expert sent to Jaffna by Messrs Harrison & Crossfield to start the cement industry, completes his investigations and returns to Colombo.

—April. 24 - Death at Karampan from paralysis of Thankam, wife of Mr. S. Soosaipillai, Udaiyar of Kayts, and mother of S. Santiapillai, Local Board, Jaffna.

April. - The Hon. P. Ramanathan secures a plot of land at Tinnevely for the purpose of erecting a new college.

—April. - Mr. A. M, Tampoe Philips, B. A., L. L. B., Cantab, a son of Mr. J. E. Philips, Planter, Pallai, and grandson of Mr. T. M. Tampoe, retired P. M. of Jaffna, establishes himself in practice at Singapore. He is the third Barrister-at-law to settle in the Straits.

—April. 28 - Inquiry into the claims for Riot damages commenced to be made at Jaffna, Mallagam and Chavagachcheri and continued till the 30th instant. See Note 374.

—May. 9 - Food control introduced for the first time in the history of the Island. Mr. B. Horsburgh appointed Food Controller. The average monthly consumption of 30,000 tons of rice cut down to 20,000.

—May. 10 - Death at Sandilipay of Rao Bahadur Murugasampillai, retired officer of the Indian Government. He is the father of Dr. M. M. Coomaraswamy of Colombo. See Note 385.

—May. - A proposal set on foot to establish an experimental station and agricultural school at Jaffna, of which the estimated cost is Rs. 30,000.

—May. - The Food Production Committee ask Government to sell lands adjoining the Karachi Tank with a view to paddy cultivation.

—May. 16 - Death at Tellippalai of E. Arumainayagam, Chief Clerk, Sanitary Board, Jaffna Kachcheri.

1919—May. 25 - Death at Colombo of Mr. S. T. Spencer, Proctor. See Note 386.

—May. - Dr. Gunam, F. Cooke, son of Mr. Thambiah S. Cooke, Proctor, Jaffna, obtains the M. B. S. degree, London. See Note 417.

—May. 30 - Every Government Agent and every Assistant Agent appointed Deputy Food Controller and empowered to issue orders providing for the fixing of maximum prices of articles in their respective provinces and districts.

May. 31 - Death of Dr. John Attigalle, M. D., a former Colonial Surgeon of the Northern Province.

—June. - Death of Mr. V. N. Sivaya, Barrister-at-law. See Note 387.

—June. 2 - Vernacular Teachers' Conference commenced at Jaffna and closed on the 4th instant.

—June. 3 - Native rank conferred on Messrs C. S. Kandiah, V. Muttukumaru, and T. Karalapillai.

—June. 5 - The North Ceylon Tennis meet comes off in the Jaffna Esplanade. Outside players from India take part. Cups are offered by the G. A., N. P., Sir A. Kanagasabai, Mr. Coomaraswamy, D. J. Batticaloa, and Mr. V. Markandu, Planter and Renter.

—June. 20 - Death at Manipay at the age of 25, of Mr. Navaretnam, son of Mr. S. K. Lawton, the well-known photographer.

—June. 26 - The corner stone of the new Church of the American Mission at Changanai laid by Miss S. R. Howland.

—June. 28 - Death at Mannar of the Rev. Fr. T. Hyppolyte, O. M. I. an erudite Tamil scholar.

—June. 30 - Death at Jaffna at the age of 25, of Rosebella Ranimuttamma, wife of Mr. W. D. Niles, the well-known advocate, and the daughter of the late Mr. S. T. Arnold, an able lawyer and sound Tamil scholar.

—July. 1 - Mr. S. S. Santiapillai, of the Jaffna Local Board, son of Mr. S. Soosaipillai, Udaiyar, Karampan, appointed chief clerk, Sanitary Board, Jaffna Kachcheri.

—July. - Mr. Chinthamani appointed Secretary of the Flood Relief Committee.

—July. 19 - The inhabitants of Ceylon of all races and creeds join the teeming millions of the British Empire in celebrating the conclusion of Peace between Great Britain and her Allies on one side and Germany on the other. The result of the terrible war which had been raging for five years has been complete victory for the cause of Justice and Liberty against Ambition and Might.

1919—July. 21 - Death of Mr. James Visuvanather (Donald Velupillai). He was one of the early adventurers to the Straits.

—Aug. 1 - A reception accorded to Mr. William Black n honour of his being appointed Justice of the Peace for the District of Jaffna. See Note 379.

—Aug. - A shipment of five lakhs of rupee silver coins received in Colombo from Madras.

—Aug. 1 - Mr. A. S. Johnpillai of the Postal Department promoted to Class I. See Note 372.

—Aug. 4 - Death of David Thambiah, Surveyor, father of Proctor Thambiah. See Note 250.

—Aug. 5 - Very Rev. Fr. J. A. Brault, O. M. I., elected Bishop of Jaffna. See Note 389.

—Aug. 8 - Dr. Eddy and Prof. W. T. Hutchins, who came on a visit to Jaffna and gave addresses, leave for England.

—Aug. 8 - An unusually beautiful phenomenon seen in the sky when the sun was surrounded by a luminous circle containing all the colours of the rainbow.

—Aug. - A series of lectures on First Aid for the benefit of Vernacular Teachers, for which arrangements were made by the Director of Education, commence.

—Aug. - The Director of Education makes a promise to provide at the expense of Government a school for the training of children in industrial and artistic work in Jaffna. See Note 381.

—Aug. 17 - The Brothers of St. Joseph, and the sisters of the Holy Family established at Mannar, celebrate the silver Jubilee of their arrival in the "Island of Martyrs."

—Aug. 18 - At a meeting of the Freeman Memorial Ward Committee held at the Jaffna Law Library, it was decided to pay the authorities of the Inuvil Hospital a sum of Rs. 1500 to be devoted for a Maternity Ward for poor patients who resort to the Hospital and to be named the Freeman Memorial Ward. See Note 395.

—Aug. 20 - The unveiling by the Major of Colombo of the Memorial erected at the General Cemetery, Borella, to the Ceylonese fallen in the great European War.

1919—Aug. - Mr. H. R. Freeman, formerly Government Agent of Jaffna, retires from the service and leaves for England.

—Aug. - Mr. Geo. DeNiese of Kandy obtains 4 prizes and one Hon. mention for five paintings he sent in to the Ceylon Art Exhibition.

—Sept. 10 - The new two rupee notes put in circulation.

—Sept. - Announcement received of the death of Abraham Pandither, well-known for his "Kurunatha Medicines."

—Sept. 10 - Death at Manipay of Mr. S. K. Lawton, the well-known and popular photographer. See Note 390.

—Sept. 11 - A grand Shakespearean recital in the Hall of St. Patrick's College given by Leo. Wallace Young, the renowned dramatic impressionist.

—Sept. 15 - Reception at the public hall, Colombo, to Mr. C. S. Kandiah, Chief Shroff, Government Railways, in honour of his being invested with the title of Mudaliyar.

—Sept. 18 - The Mahajana Sabha started—a movement to form people's associations throughout the Island for political, social and economic improvements.

—Oct. 11 - Death at Kokuvil of M. Thampapillai, first Adigara Mudaliyar among the Tamils. See Note 392.

—Oct. - The draft of an Ordinance for the Registration of Midwives in Ceylon published in the Government Gazette.

—Oct. 18 - Death of Mr. B. Bell, employed on the Burma Railway, for about 15 years. See Note 394.

—Oct. 20 - Arrival in Colombo of the New Colonial Secretary, Sir Graeme Thomson.

—Oct. 22 - Mr. A. S. Inayatulla, Riot Compensation clerk, appointed Asst. Secretary, Local Board, Jaffna.

—Oct. 25 - Mr. B. Constantine, G. A. N. P., leaves Jaffna on furlough.

—Oct. 25 - Mr. H. W. Codrington arrives and assumes duties as acting Government Agent of Jaffna.

—Oct. 29 - A lecture on "Forensic Humour" delivered by Mr. S. D. Tampoe, Advocate, at the Otley Hall. Vaddukoddai.

—Nov. 3 - A lecture on the "Origin and Styles of Ancient Ceylon Architecture" delivered at the Jaffna Wesleyan Central College Hall, by Andreas Nell.

1919—Nov. 11 - Death at Hatton of Mrs. Thangamma, relict of Arulampala Mudaliyar of the Jaffna Fiscal's Office.

—Nov. 28 - Opening of the Freeman Memorial Ward at the Inuvil Hospital. See Note 395.

Dec. - A Society known as the Jaffna Historical Society formed. See Note 396.

—Dec. 7 - Mr. Talaivasingham assumes duties as Acting Commissioner of Requests and Police Magistrate of Jaffna and Mallagam.

—Dec. 8 - The Silver Jubilee of the admission to the O. M. I. of the Rev. Bro. E. Groussault, celebrated in Jaffna. See Note 397.

—Dec. 11 - First Sessions of the Ceylon National Congress held at the Public Hall, Colombo.

—Dec. 19 - Mudaliyar J. G. Puvimanasinghe, Interpreter, District, Court, Jaffna, presented with a gold medal by the members of the Jaffna Bar, on his retirement from the public service.

—Dec. - Mr. Ernest Abraham of the P. W. D., Colombo, wins the first prize in the all Ceylon competition for the best design of the Victory Column proposed to be erected in Colombo. See Note 398.

—Dec. 23 - Death at Manipay, at the age of 86 of Mr. Joel Fitch, Evangelist. See Note 424.

—Dec. - Mr. Alfred M. Handy, a son of the late Rev. Charles Handy, B. A. appointed Private Secretary to the Chief Justice, Straits Settlements (Sir John Bucknil K. C.) in succession to his brother Mr. J. T. N. Handy, who has received appointment in the Straits Civil Service.

—Dec. 31 - The Biennial Election of members for the Jaffna Local Board. Messrs R. R. Nalliah, C. Arulampalam, and M. Asaipillai, elected respectively for the Central, Eastern and Western Wards. See Note 399.

1920—Jan. 5 - Death at Jaffna of V. F. Joseph, P. W. D., Negombo, and of Mrs. Joseph. This is the first instance in the town of both husband and wife passing away on the same day.

—Jan. 6 - Death at Colombo of A.D. Saverimuttu, Cashier, Walker Sons & Co. See Note 180.

—Jan. 7 - First intimation received with regard to the price of rice to be supplied to Ceylon.

1920—Jan. - The new one cent stamp put in circulation.

—Jan. 9 - First meeting of the Jaffna Historical Society held at the Jaffna Central College Hall, when Rasanayaga Mudaliyar, Secretary of the District Court of Jaffna, read a paper on "Achchunan."

—Jan. 13 - Death at the General Hospital, Colombo, of Miss Elizabeth, the infant daughter of Mr. H. W. Codrington, G. A., N. P.

—Jan. 14 - Death of Mr. M. Ayniahpillai, a well-known member of the Moorish community of Jaffna, and one of the oldest and most popular shop keepers of the town. See Note 425.

—Jan. 18 - Death at Calcutta of John Chinnadurai, Secretary, Y. M. C. A., Nagpur, and second son of the Rev. S. Eliathamby, Pastor, Uduvil.

—Jan. 22 - The building of the V. S. Oriental College at Chunnakam completed and the purificatory Sancte Ceremonies performed.

—Jan. 23 - A meeting of the Jaffna Historical Society. Revd. Fr. Gnanapragasar, O. M. I., reads a paper on "The Kings of Jaffna and their forgotten Coins".

—Jan. 27 - Messrs J. S. Mather, N. K. Nalliah, and Ramalingam Samuel, ordained in Colombo as full ministers of the Wesleyan Church.

—Feb. 4 - Announcement made in the Legislative Council of the formation of a new Department to be known as the 'Food' Production Department.'

—Feb. 6 - At a meeting of the Jaffna Historical Society held at the Jaffna Association Rooms, Mr. H. W. Codrington reads a paper on "A few notes on the Re-construction of the History of Jaffna."

—Feb. 13 - Death at Jaffna of Mr. Thambyah S. Cooke, Proctor, S. C. See Note 400.

—Feb. 15 - Consecration at Colombo of the Rt. Rev. Dr. Jules Andrew Brault, O. M. I., as Bishop of Jaffna.

—Feb. 15 - Rice rationing started in Jaffna.

—Feb. 16 - The new church of St. Joseph at Kayts blessed by the Rev. Fr. Aseervatham.

—Feb. 17 - A reception accorded to His Lordship Dr. J. A. Brault, the new Bishop of Jaffna, at the Kotahena Young Men's Association Hall, when a large and representative gathering of Jaffna Catholics and Old Boys of St Patrick's College was present. A special feature of the function was the offer, made by Mr. Samuel F. Johnpullae, Head Clerk, Loan Board, Colombo, and accepted by His Lordship, of a gift of thousand rupees for founding a scholarship intended to educate a poor but intelligent Catholic youth, and commemorate His Lordship's elevation to the Episcopate. The new Episcopal Throne fitted up at the Jaffna Cathedral was also presented to His Lordship on this occasion. See Note 401.

1920—Feb. 20 - The Ceylon deputation to the Viceroy of India re the issue of rice to Ceylon by the Indian Government leave by the Indian train. The deputation consisted of Mr. A. F. B. Sweaton, Mudaliyar A. E. Rajapakse, Hon. Mr. A. Sapapathy, Messrs E. G. Adamaly, M. S H. Adamaly, M. S. H. Abdul Ally, V. P. Somasundram, M. C. Raju, K. Cassim and L. Muttukrishna.

—Feb. 20 - Death at Jaffna of Mary Magdalene, relict of Jacob A Tisseverasinghe, Notary Public. See Note 104.

—Feb. 23 - A lecture on "Westminister and the House of Parliament" delivered at the Central College Hall, by the Right Hon. Sir John Randles, M. P.

—Feb. 24 - The new Local Government Ordinance passed.

—Feb. 25 - Arrival in Jaffna of His Lordship Dr. J. A. Brault, O. M. I., the new Bishop of Jaffna. See Note 389.

—Feb. 26 - Death of Dr. L. Joshua of Changanai.

—Feb. 27 - Mr. B. Constantine, G. A., N. P., returns from England and resumes duties.

—Mar. 1 - Mr. V. Murugasapillai of 'Sherman Lodge,' Vannarponne, donates a sum of Rs. 500 to St. Patrick's College for the education of a poor deserving student. This scholarship is in memory of his deceased wife, Selvakanmany Ammal. See Note 401.

—Mar. 2 - Death at Jaffna of Mr. Henry Joseph, Chief Clerk of the Provincial Road Committee and Secretary of the Local Board, Anuradhapura.

—Mar. 3 - Dr. (Miss) H. R. Williams appointed assistant to Dr. Curr at the Inuvil Hospital. See Note 402.

—Mar. 6 - His Excellency Sir W. H. Manning leaves for England, and Sir Graeme Thompson sworn in as Acting Governor of Ceylon.

—Mar. - A receiving Post Office opened at Kudatanai.

1920—Mar. 7 - Death at Jaffna of Mr. George Stanhope Aseervatham. See Note 403.

—Mar. 12 - Death at Uduvil of the Rev. G. G. Brown of the American Mission. He was for some years Principal of the Jaffna College. See Note 404.

—Mar. - Mr. C. L. Wickremmesinge assumes duties as Police Magistrate, Jaffna.

—Mar. 18 - C. Rajanayaga Mudaliyar, Secretary D. C., Jaffna, delivers a lecture at the St. John's College Hall on "The outline of the History of Ceylon."

—Mar. 20 - Ordination at the Jaffna Cathedral of the Rev. Bro. Abraham. This is the first ordination held by the new Bishop of Jaffna, Mgr. Brault, O. M. I.

—Mar. 20 - Dedication of the new church built at Delft by the native Evangelical Society.

—Mar. 24. - At a meeting of the Jaffna Historical Society. Mr. S. R. Rajaretnam, B. A., Advocate, reads a paper on "Ceylon and the Chola Empire. Part I (a Study in Imperial History).

—April. 1 - The "Ceylon Observer", the first Ceylon newspaper, established 4th Feb. 1834, passes from private ownership into the hands of a new company, "The Ceylon Observer Ltd." See Note 107.

—April. 5 - The new house of Mr. Joseph Cherubim blessed by His Lordship Dr. J. A. Brault, O. M. I. in the presence of a large and representative gathering.

—April. 10 - His Lordship Dr. J. A. Brault, O. M. I., Bishop of Jaffna, leaves here en route to Europe, taking steamer from Colombo on the 23rd.

—April. 14 - The new Salaries Scheme involving an expenditure of 7⅛ million rupees per annum passed.

—April. 20 - Sir A. Kanagasabai, who acted as District Judge of Jaffna for 14 months, retires: Mr. G. W. Woodhouse succeeds him. See Note 427.

—April. - P. C. Nicholas Mudaliyar promoted to class V of the Ceylon Civil Service. See Note 434.

—April. - Dr. W. A. Rogers of Ipoh created a J. P.

—April. 24 - At a meeting of the Jaffna Historical Society held at the Jaffna Central College Hall, the Hon. Mr. Balasingham delivers a lecture on the "Aryans".

1920—May. 1 - A life size portrait in oil of the Hon'ble Mr. Horsburgh who was Government Agent of the Northern Province, presented to the Kachcheri by the officers. This is the fourth of its kind done to perpetuate the memory of the Government Agents who have held office in the Northern Province, the three others being those of Sir William Twynam, Mr. R. W. Ievers, and Mr. J. P. Lewis.

—May. 3 - H. E. Sir Graeme Thompson, Acting Governor, visits Jaffna. He is accompanied by Lady Thompson.

—May. 7 - Rev. Fr. C. Beaud assumes duties as Director of St. Joseph's Orphanage, Colombogam. See Note 405.

—May. 10 - The celebration by Mr. & Mrs. William Mather of the Golden Jubilee of their marriage.

—May. 17 - The card system of food rationing suspended in the Jaffna Maniagar's division.

—May. 23 - Arrival in Colombo of Dr. Gunam F. Cooke, M. B. B. S. (Lond) L. R. C. P., M. R. C. S. (Eng.) eldest son of Mr. Thambiah S. Cooke, Proctor. See Note 417.

—May. 26 - The centenary of the foundation of the Holy Family of Bordeaux celebrated at the Holy Family Convent, Jaffna. See Note 126.

—May. - Mr. M. A. P. Sandrasagra, son of Mudaliyar Jos. N. Sandrasagra, J. P., Maniagar, Valikamam West, comes off successful in the London Matriculation Examination.

—May. 31 - A reception accorded to Mr. Henry Peto, M. A. (Cantab), the new Principal of St. John's College, by the masters and boys of the College.

—June. 3 - Birthday honours conferred on Mr. Philip Moses, Gate Mudaliyar C. M. Chinniah, P. C. Nicholas Mudaliyar, M. S. Ramalinga Mudaliyar and Messrs C. Rasanayagam and S. Vaithianathan. See Note 406.

—June. - An honorarium of Rs. 250 granted to Mr. A. Kumaraswamy Pulavar by Government in recognization and encouragement of literary work. See Note 432.

—June. 9 - A reception held at 'Sirivasa' Anaikoddai, in honour of the investiture of C. M. Chinniah Mudaliyar with the title of Adigara Mudaliyar.

—June. 10 - A thanksgiving service held at St. Mary's Cathedral, Jaffna, at 5 p. m. and afterwards a reception at his residence, Martyn's Walawoo, Jaffna, in honour of the investiture of Mr. P. Moses with the title of J. P.

1920—June. 11 - Death at Manipay of Mr. William Mather, Managing Director of the Jaffna Commercial Corporation. See Note 407.

—June. - Lieutenant K. V. Muttukumaru, I. M. S., brother of V. M. Muttukumaru Mudaliyar, Maniagar of Jaffna, appointed Officer commanding the Bagdad Indian Section Hospital, Moultan, Punjab.

—June. - C. Rajanayaga Mudlr., Secretary, D. C., Jaffna, promoted to the post of Deputy Registrar of Colombo. During the time he was employed in Jaffna, he proved himself highly efficient as an officer and took a prominent part in all public movements. See Note 414.

—June. 16 - Mr. H. A. P. Sandrasagara, President, Ceylon National Association, called to the Bar at the Middle Temple.

—June. 22 - The Annual Police Sports come off at the Police Grounds, Jaffna.

—June. 23 - Death at Madras of Rao Bahadur K. V. Lingham, Presidency Postmaster of Madras. He is a native of Mallagam.

—June. - News received of the success in England of Mr. C. Sittampalam, in the Mathematical Tripos, Part II. See Note 410.

—July. - A Commission appointed to inquire into, and report on, the existing system of Native Headmen, paid and unpaid, with a view to its improvement.

—July. 2 - Death at Nallur of Mr. C. Periathamby, Sub-collector of Valvettiturai. He was a good Tamil Scholar. See Note 249.

—July. - The Jaffna Food Products Company floated with a Capital of Rs. 100,000.

—July. - The Honorary Rank of Mudaliyar conferred on Mr Joseph Gabriel Puvimannasinghe, late Interpreter Mudaliyar of the District Court of Jaffna, and that of Mudaliyar of the Governor's Gate on S. Sabaratna Mudaliyar, late Deputy Fiscal of Jaffna.

—July - Publication of the work entitled "Kingdom of Jaffnapatam" by Dr. P. E. Pieris. The book gives an account of the administrative organization of Jaffna in 1645, as derived from the Portuguese archives.

—July. 15 - A demonstration of the working of a new pump, invented by Mr. Varitamby Arumugam of Valvettiturai, for baling large volumes of water, given at the Provincial Engineer's Office, W. P. See Note 411.

1920—July. - Death at Colombo of Dr. F. G. Spittal, who was Provincial Surgeon of Jaffna for some years.

—July. 17 - The Vadamaradchy Friend-in-need Society formed. Mr. P. Vytilingam, Police Magistrate of Point Pedro and Chavagachcheri, took the initiative in the movement.

—July. 21 - Announcement received of the death in England, on the 25th June, of the Rev. J. G. Trimmer, Superintendent of the North Ceylon Wesleyan Mission. See Note 433.

—July. 28 - Death at Colombo, from Cerebral hemorrhage, of A. G. Saverimuttu Mudaliyar, Chief Post Master, Colombo. He was conferred the title of Mudaliyar for distinguished services. His eldest daughter is married to Dr. V. Ratnavelu of the Civil Medical Department.

—July. 29 - Death at Colombo from heart failure of Mr. C. Namasivayam, J. P. See Note 412.

—July. 30 - Mr. S. O. Canagaretnam, Deputy Fiscal, Jaffna, leaves for Batticaloa, having been appointed Chief Mudaliyar of the Batticaloa Kachcheri.

—Aug. 1 - Death at Bombay of B. G. Tilak, the great Indian political leader.

—Aug. 6 - Paddy to the amount of 7,000 bushels, the gift of Mr. Markandan and brothers and of T. Karalapillai Mudaliyar, commenced to be distributed to the poor in the divisions of the different Maniagars of Jaffna, each pauper receiving a quarter bushel of paddy.

—Aug. 6 - P. Nicholas Mudaliyar of the Jaffna Kachcheri who was recently drafted into the Civil Service, on a merit promotion, leaves for Batticaloa, having been appointed Office Asst. to the Government Agent, and Additional Police Magistrate, Batticaloa. See Notes 406,434.

—Aug. 7 - The will of the late Mr. Namasivayam produced at the Colombo District Court. The estate is valued at Rs. 1,702,435. 30 cents. Movables Rs. 438,235.30 cts, Immovables Rs. 1,244,200. See Note 412.

—Aug. 7- The Sovereign ceases to be legal tender.

—Aug. 12 - Death at Panadura of Dr. M. Sinnatamby from heart failure. See Note 413.

—Aug. 18 - Death at Colombo of Annapurani, widow of the late Dr. Savanamuttu Hallock. See Note 414.

1920—Aug. 19. - Death at Jaffna of Annaletchumy, wife of Mr. C. Sundram, C.C. S., Chief Appraiser, Colombo Customs, and Asst. Deputy Food Controller, Chalmer's Granaries, Colombo.

—Aug. 21 - The Hon. Sir A. Kanagasabai appointed Tamil Member of the Legislative Council in lieu of the Hon. Mr. A. Sapapathy who is incapacitated owing to ill-health. Mr. Sapapathy has done useful work in Council in connection with many important questions.

—Aug. 22 - A lecture on 'The Revival of Catholicism in England in the 19th century' read at the Jaffna Catholic Club by Mr. R. C. Fernando, District Engineer, Pallai.

—Aug. 23 - A home for the aged and destitute, to be associated with the name of the late Mr. William Mather, proposed to be erected at a cost of Rs. 100,000. See Note 407.

—Aug. 25 - Celebration at Tellipaiai of the sixtieth anniversary of the founding of the Tellipalai Training and Industrial School under the American Mission of Jaffna. See Note 415.

—Aug. 25 - V. M. Muttukumaru Mudaliyar, Maniagar of Jaffna, who took some Jaffna exhibits, such as local made iron locks, pruning knives, cloth fans, brooms and leather sandals, secures at the show nine silver medals.

—Aug. 28 - Dr. C. Candiah, M. B. C. M. (Madras) the popular House Surgeon, Jaffna Civil Hospital, entertained at a Farewell dinner at the Jaffna Rest House, on the eve of his departure to Europe to obtain British qualifications.

—Aug. 28 - Death at Maviddapuram of Mr. K. Thambaiya, retired shroff of the General Treasury.

—Aug. 29 - The Government Clerical Examination held. 548 candidates presented themselves.

—Aug. - Mr. P. J. Sabapathy obtains tho licence in Medicine, Surgery and Midwifery in the last Medical Examination, passing the final in the 1st class and winning the Garvin Gold Medal for operative surgery.

—Aug. - Government sanctions the estimates for the construction of the proposed agricultural school in Jaffna.

—Aug. - The roadside drains in the town of Jaffna are being cut, deepened and cleared with a view to the easy flow of flood water.

—Aug. - The Ceylon Legislative Council is allowed by the New Reforms only 16 elected members out of a total of 38 with the Governor to preside.

1920—Aug. - Mr. M. Arumuga Upathiyayar of Vaddukoddai, a Tamil Scholar, granted an honorarium of Rs. 250 by Governent. See Note 416.

—Aug. - Mrs. S. Sapapathy of Teluk Anson, F. M. S., makes an offer of Rs 5,000 to the founding of a scholarship to enable Tamil Christians to prepare for the ministry.

—Sept. 2 - Dr. Gunam Cooke assumes duties as House Surgeon of the Jaffna Civil Hospital vice Dr. C. Candiah who leaves for Europe to obtain British qualifications. See Note 417.

—Sept. 13 - Return to the Island of H. E. Sir William Manning.

—Sept. 25 - A garden party in the Jaffna Fort to bid farewell to Mr. E. B. Denham, late Director of Education in Ceylon.

—Oct. 1 - Dr. V. Gabriel, Surgeon, Outpatient Department, General Hospital, appointed lecturer in Anatomy in the Medical College. He is a son of the late Vraspillai Adigar of Musali.

—Oct. 1 - Death at Araly of Arumugam Newton Sabapathipillai, retired overseer. See Note 386.

—Oct. 1 - Regulations made with regard to the importation of British gold coins into Ceylon revoked.

—Oct. Dr. Mylvaganam, a Jaffna gentleman, appointed P. C. M. O. of the State of Mysore.

—Oct. - Notice published re the Registration of Voters for the Northern Constituency.

—Oct. 21 - A meeting held at Pandaterruppu to commemorate the 100th anniversary of the first Medical Mission to the East started by Dr. John Scudder. Dr. L. R. Scudder of the Arcot Mission, a representative of the Scudder Family, attended and addressed the centenary meetings. See Note 418.

—Oct. - Mr. P. Ramalingam of Nallur comes off successful in the Indian Civil Service Examination, taking the first place. See Note 419.

—Oct. 25 - Marrriage of Mr. R. R. Nalliah, Proctor, Jaffna, with Miss Sornammah, daughter of M. S. Ramalinga Mudaliyar, Chief Mudaliyar of the Jaffna Kachcheri.

—Oct. 25 - Marriage of Miss Kirupainasam, 4th daughter of the late R. W. Allegacoen, C. C. S., with Mr. S. Saravanamuttu, eldest son of the Hon. A. Sapapathy.

—Oct. 25 - Death at Tinnevelly, South India, of Chelliah Christmaspillai, Rao Sahib. See Note 420.

1920—Oct. 30 - A farewell function held in the P. W. D. Office grounds in honour of Mr. William Black, J. P., on his retiring from the Public Service. See Note 379.

—Oct. 31 - A Book Stall opened at St. Mary's Cathedral, Jaffna.

—Oct. - News received of the success of Dr. S. G. Sinnatamby, son of Mr. G. V. Sinnatamby of Vaddukoddai and of Dr. Thambinayagam Saravanamuttu, grandson of the late Dr. Mills of Manipay, in the L. R. C. P. and M. R. C. S. Examinations of London.

—Nov. 4 - Death in Madura of the Rev. C. D. Veluppillai from fever. He was Pastor at Tellipallai under the American Mission. See Note 421.

—Nov. 7 - Death at Singapore of Dr. J. M. Handy. See Note 422.

—Nov. 11 - Rev. William Goudie, General Secretary of the Wesleyan Missionary Society, and Mr. Robert Simpson, arrive in Jaffna on an official visit.

-Nov. 12 - Rain commences and continues to fall heavily and incessantly, day and night, till the 30th.

Nov. 12 - The Catholic Church at Maduvil North registered for the solemnization of marriages.

—Nov. 22 - The annual almsgiving by Mr. K. Kathirasapillai, arrack renter. Fifty bags of rice, 2500 cocoanuts and Rs. 250 distributed.

—Nov. 25 - Laying of the Foundation stone, by H. E. Sir W. H. Manning, of the Hostel intended for the Denham Scholars from the Vernacular Schools H. E. expressed a desire to contribute Rs. 1,200 as a fund for the education of a scholar to be known as the Manning Scholar.

—Nov. 26 - A drama entitled "Truth Will Out" staged at St. Patrick's College Hall by the Patrician Dramatic Society.

—Dec. - Total number of voters registered in the Jaffna District for the Northern Constituency is 13,366.

—Dec. 9 - The Jaffna Inthirai Oil Mill, the first Oil Mill, erected in Jaffna by Kandiah Chetty for the manufacture of cocoanut oil, formally opened by Sir W. C. Twynam. See Note 423.

—Dec. 11 - Marriage of H. E. Sir W. H. Manning with Miss Olga May Septon, Jones. The ceremony was performed at Queen's House, Colombo, by the Hon. J. G. Fraser, G. A. W. P. in his capacity as Provincial Registrar.

1920—Dec. 15 - The Rev. Fr. Timothy M. F. Long, O. M. I., a young Irish Missionary, who recently arrived in Jaffna, placed on The Tutorial Staff of St. Patrick's College.

—Dec. 22 - The Sacerdotal Silver Jubilee of the Rev. Fr. B. A. Marcellin, O. M. I., celebrated in Jaffna.

—Dec. 27 - The Sacerdotal Silver Jubilee of the Rev. Fr. Charles Beaud, O. M. I., Manager of Schools under the Catholic Mission of Jaffna, celebrated at Colombogam. See Note 405.

—Dec. 30 - Mr. Samuel F. Johnpulle, Chief Clerk, Loan Board, Colombo, Mr. Philip Moses, J. P., and others leave Jaffna, to be present at the Marian Congress, which is to commence at Madras, on the 4th January 1921.

NOTES

1

The Portuguese visit Ceylon.

In the year of our Lord 1444 Nicola de Conte, a Venitian, gives a particular account of the talipot-tree, its leaves, size, etc., and describes the mode of preparing cinnamon. and the precious gems and pearls that were found in Ceylon. From the fourteenth to the sixteenth century, we have much valuable information given us by various authors, concerning the trade of the Island; but as our principal business is connected with it after it came into the possession of Europeans, we will at once state, that, in 1505, the Portuguese, under Don Lorenzo de Almeida, visited the Island, and were permitted to trade...... History asserts that it was chance, or rather adverse winds, which drove the Portuguese vessels on the shores of Ceylon, whilst in pursuit of some moorish pirates whom they had seen sailing in the direction of the Maldives, and the winds proving adverse, they sought refuge in the Bay of Colombo...... From a curious antiquarian work in Sinhalese, the following description of the Portuguese, their diet, and guns is extracted:—"And now it occurred, in the Christian year 1505 that a ship from Portugal arrived and anchored in Colombo. The race of men are exceedingly white and beautiful; they wear a covering to the feet and head made of iron, and they are always in motion. Their drink is the colour of blood, and they eat what looks like a white stone. They have weapons of warfare which make a noise like thunder when it breaks upon Jugandere Parivata, and a ball of iron shot from one of them, after flying some leagues, will break a castle of stone. *"Ceylon and The Cingalese" by Henry Charles Sirr,* M. A.

2

Catholic Religion Preached at Mannar.

The Island of Mannar was in early times the hereditary property of the Kadeyas, and exclusively occupied by them, subject to the King of Jaffna. About the eighth century Mahomedan emigrants from Arabia formed a considerable settlement on the Island.... In 1544, when the Roman Catholic Religion was first introduced into the Island by St. Francis Xavier, or one of his colleagues, the Kadeyas were the first to embrace it, which raised a great persecution against them. The King of Jaffna, who viewed its progress with a jealous eye, ordered 600 persons of both sexes, who had embraced Christianity, to be impaled; and issued a proclamation that no priest of any other religion than the Hindoo should approach the shores of the Island, under a severe penalty. Xavier, who was then labouring on the opposite coast, being apprized of this event, immediately repaired to Cochin, and having obtained from the authorities there a fleet, with a sufficient number of troops to co-operate with him in destroying the tyrant, he appeared off Mannar in April 1545, but failed in his enterprise. The Portuguese, however, took possession of the Island in 1590; and notwithstanding the attempts made by the King of Jaffna to retake it, they retained it till 1658, when the Dutch, after a short resistance, made themselves masters of it. During the Government of the Portuguese it was their head-quarters in the Northern Province, and a Captain General permanently resided there. They no-where appear to have exerted themselves so much for the propagation of their faith as at this place; and the success which attended their labours is sufficiently proved by the circumstance of their being very few persons of any other sect or religion at Mannar, and none in the adjacent province of Mantotta. It was here that the Portuguese detained the Empress Donna Catharina as a state prisoner, previous to their raising her to the throne of her ancestors at Kandy, and on this account it has been rendered memorable in the annals of Ceylon.—*The Ceylon Gazetteer by Simon Casie Chitty.*

Tatavaly, patron St. Andrew, represented the first converts under St. Francis Xavier, and from among them came the six hundred martyrs.—*Rebeiro's Ceilao by P E. Pieris*

Tatavaly, or more properly Thotavelee, in Mannar Island, was the original home of the Kadeyas.

3

St. Francis Xavier in Ceylon.

The neighbouring peninsula of Hindustan was, at the time to which we wish to refer, being traversed by the foot-steps of an Apostle—an Apostle like one of the twelve—possessed of the gift of tongues and of the gift of miracles, the great St. Francis Xavier. The inhabitants of Ceylon sent messengers to the Saint, begging that he would visit and instruct them in the Christian faith. In 1548 he set foot on the island, and the same marvels that had accompanied his missionary labours elsewhere, followed his preaching in Ceylon. The rites of Brahminism in the North and of Buddhism in the South of the Island, gave way to the teachings and the practices of the Christian faith. The blood of Martyrs began soon to fertilize the vineyard planted by the Apostle of the Indies—St. Francis Xavier. The glory of furnishing the first legion of Martyrs for the faith in Ceylon was to belong to Jaffna, that part of the Island which St. Francis had himself, in person, evangelized. Six hundred Martyrs were put to death by the King of Jaffnapattam, for having embraced Christianity. Among those who perished thus gloriously was the King's own son. These events led to the possession of the Island being taken by the Portuguese.—*The Sketches of the Life of Mgr. De Mazenod, By Rev. Robert Cooke, O. M. I.*

4

Roman Medals.

Pliny affirms, that during the reign of the Emperor Claudius, a Roman vessel from the coast of Arabia, was driven upon that of Taprobane, or Ceylon; that the King of the country treated the Romans with hospitality and kindness during their sojourn of six months, and upon their departure they were accompanied by four ambassadors from the Eastern to the Roman Monarch. Many modern writers treat this account as fabulous; but in our opinion, Pliny is borne out in his statement by the fact, that Roman medals of an ancient date were found, in the year 1574, at Mantotta, in Ceylon. We learn also, from Pliny, that a fleet, consisting of more than one hundred sail, went each year from the Red Sea to the coasts of Malabar and Ceylon, for the purpose of trade. Doubt has been thrown on this assertion, as writers state that it would have been impracticable for the ill-constructed vessels of that period, and with imperfect knowledge of navigation, for the Romans to have traversed the Indian Ocean; and although it must be allowed that such a voyage must necessarily have been a perilous one, still it was perfectly practicable to have sailed with one monsoon, and to have returned by the opposite, as is the custom, in the present day, with the unwieldy junks of Siam.—*'Ceylon and The Cingalese" by Henry Charles Sirr.* M. A.

5

The Dutch and Ceylon.

It was in the year 1602, that the Dutch first turned their attention towards Ceylon; their possessions in the East Indies were vast and lucrative, and this Island would open a new gate to gain, could they obtain a footing: consequently in furtherance of their design, Admiral Spillbergen was despatched by the Prince of Orange and States General of Holland, with three men-of-war, fully armed and equipped, to open communication with the Natives — *Ibid.*

6

The Portuguese in Jaffna.

In 1591 Andre Furtado de Mendonca, who subsequently rose to be the greatest Portuguese General in the East, invaded Jaffna. The Rajah of the country fled after an unsuccessful attempt at resistance and was subsequently discovered concealed in a temple and put to death, while Hendarmana Sinha Kumara, a youthful member of the Royal family, was placed on the throne at Nallur with the name of Para Rasa Sekara Pandara. It was not long before the energetic Franciscans followed with the spiritual invasion of the Kingdom. They commenced with a modest Hermitage which was erected at the spot, where Furtado had landed, and there they remained till the king presented them with a house which belonged to one of his courtiers, and which they called after our Lady of Victory. This continued to be their head quarters till 1614 when the Father Fray Pedro de Betancor, who had erected several churches in Mantotta and the Wanni districts, determined to construct a larger building nearer to the Portuguese Settlement, the Parangi Theru. The Moors at the time had a mosque close to the landing place on the Lake, and this site which lay within the Fort of to-day, the Father succeeded by a stratagem in obtaining for his purpose. The Hindu Raja of Tanjore gave him generous assistance, and on 8th May, 1614, the foundation of the new church of our Lady of Victory was laid.

In the meantime a certain Father Fray Francisco had come from Cochin bringing with him a log on which he had begun to carve an image of his patron, Saint Antonio. He now decided to convert it into an image of the Lady of Victory, and entrusted it to an artist named Anakutti for the purpose. Many days had not passed before strange rumours began to be spread abroad. It was whispered that Anakutti who had sat down on the log while at his task, had been forcibly hurled to the ground, and that people suffering with disease had been healed by drinking the water in which a fragment of the wood was dipped. The rumours were persistent, and crowds assembled to gaze at the unfinished image. The alleged miracles increased in number and the terrified Anakutti refused to continue the work and begged the Father to remove the marvellous object before harm should befall his household. An inquiry was therefore ordered, and the judges arrived at the decision that several miracles had been proved. The Fathers therefore decided to remove the Image to their church and this was accordingly done on the 24th July, the king himself appearing to view the procession which escorted it. The name of the church was at the same time changed to that of Our Lady of Miracles, and there the Image continued performing miracles, details of very many of which have been preserved.

In the meantime Father Pedro was busy with the construction of his new church and after eighteen months the Capela Mor was completed with a vaulted roof, while the walls of the nave had been raised up to the level of the clerestory (upper row of windows.) The miraculous Image was conveyed to this new abode on the Festival of S. Simon and S. Jude accompanied by a great concourse of people, the priests chanting the Psalm Dixit Dominus along the road. Not long after the Father himself died at the age of seventy years and was buried in the middle of the Capela, and was succeeded by the Father Fray Antonio de Santa Maria.

In 1615 Para Rasa Sekara Pandara died leaving as his heir a child of three years. It was not long before a conspiracy led to the assassination of the Regent, and Changill Kumara seized the chief power. The Portuguese in Colombo now determined to make another attempt to reduce the kingdom, and this was successfully accomplished by Phelipe de Oliveira in 1617. Changili who attempted to escape by way of Paritti Turai, was taken prisoner on the sea along with the rest of the Royal family, and was sent to Goa, while Jaffna was declared a Portuguese Province with de Oliveira as its first Governor. The Tamils headed by Migalpulle Arachchi and assisted by warriors from Tanjore kept up the struggle for independence a few years longer, but after a great battle which was fought near Valvedditurai in 1621 they ceased from their opposition and accepted the Portuguese rule.

A new capital was now formed at Jaffna, and a fort also called after Our Lady of Miracles, was constructed so as to enclose the new church, which was still unfinished. Deogo de Mendonca Furtado, who was subsequently Governor of Brazil, seeing the unprotected condition of the Image, offered up to it a coffer which he had brought with him, and this was subsequently replaced by a *ratabolo* which was made in Negapatam. Our Lady was also solemnly proclaimed the Protectress of the New Kingdom, and the standard of de Oliveira was always placed before her altar. The Governor was a devoted son of the Church, and with the encouragement given by him the work on the fabric was fast completed, some of the ironwood beams from the Nallur palace being utilised for the roof, and tiles obtained from a vessel which was on its way to Mannar. A *casado* of Negapatam offered a bag of silver coins, and a cross was prepared out of 120 patacas for the altar. Manoel Rodrigues who was on his way to Malacca made a further offering of a hundred cruzados and two large carpets, in gratitude for his miraculous preservation from a storm on the coast. For a subsequent similar deliverance he made an offering of three lamps as well. The fame of the Image spread over India, and offerings poured in from all parts, especially from sea-faring men. The effect of all this was soon felt on the populace. Para Rasa sehara's Queens and a young Princess were baptized, receiving the names of Dona Clara de Silva, Dona Antonia Rapoza and Dona Catherina de Sa de Rebolo. Numerous royal and other prominent personages followed their example, and finally the whole of the Tamil population was baptized into Christianity.

It was within this Church that de Oliveira was invested by Constantino de Sa Noronha with the insignia of the ancient Portuguese Military Order of Christ in recognition of his eminent services.

On 20th February 1627 a great tidal wave passed over Jaffna. The water swept within the Fort up to the very porch of the Church, but the building itself, where hundreds were seeking shelter, escaped undamaged, it was believed owing to the power of Our Lady. From the account which has been left of this storm, it appears to have been the worst ever recorded in the history of the country, some vessels having been carried inland as far as a mile and left stranded there. The exposure which de Oliveira underwent at the time led to a serious illness of which he died on the 22nd March, 1627. He was buried in the Capelo Mor with great ceremony, and a few years later his bones were placed in an urn which was let into the wall of the Chapel. A stone engraved with his arms over three crowns and sceptres, emblematic of the kings he had defeated, and bearing a short inscription in letters of gold, was placed over the niche.

It was the 23rd June, 1658. The Hollanders had, after a terrible siege lasting over three months, reduced the Fort of Jaffna, the last strong-hold of the Portuguese in Ceylon. Without the Church of Our Lady of Miracles, were all the horror and desolation of war. Within, the armed soldiers of the Hollanders were drawn up in rigid lines. The Dominie Philippus Baldaeus was standing in his stiff black gown near the spot where the Image of our Lady of Miracles had stood the week before. Led by him the Hollanders lift up their deep voices in Thanksgiving for the victory which had crowned their arms.

The curious visitor to the Church within the Jaffna Fort will see in the Vestry a large bell. Round this runs the legend *N. S. dos milagres de Jaffna-patao 1648.* That is all that remains of the Portuguese Church.—*P. E. P. The "Jaffna Catholic Guardian," April 15, 1916.*

7

JAFFNA FORT

Jaffnapatao, a quadrangular fortress, had four bastions and four half-moons or cobelos in the middle of the line of ramparts, all of which were built of pumice stone. Here was kept the necessary artillery, and it was also the residence of the Governor of that Kingdom. On one side outside the walls stretched the town, where resided three hundred families of Portuguese, and seven hundred of service holders, with the convents of St. Francisco and St. Domingos, the College of the Society, the Mother Church, the House of Sancta Misericordia and the Hospital. Two leagues from the mouth of the harbour, was a fort similar to the one of Bugio with good artillery and garrisoned by a company of infantry. The full number of men-of-war for the defence of this kingdom was two hundred Portuguese forming six companies with some native Lascarins.—*Ribeiro's Ceilao by P. E. Pieris.*

The fort built by the Portuguese was taken down by the Dutch, who erected, of shell-and coral breccia quarried from the sea, the present compact and well finished pentagonal structure. It is surrounded by a moat, and encloses houses for officers, soldiers and artificers. The chief building, never wanting within Dutch fortifications, is the Church, in the shape of a Greek Cross, one of the best places of worship in Ceylon. It was reserved by the Capitulation of 1795 for the Presbyterian consistory, ever to the present moment a courteous and loyal Board. Almost appointed to Jaffna by the colonial authorities, the Rev. Thomas H. Squance, the Wesleyan pioneer, was gladly allowed to officiate within its sacred walls. It is now used only by the Ministers of the Church of England and though unconsecrated in the episcopal sense, may be regarded as in their hands.—*Hindu Pastors by the Rev. E. J. Robinson, Late Wesleyan Missionary in Ceylon, 1867.*

8

Jesuits in Jaffna

A report made in the year 1644 by the Father Provincial to

the Superior-General of the Society supplies the following details:—
In Ceylon there were two Colleges, at Colombo and Jaffnapattam respectively.

Under the College of Jaffnapattam were the following residences:—

Cutandaculam : Patron, Saint Michael.
Palle (Pallai) : patron, Crucifix.
Tambamma : patron, Nativity of our Lady.
Mugamalle (Mohamalai) : patron, all Saints.
Achivelli (Achuveli) : patron, Holy Ghost.
Mailatti (Mayliddi): patron, Our Lady of Angels.
Telipulle (Tellippalai) : patron, St. Peter and St. Paul.
Malagam (Mallakam) : patron, St. Ignatius.
Panditiripu (Pandaiteruppu) : patron, our Lady of Remedies.
Changane (Changanai) : patron, the Holy Trinity.
Vatucote (Vaddukkoddai); patron, the Assumption of Our Lady.
Cardiva, patron, Our Lady of Remedies.

(Apparently this last Island was gifted to the Society by Don Hireonymo de Azavedo. King's letter to Viceroy, March 28, 1608.) *Ribeiro's Ceilao by P. E. Peiris*.

9

The Portuguese in Jaffna

It was not till the year 1617, that they took forcible possession of Jaffna, and having deposed the last sovereign of the Malabar dynasty, assumed the direct Government of the country. Jaffna had long been coveted by them, less from any capabilities which it presented for extending their commerce than for the security it gave to their settlements in the richer districts of the South; and apparently for the opportunity which it presented of displaying their missionary zeal in a region insusceptible of political resistance. Their first attempts to reduce this part of the Island had been made in 1544, when an expedition fitted out to plunder the Hindu temples on the south coast of the Dekkan, summoned the chief of the peninsula either to submit and become tributary to Portugal, or to prepare to encounter the marauding fleet. He chose the former alternative and agreed to pay 4000 ducats yearly. In the same year such numbers of the inhabitants of Mannar embraced christianity at the hands of the Roman Catholic Missionaries under the direction of St. Francis Xavier that the Raja of Jaffnapattam sought to exterminate apostacy by the slaughter of six hundred of the new converts. The heresy, however, reached his own palace, his eldest son embraced the new faith, and was put to death in consequence, and the second fled to Goa to escape his father's resentment..... *History of Ceylon, by Sir Emerson Tennent.*

Till the advent of Europeans, Jaffna including Wannarponne and Nallur, was almost uninterruptedly the Metropolis of a Tamil Kingdom varying in extent. The Portuguese found it the seat of Government for all Pihiti—(the Northern division of the Island, was anciently denominated Pihiti or the Rajaratta.) Its Rajah was compelled to pay them tribute from 1544 to 1617, when they took it into their own hands: the last of their strong-hold it was yielded by capitulation to the Dutch in 1658, the terms being that its ecclesiastics should depart to the Coromandel coast, and 'its garrison return to Europe.—*Hindu Pastors by the Rev. E. J. Robinson, Late Wesleyan Missionary in Ceylon, 1867.*

10

The Dutch in Jaffna

Not contented with the victory they had already obtained, the Dutch pursued the Portuguese to Jaffnapattam, thereby violating the articles of the capitulation; and after a siege of four months, it was surrendered, and the inhabitants made prisoners of war. The Portuguese Historian vituperates most bitterly the indignities offered to his nation by the Dutch—houses pillaged, plantations destroyed, wives dishonoured and daughters ravished, are amongst the crimes that he attributes to the Dutch Conquerors. *"Ceylon and the Cingalese" by Henry Charles Sirr,* M. A.

11

Portuguese churches and schools in Jaffna

The whole extent of the peninsula was brought by the Portuguese under the authority of the Church. It was divided into parishes, each of which was provided with a chapel and school-house, and where required a glebe for the residence of the Priest who was to officiate. The ruins of these ecclesiastical edifices, even at the present day, attest the care and expenditure which must have been applied to their construction. In Jaffna itself they had a church and college of Jesuits at the west end of the town; a church and convent of Dominicans on the East, besides a convent of St. Francis. Between forty and fifty Priests resided then in Jaffna. In short, there is sufficient evidence extant connected with this province of Ceylon, to justify the assertion that within a very few years of its occupation by the Portuguese, almost the entire population of the Jaffna Peninsula, including even the Brahmins themselves, had abjured idolatry and submitted to the ceremony of Baptism.—*Christianity in Ceylon, by Sir J. E. Tennent.*

12

Conspiracy.

"Shortly after the conquest our army removed to the coast of Coromandal in order to overwin Nagapattam, but, Jaffnapattam was provided with a few soldiers only, and of these, almost the greater part were Portuguese, who forgetting their allegiance to the king of Portugal, had put themselves under the obedience of the noble Company. It must also be noted that there were in the castle a large number of prisoners of war."

"All these gathered together and made a conspiracy with the natives even not without the knowledge of Rajasinghe..... The leader of this impious conspiracy was a native of Mannar, together with a Don Louis Poothatamby and five Portuguese. *Baldaeus*.

13

Religious Intolerance of the Dutch.

The same fury against the Church of Rome continued at all times to inspire the policy of the Dutch in Ceylon. In 1658 a proclamation was issued, forbidding—on pain of death—the harbouring or concealing of Roman Catholic Priests. In 1715 a proclamation was issued, forbidding public assemblies or private conventicles of the Roman Catholics, under heavy fines. Notwithstanding every precaution, however, the Roman Catholic religion retained its influence and was adhered to by large bodies of the natives, both Singhalese and Tamils, whom neither corruption nor coercion could induce to abjure it. No native could aspire to the rank of Modaliyar, or be permitted to farm land or hold office under government, unless he became a Protestant. Roman Catholic marriages were heavily taxed, their celebration by a Roman Catholic Priest was at last absolutely prohibited and declared void. Their burial was prohibited in cemetries of their own and extravagant fees were exacted on their interment in those attached to the Protestant Churches. Roman Catholics were declared equally with heathens to be ineligible to office. Freedom was conferred upon all children born of slaves who were Protestants, whilst those of Catholic parents were condemned to perpetual servitude. In the Peninsula of Jaffna they took possession of the Roman Catholic churches:- *"Christianity in Ceylon", by Sir J. E. Tennent.*

14

Point Pedro

Point Pedro, a large village and parish of Jaffna, in the province of Wadamarachy, situated at the Northern extremity of the Island..... Here was formerly a handsome church built by the Dutch, and when Baldaeus visited it in 1661, numbered 300 auditors, besides 1000 children, who were taught in the school attached to it; but it has lately been demolished, and the Hindu religion has regained its predominancy. The Wesleyan Missionaries have however formed an establishment and erected a chapel, and the Roman Catholics too have their place of worship at Point Pedro. In a war between the Dutch and English, the former built a fort here, but scarcely a vestige of it remains at present. Baldaeus mentions a smart engagement having taken place between the Dutch and the Portuguese, and that during the siege of Jaffnapattam, the latter expected to land their succours at this place, but were frustrated in the attempt.— *The Ceylon Gazetteer by Simon Casie Chitty.*

15

Batticotta Dutch Church

Laurens Pyl, who was Governor of Ceylon from 3rd December, 1680, to 10th January, 1693, had been Commandeur of Jaffnapattam before that. It was on his way to Colombo to assume the Government that Knox was entertained by him at Mannar and afterwards accompanied him to Colombo. There is a stone inscription on the Baticotta Church, now used by the American Mission, with Commandeur Pyl's name as its founder:—*Doen Maken Door Den Heer Commandeur Lourens Pyl Anno 1678.*

Caused to be built by Commandeur Lourens Pyl, 1678.

In the Jaffna Church there is also a tombstone marking the grave of a son of his who died in 1679— *Report on the Dutch Records by R. G. Anthonisz, Government Archivist.*

16

Rev. Fr. Joseph Vaz

Father Joseph Vaz, a Goanese priest arrived at Jaffna in 1687, and assuming the garb of a mendicant secretly went about preaching at Chillalai and the neighbouring villages. In A. D. 1696 he was appointed Vicar-General of Jaffna and was joined by several other priests of his order from Goa; and thus they took the spiritual charge of, and ministered to, the Catholics. In 1690 the Catholics invited Father Joseph Vaz from Chillalai to celebrate the Christmas midnight Mass in the town, and while they were secretly assembled for the purpose at the house of one Bowdewyn (a man noted for his zeal in the cause of religion) and were engaged in the recitation of the Rosary awaiting the arrival of the priest, a body of Dutch soldiers rushed in and made captives of about 300 Catholics. Eight of the boldest among them were severely scourged upon the order of the Dutch officer. One of them Pedro, by name, breathed his last, boldly confessing the truth and exhorting the rest to fearlessly undergo the punishment inflicted on them. The rest of the number were chained and condemned to penal servitude for life.—*Centenary Sketch of the Jaffna Cathedral.*

17

"From Kandy, where they had been alternately invited and proscribed by the Kings, the Roman Catholic Priests made their way into the low country, visiting in secret their scattered flocks, and administering the Sacraments in spite of the plakaats and prohibitions of the Government. Among the most distinguished of those preachers was Joseph Vaz of the Oratory of St. Philip Neri, at Goa, whose adventurous journeys and imprisonments, and his extraordinary zeal in the service of his Church, have obtained for his memory among the Roman Catholics of Ceylon, a veneration little short of that accorded to St. Francis Xavier in India. He prosecuted his labours with such success, that in an incredibly short time he had re-established the Catholic Communion in its former strong-holds in Jaffna and Mannar, extended its influence in the maritime provinces, and added to the Church upwards of thirty thousand converts from the heathen. He died at Kandy in 1711.—*Sir Emerson Tennent.*

I8

Thesawalamai

From time immemorial, the Tamil inhabitants of the Province of Jaffna had their Civil intercourses and rites determined by a traditional "Country-Law" known among the people by the name of *Thesawalamai* or "Customs of the Country":—Under the Portuguese Governor Don Philip Mascarenhas, it received some alterations; and it is probable that in course of time, it was further altered. In the year 1707, a compilation of these customs was made by Claas Isaaksz by direction of the then Dutch Governor, Cornelis Joan Simons, which compilation having been revised, translated into Tamil, and declared correct by a body of 12 Moodaliars specially appointed for that purpose, was subsequently confirmed by and published under the authority of the said Governor, and "Authenticated copies" thereof were sent to the Civil Courts for their guidance. (4th June 1707). In Regulation 18 of 1806 the "Thesawalamai" or customs of the Malabar inhabitants of the Province of Jaffna, as collected by order of Governor Simons in 1707, were declared to be "in full force."—*The Rev Ch. Bonjean, O. M. I.*

The translations were returned by the Mudaliyars with the following observations:—

We, the undersigned twelve Mudaliyars, have received from the Commandeur the Malabar Laws and Customs composed by the Dessave, Mr. Claas Isaaksz, in order to be perused and revised by us, and afterwards to state our opinion whether or not the same agrees with such laws and customs as are in use at this place.

We were also desired to confirm the translation of the Malabar Laws and Customs with our signatures, should we agree to the correctness of the same.

We, Don Philip Villaivarasa Mudaliyar, Don Anthony Narayanan, Don Vaz Mudaliyar, Don Francisco Arulampala Mudaliyar, Don Juan Caytheruperanatha Mudaliyar, Don Joan Chantirasekara Mana Mudaliyar, Don Martinho Manappuli Mudaliyar, Don Francisco Wanniyarasa Mudaliyar, Don Joan Chayampunata Mudaliyar, Don Joan Chatukavala Chenatiraya Mudaliyar, Don Louwys Putar, and Don Francisco Rasarattina Mudaliyar are the persons who have perused and revised the translation of the Malabar Laws and Customs, in consequence whereof we confirm the same with our signatures.

19

Appointment of Parpattiagara

I, Alexander Wood, Commissioner of Revenue, by virtue of Powers to that effect granted to me by His Excellency the Governor, do hereby nominate and appoint you, Erroomaravoo-yanda Mana Mudaliyar, Velale of Calapoomi, to be Parpattiagara of the village of Calapoomi, in the parish of Carativoe within the District of Jaffnapattam until further orders. All inferior Headmen and others under you in the above situation are hereby ordered and directed to acknowledge and obey you, the said Erroomaravooyanda

Mana Mudaliyar as Parpattiagara accordingly. Given under my hand at Colombo, this 1st day of February, 1811.

A. Wood.

20

By virtue of Powers in me vested by His Excellency the Governor, I do hereby confer on you, Mana Mudaliyar Ehamparam, Velale, the appointment of Parpattiagara of Calapoomi in Carative, to hold and to execute the duties of the said office under the orders of the British Government during pleasure.

Given at Condachy the eighteenth day of March 1829.

Robert Boyd.

21

Fr. Gonzalves.

Father Jacome Gonzalves of the order of St. Philip Neri arriving in Ceylon in 1703, worked till 1742—the year of his death. He was Superior General of the order and Vicar General of the Island. He was assisted by Fr. Peter Fenous in converting the Vedas. He was the author of several devotional works in Tamil —the most popular of them being his nine Sermons on the Passion of our Divine Lord—a work, which for beauty of style, simplicity of language and for the depth of devotional feelings it excites, has seldom been equalled by any similar work of its kind·

22

Father Nobili.

The Jesuit Mission to the Madras coast dates from 1606, and is associated with the names of Robert de Nobili (its founder, who died 1656), John de Britto (killed in Madura 1693), Beschi, the great scholar (who died about 1742) and other illustrious Jesuits, chiefly Portuguese.—*The Indian Empire by W. W. Hunter, C. S. I. C. I.E. L. L. D.*

Fr. Robert de Nobili was a great scholar. His attainments in Sanscrit and Tamil were extensive. He is regarded as the Father of Tamil Prose.

23

Father Caldeiro beheaded.

In Jaffna eleven Portuguese, suspected of conspiracy, were hanged and quartered, and the Jesuit Father Caldeiro beheaded for not revealing the conspiracy.—*History of Ceylon for the use of Schools, by an. Oblate Missionary of Jaffna.*

24

St. Francis Xavier visits Mannar and Kandy.

In 1545, St. Francis came to Mannar, and by his prayers, obtained the cessation of an epidemic which caused 100 deaths daily. He wished to visit Jaffna also, but he was not able to effect his design till three years later......

In 1548, Francis Xavier went to Kandy without an escort, and such was the honor in which he was held, that the Rajah received him with great respect and veneration. Many conversions took place at Kandy during his stay there. The saint also visited Jaffna, persuaded the king to cease his persecutions, and even to enter into an alliance with Portugal.—*Ibid.*

25

Floris Blom.

Floris Blom, Commandeur of Jaffnapattam, 1689—1694. He had previously served in other posts at Colombo and elsewhere. He died at Jaffna on 3rd July, 1694, and was buried in the church, where his tombstone is still preserved. His wife, Susanna Serringiers, predeceased him on 12th February, 1693, and was also buried in the church.—*Report on the Dutch Records by R. G. Anthonisz.*

26

Rev. Schwartz.

It was the writer's privilege in his school days to worship at St. Peter's Church, Tanjore, India, where Schwartz lies buried.It may not be a matter of common knowledge, that Schwartz did visit Ceylon in 1760 at the request of some Christians in Colombo and Jaffna "who were desirous of enjoying more spiritual instruction and edification."—*A Centenary Record of St. Thomas' Church, Colombo.*

27

Zwaardecroon's Memoirs.

Among the Memoirs of the Commandeur's and Dissaves, I would particularly refer to the exhaustive and valuable work of Commandeur Zwaardecroon of Jaffnapattam in 1697, a standard authority on matters relating to the Northern possessions of the Dutch East India Company in Ceylon, to which frequent allusion is made by subsequent Governors and Commandeurs. Other Commandeurs who have made important contributions to this series have been Commandeur Floris Blom of Jaffnapattam in 1690; Commandeur Jacob de Jong of Galle, in 1748; Commandeur Anthony Mooyaart of Jaffnapattam, in 1762; and Commandeur Arnoldus de Ly of Galle, in 1783; while many of the Dissaves of Matara have also, from time to time, recorded in the Memoirs left by them, nformation of great interest and value touching that part of the

Island.....*Report on the Dutch Records by R. G. Anthonisz, Govt: Archivist.*

Hendrick Zwaardecroon was Commandeur of Jaffnapattam from 1694 to 1697. In the latter year he went as Commissioner to the coast of Malabar, and for a few months previous to the arrival of Governor Gerrit de Heere, appears to have administered the Government of Ceylon.—*Ibid.*

28

Thombus.

If small things might be compared with great, it should be said that the Thombu was the Doomsday Book made by the Dutch of the lands in the thirty-two Parishes of the Jaffna District, on lines somewhat similar to the survey undertaken by William the Conqueror of all the lands in England. This book or register containing particulars as to the names of the lands, of their owners and of the gotras or castes to which they belonged, was in charge of a special officer of the Jaffna Kachcheri; while copies thereof, for the different parishes, were entrusted to the Udaiyars, who granted extracts from these copies, called schedules for such lands as their owners intended to sell or mortgage or otty or donate, certifying, after due publication of such intention, that there was no objection raised to such sale or mortgage or otty or donation. The granting of schedules having led to provoking delays and exactions, on the part of the Udaiyars, the first Ordinance passed in the year 1842, prescribed the fees to be legally claimed by them. The Thombu, long recognized as an effective check on fradulent transactions affecting lands, was, however, practically superseded by the system of Land Registration introduced in 1864; and its death-knell, frequently suggested by the decisions of the Supreme Court, was finally rung by the passing of Ordinance No. 4 of 1895.—*J. A. T.*

29

Fr. Beschi.

Father Constantine Beschi, better known here as Veeramamunivar, landed in India as a young Italian Jesuit Missionary in the year 1700;.....Fr. Beschi was a great literary genius and a perfect Tamil scholar endowed with poetical gifts of a high order. The output of his pen is almost stupendous. He published no less than 23 works in his life time.—*Madras Catholic Watchman.*

The Tamil writers of the 18th and 19th centuries are classified as modern. The honours of this period are divided between a pious Sivite and the Italian Jesuit, Beschi. This missionary of genius and learning not only wrote Tamil prose of the highest excellence, but he composed a great religious epic in classical Tamil, which has won for him a conspicuous rank among Dravidian poets. His work, the Tembavani, gives a Tamil adaptation of the narrative and even of the Geography of the Bible suited to the Hindu taste of the 18th century,—*The Indian Empire, by W. W. Hunter, C. S. I., C. I. E., L. L. D.*

30

Jacob de Jong (Jr.)

Jacob de Jong was Commandeur of Galle from 1742 to 1748, then Commandeur of Jaffnapattam from 1748 to 1763. He used to be sometimes referred to as "Jacob de Jong, junior," to distinguish him from his father Jacob de Jong, who was also at one time (1722-1723) Commandeur of Jaffnapattam. There are tombstones in the Dutch Churches at Galle and Jaffna bearing epitaphs of three of his wives. When Governor Vreelandt died on 26th February, 1752, he had to come down to Colombo and administer the Government for seven months.—*Report on the Dutch Records, by R. G. Anthonisz. Government Archivist.*

31

Philip de Melho

நாமம் பிறபாஷை நாமமாய்த்தொனிப்பினும் சாதியாசாரத்தால் இவர் சுத்ததமிழன். சமயாசாரத்தாற் கிறிஸ்தவன். இவர் கி. பி. 1723 ம் ௵ சித்திரை மீ 27 ந் திகதி கொழும்பு இராசதானியிற் றானே ஜெனனஞ்செய்து தலைத்தனத்தவரால் 1705 ம் ௵ ஸ்தாபிக்கப்பட்ட கலாசாலையிலே, எபிரேயு, கிரேக், லத்தின், ஒலாந்தா, போர்த்துக்கீஸ், தமிழ் என்னும் ஆறுபாஷைகளையுங் கற்றுத்தேற்ற முற்று, இவற்றிற்கு மேலதிகமாக வேதசாஸ்திரமுங்கற்று அதிலே மிக்க பாண்டித்தியரானூர்.

ஆசாரி அபிஷேகம் பெறுவதன்முன்னரே இவர்சத்தியவேதாகமத்தைத்தமிழிலே மொழிபெயர்க்க ஆரம்பித்திருந்தார். 1753 ம் ௵ இவர் வடமராட்சிக்குருவாய் நியோகிக்கப்பட்டு யாழ்ப்பாணம் வந்தார். 1759 ம் ௵ புதிய ஏற்பாடு முழுவதும் இலங்கையில் அச்சிடப்பட்டது. இதைமாத்திரமல்ல பழைய ஏற்பாட்டின் சிலபாகங்களையும் மொழிபெயர்த்தார். மண்டலபுருடர்செய்த சூடாமணிநிகண்டு 2 ம் தொகுதிக்கு அனுபந்தமாக இருபது உவமைப்பாட்டுகளைப் பாடிச் சேர்த்தனர். இவை பெல்லோபாதிரியாராற் செய்யப்பட்ட உவமைப் பாட்டுகள் என்றபெயரோடு மானிப்பாயில் அச்சடிக்கப்பட்ட நிகண்டுடன் சேர்ந்திருக்கின்றன. பன்னிரண்டாவது தொகுதியோடு நூறு பாட்டும் பின்னும்பல தொகுதிகளோடு வேறுசிலவும் பாடிச்சேர்த்தனர். 1790 ம் ௵ ஆவணி மீ 10 ந் திகதி இப்பண்டிதர் சமாதியை அடைந்தார். இறக்கும்போது இவருக்கு வயசு அறுபத்தேழு.—பா. ச. தீ.

32

Appointment of the Dutch Company's Physician

"Whereas by the death of the First Physician of the Jaffna Commandements, Don Joan Candappen Ilenge Kandela Modliaar, of the Maddappally Caste, his post has become vacant, we therefore, considering the urgent prayer of Poelogisinga Modliaar Philippoe Comarewelen, Welala of Tillepalle, and in view of his having on various occasions proved himself one of the ablest physicians among the natives there, deem it desirable and proper to appoint him, as the company's First Native Physician for the commandements of Jaffnapattam, as we do appoint him by these presents, with the monthly salary of one rix-dollar besides the services of four Coolies free of oelie * duty.

"Wherefore all whom it may concern are commanded to regard and respect, as it behoves them, him as such.--Colombo, 29th September, 1756.—*Report on the Dutch Records by R G. Anthonisz. Govt. Archivist.*

33

Appointment of the Dutch Company's Broker

Don Philipoe Chitambela Mudaliyar, of the Welala Caste, resident of Wannarponne within the jurisdiction of the Commandements of Jaffnapattam, is by these presents, as being one of the most respectable, influential, and able of the natives there, in the expectation that he would watch the Company's interests to the best of his ability, appointed the Company's Broker, in order to treat with the expected Elephant traders at the said Commandements, and to dispose of these animals to the profit of the Honourable Company; and we allow him twelve men free from oelie service, with the further permission to wear on his head a turban which he will not be obliged to take off anywhere, as well as to use and allow himself to be conveyed in a palanquin with a bent bamboo by Malabaars of the so-called Tandige Class, and above all, to have carried in state over him an umbrella. Wherefore all whom it may concern are enjoined to regard him as the Company's Broker, and in testimony thereof these presents are granted to him under our hand and the seal of the Honourable Company.--Colombo, 26th June, 1758.... *Report on the Dutch Records, by R. G. Anthonisz, Government Archivist.*

---

* Oeli is probably from the Tamil "Ulujam," corrupted into oelian. Having originally meant the obligation of a slave to his master, it came in Dutch times to mean compulsory service of a menial character which certain inferior classes were required to render.

34

Appointment of the Dutch Cannekappillai

Whereas Don Manual Rasakarie Mana Modliaar, first Cannekappel of the Gate of the Opperhoofd (Chief Govt. Officer) of Mannar, in consequence of advanced age and infirmity of body, is no longer able to perform his said duties in a proper manner, we therefore have considered it desirable to relieve the said Don Manual Rasakarie Mana Modliaar of the same, and reflecting on the good qualities and the urgent application of his son-in-law, the Welala Welayren Joan Ramenaden, residing at Manipay in the Jaffna Commandements, deem it proper to appoint him the said Welayren Joan Ramenaden as first Cannekappel of the Gate of the Opperhoofd of Mannar, in the place of the said Don Manual Rasakarie Mana Modliaar, as we do appoint him by these presents, with the title of Don Joan Rasakarie Ritnasinga Modliaar, with the allowance of six coolies besides the pay and dignity belonging to his office.

"Wherefore one and all whom it may concern are commanded by virtue of this open Act granted to him Don Joan Rasakarie Ritnasinga Modliaar under our hand and the seal of the Honourable Company, to regard him as first Cannekappel of the Gate of the Opperhoofd of Mannar.—Colombo, 10th August, 1761...... *Report on the Dutch Records by R. G. Anthonisz, Govt. Archivist.*

35

Anthony Mooyaart

Anthony Mooyaart, Commandeur of Jaffnapattam from 1763 to 1766, was the son of Nicholas Mooyaart and the grand son of Anthony Mooyaart of Amsterdam, who came and settled in Ceyin, 1662. He entered the Company's Service in 1712 and rose step by step to the Commandeur-ship. On the death of Baron Van Eck he was called upon, as the next in rank, to administer the Government of Ceylon during a very critical time (viz., during the hostilities with Kandy) until the arrival of Governor Falck.—*Report on the Dutch Records by R. G. Anthonisz.*

36

Pearl Fisheries

In the year 1745, the estimate of the native chiefs for the farming out of the Fishery, viz., 600 divers working 36 days each, was founded on the inspection of the Chiwela, the South side of the large bank, the Aripo, and the Bengal banks, by 16 days diving on the first, 12 days on the second, 4 on the third, and 4 on the fifth bank, respectively. During the next year, 1746, no such decrease of oysters occurred on the inspection of the banks as the divers had found during their lease of 30 days. In a conversation which I had with Joan de Kroes Patseko, the Mannar Addeppanaar over the Parawas, and Aresenileitte Mudaliyar of Carreoer under Jaffnapattam, I was told, on questioning them, that during the lease of 30 days in 1746 nearly 8 days were spent in diving for oysters on the front reef of the Chiwele banks situated right opposite Moderganemo, at a depth of 6 fathoms of water, which the year before had not been discovered at all. The statement of these two Native Chiefs seems to me acceptable.—*Report on the Dutch Records by R. G. Anthonisz, Government Archivist.*

37

Dutch Mint

The first regular Mint of the Ceylon Government (Dutch) was established about the middle of the 18th Centuary at Tuticorin. In 1781 owing to the war with England, the Mint was transferred to Colombo and the issue of Ceylon rupees began in 1784. The Colombo Mint was situated at the Bankshall near Kayman's Gate..... *Lecture on Numismatics by Mr. H. W. Codrington, C. C. S., read before the members of the Ceylon Branch of the Royal Asiatic Society.*

38

Cornelis Simons

Cornelis Joan Simons, Governor of Ceylon from 11th May, 1703 to 22nd Dec., 1707, was one of the most scholarly rulers of Ceylon under the Dutch. He was a Doctor of Laws, and it was at his instance that the Tamil Code of laws, the Thesawalamai, was digested and rendered into Dutch by the Dissave Claas Isaacsz.... *Report on the Dutch Records by R. G. Anthonisz, Government Archivist.*

39

Kanapathy Ayer

இப்புலவர் யாழ்ப்பாணம் வட்டுக்கோட்டையில் வசித்த ஓர் பிராமணர். தமது சுற்றத்தவருள் ஒருவராகிய சண்முக ஐயர் என்பவர் சிலதருக்கள் கீர்த்தனைகளோடே தொடங்கியும் நிறைவேற்றச் சக்தியற்றுவிட்டிருந்த சுந்தரிநாடகத்தை வாளபிமன்னாடகம் என்று மாற்றி, எவரும் வியக்கப்பாடி முடித்தனர். இந்நாடகம் நாட்டுமொழி நியாயிலும் மிகுபளப்பளப்பும் மணமணப்புங்கொண்டது. இஃதன்றி, வயித்திலிங்கக்குறவஞ்சி, மலையகந்தினி நாடகம், அலங்காரரூபநாட

கம், அதிருபவதிநாடகம் என்பவைகளோடு, வட்டுக்கோர்ப்பிட்டி வயத்பத்திரகாளியேசிற்பதிகமும் ஊஞ்சற் பிரபந்தமும், பரித்தித்துறைக்கணேசர் பேரில் வெண்பா, ஆசிரியம், கலி, வஞ்சி, மருள் என்னும் பாவிகற்பம் பெற்ற நூறுகவிதைகளும்பாடினர். பிரமசாரி விரதம் பூண்ட இவர் இற்றைக்கு நூறுவருடங்களின் முன் எழுபத்தைந்து வயதிலே தேகவியோகமாயினர்...... பா. ச. நீ.

40

St. Mary's Church Jaffna

A. D. 1789. In this year was laid the foundation of St. Mary's Church (now the Jaffna Cathedral). Prior to that the Catholics assembled for worship in a thatched house of wattle and daub under a large tamarind tree which then stood at the present entrance to the Cathedral by the big door. Those who gifted lands for the church were the ancestors of the present celebrants of the Tenth and the Eleventh Novenas of the Cathedral Feast viz, the August Festival of the Assumption. Of the said donors of lands, may be mentioned the names of Tomaipillai Anthonipillai, Mariapillai, wife of Arasunilayitta Mudaliyar, Swampulle Susepulle, Philip Nicholapillai, and Bastiampulle Nallatamby Mudaliyar and others. The contributions in money for the purchase of lands were mostly made by the ancestors of the present celebrants of the Twelfth and Thirteenth Novenas. Some of them surrendered to the Church for sale the very lands they were living in. The descendants of the Portuguese who celebrate the Fourteenth Novena of the August Festival were then, as they are now, distinguished for their zeal in contributing readily towards all such undertakings.—*Centenary Sketch of the Jaffna Cathedral.*

41

Don Nicholas Tisseveerasinghe Mudaliyar appointed Thombo-holder.

In 1790 Don Nicholas entered the service of the Dutch Government, as a volunteer assisting the Thombo-holder or keeper of the Dutch Records in the Kachcheri of Jaffna. He made a most careful study of the Dutch Records and gave, in the discharge of the duties assigned to him, so much satisfaction to his immediate superior, that on his retirement in 1798, when the English had already gained a footing in Ceylon, he was appointed Thombo-holder, as the most competent Tamil and Dutch scholar available and as the fittest of the candidates aspiring to the post.—*Biographical Sketch of Don Nicholas Tisseveerasinghe Mudaliyar.*

42

Kulangkai Tampiran

இவர் காஞ்சிபுரத்திற் பிறந்த மகாவித்துவான். பதிசாஸ்திரம் அனைத்துங்கடறத்தேறிய கலைஞானி. தென்மொழியாகிய தமிழிலன்றி வடமொழியாகிய ஆரியத்திலும் பாண்டித்தியம்பெற்ற இவர் யாழ்ப்பாணம்வர, இங்கே வண்ணார்பண்ணையிலே வைத்தியலிங்கச் செட்டியார் என்னும் வணிகர் திலகர் இவர்க்கு நண்பராய் இவரைப் பரிபாலித்துவந்தனர். இவர் நல்ல இலக்கணக் களஞ்சியமாகையாற் பவணந்திமுனிவர் செய்த நன்னூலுக்கு வியாக்கியானம் எழுதினது மாத்திரமல்லாது, பற்பலபுலமைகளையும் இயற்றினார். ஞானநூல் வல்லவராதலால் எம்மதத்துக்குஞ் சம்மதமான நடையினராகி யோசேப்புப்புராணம் என்னுங் காவியத்தை இருபத்தொரு காண்டத்தில் ஆயிரத்திருபத்துமூன்று விருத்தத்திற்பாடித்தமது நேசராகிய மெல்லோப்பாதிரியாருக்கு அதைப்பிரதிட்டை செய்தனர். இப்புராணமன்றி கல்லைக் கலிவெண்பா, கூழங்கையர் வண்ணம் ஆதியாம்பல பாடல்களை இவர்பாடி இருக்கின்றார். பிற்காலத்திலே சண்டிக்குளிக்கோவிற்பற்றைச் சார்ந்த சிவியாதெரு இவர்க்கு உறைவிடமாய் இருந்தது. அதி விருத்தாப்பிய வயதில் 1795ம் ஆண்டு இவரது மரணசம்பவம் நடந்தது. பா. ச. தீ.

43

Old Jaffna Town

Some outline of Don Nicholas Tisseveerasinghe Mudaliyar's residence and the neighbourhood in which he moved about is here attempted for the information of the young generation. At the time of his birth, the original Portuguese town, as improved by the Dutch, was a comparatively small square, crossed by roads at right angles, and bounded on the North by Chapel Street, West by the Esplanade, South by the Beach Road and East by the Third Cross Street. To the North of this square, lay the tank called Taarakulam and fields, to the North-East Manjetkaraichankulam and Teverikulam with the adjoining fields, to the South, Vannankulam and to the South East, the village of Karayoor proper. The houses to the North and South of this square, belong to the latter Dutch and early English periods.

Tisseveerasinghe Mudaliyar lived in an old fashioned, stone-built, four-sided, tiled house, with an open yard in the centre, letting in plenty of light. This house still remains intact adjoining Chapel Street or rather its Eastern extension, as opened by Mr. Dyke some years after the death of the Mudaliyar. Barring the Main Street starting from the Fort to the Kachcheri and beyond as far as Matale, some of the roads branching off on either side, such as Martyn's Road, the Odaikarai Road, David's Road and other Roads (the Rasantotam Road excepted) are of recent construction. There was a large number of lanes in the neighbourhood or outskirts of the town occupied by respectable natives. On a lane (now Martyn's Road) stood the old house of Kuru. kulum used in the early days of British rule as the Civil Engineer's Office, but demolished after the death of its last tenent and owner, Tisseveerasinghe Mudaliyar Abraham. Most of these lanes have disappeared and this quarter is well roaded, with a large number of good houses, though the drainage continues to be as defective as ever.

The buildings of the Wesleyan Mission and of the F. N. S. Hospital were erected during the latter half of the Mudaliyars's life, on sites which had been farms or fields. In the erection of an earlier and more important building, St. Mary's Cathedral, the Mudaliyar's father-in-law, Tomaipillai Anthonipillai, took an active part, under the direction of the Goanese priest, Leonardo Rebeiro. The tanks afore-mentioned remained, as such, for years after the Mudaliyar's death. Taarakulam quarter though still low and ill drained, is now thickly populated with houses risen or rising on every side. Manjetkaraichankulam forms the North-west portion of the walled premises of the Jaffna Convent. Vannankulam, opposite to the Jaffna Convent, filled up by the late Mr. Russell and called after him "Russell's Square" is crossed by the railway siding to the Customs, and now used as the Firewood Depot. Teverikulam, lying in the midst of the paddy fields between Rasantotam road and Mooyaart's garden (now St. Martin's Ecclesiastical Seminary) was deepened by the Catholic Mission, the earth removed being used in filling up Manjetkaraichankulam; and it remains the only tank near the town, for washing clothes, horses and cattle; but the fields adjoining have been encroached upon, for dwelling purposes. Similar encroachments for the same purpose, while far advanced in the Passiyoor, Muthalaikulam, and Maravakulam fields, have already begun in the Moondukulam fields adjoining St. Mary's Cathedral. These fields and those at Colomboturai, with most of the gardens and plantations in their vicinity, were the property of Tisseveerasinghe Mudaliyar and his contemporaries, so much so that it was the proud boast of some of them that they could get to their fields through their own lands. More than half of these fields and gardens have changed hands, during the last fifty years. A stone-built, four-sided, tiled house was the best form of the rich or respectable native habitation. Similar houses of mud and wattle, covered with cocoanut or palmirah olas and built by the middle classes, were numerous.

Houses or rather huts of one or two rooms of mud or thatch were still more numerous. Excepting the two houses in Mooyaart's Garden and Stewart's Garden, now demolished, there stood no house of any pretension to modern architecture on the Main Street (from St. James Church to the Kachcheri) a literally sandy track till the inauguration in 1833 of a local Public Works Department. The first upstair house on this street and still the only one on this section, was erected by Aseerwatha Mudaliyar in 1850.—*Biographical Sketch of Don Nicholas Tisseveerasinghe Mudaliyar.*

44

Present Town of Jaffna

Jaffna is the queen city of the North, the "Northern Capital" of Ceylon, where dwell a splendid people, cultured, wealthy and industrious. Jaffna is a well-kept and a clean city, and in its centre are to be found many relics of the old Dutch architecture.

Thanks to the work of the P. W. D. and its efficient officials, the old Dutch Church, and many other worthy buildings of the past are being rehabilitated and restored, so that the present generation may enjoy and use them, and hand them on to their children with veneration.

The picturesque clock-tower is famous for its faithfulness in marking the hours by which Jaffna and her people work and play.—*Amicus, Special Edition, April 17th, 1914.*

45

The Fort and Fort Church

The old Fort at Jaffna is probably the finest specimen of its kind in Ceylon. Although the Portuguese erected something of a fort on the shores of the lagoon, it was the Dutch, who in fact built this compact and spacious structure which has been well preserved by the British Government. Here we see moat, draw-bridge, escarpment, bastions, embrasures, corner towers etc, etc—all in excellent preservation, the dark grey stone harmonising beautifully with the green turf around and within. From the top of the ramparts on the landward side a fine view is obtained over the green esplanade which divides the Fort from the town. On one of the bastions an old banyan tree runs riot with endless ramifications. In the interior is a grassy court-yard with an old sun-dial in the centre and surrounded by several Dutch houses with spacious verandas, among which King's house is the most notable, having a series of four or five magnificient rooms with tremendously thick walls. One bedroom is more like a banquetting hall in its proportions. The verandah of the house is about 70 yards long and wide in proportion.

But the chief object of interest in the Fort is the old Dutch Church built about 1730. The ground plan is in the shape of a Maltese cross, outside the church is very plain but inside it is most impressive in its vastness and height. It has a quaint pulpit and a still more quaint singing gallery with a painting of David playing on the harp. There are a few old box pews which evidently belonged to well known Dutch families including a very spacious one for the Governor. The pews are now all attached to the walls, leaving the floor quite unoccupied and in some parts paved with massive flat tomb stones each with its escutcheon and Dutch inscription and all excellently preserved. The church is rarely used for services but is a striking monument of the past. It seems to witness eloquently to the solid work of those old Hollanders. Whatever their limitations, they built for posterity as well as for their own day. There was no scamping or jerry building.—*Miss de Winton.*

46

Kumarasinghe Mudaliyar

இவர் மாதோட்டத்திலே உள்ள காவற்குளத்திலே பிறந்தவர். சமயாசாரத்தாற் கதலிக்கிறிஸ்தவர். பேர்பெற்றபுலவரும் அனுபவசாலியான ஆயுள்வேதியருமாயிருந்தார். இதனால் சனங்களுக்குள்ளே இவர்க்கு மிகச்செல்வாக்கிருந்தது. 1800ம் ஆல நோர்துதேசாதிபதி பூனைவரி ஒன்றைச்சனங்கள்மேல் ஏற்ற, அதனால் மாதோட்டப்பிரசைகள் அரசாட்சியோருக்கு விரோதமாய்க்கலிபிலி ஆரம்பித்தார்கள். இவரின்றிக்கலகம் நிகழாதெனை அரசாட்சியோர் நினைந்து இவர்பேரிற் பிராதுதொடங்கினர். அபராதியென விளங்கியதால் இவரைப்பிடித் துக்கசைபடியடிப்பிக்க இவர் உள்ளம் சார்ந்து தேவமாதாபேரிலே ஆசுகவியாய் அனேகபாடல்கள்பாடினர். பா. ச. தீ.

47

Franciscus and Morgappa

The Tamil Christians of the time were extremely fortunate in having the services of two chief Proponents or preachers of the Gospel, one of whom Gabriel Jurgen Ondaatjee was accepted as a Presbyterian Minister of the first class, the other was Manuel Morgappa, who was ordained in Holland and got the degree of Doctor of Laws and Divinity, Utretcht. He became Presbyterian Chaplain at Jaffna, his predecessor there being William Franciscus, who afterwards joined the Church of England and became a Proponent.—*A Centenary Record of Saint Thomas' Church, Colombo.*

"Proponent"—According to Sir Emerson Tennent it was "a clerical office peculiar to the Church of Holland with functions intermediate between those of a catechist or deacon of the Church of England and those of a probationer or licentiate of the Church of Scotland". The word itself is Latin and means "laying on a table" or "serving up" and refers probably to preparing the Communion table, chief amongst the other duties of this lay officer.

48

Treaty of Amiens

The definitive treaty of peace was signed at Amiens, on the 27th March, 1802. Its conditions varied in no material circumstance from the preliminaries agreed to at London nine months before. The cession of Ceylon and Trinidad to Great Britian, and the restoration of all the other conquered colonies to France and Holland, the integrity of the Ottoman dominions, and the recognition of the Republic of the Seven Islands, were provided for as in the preliminary articles.—*History of Europe by Sir Archibald Alison, Bart. F. R. S. E.*

49

Protestant Christians

In 1802 the nominal Protestant Christians amongst the Tamils of Jaffna were 360,000; in 1806, Buchanan (Revd. Claudius) who then visited Ceylon described the Protestant religion as extinct, the fine old Churches in ruins, the clergy who had once ministered in them forgotten, and but one Hindoo (evidently Tamil) Catechist in charge of the Province.—*Sir E. Tennent.*

50

Delft

The long island of Delft, called by the natives "Neduntivu," which means "Long Island" is situated 16 miles to the South West of Kayts Island, and is about 6 miles long by an average of 3 broad. It is of coral formation and perfectly flat, the northern part consisting of groves of Palmyrahs, and the Southern of "Stone-strewn plains covered with good grass and dotted with Sooriya trees." Its extent is about 11,500 acres (or 18 sqr. miles) of which 2,500 are under dry grain cultivation, 1100 under palmyrahs, and 4700 pasture land. It comprises three villages known as Delft East (Kilakku Kurichchi) Delft Centre (Nadu Kurichchi) and Delft West (Metku Kurichchi). The people possessed in 1905 four boats (Vattai), all under 8 tons under

20 Kadmarama. The chief exports are mats, Shark fins, ghee in bottles and pots, copra in bags, Pinnaddu, dried palmyrah seeds, coconuts, cotton thread, cuttle fish bones, and cattle. Delft ghee is in demand at Jaffna. The horse-breeding, under the Portuguese, gave the island a new name, Ilha das Cavalhos, Isle of Horses. Under the Portuguese, and after them under the Dutch, the whole Island was given up to it. In British times, for the first third of the 19th century, the South of the Island was reserved for horse breeding, and the end of that century saw a revival of it. but in 1906 the horse breeding establishment was finally abandoned. Extensive ruins of stables at Sarapiddi and a mile or so west of the Government Bunglaw on the North of the Island, the latter known as the "Thirty Pillars" still remain standing, gaunt among the coral stones, the prickly pear, and the scattered palmyrah trees of the plains, to show on what an extensive scale these operations were at one time carried on.

Nolan took charge of Delft in 1811 and was confirmed in his appointment as Supt. of Delft Island June 8, 1814. He was also "Sitting Magistrate and Fiscal of the Province of Delft". He retired on January 1,1826, returned to Ireland and died in 1840. He was succeeded as Superintendent and Sitting Magistrate by Robert Atherton. These posts were abolished in 1833. Nolan had a salary of £ 600 a year,—*J. P. Lewis. C. C. S.*

51

The American Board

The "American Board of Commissioners for Foreign Missions,' under whose auspices the American Mission in North Ceylon was established, was organised on the 29th of June, 1810. It originated in the long cherished desires and matured resolutions of six youngmen, at that time students in Theology, to consecrate themselves to the service of God, in preaching the Gospel of Christ in heathen lands. At that period, the subject of Foreign Missions was almost unknown to the American Churches.—*Revd. Dr. Poor's letters to His late pupils.*

52

First Am: Missionary to Ceylon

In Feb., 1813, Mr. Newell started as he supposed for Bombay but was landed, providentially, on the Island of Ceylon. He spent ten months in Colombo, constantly preaching in English to the foreigners and Eurasians and gaining a knowledge of the situation which he passed on in urgent letters to the Board. He strongly recommended establishing a mission in Ceylon, —*A. Century in Ceylon by Helen I. Root.*

53

The Wesleyan Methodist Mission, North Ceylon

The Ceylon Mission is the oldest in the East belonging to the Wesleyan Missionary Society, and owes its origin humanly speaking to the powerful advocacy and quenchless zeal of Dr. Coke. In 1813, after a lengthy debate, the British Conference was induced to sanction the proposed Mission at Ceylon, Java, and the Cape of Good Hope, and appointed seven Missionaries (two of whom were married) to accompany Dr. Coke on this new enterprise. They embarked at Portsmouth on December 30th, 1813. Two of their number, however, were destined to end their course before they landed on "India's coral strand." On February the 10th Mrs. Ault, the wife of one of the oldest missionaries, succumbed to a wasting disease. But a greater trial yet awaited the little band: on the morning of May the 2nd, Dr. Coke was discovered a lifeless corpse on the cabin floor. Apoplexy had suddenly deprived the missionary party of its leader. A greater trial could not have happened to them, for none of them had power to touch the doctor's papers, or to cash any of the bills he had brought with him. They were thus cut off from all resources, and when they landed they were not able to muster money enough to pay the usual fees of the steward, or to pay the hotel bill for their first day's dinner in Bombay. Their circumstances, however, were soon noised abroad and secured for them friends in unexpected quarters. Sir Evan Nepean, the Governor of Bombay, kindly entertained them till they were able to secure a vessel for Ceylon, and a Bombay merchant (W. T. Money) offered to advance them any sum that they might need on the credit of the Society. Sailing from Bombay on the 20th of June 1814, they arrived safely at Galle on the 29th of the same month.

On July 11th, they assembled themselves in conference to divide the load and to appoint their stations. Messrs. Lynch and Squance were sent to Jafina, Mr. Ault to Batticaloa, Mr. Erskine to Matara, and Mr. Clough remained in Galle, where he was afterwards joined by Mr. and Mrs. Harvard, who had remained a while in Bombay.

In January 1819, the missionaries met together again in Galle to hold their 3rd annual Conference. The most important resolution of this meeting was the division of Ceylon into two districts, to be designated the Singhalese and Tamil districts. The following year the Northern District was strengthened by the arrival of three young ministers, one of whom, the Revd. Joseph Roberts, was destined to make his mark in the mission both in North Ceylon and Madras, and to become widely known as an author by his work on Oriental Illustrations.

The first property purchased by the Wesleyan Mission in Jaffna was the old orphan-house and Lutheran Church on the esplanade. This building had been converted at a small expense into a school and chapel. The chapel, however, soon became too small, and Mr. Roberts resolved to build a new and larger edifice on the opposite side of the road. The new chapel was completed at a cost of £ 702, and it was dedicated to the service of God in the early part of 1823.

The returns for 1825 contain 26 schools with 795 scholars, taught by twenty-six teachers. One of these schools was a girls' school in Jaffna with forty pupils, taught by a highly respected Dutch Lady, Mrs. Schrader.

Something had also been done towards the creation of a native ministry. John Philip Sanmugam was the first Tamil Minister in connexion with the Wesleyan Missionary Society.

In 1833 the Revd. Joseph Roberts returned to England and the Revd. Peter Percival returned to Jaffna. In Calcutta, Mr. Percival had been associated with Dr. Duff, in connection with his gigantic educational operations. He had there seen the value of a Christian education as a Missionary agency. As soon therefore, as he returned to Jaffna, he began to give his attention to the schools. His first care was to establish a superior English school, which bears to this day the name he gave it, the "Jaffna Central School." Similar schools were commenced in each of the principal stations.

1835-1845. This was a period of considerable activity. In Jaffna Mr. Percival was diligently employed in strengthening, and developing his educational schemes. In 1837 a girls' boarding school was added. It commenced with six pupils. It has now become one of the largest in the Island. A training class was also formed to prepare teachers for the numerous schools. Mr. Percival next gave his attention to the training of young men for the more important work of preaching.

In the midst of this educational activity, Mr. Percival applied to the Local Government for the transfer of the old Dutch

Churches at Wannarponnai, Puttur, and Cattavelly to the Wesleyan Mission, which after due reference to the Secretary of State was successfully accomplished. Funds and materials were then gathered for the renovation or re-building of these old Churches; the Wannarponne Church was restored in 1837 at a comparatively small outlay, but the Puttur and Cattavelly Churches were so far gone to decay and ruin that the walls had to be taken down and rebuilt.

It was also a time of change. In the end of 1852, Mr. Percival, after twenty-six years service in India and Ceylon, retired from the district and was succeeded as Chairman by the Revd. R. D. Griffith, who after about three years gave place to the Revd. John Walton.

1855-1865. The whole of this period was characterized by hard and steady work. In some parts of the district, mission operations were almost suspended, month after month, on account of the ravages of cholera and small-pox.

On the return to England of Mr. Walton, in the end of 1859 Mr. Kilner became General Superintendent and Chairman of the district. One of the first things which claimed his attention was the formation of a class of converted young men to train them for the work of the ministry.

1865-1879. This period began gloomily. During the year 1866, whilst the Chairman was on a visit to England, two of the English Missionaries died and one proved unfaithful, so that at the end of that year only two missionaries remained in the field. Mr. Kilner returned to the district in the beginning of 1867, two additional young missionaries having been sent out to Jaffna a few months previously. Taking up the thread where he had dropped it on proceeding to England in 1865, Mr. Kilner threw his whole soul into the creation of a vigorous native agency, to the strengthening of all local institutions, and to the building of a healthy native Church.

In 1875 the Revd. John Kilner finally returned to England and the Revd, E. Rigg was appointed as his successor. The work continues to grow and in the matter of education especially, the mission has occupied a prominent position in Ceylon. There are now five central stations, Jaffna, Point Pedro, Trincomalee, Batticaloa, and Kalmunai. Each station (except the last, which has but recently been occupied by an English missionary) possesses a girls' boarding school, an English Central school and from a dozen to a score of vernacular schools. At Jaffna there is a training institution for male teachers, containing at present thirty five students. At Batticaloa, there is a printing establishment. which is doing its best to supply the mission with such books, as cannot elsewhere be obtained. The aggregate value of mission property in chapels, parsonages, school bungalows, printing establishments etc., at the end of 1878 was £ 24,000.—*The Rev. J. Brown's Report to the Missionary Conference, South India and Ceylon, 1879,*

54

The first American Missionary to Jaffna

Rev. E. Warren was the first to reach the field, on July, 11,1816, coming overland in a planquin, a laborious journey. The others soon joined him and they took a house in Jaffna Town. Wesleyan Missionaries from England were by this time established there, and this fact influenced the decision of the Americans to press out into the country, thickly settled and wholly unreached by Protestant Christian influences.—*A Century in Ceylon by Helen I. Root.*

55

A. M. Med. Establishment

"The History of the Medical establishment dates from the commencement of the American Mission. Two of the first company sent by the American Board of Commissioners for Foreign Missions to this Island, Rev. Messrs. Warren and Richards, had a knowledge of Medicine, and commenced at an early period, its practice among the people. Mr. Warren established a small hospital at Tellipallai as early as 1817 having received aid in its erection, and in part for sustaining it, from a few European friends in the province. Dr. Scudder arrived and entered upon his labours as a Missionary physician in 1819. In addition to his personal labours in his profession among the people, Dr. Scudder commenced the training of a few native youngmen to practise medicine in the country upon European principles. In 1833 Dr. Ward joined the mission and took charge of the Medical Department. He continued to some extent the instruction of native youth in medicine. He left the island for America early in 1847. Dr. Green became connected with the mission in October 1847 and has had charge of the establishment up to the present time."

The above is the introduction of a Paper drawn up by the Rev. Mr. Hastings and presented to Dr. Rufus Anderson and Rev. C. A. Thompson, who in 1855, came to Jaffna as the Deputation of the Prudential Committee of the American Board of Commissioners for Foreign Missions. At the time Mr. Hastings, paper was presented Dr. Green had trained several students of whom 14 were living and of them five were in Mission Service, four in Governmeut employment, two connected with the Jaffna Friend-in-Need Society's Hospital, two employed by the Planter's Association in cocoanut estates and one in independent practice in the town of Jaffna. Dr. Green's Medical School at Manipay was at the time in receipt of an annual grant of £. 50 from Government.

56

The Church Mission

At the close of the year 1817, the C. M. S. appointed four English clergymen—the Revs. Samuel Lambrick, Benjamin Ward, Robert Major, and Joseph Knight—to commence operations in the island. They left England on the 20th December, 1817, in the ship Vittoria, and arrived in Ceylon about the end of June in the following year.

It was arranged that Mr. Lambrick should be stationed at Colombo, Mr and Mrs. Major at Galle, Mr. Knight at Jaffna and Mr. and Mrs. Ward at Trincomallee.

The Rev. Joseph Knight, the first church missionary to Jaffna, commenced his work in 1818, at Nallur, a village situated at about two miles to the north-east of the town of Jaffna. Innumerable were the difficulties and bitter the opposition he had to encounter: The people considered missionaries as outcasts, and deemed it pollution to admit them to their dwellings. It was always usual for the Pundit to go to the tank—and bathe on his way home, after giving his morning lesson at the bungalow. In 1841. Chundicully, and in 1849, Copay, were taken up as seperate mission districts, at both places substantial churches have been erected as well as at Nallur.

The Nallur Girls' Boarding school, opened in 1841, is one of the most interesting and hopeful of our educational labours. Many of those who passed through the school are now heads of families.—*The Rev. W. Oakley's Report to the Missionary Conference, South India and Ceylon, 1879.*

57

Dead Chanks.

Dead chanks, according to Mr. Charles Scott, the predecessor of Mr. Dyke, were first discovered in the Jaffna lake in 1821. The annual revenue derived from this source is small; and Mr. Dyke in his dav urged that the money derived should be handed over to the local authorities for local improvements. This however, has not been done. From the records in his office, Mr. Twynam gives the Jaffna chank revenue for 50 years from 1841 to 1891, which sums up. Rs. 191,930.—*The Jaffna Catholic Guardian, 8th Oct, 1892.*

58

The Batticotta Seminary

The Batticotta Seminary was started in the year 1823. It came into being four years before the Cotta Christian Institution of which the foundation was laid by Sir Edward Barnes in 1827; eleven years before the Jaffna Central School, now the Central College, started by the Revd. Peter Percival of the Wesleyan Mission, in 1834; thirteen years before the Colombo Academy, now the Royal College; established by Sir Robert Wilmot Horton in 1836; eighteen years before the Chundikuly Seminary, now St. John's College, started by the Rev. John Talbot Johnstone of the Church Missionary Society, and the Central School Commission for the instruction of the population of Ceylon, established by Sir Colin Campbell, in 1841; twenty-six years before St. Thomas' Collegiate Institution, now St. Thomas' College, founded by Dr. Chapman, the first Anglican Bishop of Colombo, in 1849; and twenty-seven years before the Jaffna Catholic School, now St. Patrick's College, opened by Dr. Bettachini, first Bishop of Jaffna, in 1850. It was so late as 1870, during the administration of Sir Hercules Robinson, afterwards Lord Rosemead, that the Central School Commission was superseded by the present Department of Public Instruction. Sir James Emerson Tennent, the accomplished Colonial Secretary and Lieutenant-Governor of Ceylon, has the following record of his impressions of Batticotta and of its far-famed seminary.

"Batticotta, the head-quarters of the Mission, stands about six miles westward of Jaffna, in the midst of well cultivated rice farms and groves of palmirah and cocoanut palms. The whole establishment is full of interest and forms an impressive and a memorable scene—the familiar objects and arrangements of a College being combined with the remarkable appearence and unwonted costumes of the students; and the domestic buildings presenting all the peculiar characteristics of oriental life and habits. The sleeping apartments, the dining-hall and the cooking room are in purely Indian taste, but all accurately clean; and stepping out of these, the contrast was striking between them and the accustomed features of the lecture room with its astronomical clock, its orrery and transit instrument, the laboratory with its chemical materials, retorts and electro—magnetic apparatus and the museum with its arranged collection of minerals and corallines to illustrate the geology of Ceylon. But the theatre was the centre of attraction, with its benches of whiterobed students and lines of turbaned heads with upturned eager countenances, "God's image carved in ebony." The examination, which took place in our presence, was in History, Natural Philosophy, Optics and Algebra. The knowledge exhibited by the pupils was astonishing; and it is no exaggerated encomium to say that, in the extent of the course of instruction and in the success of the system for communicating it, the Collegiate Institution of Batticotta is entitled to rank with many an European University."

To the American Missionaries, then, is due the praise of being the earliest and most enterprising pioneers, during the British period, of Western education in "India's utmost isle, Taprobane."* In 1816, the year of their first coming among us, they started two native free schools for the instruction of the people of this Tamil country. In 1822 there were 42 schools with 1800 pupils maintained at a cost of £ 270, including presents, premiums and the wages of the teachers, who, instead of receiving a regular salary, as at present, were paid according to the progress of the scholars, which was determined by a monthly examination. For seven years the work of education was so sedulously and zealously carried on that the five principal stations where the Missionaries had established themselves—viz, Tellipalai, Ooduvil, Manepay, Batticotta and Panditarruppo, were provided with large Boarding schools. Not a few of the pupils in these schools had made such advancement in their studies and given such promise

* Such was the general success of the educational measures of the Hon. Mr. North, afterwards Earl of Guilford, who first administered the affairs of Ceylon as a British colony, that in 1801 the number of schools throughout the Island was 170; and his successor Sir Thomas Maitland exhibited an equal appreciation of the importance of popular instruction and an equal assiduity in its promotion. But his operations, like those of his predecesor, were unfortunately circumscribed by the embarrassed state of the colonial finances, from which, by order of the Secretary of State, no larger a sum than £ 1500 per annum was for many years appropriated to the maintenance of Native education. Christian David, the first Protestant Tamil Minister in Ceylon, relates in his antobiography that, having been appointed by Mr. North in 1800 to the superintendence of 47 schools in the peninsula of Jaffna, they were all suddenly closed by Sir Thomas Maitland in 1806, most probably in consequence of the want thus caused of the means applicable to their maintenance.

of further advancement as to warrant an attempt to place within their reach the advantages of higher education in a Central High School. According to an early American Report, which has come to hand:

"The plan of such an institution was prepared and published and, though by some thought rather large, was warmly approved by the friends of the Mission in America and generally also in India. Funds to a considerable amount were conditionally pledged in America and would have been given, had not unexpected obstacles from the local Government prevented its projectors from carrying the plan fully into effect. *

The institution was commenced in a modified form at Batticotta in 1823 by bringing together the most forward lads from the different Boarding Schools and placing them under the care of one of the missionaries, who with assistant teachers, was to devote himself principally to their instruction in literature, science and religion. The number at first received was forty-eight, who, after qualifying themselves by farther attention to some elementary subjects, entered upon a course of study both in English and Tamil, similar to that laid down in the original plan of the College."

The expenses of the Seminary were defrayed by the American Board of Commissioners for Foreign Missions, which is also called the Foreign Missionary Society of the American Congregational Churches. Most of the pupils were supported by patrons in the United States after whom they were called § and who made specific yearly donations of not less than twenty dollars for their beneficiaries.

* Sir J. E. Tennent refers to one of these obstacles as follows:- By some singular misconception on the part of the Governor, Sir Edward Barnes, the Mission was uncourteously refused the permission to use their own types; and the printer, who had actually arrived from America, was ordered, within three months, to take his departure from Ceylon. The printing presses were handed over to the Missionaries of the Church of England and for several years afterwards the liberty to use them was withheld from the Americans. This unwise decision was ultimately rescinded by Sir R. W. Horton in 1832.

§ Both at Batticotta, and at Oodooville, it is a part of the system to apply the annual contribution of some one friend of the Mission if it amount to the stipulated sum (which was £ 4 3s per annum) to the exclusive education of one individual, who, on admission, assumes, in addition to his own name, that of the distant benefactor to whom he is indebted for his presentation. Thus at Oodooville the Tamil girls each bear the Christian and surname of an American lady: and at Batticotta one of the native students was presented by a name somewhat familiar to me as Mr. William Tennent—Sir J. E. Tennent.

The term of study was six years. The course of instruction embraced the Bible, English Grammar, Arithmetic, Algebra, Negando, Nannool, English Language and Literature, Natural Philosophy, Mental Philosophy, Logic, History, Kural, Euclid, Trigonometry, Mensuration, Chemistry, the evidences of Christianity, European and Hindu Astronomy, the principles of Law, Sanskrit and English and Tamil Composition*

This course will bear favourable comparison with the course of the present day in many of the Colleges in Ceylon, which it is worthy of remark, is generally too commercial in its aims and tendencies to be either liberal or comprehensive, on the one hand, or free, on the other from the prevalent evils of injudicious forcing and hasty cramming.

The first Principal was the Rev. Daniel Poor, D. D., who was in responsible charge of the Seminary for thirteen years from 1823 to 1836. In 1833 Dr. Nathan Ward and the Rev. James Read Eckard joined the Seminary as Professors. Of the excellent work of Dr. Poor, as the first and foremost educational pioneer, the best evidence was afforded by his own pupils, of whom or rather of the more brilliant of whom, it was truly remarked that "they would not suffer by comparison with the young men of their age in any country". His resignation was accepted with a high sense of his invaluable services and in response to his earnest desire to proceed to Madura where he established and conducted a new mission, with the assistance of some of the pupils he had trained at Batticotta, such as J. S. Tappan (father of the late Messrs Chelliah and Muttiah, the well known Colombo brokers) Francis Asbury of Sandilipay (father of the late R. O. D. Asbury) Nathan Strong of Manepay, afterwards connected with the well known firm of printers, under the name and style of Ripley and Strong, Eli. F. Cooly, of Putoor (father of Mr. P. C. Chellappah, sub-Inspector of schools) and Thomas Spencer (father of Mr. L. P. Spencer B. A. of the Wesleyan Central College), When at length the springs of life began to give way and Dr. Poor returned to Jaffna to spend his last days among the people to whose welfare he had devoted his best energies, he was suddenly prostrated by the cholera of 1855; but even then he was as cheerful as ever and his dying conversation with Dr. Green has often been quoted in illustration of the flashes of his wit and humour, so playful, edifying and lively, even when he lay on the threshold of eternity. There are a few of Dr. Poor's

* The curriculum embraced all the ordinary branches of historical and classical learning and all the higher departments of mathematical and physical science—Sir J. E. Tennent.

171

pupils, still in the land of the living, who speak in terms of the highest commendation of his services as an educationalist and of his character as a philanthropist.

Dr. Poor's successor was the Rev. Henry Richard Hoisington D. D., who joined the Mission in 1834 and whose still surviving pupils— notably Mr. Samuel Merwin, a Government pensioner, now in his 84th year and the Rev. George Champion of the Church Mission, now in his 80th year—are enthusiastic in their praises of him, as the ablest scholar among the American Missionaries who have come to the Island during the last 88 years. He knew Latin, Greek and Hebrew well, and his linguistic attainments on his arrival, were already so extensive that he soon mastered the Tamil and Sanskrit languages well enough to be able to do into English, in a most creditable manner, some of the standard works in those languages on Savaism and Hindu Astronomy. His great desire was to build an observatory at Batticotta, for which he collected the necessary funds on his first return to the United States. He even laid the foundation of the proposed building; but his colleagues, perhaps wiser in their generation and more practical in their views, were so opposed to a project, clearly beyond the sphere of the useful among a people taking their first steps in Western knowledge and civilization, that it fell through. *The life and Times of C. W. Kathiravetpillai. By James H. Martyn.*

59

The Uduvil Girl's Boarding School

This institution was founded in 1824 by Revd. and Mrs. Miron Winslow, American Missionaries. At first, all education was free, and in addition, every student was given a dower of £ 4. 10 s. In 1843, this giving of dowry was abolished, although education was still free. In 1852 fees were charged, a custom which has continued ever since. In 1840, Miss Eliza Agnew became principal of the school - - - - From 1881—1913, Miss Susan P. Howland has been its Principal. During this time the educational standard of school has risen steadily. In 1886, a normal department for training teachers was started. In 1897 an English department, where all subjects should be studied in English was started. First Christian Endeavor Society in girl's school in India or Ceylon started at Uduvil in 1884. The school has greatly benefited by the long terms of service of these two principals :—*Amicus, Special Edition, April 17th, 1914.*

60

Puttur Well.

The Puttur Well is a large rectangular pit in the lime-stone rock, and its dimensions are about 40 ft. in length by 25 ft. in width. The only *previous experiments* made were in 1824 when engines of considerable power were employed to raise water from the well with a view of irrigating the district. The *only result* obtained, however, was the establishment of the fact that it was impossible to affect the level of the well or check the curious rise and fall of its water. This latter phenomenon has earned for it the title of the "Tidal Well of Puttur :—*Journal of the Ceylon Branch of the Royal Asiatic Society*.

61

Klaly St. James'

அஞ்ஞானமார்க்கத்திலிருந்து முதல்முதல்மனந்திரும்பி ஞானஸ்நானம்பெற்றுத் திருச்சபையுடன்சேர்ந்தவன் கனம்பொருந்திய எற்லி ஐயருடைய குதிரைவேலைபார்த்த ஒருவனே. இவன் 1825ம் ஆண்டின் முடிவில் சாமுவேல் என்னும் நாமத்தினால் ஞானஸ்நானம் பெற்றான். தன் மனைமக்களுக்குச் சுகவீனமான காலத்தில் சுத்தவாளரின் தயவைப்பெறும் நோக்கமாய் யாழ்ப்பாணத்திற்குக் கிழக்கே இருபது கட்டை தூரத்திலிருக்கும் கிளாலியென்னுமிடத்திலுள்ளபெயர்போன றோமான் கத்தோலிக்க கோவிலுக்கு நேர்த்திக்கடன்செய்து அங்கே, வருஷாவருஷம் போக்குவரவுபண்ணி, சந்தியோகுமையோருக்குக் காணிக்கையாக ஒருவெள்ளிப்பட்டயத்துடன் பரிசையையும் அக்கோவிற் சுவாமியார்வசம் ஒப்பித்தான்.—*The Christian Friend, October, 1871.*

62

Don Diego Warnasooria Arasunilayitta Mudlr

He was a Tamil Respadore, co-equal in position and authority to a Singhalese Chief or Dissave. Residing in the Jaffna Division, he took precedence of the other Headmen of the Jaffna district under the Dutch administration. He was highly respected; and generally moving in a Palanquin was looked up to with feelings akin to awe and veneration by the populace. To his enlightened patronage, we are indebted for the Gnananantha Puranam. It is clear from the following stanza that this poem was completed in the year 1823 when Father Joa Baptista (John Baptist) was Parish Priest of Jaffna.

போற்றியபரமஞானிபுனிதமாதவத்தின்மிக்கோன்
ஏற்றியசேகரங்கோன், தூயசந்தத்திலுள்ளோன்.
பெற்றிலையடையுஞ்சுத்தபேர்சுவாஞானகான,
மாற்றுநற்குருவின்பாதமடியனென்தலைமேற்கொண்டேன்.

Don Diego Warnasooria Arasunilayitta Mudaliyar died in his 92nd year, in 1825, when, on the abolition by the English of the office of Respadore, his son, Don Nicholas Arasunilayatta Mudalyar, became the first Maniagar of Jaffnapatam. Don Nicholas served with much acceptance till 1839.— *Biographical Sketch of A Mudaliyar Santiagopillai.*

63

Matthew Philips

Mr. Matthew Philips was born in the year 1794. He was educated under the Revd. C. David (a convert of Schwartz's) who was then Colonial Chaplain of Jaffna. He became pundit to the Revd. Mr. Meigs, and about 1817 was a teacher in the American Boys' Boarding School, then at Pandaterruppu. When the Revd. Mr. Knight arrived in Jaffna, in the year, 1818, being in want of an intelligent man to help him in his work, he applied to the American Mission, and Dr. Spaulding recommended Mr. Philips to the post. The latter then removed to Nallore, where he laboured in the full confidence of the Mission for upwards of thirty five years as head Catechist and General Agent. He appears to have been a very successful, earnest and laborious worker.—*C. M. S. Gleaner.*

64

The American Mission Press

For the first few years of the American Mission, tracts were written on the leaf of the Palmyrah, but in 1821, Mr. G. Garret arrived with a press. The local Government being at that time hostile to the operations of the Mission, he was peremptorily ordered to leave the Island within six weeks.

He accordingly went to the Continent and the press was taken by the Church Mission and thus made available for printing the necessary tracts and books. This continued till 1834. when the restrictions of the Government having been removed, the press was transferred to our Mission and set up at Manepay.--*The Rev. Mr. W. W. Howland.*

65

Mutta Kumara Pulavar

இவர் வட்டுக்கோட்டையைச்சார்ந்த அராலிக் குறிச்சியிற் பிறந்து, அனலைதீவில் விவாகஞ்செய்து, ஊர்காவற் றுறையில் நடமாடினவர். அதிகவிரைவிற் பாடுந்திறமையாற் பேர் பெற்றவர். இவர் ஊர்காவற்றுறையிலே ஒருபாடசாலையை ஸ்தாபித் துப் பல மாணாக்கர்க்குப் பாடமோதிவைத்தார். நயினாதீவு நாகம்மாள் பதிகம், அனலைதீவு ஐயனார் குறவஞ்சி, தேவசகாயநாடகம், சேமந்தனி

நாடகம், பதுமாபதிநாடகம், எனப் பெயரிய சிலவற்றைப் பாடியிருக்கின்றனர். 1827 ம் வருஷம் வரையில் அராலியில் இறந்தனர்.

—பா. ச. தீ.

66

Mappana Mudaliyar

இவர் தென்மராட்சியிலுள்ள எழுதுமட்டுவாளிலே இற்றைக்கு முன்பின் நூறுவருஷங்களின்முன்னே இருந்தவர். அரசாட்சியாரிடம் தென்மராட்சி மணியவேலையை ஒப்புக்கொண்டு பெருஞ்செல்வாக்குடையவரானார். இலக்கணம், சோதிடசாத்திரங்களிற் சமர்த்தராய்ப் பேரெடுப்புற்றிருந்தார் அல்லாமல் வித்வ சிரேஷ்டராய்த் திருச்செந்தூர்ப் புராணத்துக்கு வியாக்கியானஞ்செய்து, சோமகேசரிநாடகம், பரிமளாசநாடகம், குறவஞ்சி என்பவற்றைப்பாடி, விரதநிச்சயம், ஆசுசவிதி, என்னும் இரண்டு பத்ததிமுறைகளைப்பலநூல்களிலிருந்து தெரிந்து திரட்டியெடுத்தனர். இவர் 50ம் பிராயத்திலே 1827ம் ஆண்டிலே தேகவியோகமாயினர்.—பா. ச. தீ.

67

Visuvanatha Sasthiriar

இவர் யாழ்ப்பாணம் வட்டுக்கோட்டையைச்சார்ந்த அராலிக்குறிச்சியில் இருந்த ஓர் பிராமணர். இவரது கணிதத் திறமையைப்பற்றிக் கேள்வியுற்ற இலங்கை நீதிராசாவாகிய சேர் அலெக்சாந்தர் யோன்ஸ்தன் (Sir Alexander Johnston) இங்கிலாந்து அரசராகிய நான்காம் ஜோட்சுக்கு இவரைப்பற்றிப் பாராட்டி வியந்து நிருபம் அனுப்பி "இராசாவின் கணிதர்" என்னும் பட்டப்பெயரை இவர்க்குப் பெற்றுக்கொடுத்தனர்.

இவ்வாறு கோவறிந்த கணிதசிங்கமாகிக் கீர்த்திப்பிரஸ்தாபமுற்றிருந்தாரேனும் சந்திரகிரகணம் ஒன்றைவிட்டு, வட்டுக்கோட்டைச் சாஸ்திரசாலைத்தலைவராகிய பூர் பண்டிதர்க்கு (Rev. Dr. Poor) இவர் பரிதிமுன் பனியெனச் சவிமழுங்கித் தோல்விபோயினர். 1828 ம் வருஷம் பங்குனி மாதம் 28 க் திகதி தோற்றிய அச்சந்திர கிரகணம் பரிசத்தில் 15 நிமிஷங்களும், விமோசனத்தில் 24 நிமிஷங்களும் இவரது கணிதத்திற் பிழைப்பட்டன. இவர் வல்ல கணிதரேயல்லாது பெரும்பெயர்வாய்ந்த புலவருமாகி, மாவைக்குறவஞ்சி, வண்ணைக்குறவஞ்சி, குருநாதர் கிள்ளைவிடுதூது என்னும் பெயரிய மூன்றுபாடல், களை இயற்றினர். இவரிடம் சோதிடங்கற்ற மாணவர் பலருள் வட்டுக்கோட்டைச் சாத்திரசாலை ஆசிரியருள் ஒருவராகிய அமரிக்க மிஷனுக்காகப் பஞ்சாங்கம் கணித்த சேமசேகரம்பிள்ளை (Mr. Dashiel) ஒருவர்.—பா. ச. தீ.

68

Nicholas Puvirajasinghe Mudaliyar

Nicholas, the third son of Manueltamby Puvirajasinghe Mudaliyar, was born in the year 1811. After a course of elementary instruction in Tamil, he was sent in 1823, in his twelfth year, to the Nallur English School, started by the Revd. Mr. Knight, and continued by the Revd. Mr. Adley, of the Church Missionary Society. He pursued his studies for about six years. He belonged to a class of intelligent boys. To some of these boys, including Mortimer (afterwards the Revd. Thomas Mortimer) and Marsh (afterwards Proctor William Marsh) Mr. Adley took a fancy. and in 1828, when he had to attend the Annual Conference of the Church Missionaries in Colombo, he was accompanied by these boys. In 1831 Mr. Nicholas had to return to Jaffna. In 1833, Mr. Dyke inaugurated his truly memorable administration of the North. Close upon his heels followed Mr. Parsons to open a branch office of "the Civil Engineer and Commissioner of Roads" since called " the Director of Public Works."

The Revd. Mr. Adley recommended Mr. Nicholas to the favourable notice of Mr. Parsons as a young man of parts and promise. Mr. Parsons engaged Mr. Nicholas in 1833, to serve as Interpreter, Translator and Paymaster, in his office. Thus did Mr. Nicholas become connected with the Department of Public Works, from its very inception in Jaffna.—*Life of Nicholas Puvirajasinghe Mudaliyar.*

69

Nayanmarkadu Hospital

This is the only hospital in the Island where the purely Ayurvedic system of treatment is pursued in its integrity. The Jaffna Catholic Guardian of June, 23rd 1888 says :- This hospital is a consolation for all. It lies about 3 miles from the Town receiving daily a good number of patients who suffer from carbuncles, tumours, boils, dislocations, wounds etc. All these defects of the human body are easily cured by the able treatment of the Doctor. He has inherited his father's dexterity in Medical practice and leaves no marks of stain to blot out his fame. He also possesses a knowledge of English Medicine. One thing we regret is that the hospital is not large enough to receive its numerous patients."

This hospital was commenced by Mr. Arumugam Vettivelu who had a knowledge of medicine and who acquired some skill in treating fractures, dislocations and sprains. For these disorders, he prepared a special poultice, for which this hospital is still famous. His son Mylvaganam who succeeded him in the management of the hospital possessed considerable skill in surgical operations. Since his death, his brother Mr. SivaSuppramaniam is in charge of the hospital. He is both a surgeon and physician and he has effected some very remarkable cures.—*C, N. P.*

70

Revd. John Hensman

In 1828, John Hensman was admitted as a boarder in the Nalloor C. M. S. Boy's Boarding School. His conduct was exemplary. Mr. Adley took a great liking to him, and got him admitted into the C. M. S. Seminary at Cotta, in 1832. The Rev. J. Marsh was Principal of the Cotta Institution during the latter part of young Hensman's stay there, and the latter so won the affection of Mr. Marsh by his conduct and progress, that afterwards when he was appointed Principal of the Colombo Academy (Now Royal College) he got Mr. Hensman a position in the Academy. One of Mr. Hensman's pupils at the Academy was Mr. de Saram, afterwards District Judge of Jaffna, and it is related that once he good humouredly said to Mr. Alfred Hensman, Proctor, when the latter was rather too vehemently arguing a case, that he was obliged to show unusual patience on account of his having been his father's pupil at the Colombo Academy.—*The Life of the Rev. John Hensman.*

71

Henry Martyn

இவர் முதற் தெல்லிப்பழையில் ஸ்தாபிக்கப்பட்டிருந்த அமெரிக்க மிஷன் தருமப்பாடசாலையிற் சேர்ந்து, அவ்விடத்தால் வட்டுக்கோட்டைச் சாஸ்திரசாலை சென்று, எதொரு காடினியபாடத்தையும் ஒருதரத்துக்கு மேலே இருதரம் பார்க்கவேண்டா ஞாபகசாலியாய் இருந்தமையாற், பிடித்ததெல்லாம் இரும்பென்றாற்போற், படித்ததெல்லாம் மனசில் அமையப்பெற்றவராய், விரைவிலே பாண்டித்தியமடைந்து, மைந்தன் ஒருவன் தந்தையானாற்போல, அச்சாஸ்திரசாலையிற்றானே ஆசிரியருமானார். "என்னிருகண்ணினு மிதயமாமலரினும் துன்னியெக்காலமுந் துலங்குகொழுந் தோன்றல்" என எட்டுவருடக்காலமாக எமக்கும் இவர் சிரேட்ட ஆசிரியர். இங்கிலிஷ இலக்கண இலக்கியங்கள், சாத்திரங்கள், கணிதங்களில் அன்றித், தமிழ் இலக்கண இலக்கியவல்லவராய்ப் பதிசாஸ்திரக்கரைகண்டோர் இவரொன்ன அதிலும் மிக்க விற்பன்னம் அடைந்தவர். தேவபத்தியில் முதிர்ந்த பிரசங்கியாகவும் தெரிவுசெய்யப்பட்டார்.

நாற்பத்தாறு வருடம் நிலைகொண்டிருக்கும் "தாரகையை" ஆரம்பித்து நடத்தினருளும் இவர் ஒருவர். மணிவட்டம், நாழிகைவட்டங்களைத் திருத்தச் சுதேசிகளுள் முதன்முதல் அறிந்தோர் இவரே. செப்படிவித்தையைத்தானும் மிக ஒப்பிதமாய் விளையாட வல்லவர். இவ்வகைச் சாமர்த்தியராய் 1843 ம வருஷம் வரையிலாக்கும், அச்சாத்திரசாலையோடு சம்பந்தப்பட்டிருந்து, அப்பால் டைக் மன்னவரின் தாட்சணியத்தால் அரசாட்சி "ஸ்தோர்க் கணக்கப்பிள்ளை"யாயினர். சப்பிறீங்கோட் கூடுங்காலத்திற் துவிபாஷித முதலியார் வேலையையும்

நடத்தினர். 1861 ம் வருஷம் வரையில் அச்சியந்திரம் கொண்டுவரும் கருத்தோடு சென்னபட்டணம்போய்த் திரும்பிச் சிலநாட்களுட் தேக வியோகமாயினர். பற்பலதனிப்பாக்கள், தேவஷிசோடு எஸ்தர் விலாசம் முதலாம் சிலபாடல்களையும் பாடினர்.— பா. ச. தீ.

72

King's House,
Colombo,
January 7th, 1833.

Henry Martyn

I have received your letter of the date of December 15th 1832, containing a statement of your qualifications, of the accuracy of which I entertain no doubt from the favourable impression I received during your late examination. The qualifications you possess are precisely those which will enable you to carry on the important duty of tuition, with the certainty of rendering inestimable benefits to the Colony, if you persevere fearlessly and zealously in that course. I trust, therefore, that I may rely on your devoting yourself to that duty and you may depend upon receiving every support from me in my power. I have heard that you have met with some reproach from your brother students, in consequence of your having turned your attention to various kinds of manual labour, which are not carried on by persons of your caste; but I beg to assure you that, so far from that circumstance exciting my disapprobation, it has precisely the contrary effect, as it evinces that you are superior to those prejudices, which cannot long remain, when that system of improvement shall have been more generally developed, which is now so successfully commenced in this Island. Feeling satisfied that you will continue to show unremitting zeal in furthering the views of those benevolent men with whom your happy destiny has connected you.

I remain,
Very truly yours,
R. W. Horton.

73

Watch Repairing.

Mr. Henry Martyn when at Batticotta used of a Saturday morning to pay a visit to Jaffna, and, on such occasions, to do various little errands for the Missionaries. One of these errands was to take the clocks and watches out of repair, to be put to rights by a Burgher named Alvis. He was anxious to see the watch-maker at work; but the watch-maker always avoided him being too jealous to afford an opportunity to a stranger to learn his craft. But Mr. Martyn thought he might try his hand at watch-repairing. Setting out one morning, with a watch belonging to Dr. Poor, he halted at a Madum. He examined the watch for sometime and then carefully took the mechanism to pieces, the only tool he had, being a penknife. After cleaning the different parts, he put them together, and found, on winding, that the watch resumed its normal motion. So elated was he with his success that, instead of going to Jaffna, he returned to Batticotta much sooner than usual. Dr. Poor, on receiving the watch, remarked humourously enough that Mr. Martyn must have taken to that wonderful mode of locomotion known as the seven-leagued boots to have done his errand in so short a time. The true explanation followed and Dr. Poor was so pleased with Mr. Martyn's performance that he soon obtained for him all the tools and implements of a watch-maker. Thus was Mr. Martyn led to pay special attention to watch-making. A noticeable feature of his study at Batticotta was the number of clocks, watches and musical instruments which caught the eye of the visitor. During the last 18 years of his life, he found much more leisure, as a Government storekeeper, to practise the art. He gave the public so much satisfaction that Mr. Gillman, Office Assistant to the Government Agent, and latterly a Judicial Officer highly esteemed for the acumen and close reasoning displayed in his judgments, wrote to him to say that with such an artist in Jaffna, it was unnecessary for him or his friends to send their watches to Colombo or Madras—a course then involving risk and delay—*The Life of Henry Martyn.*

74

American Mission Press & Infant School

In 1833 the restrictions laid upon the Mission were removed and additions to the force made. This followed upon the visit of the new Governor, Sir Robert Horton, who became greatly interested in the plans and progress of the Vaddukoddai Seminary.

Mr. & Mrs. Minor took up the printing work at Manepay, where the long wished for press was set up and with it the other press shipped out years before, lost in India, recovered and since loaned to the neighbouring Church Mission at Nallur. Mr. & Mrs. Hoisington settled at Vaddukoddai. He became the head of the Seminary faculty and took the place of Dr. Poor when the latter removed to India. Mr. Hoisington proved to be of unusual scholarly tastes, and gifts and his learning commanded respect among the people every-where. His devotion to the Seminary was unbounded.

Mr. and Mrs. Eckard were stationed at Panditerippu, where Mrs. Eckard opened the first "Infant School" in Ceylon modelled after the ones popular in America at that time :— *A Century in Ceylon by Helen I. Root.*

75

The Jaffna Wesleyan Central School.

The Central College was originally and popularly known as the "Vembadi Wesleyan School," on account of a number of big Margosa trees that stood in front. It was also known by the name of Percival's school. There was an English School in the time of Revd. Roberts, predecessor of Revd. Peter Percival, who engaged Mr. Brown Sinnatamby, as Head Master, and Messrs Meckenstry Kanagaratnam, Wyman Katiravetpillai, Jonathan Crowther, John Koch and several others as assistants. The prominent scholars in these days were Messrs. Muttukistna, who became afterwards Deputy Queen's Advocate and B. L. Stoner Modlr., Samuel Grenier, Chellappahpillai and Arianayagam and others. Messrs. Chellappahpillai and Arianayagam were recommended by Mr. Percival to the Normal College in Madras where they passed their B. A. and B. L. examinations creditably. Mr. Percival was compelled to join the Madras University. The Revd. R. D. Griffith who succeeded him died on his return home. Revd. John Walton took the chair with Revd. William Barber as principal of the Central School. The old staff of teachers resigned. A new staff was employed with Mr. Samuel Grenier as Head Master, Mr. John Koch as Roll-caller and Messrs Frederick Grenier, Peter Vyramuttu, Joseph Vallipuram, Philip Tamber and several other graduates of the Central school as assistants. Rev. J. Walton was succeeded by Revd. John Kilner. Mr. Samuel Grenier having lost his father resigned and went to Colombo. Mr. William Nevins took his place and the school was affiliated to the Madras University :—*The Central— June 1907.*

76

Church Repair and Appeal to European Priests

In 1834 His Holiness Pope Gregory xvi separating Ceylon from the Jurisdiction of the Bishop of Cochin, with a view to its better administration, erected it into an independent vicariate appointing the then Superior of the Island Mission, the Revd. Father Francis Xavier the first Vicar Apostolic directly responsible to the Holy See. Father Xavier having died soon after his nomination, Father Vincente de Rosario was the first Goanese to assume duties as the Vicar Apostolic of Ceylon, with the title of Bishop of Tamacene. Him succeeded another Goanese Missionary

Father Caitano Antonio who was raised to the dignity of Bishop of Usula. It was about the year 1839 when the rebuilding of St. Mary's Church in Jaffna was proceeding apace, that the Catholics of Colombo petitioned the Holy See to send a few European priests to the Goanese Fathers labouring in their midst. The Goanese Missionaries were doubtless most zealous and self sacrificing and many of them were also well versed in Tamil, but they were found unequal to the growing requirements of the Catholic Community in a progressive, English Colony. This was so strongly felt by the principal members of St. Mary's Congregation, that following in the wake of their Colombo brethren, they also made an earnest appeal to the Propaganda in Rome for European Priests. Chevalier Saverimuttu Mudaliyar and Mr. Abraham took the lead in getting up this appeal, which, in due time, was responded by the Propaganda sending a small band of Italian Missionaries, of whom Father Bettachini was the first to arrive in 1843. He was followed by Drs. Bravi, Cingolani, Sellani and others. This band received two Spanish accessions in Fathers Oruna and Florentine Garcia, the latter of whom becoming the first European Parish Priest of St. Mary's Jaffna in 1848, lived to a good old age and died as Dr. Joulain's Honorary Vicar-general at Bolawatta in 1894. In 1847 another band consisting of Fathers Semaria, Keating and Ciamin and Brother Gaspard de Stefanis was sent at the request of Dr. Bettachini by Dr. Mazenod, Bishop of Marseilles, and Founder of the Order of the Oblates of Mary Immaculate:—*Biographical Sketch of T. Mudaliyar Abraham.*

77

Chevalier Saverimuttu Mudlr

A. D. 1869—A. D. 1882. Sandrasagra Mudaliyar Saverimuttu Mudaliyar, who was distinguished for the interest he always took in all matters connected with the Cathedral Church, brought to completion the Portico works of the church. He also furnished the church with sacred images, globe lamps, cloth etc partly from his own private funds and partly from subscriptions raised by him amongst the congregation and among his friends. His indefatigable exertions were so highly appreciated by the late Archbishop Bonjean that his Lordship brought prominently to the notice of His Holiness the Pope, whereupon His Holiness was pleased to create Saverimuttu Mudaliyar a Knight Chevalier of the order of St. Gregory the Great.—*J. H. W.*

78

Puthankuli Bridge

In 1836 Mr. Parsons undertook the construction of the Puthankuli Bridge on the road to Chavagachcheri and entrusted the immediate supervision of the work to Mr. Nicholas, who had already given proofs of his natural aptitude to direct labourers and artificers to carry out a plan in a workman-like manner. The Puthankuli Bridge, the best in the North, was so well constructed as to raise Mr. Nicholas in the estimation of Mr. Parsons who appointed him Storekeeper of the Department in 1840.—*The life of Nicholas Puvirayasinghe Mudaliyar.*

79

Terrestrial Globes

In the year 1835 in his twenty-fourth year, Mr. Martyn constructed two Terrestrial Globes, which he forwarded to the Royal Society of Great Britain and Ireland and for which he received the following graceful and encouraging acknowledgement from that distinguished body.

The Royal Society of Great Britain and Ireland,
14 Grafton Street, Bond Street.
London 18th of July, 1835.

Sir

I have the honour to inform you that, at a General Meeting of the Royal Society of Great Britain and Ireland held this day, your interesting donation, received through the Right Hon'ble Sir Alexander Johnston, of two Terrestrial Globes, ingeniously made by yourself, with the names on one written in English and on the other in Tamil was laid before the Society and I am directed to return you its best thanks for the same.

I have the honour to be,
Sir, your most obedient
very Humble Servant
H. Harkness
Secretary.

To Mr. H Martyn,
Batticotta,
Jaffna,
Ceylon.

80

Tirupanichangam

About the year 1837 a Society was formed composed of the members of the church and this Society carried out all works in connection with the church. It was composed of the following gentleman as Office Bearers viz. President, Sandrasagra Mudaliyar Saverimuttu Mudaliyar; Secretary, Philip Bastiampillai; Treasurer, Bastiampillai Anthonipillai; Accountant, Nicholapillai Sinnetamby; and the following Committee Members; Arasunilayitta Mudaliyar Santiagopillai, Tisseverasinghe Mudaliyar Abraham, Tisseverasinghe Mudaliyar Joseph, Anthonipillai Santiagopillai, Susaipillai Swampillai, Bastiampillai Santiagopillai, Markupillai Gnanapragasam, Santiagopillai Simeon, Gabrialpillai Yakopillai, Swampillai Anthonipillai; Santiagopillai Philipu, Anthonipillai Pedropillai and Sanjupillai Anthonipillai. This Society collapsed in 1852. Prominent amongst the members of the Society was Mupu Gnanapragasam. He commanded more influence than any lawyer of the day. He was the first Catholic Registrar. A great Peacemaker, he was instrumental in preventing breaches of peace amongst the members of the church. The melody of his stentorian voice and his exemplary administration of office as "Mupu" are still the theme of admiration amongst posterity. —*Centenary Sketch of the Jaffna Cathedral.*

81

Chenathiraya Mudaliyar

இவர்கோப்பாயைச் சேர்ந்த இருபாலைக் கிராமத்திற்பிறந்தவர். இலக்கண இலக்கியங்களில் மாத்திரமன்று அக்காலத்துக்குரிய அரசியல் நியாயப்பிரமாணங்களிலும் வல்லவராய், மாகாணநியாயஸ்தலங்களில் நின்று நியாயதுரந்தரர்க்குரிய கடமைமையையும் நடத்தினவர். இவர் தமிழ் அகராதிவேலையில் ஏற்பட்டிருந்தநைற்தேசிகருக்கு (Rev. Mr. Knight) அதி உபயோகியாய் இருந்தார். ஞாபகத்தில் இவருக்கு மிஞ்சினோர் இலர். பவணந்திமுனிவர் செய்த நன்னூலை இவர் நாற்பதுநாளில் படித்துமுடித்தார். இவர்பாடிய தனிப்பாக்களும் பல. நல்லைவெண்பாவெற்றி மாவிட்டபுரக்கோவில் மீது ஊஞ்சல் இசையும் நல்லைக்குறவஞ்சியும் பாடினர். பா. ச. தீ.

82

The Morning Star

The Morning Star printed semi-monthly, in English and Tamil, was commenced in 1841. It was at first edited by two Natives and devoted to education, science and literature and to the dissemination of articles on agriculture, government and religion with a brief summary of important news:—*The Revd. Mr. W. W. Howland.*

The two natives referred to were Henry Martyn and Seth Payson whose names were printed, as editors, at the foot of the last page of every number of the first volume.. Mr. Martyn contributed the bulk of the editorials. The English translations of the *Panchatantra* and the *Paramatha Kuru Kadai*, the controversial papers on Tamil Grammar, and the summary of news in

English were also from his pen. With the close of the first volume Mr. Martyn's connection with the *Star* ceased.

The *Morning Star* is the oldest newspaper in Jaffna. The newspapers started elsewhere in the Island, prior to its publication were edited by Europeans. Mr. Martyn is therefore entitled to the distinction of being the first Native Journalist of Ceylon:— *Biographical Sketch of Henry Martyn.*

83

Friend-in-need Society

A public meeting was convened at the Court House, on Tuesday evening the 9th instant, according to appointment, for the purpose of forming a Friend-in-need Society. Captain Cochrane having been called to the chair, opened the meeting by a brief address, stating the object for which they had assembled. The meeting was then addressed by the Rev. P. Percival, and Mr. F. C. Grenier, showing the importance of forming such an institution, and the great usefulness which it might be hoped would result from its formation, if liberally supported by its friends. We understand that the monthly subscriptions amount to £ 8.— *The Morning Star. March 18, 1841*

84

P. Kandapillai

இவர் 1766 ம ஆண்டு பிறந்து தமது சுயபாஷையோடு உலாந்தா, போர்த்துக்கீஸ், ஆங்கில பாஷையுங்கற்றவர். பதினெட்டு வருஷங்களாக ஆராச்சி உத்தியோகத்திலிருந்து வழக்கமாய் ஆராச்சிகந்தர் என்னும் பெயரால் அறியப்பட்ட இவருக்கு ஆறுபுத்திரரும் ஆறுபுத்திரிகளும் பிறந்தார்கள். உத்தியோகத்தோடு வைத்தியமும் கல்வியறிவும் விளங்கியதால் சென்றவழி எங்கும் கண்ணியமும் மரியாதையும் இவர்க்கிருந்தன. உத்தியோகத்தை விட்ட பின்பு, தம் காலத்தை நாடகம்பாடுவதிலே போக்கினர். இவர்பாடிய நாடகங்கள் சந்திரகாசநாடகம், இராமவிலாசம், நல்லை நகர்க்குறவஞ்சி, கண்டிநாடகம், எரோது நாடகம், சந்நீக்கிலார் நாடகம், இரத்தினவல்லிவிலாசம் ஆகிய 21 எனக்கேள்வி. இறுதியிற் சொல்லப்பட்டதைப் பாடிக்கொண்டிருக்குந் தருணம் 1842 ம் ஆண்டு ஆனிமாதம் 2ம் திகதி புதன்கிழமை 76 பிராயத்திலே சட்டென யாதோர்நோயும் இன்றி இறந்தனராம். இவர் புத்திரர் ஈ. ஈ. தம்பு என்பார் நெடுங்காலம் யாழ்ப்பாணக்கச்சேரி ஆராச்சி வேலைபார்த்து வந்தார். பரமானந்தர்நொத்தாரிசுப்புலவருமாயிருந்து இறந்துவிட்டார். இவர் பாடத்தொடங்கிவிட்டிருந்த இரத்தினவல்லிவிலாசத்தை இவர் குமாரர், ஆறுமுககாவலரே பாடிமுடித்தனர். சில வைத்தியநூல்களு

க்குடரையும் இயற்றினர். இவரது தௌகித்திரபௌத்திரருள் த. த. பொன்னையாபிள்ளை, த. த. கைலாசபிள்ளை என்பார் சிரேட்டர். யா. ச. ஜ.

85

Saivite School

On the last day of September 1842 some of the Hindus met by agreement at a house in the Tamil City, spoke to one another with contempt and pity of converts to the religion which they said the missionaries had invented, and resolved upon establishing a school with a view to the defence and propagation of the ancient faith of Siva. Though an attempt to make a collection for this purpose had the effect of suddenly thinning the meeting, yet the new school was openned on Saturday, October 22nd 1842 "it being an auspicious day":—*Hindu Pastors by the Revd. E. J. Robinson, Late Wesleyan Missionary in Ceylon, 1867.*

86

S. Ambalavanan

The appointment of Mr. Supramania Ambalavanan to the District Judgeship of the Islands is an event of no ordinary interest to the local community. Descended from the most respectable parentage, possessed of wealth with good native talent improved by an English education in the Batticotta Seminary, engaged for the last four years as a Proctor, and for about 18 months as Deputy to the Queen's Advocate in the District Court of Walligamam, he is entitled to the patronage and favour of the Government. The mass of the natives have known him to be upright and honest in his management of cases in Court, and they have the confidence that he will act on similar principles in the more important and responsible capacity of Judge:—*The Morning Star, April 27. 1843.*

87

Mr. Martyn and his pupils

Mr. Martyn served on the Staff of the Batticotta Seminary for about eleven years. During these years, he had much to do with the education of most of the promising young men whom the Seminary had attracted from the different parts of the Peninsula. Of his numerous pupils, mention may be made of

1. E. Cornelius, Alias Sinnatamby Saravanamutto of Manepay, Surveyor under the District Road Committee, Jaffna.
2. Gerard H. Hallock, Alias Saravanamutto Murugasu Mudaliyar of Manepay, Head Clerk of the Jaffna Customs.

3. David Riggs, Alias Valauthar Sidemparapillai of Puttoor Surveyor.

4. Ponnampalam Sinnacutty of Pannalai, Proctor, D. C. Jaffna.

5. J. R. Arnold, Alias Arunasalam Sathasivam of Manepay, Editor of the Morning Star and Professor of Vernacular Literature in the Jaffna College.

6. Daniel L. Caroll, Alias Vyravanathar Visvanatharpillai of Manepay, first B. A. of the Madras University and Registrar of Tanjore.

7. William Nevins, Alias Muttar Sidemparapillai of Uduville, Headmaster of the Wesleyan Central School.

8. Elisha Rockood, Alias Sinnatampy of Alavetty, Sub collector, Kankesanturai.

9. Joseph W. Barr, Alias Appukutty of Tellippalai (Kumarakulasinha Mudaliyar) Chief Clerk and Interpreter, Minor Courts Jaffna.

10. George Champion, Alias Kanapathipillai (Jacob Ruben) of Manepay, Native Pastor, C. M. S. Jaffna.

11. Ira Gould, Alias Antho Simon of Panditeripo, First Dispenser of the Jaffna Friend-in-Need Society's Hospital.

12. David Stowell, Alias Saravanamuttu Sinnatamby of Manepay, Head Clerk, P. W. D, Jaffna.

13. Robert Breckenridge, Alias Ambalavi Kathirasar of Tellipallai, Sub-Inspector of Schools.

14. Joshua Danforth M. D., Alias Kathiraser Periatamby of Changanai, Resident Surgeon, Jaffna Friend-in Need Society's Hospital and Medical Officer, Vavuniya Vilankulam.

15. B. C. Graves, Alias Chittampalalam Vyramuttapillai of the well known Firm of L. C. Graves and. Co., Madras and sometime Maniagar of Batticotta.

16. Samuel Mervin, retired 2nd Clerk, Jaffna Kachcherri:— *Biographical Sketch of Henry Martyn.*

88

Government Storekeeper

Mr. Martyn applied for two appointments—a Government Surveyorship in the Eastern Province and the Government Storekeepership at Jaffna—then vacant. He accepted the Storekeepership, which Mr. Dyke was pleased to confer on him. This acceptance the late Mr. Solomon Johnpulle, in an article on the "Worthies of Jaffna", contributed forty-five years later, to his paper, the

"Ceylon Patriot," deplored as a most untoward and unfortunate event, in the life of one who, under favourable circumstances, might have been the Faraday of Ceylon, but whose ingenious and inventive mind was diverted from scientific and philosophical pursuits to the calculation and distribution of such trifles as "Ola" mats and "Naar" baskets.

From 1843 to 1860, Mr. Martyn was the General Storekeeper at Jaffna. During the period under notice the office was held in a rented house to the North and the Storehouses for salt were located on the grounds to the South-East ot the Jaffna Customs. The Storehouses constructed of timber and palmirah leaves, were reduced to ashes by a disastrous fire that broke out accidentally in the year 1850. They were then built anew on more spacious grounds to the South of the same road (Beach Road) at some distance from the original site. The present Stores and the permanent buildings serving as the office were constructed during the administration of Sir William Twynam.

The Storekeepership has of late been shorn of much of its importance. Salt is now the principal article in charge of the storekeeper. In Mr. Martyn's day over and above the custody of arrack and salt, the storekeeper had to take charge of all the timber felled and removed from the Crown Forests, now entrusted to the supervision of a separate department. He had also to supply all the provisions for the patients suffering during an outbreak of cholera or small-pox—a duty now transferred to the Civil Medical Department.

During his term of office the worst visitation of cholera was in 1845 and of small-pox in 1854.

For many years Mr. Martyn, at the request of Mr. Dyke, acted as Interpreter during the Criminal Sessions of the Supreme Court at Jaffna whenever the work was heavy. He was often complimented by the presiding Judge for the accuracy and fluency of his interpretations:—*Biographical Sketch of Henry Martyn.*

89

Kathirasa Pulavar

அச்சுவேலிச் சோதிட சாஸ்திரிகளுள் ஒருவராகிய இவர்பாரெஞ்சத்தியிற்சிறந்தவராதலிற் பதுமபூரணி நாடகம் என்னும் ஒருபாடலுடன், அச்சுவேலி செல்லி ஓடை அம்மன்பேரிற் பலவிருத்தங்களும்பாடினர். இவர் 1844 ம் வருஷம் 40 வயதில் அகாலமரணமடைந்தனர். பா. ச. தீ.

90

Ceylon Branch of the Royal Asiatic Society

This Society was formed in 1845 for promoting enquiries into the History, Religion, Literature, Arts and Natural History of Ceylon together with the social conditions of its present and former inhabitants. The members are elected by ballot and pay an admission fee of half a guinea. The General meetings are held quarterly in the first weeks of February, May, August and November, when all papers and other communications to the Society are read. The papers are open to free discussion and are either printed in the Journal of the Society kept among its manuscript record or returned to its author, as may be determined by the votes of the General Meeting:—*The Ceylon Almanac, 1849*.

91

Swaminathar

இவர் மானிப்பாயிலே இற்றைக்கு முன்பின் 120 வருடங்களின்முன் பிறந்தவர். இவர் தம்பியார் சலாபக்குத்தகைகொண்டு, இலங்கை, இந்தியா எங்கும் பேரெடுப்புற்ற முத்துச்சாமியாபிள்ளை. இப்புலவரது புத்திரர் இலங்கைச் சட்டநிருபண சபையில் அநேக ஆண்டுகளாகப் பிரதிநிதியாய் இருந்த எதிர்மன்னசிங்கமுதலியார். இவர் சங்கீதசாஸ்திரத்தில் மிக்க பேர்பெற்றுச் சந்தமும் இன்பமுமாய்க் கோவைத்துறை படிக்கும் காரணத்தாற் கோவைத்துறைச் சுவாமிநாதர் என்றும், நாடகம்பாடும் காரணத்தால் நாடகச்சுவாமிநாதர் என்றும் இருநாமங்கள் வாங்கினவர். நாடகங்கள் விலாசங்களுள் இவராற் பாடப்பெற்ற இராமநாடகம், தருமபுத்திரநாடகம் இரண்டிற்கும் மேற்பட்டனவில்லை. பதிகங்கள் ஊஞ்சலிசைகளாதியவும் பாடினர். பா. ச. தீ.

92

Saravanamuttu Pulavar

இவர் நல்லூரிலே இற்றைக்கு முன்பின் 40 வருடங்களின் முன்னே இருந்தவர். வேதாந்த சயஞ்சோதி என்னுநூலை இயற்றினதன்றி, ஆத்மபோதப்பிரகாசிகை என்னும் பின்னோர் நூலைச் சமஸ்கிருதத்திலிருந்து மொழிபெயர்த்தார். இவர்வடமாகாண மன்னவராகிய டயிக்துரையிடம் பலவருஷங்களாக உடையார் உத்தியோகத்தில் அமர்ந்திருந்தனர். 1815 ம் வருஷம் சிவபதித்தேகவியோகமாயினர். பா. ச. தீ.

93

St. John's College

St. John's College is the Chief Educational Establishment of the Church Missionary Society's North Ceylon Mission. In 1823 a Boy's English School established at Nallur by the Church Missionary Society was conducted by the Revd. William Adley. In 1841 it was transferred to Chundicully in order to make room for the Girl's Boarding School which still exists at Nallur. In 1846 the School was removed to its present position adjoining St. John's Church. Part of the ground was granted by Government, and for the remainder the Seminary was indebted to the late P. A. Dyke Esq. The materials of the Old Dutch Church were used by the Revd. Pargyter for the construction of the School.

In 1876, the Revd. D. Wood bought an additional piece of land on which, in 1888, a Boarding House was erected by the Revd. G. F. Fleming with funds collected from Old Boys to perpetuate the memory of Mr. J. Evarts, whose name as Headmaster for 20 years, is still revered.

Our Jubilee was celebrated in 1891 and to mark the occasion it was given its, new name 'St. John's College." On the 12th October 1899 the roof of the main building collapsed. In February 1901, the Metropolitan, then Bishop of Colombo, formally opened our College Hall with its four class-rooms.

One great result of the good work done by the college for over 60 years was the founding of the Old Boys Association, in 1904 and the college play-ground intended as a memorial to the Revd. Charles C. Handy B. A. who was Headmaster of the Institution for 19 years, was opened on the 21st May 1909. *Principals.* Revds. J. T. Johnstone. 1841-1846; R. Pargyter, 1846-1866; D. Wood, 1874-1878; E. Blackmore 1878-1879; G. T Fleming 1880-1889; C. C. Handy. B. A. (acting) 1889-1892; J. W. Fall M. A. 1892-1895; J. Carter M. A. 1895-1899; R. W. Ryde M. A. 1899-1900; Jacob Thompson M. A. 1900;

Head-Masters:—Messrs. W. Santiagoe, 1841-1848; J. Philips. 1848-1853; R. Williams. 1853-1866; S. Williams, 1866-1867; J. Evarts, 1867-1887; Revd. C. C. Handy B. A. 1889-1908; T. H. Crossette, M. A. 1908:—*St. John's College Calendar for the year 1910.*

94

Philip Chinnaver

The son of an expert and painstaing farmer, Chinnaver grew a fair, lively lad. full of promise, and rather tall and stout for his age. Removed from the Tamil School in his fifteenth year, he followed his father to his farm where he was taught, day by day, to plough, to sow, to mow, to mannure, to irrigate, to reap, to bind into sheaves, to stack, to thresh, to drive a team tread ing out the corn, to winnow, to make nursery beds, to plant, to make fences and enclosures, to pen, tend and brand cattle, to make mats and baskets, to twist naar and coir ropes, to drive a pair of bullocks, yoking them to a cart, to milk a cow, to churn cream or cure into butter, to thatch a house, to make movable huts for watchers etc. Taking kindly to these pursuits he graduallv acquired a satisfactory knowledge of the practical Georgic of his father, who was much consoled in his old age, by the thought that his son had been fully trained to replace him honouralbly in Adams profession. Chinnaver whose life as a farmer, was necessarily uneventful, died in 1845 in his 78th year, leaving two sons, Joseph and Thampapillai:—*Life of Philip Chinnaver*.

95

The Oblate Mission of Jaffna

In 1845 the Island of Ceylon was divided into two vicariates—one at Colombo in the South, and one at Jaffna in the North. Monseigneur Bettachini was appointed Vicar-Apostolic of Jaffna. This zealous prelate felt the importance of calling to his aid some Society of Missionary priests. He fixed his choice on the Oblates of Mary. Monseigneur de Mazenod, whom he vistied in 1847 at Marseilles entered fully into all his views, and it was then agreed upon between both prelates that a foundation of the Oblates of Mary in Jaffna was to take place forthwith.

Father Semaria was appointed Superior of the Missionaries who were to go Ceylon. No better choice could well have been made for such a position. A Saint, a Scholar, an Apostle, he was admirably fitted for the great work which awaited him in Jaffna. At the time of the arrival of the Oblates in Ceylon, there were only eight priests in the Vicariate of Jaffna, a district nearly one-third the size of Ireland. There were then about fifty-thousand Native Catholics in that District. On his arrival in Jaffna Father Semeria was named Vicar-General. This position opened up a large field for his great administrative capabilities and Missionary zeal.

In the year 1854 the District of Jaffna was visited by a double scourge—cholera and small pox. Desolation was in every home, and the whole population was buried in a stupor of terrible despair. The streets rang day and night with the cries of the affrighted multitude. Out of the six thousand Catholics of which the mission of the town of Jaffna was composed, one thousand had at the close of the year, fallen victims to the terrible plague. Father Lacombe, a devoted young Missionary, was carried off by the frightful epidemic, a Martyr to his priestly duty. The heart of the Saintly Father Semeria was plunged in deep affliction at the sight of his perishing people. His labours among the cholera and small-pox smitten were incessant. To Christian and pagan alike he was father and friend and nurse. The year 1855 opened without any cessation of the double scourge, Early in the February of that year, a letter reached Monseigneur Semeria from the venerable founder, Monseigneur de Mazenod, announcing the definition of the dogma of the Immaculate Conception, in the following terms:—

> The Holy Ghost has spoken by the voice of Peter. The Supreme Pontiff, Pius IX, the infallible organ of the church, surrounded by two hundred Bishops, has pronounced the decree, declaring that the Virgin Mary, Mother of God, was preserved from the stain of original sin. Let us rejoice and give thanks to God that we, by the name borne by us (Oblates of Mary Immaculate), should have already proclaimed this truth.

The reception of news so important and so gladdening to the pious heart of the devoted and afflicted Oblate Father, who was a sure son of Her Whose Immaculate Conception had been declared an Article of Faith, stirred up in his soul hope for himself and his people, of escaping, through the intercession of Mary the Immaculate, from the dreadful scourge that was upon them. He forthwith resolved to order a Triduum of prayers in honour of the Immaculate Conception to be offered to God, to obtain, through Mary's intercession, the cessation of the plague. He invited the Fathers of the neighbouring missions to come to Jaffna, and take part in this devout celebration. During three days, violence was offered to heaven by Priests and people praying together to be delivered from the terrible scourge. Great crowds flocked to all the devotions of the Triduum; the voices of those who were weeping and sighing and petitioning for mercy were loud in the church from morning till night. The confessionals were besieged by eager multitudes who wished to make their peace with God and very many approached the Eucharistic Table. On each of the three days a numerous procession, in which was borne with great solemnity a statue of Mary the Immaculate issued from the church and circulated through the streets of the town, singing Hymns and Litanies, and reciting prayers for forgiveness, and for the turning away of God's anger. Arches of flowers were erected at the entrance to the chief thoroughfares, flags and festoons graced the fronts of several houses. Many Protestants willing to show their sympathy with their Catholic fellow-towns men, decorated their house fronts in the streets through which the statue of Mary Immaculate was being carried. Still the plague continued to advance with terrible strides, and to strike down its average daily number of victims. No cessation or lessening of the evil took place during the three days from the commencement to the completion of the Triduum On the fourth morning the Triduum closed. Quickly the news spread that there had been no new cases of Cholera on the previous night, no death that morning, and that all who had been attacked had recovered and were out of danger. That day forty patients came out from the small-pox hospital cured. The anger of God was appeased, and the power of prayer through the intercession of Mary the Immaculate was established. Many conversions of pagans and Protestants were the result of an event which seemed more than marvellous and nothing short of a miracle to the pious and thoughtful.

In the year 1856 Monseigneur Bettachini made successful application to the Holy See for the appointment of Father Semeria as his Co-Adjutor, with right of succession. On the 20th of August of the same year the latter was consecrated Bishop at Marseilles. Monseigneur Bettachini died in 1857, when the full charge of the vicariate of Jaffna passed into the hands of the Oblates of Mary.

The founding of Catholic Schools, in which a secular education of a high standard would be given, was one of the first works of importance in the eyes of Monseigneur Semeria. Next in importance, to the mind of the Holy Prelate, was the establishment of Orphanages on an extensive scale in his Vicariate for poor Christian children deprived of their parents, and also for the reception of poor little outcasts, the "waifs and strays" of Paganism. These two great works, which were to prove of such immense value to the Vicariate of Jaffna, were entrusted by Monseigneur Semeria in an especial manner, to the enlightened and devoted direction of Father Bonjean.

Monseigneur Semeria took his departure from Ceylon for Europe early in May 1867. The chief object of his journey was to assist at the General Chapter of the Society of the Oblates, which was to be held during the month of August of that year in Autun. He was never to see Ceylon again. When he was preparing to go to Jaffna he was taken ill at Marseilles at the house of the Oblates in that City, where he expired on the fourth day of his illness, in the holiest dispositions. His death took place on the 23rd January, 1868. We select the following from the biographical sketch of this holy prelate, written by his spiritual son and Oblate Confrere, Father Bonjean:—

"John Stephen Semeria was born at Calla, near St. Remo, in the year 1813, of an honourable family. He was remarkable during the year of his probation, for his perfect obedience, the tender delicacy of his conscience, the sweet gravity of his manners and his scrupulous charity. He was raised to the Priesthood in the year 1835. Shortly after his Ordination he became the associate of Father Albini in his Missionary works among the poor Italians at Marseilles, and became afterwards the fellow-labourer of that holy Priest in his missions in Corsica. At the call of obedience he cheerfully changed the scene of his labours from Corsica to Ceylon.

He whose words we have just cited, and who had been for many years the alter-ego of Monseigneur Semeria in virtues, in labours, and in holy sympathies, was designed by public voice as the most-fitting successor of that saintly prelate. The appointment, by the Holy See, of Monseigneur Bonjean to the office of Vicar-Apostolic of Jaffna, confirmed the expectation which existed so widely with reference to that event.

Under the active and enlightened guidance of Monseigneur Bonjean, the Vicariate of Jaffna continues to make most consoling progress. The number of Catholics in that Vicariate, which in 1850 was fifty thousand five-hundred, is now seventy-thousand. Within that period over twelve thousand pagans have been baptised, one hundred and four schools have been opened, five Orphanages have been established. A Catholic press has been created, and a Catholic Journal founded, which is printed in Tamil and English. Whilst the work of primary education is being pushed to the fullest development possible, under the circumstances, the higher branches of studies for young people of both sexes are being advanced year by year to a perfection that places them on a par with the best schools in the Island. In the Jaffna Vicariate there are 263 Churches, the greater number of which are, it is true, very humble ones, and nearly forty priests of the Society of the Oblates of Mary. There are also in that Vicariate five convents, including two for Native Nuns; a Junior Seminary for young ecclesiastics. A theological Seminary is in process of formation there.

The consecration of Monseigneur Melizan as Co-adjutor Bishop to Monseigneur Bonjean, is an event which cannot fail to give an additional impulse to the great religious movement which is astir in the Vicariate of Jaffna. We regret that our limited space compels us to close this notice of the Missions of the Oblate of Mary Immaculate in Ceylon, without our being able to include in our narrative some details of the Apostolic works of the zealous and devoted Fathers Boisseau, Mauroit, Pusaque, and of several other Oblate Missionaries in that Island, whose labours have been blessed with signal success.—*Sketches of the Life of Monseigneur de Mazenod by the Rev. Robert Cooke, O. M. I.*

96

Saivite Discourses

Saivite preachers and stewards appeared, and formed and worked a circuit somewhat on the Methodist model. In connection with the reading and recitation of passages from their sacred books, a lecture or sermon was delivered every Friday evening, in a spacious shed on the holy ground within the high wall round the temple of Siva at Wannarponne, and appointments, though not of such frequent occurrence, were also kept at the important villages of Chunnagam and Manepay. Before the delivery of the first lecture, December 31st 1847, the officiating priest of the temple broke a cocoanut in honour of Pillayar and the under taking; and at the close of the meeting he solemnly rose and said, that the omens for the association were remarkably auspicious. In the first place, the cocoanut had broken evenly into two equal parts, and secondly at the commencement of the address, he had heard the sound of a bell within the temple. The principal orators, both of whom had been day-pupils in our Jaffna school, were Arumugavar, the first and most frequent, and the presiding genius through all the movement, and a friend of his named Cattigas Ayar. The former, of the Velala or agriculturist caste, good-looking, intelligent, studious, reserved, of grave demeanour and blameless life, not better acquainted with the Hindu Shastras than with the Christian Scriptures, had been for a long period, day after day, the worthy companion and valued assistant of the gifted and plodding Mr. Percival in preparing and editing treatises and hymns in Tamil and translating the prayer-book and the Holy Bible. Cattigas Ayar, a round, oily Brahmin, physically inferior to his colleague and naturally less austere and resolute but equally learned in Hindu lore, and quite patriotic, would not alone have originated such an enterprise. He was the writer's respected and faithful Moonshee, and when bantered in the study, admitted without hesitation, and in the best temper, that he did not himself believe much of what he thought it necessary to relate to the people as unquestionable history.

The subjects of discourses supplied were the following:—Initiatory prayer; the holy necklace; the love of Siva; the sacred writings; taking away the life of animals, two lectures; festivals, the public worship of Siva, the mortality of the body, the leading doctrines of Sivaism; the duties of women; impartial judgment; earthly and heavenly treasures; adultery; charity; sacrilege, two; drunkeness, three; gratitude; alms-giving; education; unity of God; the veneration due to Cows, two; imitating the wise and the good; the vanity of earthly pleasures; and credulity:—*Hindu Pastors by the Rev. E. J. Robinson, late Wesleyan Missionary in Ceylon, 1867*

97

Temperance Movement

In 1834 when the reinforcement to the American Mission came fresh from the temperance agitation in the United States none of them used alcoholic drinks, and their example together with the conviction already growing in the minds of the Senior Missionaries led to the abandonment of their use altogether. Dr. Scudder found his first temperance mass meeting so great a popular success as to convince him that the mission ought to take a decided stand in the matter. A Jaffna Temperance Society was formed, uniting all factions in a common opposition to a common enemy:—*A century in Ceylon by Helen I. Root.*

98

Dr. Green

Dr. Samuel Fisk Green came to Jaffna in 1847. After a few months' stay at Vaddukoddai where he used the equipment and continued the work of Dr. Ward, he removed to Manepay.

Dr. Green's first classes were instructed in English but he soon found that the English terms in medical text books were practically unintelligible even to educated Tamils. The task of accurately defining in Tamil the terms used was immediately undertaken, rather the creation of a medical nomenclature in the Tamil language, a stupendous task which occupied many years. Dr. Green succeeded in getting through the press the following books, some 4000 pages in all ; Cutter's Anatomy, Physiology and Hygiene, Maunsell's Obstetrics, Druitt's Surgery, Gray's Anatomy, Hooper's Physician's Vade Mecum, Well's Chemistry, Daltoe's Physiology, Waring's Indian Pharmacopocia.

Dr. Green spent ten years in Jaffna, then after an interval of five years at home, he married and returned for a second ten years, and would gladly have returned for a third term of service had not the Board then adopted a policy of cutting down the medical works in all its missions, a policy afterwards happily reversed but too late to save Dr. Green to Ceylon.

Twice at least during Dr. Green's years in Ceylon there occurred a fearful epidemic of Cholera which he was helpful in combating. He took the disease in 1855 just after the death from Cholera of good old Dr. Poor, and on his recovery, gave himself to the cure and prevention of Cholera in the Province. In 1866 again there were many thousands swept away by this disease. Dr. Green's tracts on Cholera were distributed by thousands by the Government, and his methods widely followed:—*A Century in Ceylon by Helen I. Root, 1916.*

99

Esther Vilasam

Mr. Martyn had the gift of song and from his boyhood displayed a talent for poetical composition. Various are the Tamil songs he composed on various occasions at the request of his friends; but they were all of a fugitive or fragmentary character. His version of the Lamentations of the Blessed Virgin Mother at the foot of the cross, dictated during the last week of the lent of 1848, is the only specimen of his versification extant. In his latter days he dictated to an amanuensis, bit by bit, a poem, similar to the "Sakuntalai Vilasam," dramatising the Biblical account of Queen Esther. This poem, of which the tunes were suggested by Ponnan, a celebrated Tamil musician, was committed to writing on palmyrah leaves; and the book in this form, the only one available, was in possession of his brother-in-law, who would on no account lend it to any one, till a separate copy was made, but who was compelled by the author to lend it to one Pedro, a man with some pretentions to poetry, who was soon afterwards implicated in a murder and transported to Malacca. Anxious inquiries were made for the poem, but Pedro in trouble seems to have irrevocably lost it. A few pieces from the "Esther Vilasam" are still remembered and sung by a few persons in the town and these pieces bear traces of the elaborate elegance of the poem.—*Biographical Sketch of Henry Martyn.*

100

Commotion at the Cathedral

The solemn Christmas Service in Jaffna both at midnight and the following morning, was held in St. Mary's alone from time immemorial; and the practice was continued by Dr. Bettachini till the year 1848, when he decided to sing the Midnight Mass in St. Mary's Minor or the Church of our Lady of Refuge. This decision greatly surprised and irritated the less intelligent section of the Cathedral Congregation, who seemed to think a grievous wrong was done in upsetting immemorial Custom and depriving the Cathedral of a special and inalienable privilege. While the Midnight Mass was being celebrated in St. Mary's Minor, St. Mary's Major was alive with the hum of an excited mob. The Church was opened and prayers were read by some, while others gathering about the Belfry, pulled away lustily all night, tolling, the parting knell, as they said, of their Bishop. When, after a rainy night, the morning broke bright and beautiful, Dr. Bettachini ordered the Cathedral to be closed. Mr. Robert Langslow, a pious young Irishman, who was the Deputy Queen's Advocate, undertook to execute the order. Proceeding with Andrea, the Bishop's Italian coachman, and a few servants, he had bolted and barred all the doors on the Southern side and some on the Northern side when, as the result presumably of some concerted action, a very stout man, taller than his comrades by at least half a head, opened the first door shut. Mr. Langslow going up to the man rebuked him, threatening him with a prosecution. The man then retreated and Mr. Langslow returned to see the remaining doors shut. Thereupon the man re-appeared and hastily opened a few doors on the Southern side. Mr. Langslow had again to rebuke him in a severer tone. This scene of Mr. Langslow closing and the man opening the doors was enacted and re-enacted for some time. Mr. Langslow was at last so exasperated that he directed Andrea and the servants to have the man seized. Andrea perceiving the perilous position he was in, counselled Mr. Langslow to with-draw, deeming prudence the better part of valour; but Mr. Langslow persisting, Andrea beat a hasty retreat. The servants, in executing Mr. Langslow's order, caught a Tartar in the stout man to whose rescue his comrades came, in overwhelming numbers. Mr. Langslow found himself in an awful plight. In the melee that ensued, he was forced out of the Church and struck and stoned by hands he could not recognize, and, in the effort to make his escape, he stumbled upon a heap of stones and sustained further injuries. Father Semeria the Parish Priest, perceiving the serious commotion, hied to the scene. Mr. Abraham who had also been present near the spot, where Mr. Langslow fell, raised him up and dispersing the mob, lifted him into his carriage, and, with Brother Gaspar-de-Stefanis accompanied him to the Jaffna Friend-in-Need Society's Hospital where the wounds were dressed by Dr. Hoffman, the Military Surgeon. Mr. Langslow recovered rapidly enough, and resumed his duties; but it would appear that his death in the following July was due to the severe internal injuries he had sustained. His remains lie interred in the Cathedral. There is a large granite stone over his grave with the following inscription:—

To the Memory
of
Robert Wm. Langslow, Esqr., B. A.
Deputy Queen's Advocate
of Jaffna.

Eldest son of Robert Langslow, Esqr,, late District Judge of Colombo.

Born at Shropshire 14th August 1819.
Died 15th July 1849.
On whose soul may sweet Jesus have mercy. R. I. P.

It took some time to bring the recalcitrant congregation to their senses. *Santhappa Nather,* one of the four Jesuit Missionaries then labouring in the Jaffna District under Bishop Bettachini, used to say, with reference to this commotion:— மாமூலத்தை நாத்தினால் மாச்சலே மாச்சல்:—*Biographical Sketch of T. Mudaliyar Abraham.*

101

Chanmukach Chaddampiar

இவர் மூன்றுநான்கு தலைமுறைகளான வித்துவான்கள் வமிசத்தைச் சேர்ந்தவர். இப்பண்டிதர் அநேக ஆண்டுகளாக வட்டுக்கோட்டைப் பழையசாஸ்திரசாலையிலே தமிழ் ஆசிரியராய் மாத்திரமல்ல, அங்கேவசித்த பலமிஷனரிமார்களுக்கு ஆசானுமாயிருந்து சண்முகச்சட்டம்பியார் என்னும் நாமத்தினாலே தான் வழக்கமாய எங்கும் அறியப்பட்டவரானார். தம்மனைவிமக்களோடு கிறீஸ்துமதந்தழுவிச் சாவிலி என்ற அருத்தம்தரும் நதானியேல் என்னும் நாமமும் பெற்றார். இவர் 1849ம் வருடம் தைமாசம் 6ந்திகதி சனிக்கிழமை 55ம் பிராயத்திற் பரலோக பிராப்தியாயினர்.

மானிப்பாய்த் திருச்சபைப்போதகராய் மலைமேற்றீபமெனப் பிரகாசிக்கும் உவாரன்பூர் நதானியேல் (Rev. W. P. Nathaniel) தேசிகர் இவரது இரண்டாம் புத்திரர். பா. ச. தீ.

102

Stewart's Garden

Dr. Bettachini, who was then occupying the old house of the Goanese Fathers, that stood to the Southwest of the Cathedral, thought it both safe and dignified to reside in a house of his own, and the members of the "*Thirupanichangam*" were asked to purchase a suitable residence. Stewart's Garden, on the Southern side of the Main Street, probably so called from its having been owned or occupied by Mr. Stewart, afterwards Justice Stewart, was then in the market, and the Bishop willing to acquire it, promised to pay three-fouths of the purchase amount, leaving the Catholics to make up the balance. Aseerwatha Mudaliyar, second Interpreter of the Jaffna Kachcheri, who had already acquired the large walled premises known as Mooyaart's Garden on the other side of the road, (now St. Martin's Ecclesiastical Seminary) cast wistful eyes on Stewart's Garden and it was even reported that he was determined to have it at any cost. On the day of sale, there was brisk bidding for sometime between Mr. Abraham and Aseerwatha Mudaliyar, who, seeing the determination of the Catholics, withdrew, leaving them to buy the property. On the site of the old house occupied by Drs. Bettachini, Semeria, Bonjean and Melizan, a new Refectory has been built; and the garden extended by Dr. Bonjean on the Eastern side as far as the road, has been walled on that side by Dr. Joulian:—*Biographical Sketch of T. Mudaliyar Abraham.*

103

St. Patrick's College, Jaffna

It was about the year 1850 that the Jaffna Catholic English School was founded.

Father Mauroit, in whom centre a thousand endearing and venerable associations, was the first Manager. Mr. Foy, an Irish gentleman, was the first principal. The teachers were Mr. William Marsh, Mr. W. Santiagupillai, a Cotta Student known to this day by his "Christian Psalmody," which was the first printed edition of the poems of Anthonykutty Annaviar, the celebrated Christian poet of South India; Mr. G. S. Arianayagam Pillai, B. A. B. L. who latterly rose to a Seat on the High Court Bench of Travancore; Mr., afterwards Fr. Xavier, the first Tamil priest ordained in Ceylon; Mr. Mac. Donnell, the son of Kutty Mooper, the oldest Tamil teacher that the Mission has known; Mr. Paul, whose name has since been associated with Hambantota where he was for many years employed, and Mr. Veeravagu. One of the first students was Fr. P. O'Flanagan who subsequently prosecuted his studies in the Government College at Pondicherry and in the Scholasticate at Autin, France.

In July 1857, Dr. Bettachini died at Bollawatte. The Right Revd. Dr. John Stephen Semeria, Bishop of Olympia, succeeded him. He took a warm interest in education. He appealed to the Revd. Fr. Cooke, the Provincial of his Order in England, for European Masters, and late in 1859 we got Brothers Brown and Byrne!

In 1860 the school commission, on the persistent representation of Father Bonjean, consented to extend to the Jaffna Boys Catholic School the Government-grant, which they were giving to the English Schools under the management of the Weslyan and Anglican Missions. It was this School Commission that gave the school the name of the Jaffna Boys Seminary, by which it was afterwards known. The Circular instituting local examinations on the lines of the Cambridge local examination was issued by Mr. Scendall on the 6th December 1861. Mr. Bruce in 1880 condemned these locals as having no prestige and introduced the Cambridge Local. Messrs Scendall and Bruce were afterwards created Civil Knights and Governors of Crown Colonies. On the 31st of October 1861, Bishop Semeria left for Europe. After eight months he returned to Jaffna with Fathers Boisseau and Boutin, Brothers Conway and Dowling and Mother M. Xavier, known in the world as Mrs. Marchand, who was the first Lady Superioress of the Jaffna Convent, Sisters M. Helen, M, Teresa, M. Stanislaus and M. Joseph of the Holy Family of Bordeaux. It was in response to Dr. Semeria's appeal for European masters that Brothers Conway and Dowling were sent. With their arrival in 1862, the teaching staff of the school was materially strengthened. There were then besides the four European tutors viz. Brothers Albert Michael Bennett, John Joseph Brown, Patrick Joseph Conway and Robert Rowland Dowling, the Native teachers Messrs W. Santiagupillai, Authur Fletcher, Peter Vyramuttu, John Bastian, John Joseph Tisseverasinghe, the well known Surveyor, G. Bastian familiarly known as Chellar Master, and C. Thiagar, the genial and popular Tamil Pandit and Moonshee. Of Brothers Dowling and Conway it is necessary to say a few words. Brother Conway was a fine specimen of manhood, remarkable for soundness of judgment and decision of character. At his request two young Civilians took part in the public examination of the school in 1866. Brother Dowling is one of the ablest and most successful teachers the school ever had. Poets, they say are born, not made. Teachers of the Dowling type too are born, not made. Brother Dowling was only 18 when he came amongst us and he passed away when he was 21, having accomplished in less than three years what many people cannot hope to do in a whole life. He died of consumption on the 21st of August 1865, at Myrtle Lodge", where he was removed for a change. Myrtle Lodge was the name given by Mr. Joseph Price, District Judge of Jaffna to his large coccanut garden at Colombogam, which passed into the hands of the Catholic Mission in 1863, and is now known as the St. Joseph's Orphanage. Brother Conway survived Brother Dowling four years. He managed the school with remarkable ability for about 8 years. He died on the 22nd February 1870 of paralysis. To one of his students who visited him when he was stretched on the bed of sickness, he said that a strong man struck down by paralysis had no hope. It was the year before Brother Conway died that the Confraternity of the Sacred Heart of Jesus was formed. Dr. Bonjean had then assumed the Episcopate. Brother, afterwards, the well known Father Murphy, succeeded Brother Conway. He continued only for a short time and only to meet a pressing exigency, Father, or Brother Flanagan as he then was, succeeding him at the close of 1870. Brother, Flanagan was ordained priest with two others in December 1871 at the very first ordination of priests held in Jaffna. The two others were Fr. Vedrenne who is no more and Fr. Roux, whose name will for ever be honourably rembembered in connection with the Buddhist riots at Anuradhapura. From 1871 to 1874 Fr. Salaun had the management of the school. He was in feeble health and died of consumption at Jaffna on the 14th of April 1874. Fr. Flanagan then became Director of St. Josephs' Orphanage and manager of schools and continued as such till his death in 1889. During the time the school was conducted by the Brothers the pupils got their education for the asking. They may be said to have enjoyed a halcyon period when no fees were exacted. Three pence a month uniformly through all the classes was not much of an exaction. Rs. 6 was the sum total of the fees a scholar paid for his whole schooling in those days. At the time the school was under the management of Fr. Flanagan, the teaching staff consisted of Native youngmen trained by the Brothers during the previous decade. Fr. Flanagan however was anxious to get an infusion of new blood and we got Mr. Mac. Mahon of St. Peters' College, Agra, in 1874 and Fr. Lytton joined the school in 1875. The Inspectors who successively examined the school were Messrs Scendall, Marsh, Colscn, Helps, Alwis, Walker and Blair. About the year 1878 an agitation was set on foot by the leading Catholics of Jaffna for higher education. The late Fr. Murphy may be said to have been the soul of the movement. In 1879 the Very Rev. Fr. Soulier, Visitor General of the Oblates, of Mary Immaculate, came on a visit to Jaffna. The college under its present name was opened on the 10th of January 1881. The Revd. Fr. J. R. Smythe was the first Principal of St. Patrick's College. He was the son of a Protestant Clergyman and had, after prosecuting his studies at Trinity College, Dublin, entered the Ceylon Civil Service. It was while he was Police Magistrate of Jaffna that he resolved to join the Catholic Church and was on December 8th 1868, received into the Fold by the Rev. Fr. Salaun, the Director of the Colombogam Orphanage. The foundation stone of the large College Hall, unquestionably the best of its kind in the Province and comparing favourably with any other in the Island, measuring as it does hundred and five by 22¼ feet, was laid on the evening of Sunday the 4th December 1881. Fr. Smythe continued as Principal till 1883, June, which witnessed important changes in the ecclesiastical administration of the Island. The Central Province was detached from Colombo and erected into a separate Vicariate and entrusted to the Sylvestrian Fathers, with the Right Revd. Dr. Pagnani as Vicar Apostolic, The Colombo Vicariate was entrusted to the Oblates of Mary Immaculate with the Right Revd. Dr. Ch. Bonjean as Vicar Apostolic, the Rt. Revd. Dr. Andrew Melizan succeeding him as Vicar Apostolic of Jaffna, In the month of August of the same year, Dr. Ch. Bonjean left us for Colombo after having spent twenty-seven years of his life in our midst, devoting talents and energies, that might have graced any of the leading capitals of the World to the social, moral and intellectual improvement of the people committed to his charge. With him left Fathers Pulicani, Boisseau, Charles Collin and Smythe. The Revd. Father Lytton succeeded Fr. Smythe. In December 1883 the distribution of prizes was held for the first time in the new College hall. A class for the study of French was opened early in 1884. In March 1885 died Brother J. J. Brown after 27 years spent in the work of teaching. On the 25th of April Dr. Melizan paid a visit to the College and presented to the masters and pupils the new Principal Revd Fr. J. Collin and Brothers Dunne and Wheeler, who were about to enter upon their duties as Professors. January 1887 witnessed the death under very painful circumstances of the Revd. Fr. M. A. Murphy, one of the ablest and most zealous clergymen, that Jaffna has known. There was no public movement in his time in which he did not form a prominent figure. He will perhaps be longest remembered in connection with the Jaffna Catholic Guardian, of which he was Editor during an exceedingly eventful and sensational period. In January 1889, the death took place at Point-Pedro of the Very Revd. Fr. P. O' Flanagan whose connection with the college was almost co-extensive with his life. Revd. Fr. Patrick Dunne was the fifth Principal. Young and vigorous and gifted with rare talents he put his whole heart into the work. The successes secured by so many students during his time in the various Universities and other Examinations and the capabilities displayed by them in the various offices and professions into which they found admission justly caused St. Patrick's to be regarded as one of the best taught schools in the Island. Shorthand and Book-keeping are two subjects first introduced into the curriculum by Fr. Dunne. The former was made a subject of study in St. Patrick's College long before it found a place in the Government Code, and a student of St. Patrick's College who presented himself for the Cambridge Junior Local obtained distinction in Shorthand as early as 1892. The Revd. Fr. Dunne found time amid his many and varied duties as Principal to give the world two valuable publications. In the early part of 1898 he published a system of Shorthand he had invented for the Tamil language. The system was presented within the short compass of sixteen pages and recommended itself as much by its conciseness as by its clearness. The publication showed how great a master he was of the art of Phonography. About the middle of 1900 he published a concise Tamil—English Dictionary. Mr. (now Doctor) A. C. Evarts who put in five years excellent work at St. Patrick's both as a member of the teaching staff and as Boarding Master, joined the Civil Medical Department in February, 1890. Two successful students who became teachers and subsequently left the college in search of more remunerative occupations are Messrs. J. Gregory and B. Joachimpillai. The former is a Government Surveyor high in the esteem of the Department, and the latter is in active practice as an English and Tamil Notary in the Town of Jaffna. The year 1900 was the fiftieth anniversary of the foundation of the first Catholic School in Jaffna. In other words it was the Golden Jubilee of St. Patrick's College, once known as the Jaffna Boy's Seminary. Mr. S. Abraham who had been a student of the Jaffna Boy's Seminary under the Brothers and had been appointed a teacher in the sixties, retired on pension in May 1901. Mathematics was his favourite subject, and his proficiency in that branch of study and the special knack that he had in imparting instruction in it are well-known. In October 1901 the Revd. Fr. Dunne desired to be relieved of work in which he had been engaged without a break for sixteen years. The demonstration that took place when he left St. Patrick's and the touching displays that took place both at Jaffna and at Colombo when he finally bade adieu to Ceylon and took his departure for Europe are striking proofs of the hold that Fr. Dunne had on the affections not only of the pupils and teachers of St. Patrick's College but every one who had had the pleasure of his acquaintance. The next principal was the Very Revd. Fr. J. Collin, who was assisted by Fr. Chas. Beaud,

A valuable addition was made to the Staff in the person of the Revd. Fr. Chas. S. Matthews from the Ottawa University, who joined the College in 1903. The excellent work that he has done so far, as Professor, Discipline Master, Prefect of Games and Director of the Boarding, shows that he is quite an acquisition. The Silver Jubilee of the opening of the institution as the first Catholic College in the Island took place on the 10th of January 1906:—*St. Patrick's College Annual, 1905.*

104

The Catholic Girl's School

The Jaffna Catholic Girls' English School, conducted by Mrs. Flanagan, mother of the Revd. Fr. Flanagan of revered memory was originally held in the premises now occupied by the Jaffna Resthouse. Mr. Philip Thambapillai, well-known in his day as a Tamil Pundit and Moonshee, and father of Mr. P. A. Manners, the retired officer of the Jaffna Kachcheri, was one of the masters. The school was subsequently removed to the house in 3rd Cross Street now owned by the heirs of the late Mr. Benjamin Santiagopillai, one of the veteran lawyers of Jaffna. The two houses to the north were used as chapel and residence of the school mistress respectively. The sisters of the Holy Family when they arrived in Jaffna, occupied this house before they were installed in the new convent of Jaffna. Annamuttu, wife of Mr, S. Pedropillai, the well-known townsman of Jaffna and mother of Mr. P. Christopher of the Jaffna Premier Bakery, Victoria, the eldest daughter of the late Mr. Henry Martyn and wife of Mr. Gabriel Solomon Puvirajasinghe, Proctor, Jaffna, Mary Savirimuttu, the eldest daughter of the late Chevalier Savirimuttu Mudaliyar, Barbara Sinnamma, wife of Mr. Anthonipillai Rajakariar and mother of Mr. A. Benjamin Rajakarier, the energetic and popular Udaiyar of Jaffna Town, Mrs. Cherubim, the wife of Mr. Muttiah Cherubim and mother of Mr. Joseph Cherubim, the well-known Local Agent of the B. I. S. & Co. Steamers, Mary Magdaline, wife of Mr. Jacob Tisseveerasinghe, Notary Public, Mary Victoria widow of Mr. J. A. Tisseverasinghe, retired Sub-Collector, and mother of Mr. J. A. J. Tisseverasinghe, Proctor, and Mary Justina, wife of Arasunilayitta Mudaliyar Henry, Udaiyar of Jaffna, and Mary, wife of Joachim Sandrasegra, and mother of Mr. H. A. P. Sandrasegra, were among the first pupils.

M. A. P.

105

Translation of the Bible

The work of translating the Bible into Tamil commenced by Mr. Percival and his colleagues, was continued by his successors, and the revised Tamil Bible, which at length made its appearance, owes the purity and elegance of its diction to such scholars as Arumuga Navalar and Mr. Katiravetpillai, who were associated with the Missionaries in the work of translation and revision: —*The Life of C, W, Katiravetpillai.*

106

Christian David

Revd. Christian David was born, August 17.1771, of a highly connected and distinguished family, and his father held the post of the Judge of the High Court of Justice under the regime of the Royal Danish Government, and was one of the Elders of the Lutheran Church. Mr. David prosecuted his studies at Bishop's College, Calcutta, where he spent a course of years prior to admission to Holy Orders. In 1801, Mr. David had an offer, from the resident in the Court ot His Majesty the King, of a very lucrative situation, somewhat more in importance to a Government Agency. At the same time he received from H. E. the Governor of Ceylon an offer to be State Preacher of the Gospel in the Island. He accepted the post' of preacher of the Gospel in Ceylon and Superintendent of over forty schools in the Northern Districts of the Island. Colonel Barbet, Commander of the Fort and Commission Extraordinary, was a man deeply interested in educational and missionary works. With his help, Mr. David restored the Old Dutch Church of St. John's as a place of worship, and continued to preach there till 1841. In March 1802, His Excellency the Hon'ble North attended Divine Service at St. John's Church, where he heard Mr. David preach, and in testimony of his good opinion towards Mr. David directed Rs. 250 to be paid to him as a mark of his Excellency's approbation of Mr. David's exemplary behaviour in the exercise of his holy function:— *Memoir of the Revd. Christian David.*

In an entry of his autobiographical record the following noteworthy event is recorded.

"In the middle of March 1814, I arrived at Arrippoo, where His Excellency and Lady Brownrigg came to see the pearl-fishery. Both His Excellency and Lady Brownrigg requested me to remain there in order to perform Divine Service on the following Sunday, but I mentioned to them that my prayer book was with my clerk, who was then at Mannar, where I intended to go to perform Divine Service on Sunday. Then Lady Brownrigg told me that she would provide me with a Prayer Book, and shall also have a clerk suitable to answer the responses. This conversation we had on Friday afternoon, and on the following day notice was given that Divine Service would be held on Sunday morning precisely at 10 o'clock, in the large bungalow, which was erected for receiving visitors, etc. On Sunday morning Lady Brownrigg sent me a Prayer Book, and a little while after she came to me and said:—Mr. David, it is high time to go to the bungalow, and there you will find a reading desk and cushion for kneeling and the clerk ready for you. Immediately I went thither. Many Civil and Military and other gentlemen, who came to the pearl fishery from different places were present. I commenced the morning service at 10 o'clock, and to my greatest surprise found His Excellency, the most devout Governor, as a substitute for a clerk. His most exemplary behaviour astonished the congregation. After service was over I thanked the Governor for having condescendingly taken the clerk's part in the service. Immediately like David of old, I thanked our gracious Creator—who am I, Oh Lord God and what is my house, that thou hast brought me hitherto.

107

Ceylon Journalism

In 1853,[*] Mr. Katiravetpillai, while still a teacher in the Wesleyan School, came before the public in a new and an important capacity, which gives us an opening to pass ràpidly in review the leading events connected with the rise and progress of the Fourth Estate in Ceylon. The first attempt at Journalism was made during the admintstration of Sir Robert Wilmot Horton. The Colombo Journal, conducted by Officials made its debut on the 1st January 1831, with George Lee, the father of the late Lionel Lee as Editor, but the severe and ill-advised criticism of the home authorities appearing in its columns led to its discontinuance on the 31st December 1833, under orders from England. The Colombo Observer, of which Mr. Winter was the first Editor, was started by the merchants of Colombo on the 1st February 1834. Mr. Winter was succeeded in the editorship by Dr. Elliott, who also became the proprietor. Mr. A. M. Ferguson joined the staff in 1846 and became proprietor in 1857. Mr. John Ferguson joined his uncle in 1861. In 1867 the name was changed to "Ceylon Observer". Mr. A. M. Ferguson, who was made a C. M. G, in recognition of his services in connection with the Melbourne Exhibition, died the oldest Journalist in the East in 1892, when Mr. John Ferguson, C. M. G., M. L. C., became the editor-in-Chief of the oldest newspaper established in Ceylon independent of Government. On the 3rd May 1837 was started the Ceylon Chronicle of which the Revd. S. O. Glenie was the editor and Governor Horton, Treasurer Temple and Postmaster General Lee were the contributors. Sergeant Rough, the Acting Chief Justice, Mr. Marshall Auditor-General and Mr. Henry Staples, Proctor, wrote squibs, criticising the new journal, which was discontinued on the 30th September 1838. "The Ceylon Herald" was published from 7th September 1838, to the 30th June 1846. The first attempt at journalism in Jaffna was made in the year 1841, when the "Morning Star," devoted to education, science, literature, agriculture, Government and religion with a summary of important news appeared as a bi-monthly Anglo-Tamil Journal, under the editorship of Henry Martyn, with whom was associated Mr. Seth Payson, a licensed preacher of the American Mission, subsequently better known as "Payson Udaiyar". "The Ceylon Advertiser" and "General Intelligencer" started on the 23rd September 1845, was discontinued on the 3rd April 1846, "The Ceylon Examiner" was started on the first January and the "Ceylon Times" on the 1st July 1846. The Examiner which owed its power and popularity to Lorenz, has ceased of late to make its appearance, "the Ceylon Independent" superseding it, but the "Ceylon Times," with which Mr. John Capper was long and honourably connected, continues to be published as a leading daily paper under the title of "The Times of Ceylon." It was at this stage of the progress of the Fourth Estate in Ceylon that "the Literary Mirror," a monthly Magazine was started by Mr. Katiravetpillai. The first number was issued on the 6th May, 1853:—*The Life and Times of C W. Katiravetpillai.*

108

Copay C. M. S. Tamil School

This school was started in 1853, and was a seat of high Tamil Culture. Mr. Thamotharampillai Kingsbury, afterwards so famous in Madras, was the first Headmaster and was followed by Messrs Homer, and then Evarts, the Tamil Poet (father of Mr. Jeremiah Evarts.) It was during this time that Messrs Bren. Evarts and Hensman formed into a Committee and published that book in Tamil, so in-valuable to preachers and evangelists, called "Samaya Pareedchai." (Test of Religions). It was also then that Mr. Evarts wrote the first part of "Thiruvakupuranam" (Scripture History in verse) a masterly production used as a text book in the Mission Schools in those days, but which unfortunately he did not live to complete:—*The Life of the Revd. John Hensman.*

109

Photography

The American Missionaries were the first to introduce the Photographic art into Ceylon. They obtained the necessary apparatus, chemicals, and printed directions in 1853. and made a number of trials which were unsuccessful. It was then suggested to them by an admirer of Mr. Martyns' ingenious mind and artistic talents that he should be given an opportunity to try his hand at the new art. Accordingly Mr. Martyn was invited to a meeting of the Batticotta Church. On his arrival, the Senior Missionary, the Revd. E. P. Hastings, entrusting the photographic apparatus to him, asked him to study the process, while with his colleagues he attended the meeting. Mr. Martyn applied himself to the study of the process. On the return of the Missionaries from the meeting, which lasted for about 3 hours Mr. Martyn told them, what came upon them as an agreeable surprise, not untinged with misgivings, that he would take their photo, if they would sit to him. They then sat to him and he took their photo, to their satisfaction the first photo ever taken in Ceylon. Mr. Martyn is thus entitled to rank as the first photographer of the Island. The photographic art was introduced into Colombo by Mr. Parting in 1856. The Mission aries were so much pleased with Mr. Martyn's penetrating intelligence that they made a present to him of the photographic aparatus etc. which he had turned to account, so readily, in a few hours. Thus equipped, he soon opened a studio in his house to the East of the Custom's premises; and associating Mr. Cyrus Koch in the practice of the new art, cultivated it during the rest of his life, as one of his hobbies:—*Biographical Sketch of Henry Martyn.*

110

Kasinatha Pulavar

இவர் அச்சுவேலிக்கோயிற்பற்றில் வசித்த சோதிடசாஸ்திரிகளுள் ஒருவர். கிறிஸ்தாப்தம் 1799இல் பிறந்து 1854ல் இறந்தனர். இலக்கிய ஆராய்ச்சியும் உடையராய் வித்தாண்மைபூண்டு தாலபுராணம் எனும்ஓர் பாடல் இயற்றினர். அதைப்பனங்காய்ப்பாரதம் எனவழக்கத்திற்கூறுவர். பனைமரப்பெருமையும் அவற்றின்பிரயோசனங்களுமே அப்பாடற்பொருளாம். பா. ச

111

Siva-Dhushana-Parikaram

It had been for years the desire of Arumugavar and his friends to possess a printing-press, and there had even been negotiations to join certain Burghers in a subscription to purchase one for their common use. Now the wish had become so strong and general, that the Tamil gentry surmounted the difficulty without the help of their uncongenial neighbours, and traitor-Sepoys of the press, workmen who had been trained in the noble American establishment at Manepay, then daily employing a hundred hands, were ready to be engaged. Arumugavar began to publish, in separate volumes, a choice succession of Tamil classics, and issued a series of school books in the Native language after the model of those provided by the missionaries. The blending in conflict and compromise of Hinduism and Christianity is shown in the sentiments conveyed by several of the phrases and sentences in the first book of lessons for children of tender years. The following are "examples":—Tell no lies," "Eat no flesh," "Despise not him who despises you." "Anoint yourself every Saturday with oil," "He who commits sin will have pain in hell." "He who practices virtue will have bliss in heaven" "Though born in a low caste the upright man is great." "When you go to the temple, think of nothing but the worship of God." "Remember always that God is one." Proceeding with unabated zeal and talent, the movement crowned itself in 1854 in a work entitled "Siva-Dhushana-Parikaram" in which the author, doubtless Arumugavar, displaying an intimate and astonishing acquaintance with the Holy Bible, labours cleverly to show that the opinions and ceremonies of Jehovah's ancient people closely resembled those of Sivaism, and were neither more nor less Divine in their origin and profitable in their entertainment and pursuit. The notion of merit held by the Hindus, their practices of penance, pilgrimage and lingam-worship, their ablutions, invocations and other observances and rites, are cunningly defended on the authority of our sacred writings:—*Hindu Pastors by the Revd. E. J. Robinson*, (*Late Wesleyan Missionary in Ceylon.*)

The phamplet entitled "Suppratheepam" was written by Daniel L. Carrol alias Vyravanather Visvanathapillai of Manepay, in refutation of Siva-Dhushana-Parikaram.

II2

Daniel Poor

Revd. Daniel Poor was one of the first band of Missionaries who came to Ceylon in 1816. He was stationed at Tellipalai where as at Vaddukoddai, the property which had belonged to the Dutch Church was granted by the Government for the use of the Mission. That he was a man of good intellect is indicated by the fact that he preached in Tamil in one year from the time of his arrival. When the Batticotta Seminary was opened in 1823, he took charge of it. He laboured to establish and further a broad system of thorough religious and scientific education as a means of Christianizing heathen learning. For eleven years he presided over the Batticotta Seminary with distinguished ability. The rest of his mission life was spent at Tellipally, Manepay and Madura, India, where he threw his whole energies into the work he most loved—preaching the Gospel:—*The Church of Christ in Ceylon.*

113

A Private Tamil School

A private school was started by A Mudaliyar Santiagupillai, who engaged a good Tamil Scholar of Nallur, Vasiakone Katiritamby, a kinsman of the famous Saravanamutto Pulavar, to impart a sound practical knowledge of Tamil. A portion of the back verandah of his house on the Main Street, Jaffna, was set apart, at first, for the accommodation of the children, but as the attendants increased, a bungalow was erected, into which Mr. Katiritamby and his pupils were duly installed on the 1st May 1857. Over and above the fees charged, Mr. Katiritamby got during Christmastide a lump sum for the Chanippaddo sung by the children, from house to house, recounting the trials they had endured, and the progress they had made. Mr. Katiritamby was probably the last of the race of cruel pedagogues in Jaffna to whom the "Nettykal," "the Katterumbu" and the "Kothundum" were familiar modes of torture sanctioned by immemorial usage, the infliction of which on the little ones confided to their training, afforded them peculiar delight, as the sovereign means of repressing truant tendencies. But he was a successful teacher, and the boys and girls whom he taught were able to read and write fairly well, while the more advanced lads, could explain difficult passages from the Nâyadathum, Baratham and Kural, write essays and even compose metrical verses of some merit. In 1864 when Katiritamby passed away, he was succeeded by Aiyaturai Iyer, son of Visuvathee Iyer, the chief officiating priest of the Kandasamy temple at Nallur. The school was maintained by the Iyer, in a high state of efficiency, till the supersession of the Central School Commission paying lump sum grant to English Schools, by the Department of Public Instruction giving grants-in-aid on the result payment system in 1870. With the gradual multiplication of village vernacular schools encouraged by the new system, the Iyer found it increasingly difficult to secure even a tolerably good attendance, and the school had to be closed in 1874. It has been well observed by one of the foremost educationists of the Island, the late Dr. Bonjean, that, under the grant-in-aid system initiated by Sir Hercules Robinson

210

and developed by his successors, public instruction has lost in depth what it has gained in extent, as a partial compensation for the want of that solidity and thoroughness which the educational agencies, public and private, were able to attain under the old system, untrammelled by a code, which commenced by Mr. Lawrie, formulated by Mr. (now Sir) Charles Bruce and subjected to yearly revision by successive Directors, enforces the cramming of a certain amount of knowledge, within a certain amount of time, as the condition of obtaining a certain amount of grant:—*The Life of A. Mudaliyar Santiagopillai.*

114

Daniel L. Caroll

Mr. Caroll came into prominence, first by his vigorous phamplet entitled "Supratheepam," then by his Tamil translation of Colenso's Algebra and finally by taking the B. A. degree on the foundation of the Madras University in 1857, two years after the Batticotta Seminary was closed.

Mr. C. W. Thamotharampillai claimed with Mr. Caroll the distinction of being the only other candidate who passed the first B. A. examination of the Madras University. He subsequently took his B. L. degree and became Judge of Puthukkoddai. He was recognised as one of the ablest Tamil Scholars of his day. He was appointed an examiner and elected a Fellow of the Madras University. As a reward for his distinguished services, the Government raised him to the rank of "Rao Bahadur":—*Life and Times of C. W. Katiravetpillai.*

115

J. R. Arnold

Mr. Joel R. Arnold, Alias Arunasalam Sathasivam of Manipay, was for many years the Editor of the "Morning Star" and Professor of Vernacular Literature in Jaffna College, which is the Batticotta Seminary revived under certain limitations, after a lapse of fifteen years, through the exertions of some of its most prominent old boys, including the late Robert Breckenridge, who raised subscriptions locally, in fulfilment of what the American Board had laid down as the condition of its renewed support. It must be said of Mr. Arnold that he was not of those whose talent was "kept laid up in a napkin." His literary industry was most commendable. He will long be favourably known as a verseman by his "Meyvetha-Saram," "Tiruchchathakam," "Nannery Malai, "Nannery Koththu," "Satpothasaram" and "Illara Nondy," and as a proseman by his "Nannery Katha Sangrakam" "Universal History," "Compend of Astronomy" and the "Galaxy of Tamil Poets," to which last is prefixed an encomium in Tamil verse by the subject of our notice. Mr. Arnold's son is a Proctor practising in the Jaffna Courts:—*Ibid.*

Proctor Arnold died on the 21st December, 1906.

116

S. Davidupillai

Mr. Davidupillai entered the service of the Government at the Kachcheri at Jaffna in his 19th year, while the Dutch were yet the Masters of the Island. Under the English he was provided with a post in the Paddy Department, Jaffna Kachcheri. In this post he served faithfully and honourably till the year 1855. Eighteen years after his death, the road opened adjoining his residence and extending from the Main Street to the Beach Road in a perfectly straight line, was called David's Road by Sir William Twynam, in memory of a good and faithful servant of Government.—*Life of S. Davidupillai.*

Mr. J. Gregory, Licensed surveyor, is a grandson of Mr. Davidupillai.

117

Kamanyar

Mr. Armstrong was promoted to the rank of Commanding Officer of the Tenth Division of Pioneers which was raised by him—Such officers came to be known in Tamil Districts as "Kamanyar"—Armstrong himself being known as "Muttu Kamanyar" ever since he assumed the said command.—*Memoir of Francis Muttyah Armstrong.*

118

Controversial dialogues

Mr. Martyn made a proposal to Fathers Bonjean and Mola to have a course of controversial dialogues in Tamil on Sunday evenings, before Benediction, discussing the comparative claims of Catholicism and Protestantism. The Rev. Fathers entered warmly into his views and encouraged him to make a start, after obtaining the approval of Dr. Semeria. A spacious bungalow was quickly put up, on the North Eastern Corner of the Cathedral grounds, and just in front of the present episcopal residence, and the first dialogue was held about 4 p.m. on the second Sunday in September 1860. Dr. Semeria inaugurated the proceedings by blessing the meeting and then retired. Father Bonjean took the chair, being supported, on the right, by Fathers Mauroit and

Mola, and on the left by Fathers Chounavel and St. Geneys. The Catholic laity was fully represented. The chairman, in his opening speech, explained the object of the meeting and then the dialogue written by Mr. Martyn, in which the Catholic was pitted against the Anglican and the Wesleyan, was read by three persons trained by him so to read as if they were engaged in an animated controversy as to the merits of their respective systems of belief. Mr. Mariampillai, better known as மெல்விட்டுமரி யாம்பிள்ளை, represented the Catholic, Mr. Philip Francis, son of the aged Catechist of the Cathedral, the Anglican, and Mr. Thambimuttu (brother of Fr. Xavier) the Wesleyan. The first dialogue created a most favourable impression and the subsequent dialogues, were increasingly popular and attracted large numbers of different persuasions:—*Biographical Sketch of Henry Martyn.*

119

Last illness, Death and Funeral of Henry Martyn

Early in January 1861 Mr. Martyn accompanied by Mr. Williams of the Jaffna-Kachcheri, left for Madras for the purpose of laying his case before the Home Government in the hope of obtaining redress. After a stay of about eight weeks in Black Town, he returned to Jaffna on the 10th March 1861. The day after his return from Madras, he took a bath. The next day he was seized with acute pneumonia. Father Mola, who in the practice of medicine, was then successful and popular, saw him, day after day and tried to arrest the progress of the malady. On the 6th night of his illness, his life was despaired of and Father Bonjean who was sent for, administered to him the last sacraments. He then revived a little and willed away his property very briefly as follows:—"This is my Last Will and Testament that all my property should go to my wife." The next morning there was a considerable change for the better. A few days later, he was removed at his own request, to one of the Lodging Houses attached to the Jaffna Friend-in-Need Society's Hospital and placed under the treatment of the Dispenser in charge. Having made some progress towards recovery he made up his mind to return home early on the morning of the 31st March (Holy Saturday). He was then in the dispensary, bidding good-by to the dispenser, when he pressed him to take some liquid medicine. He expostulated with the dispenser, observing that the dose he was forcing on him was unusually and unpleasantly too near the one he had already taken. He then swallowed the potion, saying that he fully confided in him as one of his old pupils at Batticotta. It was the last medicine he took; for, in a minute or two, he was no more; to the utter amazement of the by-standers and his own attendants. His remains were forthwith removed to his residence where his widow and children and relations and friends bemoaned his loss. The funeral took place on Easter Sunday after Benediction, thirty-four-hours after death. During this long period, the hand and feet remained perfectly pliable, thus giving support to the suspicion of foul play and the report that got abroad that he was drugged. As the funeral cortege reached the pandal for the representation of the Passion, then erected, for the first time, adjoining the Northern side of the Cathedral, Father Mola, in response to the general desire expressed, taking down the coffin and lifting up the lid, found that decomposition had set in. No autopsy was held. In those days intra-mural burials were not prohibited; and the remains were interred in the Cathedral:—*Biographical Sketch of Henry Martyn.*

120

St. Joseph's Orphanage

This Institution owes its existence to, and depends for its support on the "Association of the Holy childhood," which, at first, established for the redemption of the Chinese children, has since extended its operations to India and Ceylon. The funds are to be exclusively devoted to works connected with the baptism and the Christian education of heathen born children:—*Report on the Jaffna Catholic Schools and Orphan Asylums.*

121

Sir Muttu Coomaraswamy

The Hon'ble Mr. Coomaraswamy Mudaliyar, the father of the Tamil Knight, was himself the representative of the Tamils in the Legislative Council till 1836. The academy may well be proud of having trained for Ceylon one of her greatest sons. Young Coomaraswamy was appointed a Cadet in the Colombo Kachcheri. He was transferred soon after to Mullaitivu as Police Magistrate, which place he resigned to join the Bar. After the usual term of apprenticeship, he was called to the Bar as an Advocate. A few years after, he was summoned to the Legislative Council, as the representative of the Tamil Community, on the retirement of the Hon. Mr. Edirmanesingham. His immense wealth and resources did not necessitate an active practice at the Bar. With a command of English such as few Englishmen could boast of, he was a speaker of no common order. He combined grace of diction, with fluency of speech. With hardly a taint of foreign accent, he ranked the best amongst the speakers of his time. Exhaustive on any subject on which he delivered himself, his addresses were often open to the charge of extreme length, but he never rose without propounding important sentiments in well-chosen language. In 1862, Mr. Coomaraswamy started for Europe. While in England he published a translation of a Tamil Drama entitled "Arichandra" and dedicated it to Her Majesty the Queen. The dedication and the preface are a masterpiece of English Composition. Meanwhile he was called to the Bar at Lincoln's Inn, being the first non-Christian (not being a Jew) who obtained a privilege of being registered in the rolls of the Inns of Court.... He had ventured to carry into effect the grandest scheme of his life. Lady Coomaraswamy and her infant son had preceded him to Europe and he himself expected to follow them soon. If he had lived it was his ambition to have entered the British Parliament. The day however on which he was to embark for Europe was his last. On the 4th of May 1879 Sir Coomaraswamy was no more:— *The Ceylon Review, 1894*.

122

St. James Church, Jaffna

This Church stands at the South-Western end of the Pettah, commanding a very good view of the lagoon which stretches before it. The foundations were laid some 18 years ago, to replace an older church. The plan of the church was laid out by the Revd. Father Mauriot who has from time to time superintended the works. Only one kind of timber—Ironwood—is used for the roof. The site of the church is so closely hemmed in on all sides by compounds thickly planted with trees and densely inhabited that it is deprived of the commanding prospect it would otherwise have. The upper structure, however, is open to view, and the pretty dome, quite an architectural novelty in Jaffna, with the emblem of redemption at the top, piers above all other buildings in the Town and is the first object that meets or rather attracts the eye as one enters the lagoon from the sea without.—*C. C. Messenger, May, 1876*.

The beautiful dome was completed in 1876 under the self taught architect Maistre Santiagoe of the congregation attached to the Church:—*J. C. Guardian*,

123

Adaikala Matha Church

The building of this Church is traditionally connected with the Goanese Priest, the kind-hearted Father Lobo (1783-1802), whose tomb is still shown within the Sanctuary. But the old building was found, to be behind the times for a progressive congregation and so the foundations were laid in another site within the same compound for a magnificient church. The ceremony of blessing its corner-stone was performed by Dr. Joulain on the 8th September 1907, Father J. Aloysus O. M. I. then being in charge:—*J. C. Guardian.*

124

Philip Bastiampillai

Mr. Bastiampillai (Velichorpillai), a typical lawyer of his day, was born of a respectable family in 1819, and was educated at the Batticotta Seminary. In 1844 he was admitted a Proctor of the District Court of Jaffna and practised his profession with honesty and success. He worked his way up to comfortable independence, and in him the talented Mr. Henry Martyn of Batticotta fame found a willing and an able confrere in his efforts to elevate Catholic Society in Jaffna. None of his four children, the eldest of whom was Mr. Philip Bastiampillai, Proctor, survive and in Messrs F. X. R. Bastiampillai, Planter, H. A. P. and J. N. Sandrasagra, Advocates, there are three of his grandsons living. Mr. Bastiampillai died in 1862 comparatively early in life, deeply regretted:—*J. H. Witterborn.*

125

Martyn's Road

Mr. Dyke proceeded to England on furlough on the 1st October 1860, Mr. Flanderka, a Burgher gentleman and a Ceylonese, for the first time, in the annals of the Civil Service acting for him, as Government Agent, on his own special and pressing recommendation. Mr. Martyn died on the 31st March 1861. A month or two later, Governor MacCarthy decided that the loss to Government arising from the large deficit of salt in the Jaffna stores, should be made good by the seizure and sale of Mr. Martyn's estate. But the Secretary of State to whom Mr. Martyn had appealed directed an independent inquiry to be held, in view of the various reasons which Mr. Martyn had urged, as fully accounting for the wastage, but which Mr. Dyke had failed to deal with or refute entrenching himself on the general charge of want of confidence. The Hon. Mr. Pennyfather, Auditor-General, was appointed a commission to enquire into and report upon the causes, if any, of the wastage. He arrived in Jaffna soon after Mr. Dyke's return from England and prosecuted a very careful and impartial enquiry on the spot, with all the papers before him. His report was that the causes of the wastage were so various, so long in operation, and some of them so much beyond human control as to exonerate the storekeeper from culpable negligence and from the serious responsibility of making good the deficit. The Governor thereupon rescinded his order, and it goes without saying that if he had been living, he would have been re-instated in office. In 1862, Mr. Dyke opened a road adjoining the late Mr. Martyn's residence and called it Martyn's road, as a lasting compliment to a distinguished native. This is now the approach road to the Jaffna Railway station from the Main Street.—*Biographical Sketch of Henry Martyn.*

126

The arrival in Jaffna of six Sisters of the Holy Family

These devoted ladies accompanied Bishop Semaria, on his return back from home in 1862. His Lordship, the Rev. Fathers Boutin and Boisseau, Brothers Dowling and Conway, and the Sisters, obtained from the French Government, a free passage on the steamers of the Imperial Navy. The steam-aviso L'Echo, landed them safe at Galle, on the 19th October; and through the courtesy of Sir Charles MacCarthy, who kindly placed the Colonial Steamer "Pearl" at the Bishop's disposal, they all reached Jaffna, on All Souls—Day. In January following, the Sisters received the direction of our Female Seminary, from the worthy Mrs. Flanagan, through whose well-sustained exertions, it had been placed and kept in a creditable condition. The names of the sisters are:—Rev. Mother Xavier Marchand, Superioress; Sister Mary Stanislas Quinn; Sister Mary Helen Winter; Sister Mary Ligory Roger; Sister Mary Teresa Van Murs; Sister Mary Joseph Maroilles. The "Association of the Holy Family was established in 1820, by a holy Priest of Bordeaux, the Rev. Abbe-Noailles:—*Report on the Jaffna Catholic Schools and Orphan Asylums.*

127

Journalism in Jaffna

The first attempt at Journalism in the North was made in the year 1841 when the Morning Star devoted to education, science, literature, agriculture, government and religion, with a summary of important news appeared as a bi-monthly Anglo-Tamil journal under the editorship of Mr. Henry Martyn, the father of Mr. James H. Martyn, the late editor of the Catholic Guardian. The late Mr. Henry Martyn is thus entitled to the distinction of being the first native journalist in the Island.

In 1853 was started the Literary Mirror by the late Mr. C. W. Kathiravetpillai. It was a monthly Magazine and during its short career very interesting articles on various subjects, literary and scientific appeared in it. The Mirror thereby came into prominence as a vehicle of useful information and public education and received for it a large and respectable clientele both Native and European, including Civil Servants such as Sir C. P. Layard, the father of one of our former Chief Justices.

It was in 1862 that Mr. Nicholas Gould started a newspaper known as the Jaffna Freeman. Its chief contributors were the late Messrs Solomon Johnpulle, Arnold, Schoorman, John Wittebron W. Santiagupillai and Miss Thahitha Ondatjee. The Ceylon Patriot was started on the 6th February 1863 by the late Mr. C. W. Kathiravetpillai, then a leading advocate and latterly Police Magistrate of Kayts. Rev. John Kilner, Superintendent of the North Ceylon Wesleyan Mission and Mr. L. Leisching of the Civil Service contributed to the Ceylon Patriot very interesting articles of a literary character. With the advent of the Patriot a keen competition was called into play between the two Jaffna papers, the Freeman and the Patriot. For a time the writers in both the papers exerted their powers to the utmost to excel each other and to ensure their excellence in the field of journalism. The Patriot, however, thanks to its keen sighted editors, had this advantage over the Freeman that its criticism of men and measures was well meant, fair and legitimate, and its general tone moderate and dignified, while the articles in the Freeman were charged with rancour, coarseness, partiality and personality. The Patriot changed hands in the year 1865, Mr. Solomon Johnpulle becoming its proprietor. The Freeman ceased to exist in 1867 when it was amalgamated with the Patriot which continued to be published under his auspices and remained for some time more in his family till again it changed hands some years ago. Mr. A. Canagaretnam, Proctor, S. C., is now its Proprietor and Editor. Messrs C. W. Kathiravetpillai, Solomon Johnpulle, T. C. Changarapillai, S. K. Lawton, J. J. Tisseveerasinghe, James H. Martyn, Proctor Senathirajah, C. N. Puvirayasinghe and H. F. Johnpulle were its successive Editors. Its chief contributors were Messrs G. P. Savundranayagampillai, B. A. and B. L. of the Madras High Court Bar, Vedanayagampillai, Christian Poet of South India and others.

The Jaffna News was a paper edited by Mr. Hughes for less than a year till 1871 when it collapsed.

Among Magazines mention may be made of the Jaffna College Miscellany started in 1872. The Victoria College Magazine is a quarterly started in 1898. In 1900 was started the Central, the Magazine of the Jaffna Central College. The Ceylon Law Review was edited by Mr. Isaac Tambiah from 1901. The Christian Review is a quarterly started by Mr. Tambyah in 1904.

St. John's College Magazine was started in 1904 under the auspices of the Old Boys Association of the College.

St. Patrick's Annual is the organ of the Old Boys Association of St. Patrick's College started in 1905.

For a good many years the Catholics of Jaffna had no newspaper of their own. The Jaffna Catholic Guardian was started in the year 1876 by the late lamented Dr. Christopher Bonjean O. M. I., the first Arch-Bishop of Colombo, then Bishop of Jaffna. The Jaffna Catholic Guardian which was enlarged to its present size in 1896 continues as a weekly. The late Dr. Bonjean, Mr. P. E. Morgappah, Rev. Fathers. M. A. Murphy, C. Collin, J. B. Meary, J. Collin, P. Dunne. J. Neville and the late Mr. J. H. Martyn were successively its Editors. The Hindu Organ was started in 1889 by the late Mr. T. P. Chellappahpillai, then retired Chief Justice of Travancore. Messrs Chellappahpillai, Advocate, S. Nagalingam Proctor, A. Cathiravelu and others were its Editors. Mr. A. Sapapathy continues to edit the paper now:—*The Jaffna Catholic Guardian, January, 20th 1912.*

128

The Colombogam Estate

The house and estate of the late Mr. Price at Colombogam were purchased in 1862 for the use of the orphans. The total area of the land, is 14 acres, mostly planted with cocoanut trees. About 4 acres are laid out in a vegetable garden, and planted with lemon-trees, mango-trees and jak-trees:— *Report on the Jaffna Catholic Schools and Orphan Asylums.*

129

Laying of the foundation stone of the Convent School of the Holy Family, Jaffna

The following is abridged from the report published in the Examiner :—

The foundation-stone of the Convent School was laid on the 24th May, by his Lordship, the Right Revd. Dr. Semeria, assisted by a number of the Catholic Fathers, in the midst of a respectable concurse of people of all classes. The following is a free translation of the Latin document drawn on the occasion and partly engraven on the stone:—

"On the ninth of the Kalends of June 1864, being the festival of the patronage of the Blessed Virgin Mary, under the title of "Help of Christians", under the Pontificate of Pope Pius the ninth; in the reign of Victoria, Queen of Great Britain, on the occasion of her birthday, Charles Justin MacCarthy, Knight, being Governor of the island of Ceylon; the Right Reverend Dr. J. S. Semeria, Vicar Apostolic of Jaffna, assisted by the Reverend Fathers Moukel, Mauroit, Salaun, Bonjean and Boisseau, in the presence of several generous benefactors, and amidst a large concourse of people, solemnly blessed and laid down the first stone of a Convent of the Holy Family, in honour of the Blessed and Immaculate Virgin Mary, and of St. Joseph, for the training of young ladies in piety and learning, and for the support of destitute and orphan girls."

130

The O. B. C.

A branch of the Oriental Bank Corporation was introduced into Jaffna so far back as the year 1864. It continued its operations for well nigh 30 years, with results so satisfactory that it may safely be asserted, that local causes did not contribute to the difficulty which staggered the Corporation in 1884 but which the then Governor of the Colony, Sir Arthur Gordon, afterwards Lord Stanmore, promptly averted by his courageous guarantee of its discredited notes or the final crash of 1892, which led to the winding up of an institution almost as familiar to the people here, as the Bank of England to Londoners who jocularly called it the "Old Lady of Thread Needle Street." The Jaffna branch on its first establishment, held its office in a house that stood at the South-Eastern Corner of the junction of the Main Street with the 3rd cross street, and its business steadily increased and grew so prosperous and successful that the Directors resolved to have a house of their own for carrying on the local business. With this view a plot of ground at the Eastern end of the 2nd cross street was purchased and the work of building the new house commenced. On its completion the Bank moved to the new house and this is the large upstair building which is now used as the Jaffna Post Office and which was purchased in 1893, when the Corporation went into liquidation, by Mr. Melville-Geddes, Planter, from whom it passed to other hands. In July 1899 it was acquired by Government. The old house at the main street after the Bank vacated it, became the habitat of a school known as Koch's school, from which some of the bright and prominent students went over to join the Native Town High School, which was started by the late Mr. William Nevins and which in 1893 developed into the Jaffna Hindu College. It was also in this house that the Jaffna St. Joseph's Catholic Library was established in 1884, when it was in the possession of the late Mr. Manuelpillai Rajakariar to whom it was transferred by Mr. P. S. Sandrasagra—father of Jos. N. Sandrasagra Mudaliyar, J. P., the popular Maniagar of Valigamam West—who purchased it when he was employed as the Store-keeper of the Bank, to whom was entrusted the custody of the tobacco hypothecated to the Bank as security for the money lent to tobacco cultivators and traders, and who on that account was popularly known as Bank Santiapillai and who afterwards became the Jaffna Agent of the British—India Steam Navigation Company. The last owner demolished the old building and erected on it a new house known as "Jubilee House," in which Mr. Joseph Machado, the leading and popular merchant of Jaffna, keeps his fine large shop. Mr. Charles Morrison who took a prominent and praiseworthy interest in all movements that were set on foot to promote the interests of the local population and who is still remembered and talked of as a gentleman of genial manners and charming personality, was the local Agent or Manager of the Bank. Mr. Sinnatamby Saravanamuttu of Manepay was the Shroff:—*C. N. P.*

131

Percival Ackland Dyke

இவ்வேசண்டர் முதன்முதல் 1822 ம் ஸு வைகாசி மீ 15 ந் திகதி இலங்கையாசாட்சியிலுத்தியோகம் பெற்றனர். அப்போதிவருக்கு வயது பதினேழு. இவ்வரசாட்சியிற்சேருமுன்னர் கடலிராணுவத்தைச் சேர்ந்தவோர் கப்பலிலுபதளபதியாகவிருந்தார். இலங்கையாசாட்சியிற் சேர்ந்த போதிராசாங்கலிகிதரின் தொழில்சாலையிலொருதவிக்காரனாயேற்பட்டார். பின்பு 1824 ம் ஸு பங்குனி மீ யாழ்ப்பாணத்துக்கு இரண்டாங் கலக்கட்டராகி அநேக்க 1825 ம் ஸு மாசி மீ யாழ்ப்பாணத்துக்குப் பிசுக்காலும் பொலிஸ்நீதவானு

மாயினர். 1827 ம் ௵ யாழ்ப்பாணத்திலிருந்து உத்தியோகவுயர்வுபெற்றுக் கீழ்மாகாணத்துக்கப்போது தலைவிடமாக விருந்த திருக்கோணமலைக்குப்போய் மாகாணநீதவானுங் கலக்கட்டருமாயிருந்து 1829 ம் ௵ ஐப்பசி ௴ 8 ந் திகதி யாழ்ப்பாணத்துக்குக் கலக்கட்டராகத்திரும்பினர். குறித்த ஐப்பசி ௴ 8 ந் திகதி தொடங்கியிவர் மரித்துப்போன ஐப்பசி ௴ 8 ந் திகதிவரைக்குமிவரே யாழ்ப்பாணவேசண்டராகவிருந்தவர். சிலகாலமிவர்பொறுப்பிலே சலாபத்தில் முத்துக்குளிப்பு நடத்தப்பட்டது. இலங்கையரசாட்சியில் முன்பின் நாற்பத்தைந் துவருஷஞ்சேவகம்பண்ணினர்.

இவரழகியவங்கலட்சணமும் புளகிதவதனகாந்தியுமாட்களைப்பார்த்தவரவர் குணமறியும் யூகசாமர்த்தியமுமுடையவர். இறைஞ்சலர்க்கிடியேறெருத்திருந்தார்.

கச்சேரியிற்றும் குடியிருந்தகாணியிற் சிறந்தவித தாபரங்களை நாட்டியவைகளைப் பண்படுத்திப்பாதுகாக்கவும் நீர்ப்பாய்ச்சவும் வேலையாட்களைவைத்துத் தமதிருவிழிபோலவைகளைப் பேணியவைகளிலிருந்துபார்த்தவுச்சிதவாசனையை மோந்து சுகிர்தகனிகளையருந்திவந்தார். இத்தோட்டத்தைப்பார்க்கப் பிரியமுடையவர்களுமுத்தரவுடனுட்புகுந்து பார்த்து விருப்பப்படியெவ்வளவுகனிகளையுந் தின்றுபார்க்கலாம்.

யாழ்ப்பாண ஆபத்துக்குதவிவைத்தியசாலையை இஸ்தாபித்தவரிவரே. அவரிவ்வறச்சாலையையுரப்பாய்ப் பெலப்பிக்கவதிக நிதிசேர்த்துத்தமதுஸ்ழுப்பினதிகபாகத்தையு மிச்சாலையினயத்துக்காகவே செலவிட்டார். இச்சாலையைச் சேர்ந்த கட்டடங்கள் அவுடதசாலை, புருஷர்சாலை, ஸ்திரிகள்சாலை, மேகரோகிகள்சாலை, கர்மகர்த்தாக்களினுலோசனமண்டபம் முதலியன. இச்சாலைக்குட்புகும் வாசலிராப்பகறிறக்கப்பட்டிருக்கும். உள்ளிருந்து பரிகரிக்கப்படும் ரோகிகளுக்கன்னவஸ்திராதிகளிலவசமாகக் கொடுக்கப்படும்.

காட்டிராசாக்களாயிருந்து பகற்காலத்திலே வெளிகளில் வசித்திராக்காலத்திலே நாட்டிற்சென்று வீட்டுமுற்றத்திற் தீப்பந்தம்போட்டு வீட்டுயசமானரைக்கூவி:—உம்சேமத்திரவிய மெவ்வழியெனவினுவியவர்கள் மனைதைக் கருக்கியுருக்கிக்கொள்ளையடித்துண்டுதேத்து வனங்காத்தலையராய்த்திரிந்த அம்மையன், கரியன், பாளைவெட்டியகந்தன் முதலியகள்வர் குழாத்தை மென்னக்கருவறுத்தச்சமின்றிப்போக்குவரவு செய்தற்குமமைதியாய்த் துயின்றெழுதற்குமுதவியாகச் சந்திக்காவலரை யேற்படுத்தினர்.

கொள்ளல் விற்றல் பண்ணுமிடங்களாகக்கடைகளையும் ஏழுசந்தைகளையுமிடங்கள்தோறும் இஸ்தாபித்து மக்கள்கே நிழற்றருந் தருக்களை நிரையே நாட்டிவித்தும் வெயில்மழைகளுக்கொதுங்கிக்கொள்ளக்கொட்டகைகளைக் கட்டுவித்தும், மாடாதிய மிருகங்களுணைத்து சனங்கள் விக்கிரயஞ்செய்யக் கொணர்ந்தபண்டங்களைப் பழுதுபடுத்திக் குழப்பிக்கலக்காது காத்தற்பொருட்டுச் சுற்றிமதில்கள் சமைப்பித்தரண்படுத்தியுமிருப்பதைச் சன்னாகம், சங்கானை, அச்சு

வெளி, வல்வெட்டித்துறை, பருத்தித்துறை முதலிய விடங்களிலுள்ள சந்தைகள் செவ்வேகாட்டுகின்றன. முற்றவெளியிலிராசவீதியினிருமருங்கிலுமடர்ந்து கப்புங்கவருமெண்டிசாமுகங்களிலும் விட்டு வழிகடக்கிளைழத்தோரைக் குளிர்ச்சியாக்கும் பூவரசுகளுமிப்புன்னிய புருடன்பண்ணியசெய்பயிர்.

பலவாண்டுகளாகச் சொல்லரிய சுக சீவியாயிருந்தாளுகைபுரிந்த விவரதயமொத்த நிரேகத்திற் பற்றியெழுந்த கும்பிணி யற்றுவினைத்தமுற்றிய குருவிச்சிபோலாயிவர் வலிமை வாட்டி வொடுக்கிற்று. அப்போது செடுங்காலமாகத் தம்மனைதக்கிதமானமாளிகையாகவபிமானித்துவசித்த கச்சேரிமனையைவிட்டுச் செம்பிக் கோப்பாயிற்றும் வேண்டுந்தோறுஞ் சென்றிருந்துவப்பாறும்பொருட்டுச் சமைப்பித்திருந்த சித்திரைத் தம்மிறுதிகால வாழ்வுக்குகந்ததாகத் தெரிந்தவ்விடம் போந்துறைந்தனர்.

இவரது பிரிவசன்பருமப்போதிலங்கையமரிக்க மிசியோன்மைத்தியப்பகுதிக்கதிபருமாயிருந்த மிறீன் என்னுமாயுள்வேதியர் தம் முழுயூகசாமர்த்தியமெல்லாங் கொண்டிவரைப் பிணித்தபிணி வாயாற்பறிக்கப்பெரும்பிரயாசையடையக் காலத்தச்சனே இவ்வாயுள் வேதியனினெவ்வெவ்வெடுப்புக்களையும் பொடிப்படுத்தி யேசண்டாளவினையக்காயப்படவினின்று 1867 ம் ஸு ஐப்பசி மீ 8 ந் திகதி பிரிந்துவிட்டனன்.

இவரதுடற்சுண்டிக்குளிக்குக்கொண்டுபோகப்பட்டுச் சங்குவான் கோவிற் சவக்காலையிலடக்கம்பண்ணப்பட்டது. அடுத்த 9 ந் திகதி முதனுலைக்குதினங்களாகக் கச்சேரி, கோடுகள், அலுட்பாந்தி, வங்குச்சாலைமிலைத்துமிவர்பொருட்டுத் துக்கம் கொண்டாடும்படி பூட்டப்பட்டன:—*History of Jaffna by S. John.*

132

Hindu English School

Schools have from time to time been rapidly increasing in this part of the Province. Arumuga Navalar, a rigorous Hindu of high attainments in the vernacular, who takes credit for having introduced reforms into the profession and practice of Saivaism, has lately opened an English school at Vannarponne, which is manifestly intended for the education of the children of the Hindus. The Hindu community may now enjoy the satisfaction of having secured for themselves a denominational school of their own:—*C. C. Messenger, January, 1872*.

133

The Confraternity of the Sacred Heart of Jesus, Jaffna

This Society was originated by the late Rev. Brother P. J. Conway whose untimely death cannot be too severely deplored; for whether we regard him in the character of a scholar and an educationalist or in that of a gentleman and a Christian, we should place him in the very first rank. Brother Conway so zealously interested himself in the welfare of the boys, that he hit on the bright plan of putting them into a Society. The design met with the Bishop's hearty approval, and the boys after a period of probation were formally received into the Society by Dr. Bonjean before he left us for Rome about the close of 1869 to share in the deliberations of the Vatican Council:—*C. C. Messenger, June 1872.*

134

Dr. Danforth

The late Joshua Danforth was the Resident Surgeon of the Jaffna Friend-in-Need Society's Hospital, of whom Dr. Green, the popular Medical Missionary, was so proud as his best pupil, that he obtained for him an honorary M. D. from his University in the United States:—*The Life and Times of C. W. KatiravetPillai.*

D. H. CLARKE was one of the ablest Mathematical Scholars of the Batticotta Seminary, who secured fame and fortune, as an Engineer, under the auspices of Sir Charles Trevelyan, Governor of Madras, and nephew of Lord Macaulay.

THE REV. B. H. RICE was the Native Pastor of the American Church at Batticotta.

MR. LEE of Ooduville was the father of Mr. Samuel Lee, M. A. of the City College, Colombo. *Ibid.*

DR. G. M. REID was one of the favourite students of Dr. Green, who held that he was as good a physician as Dr. Danforth was a Surgeon. He was engaged by Mr. Dyke as his Medical attendant and by the Wesleyan and Catholic Missions to look after the sick in their Boarding Establishments. He was also engaged by some of the wealthy Burgher families in the Town to visit them periodically on the principle that prevention is better than cure. He was successful and popular as a Medical Practitioner, and being careful of his money, he saved a considerable sum. He married Victoria, the eldest daughter of Nicholas Puvirayasinghe Mudaliyar of the P. W. D, in 1860, and died without issue in 1878:—*Life of Nicholas Puvirayesinghe Mudlr.*

135

The Brahmin Will Case

The conversation of all classes of Society for some time past turned principally on Mr. Gould and his accomplices whose names are now to be associated with a crime, which, notoriously disreputable in itself, has brought disgrace and misery upon them. Mr. Gould from his wide-spread popularity was talked of both in town and country more than Supper and Ramalingam, who were introduced only incidentally, and the successes which attended his previous trials, and the talismanic facility and ingenuity with which he invariably extricated the difficulties he found himself in, did in great measure authorise, as it were, those who were well disposed towards him to anticipate a favorable issue. The intelligence which was communicated on Thursday the 9th instant took air with startling, I may almost say, telegraphic rapidity in all directions, was nevertheless not so unexpected as to cause either disappoinment or surprise, for the fact of two of the accused having turned Queen's evidence with important admissions to make, had occasioned many misgivings as to the fate of Mr. Gould. There is very little talk here concerning the question of his innocence or guilt in the crime of which he has been convicted owing to the general acquiescence of the people in the justifiableness of the sentence pronounced against him. But he has a large share of public sympathy for the sad destiny of penal servitude which has become his portion to endure in the prime of life and vigour of manhood, after having occupied the highest independent position attainable by the Jaffna man in his own sphere. To Jaffna, Mr, Gould has not been a useless man, albeit he has made himself mischievous to some extent, and the career he led, has been such as to render him quite a bewitching, adventurous and romantic character. Poor and unpatronised, he worked his way manfully up to eminence and command. In 61 he entered the public stage as a journalist; and it was quite a wonder how he could have been in possession of a press, oppressed by want as he then was. In 63 he passed as an advocate; and by his wit, cunning and unrivalled excellence as a speaker, he became eminently popular and engrossed the practice of our courts. It is but right to say that he asserted himself as the friend of the people and won their affection. In the time of the late Mr. Morphew he was in the zenith of his popularity, and it was considered suicidal and the fears then entertained has been now justified. He gradually lost his influence in the court and having brought himself into difficulty and raised contention in a cause which he had better not connected himself with, he has passed from public honor into public ignominy:—*C. C. Messenger, Nov. 1871.*

மேலேசொல்லப்பட்ட வழக்கு, டைக்மன்னரின் பின் டைமா சவை · ஏசண்டராய் வந்த நசல்த்துரை காலத்தில் நடந்தது. பெரும் செல்வச்சீமானுயிருந்து 1868 ம் ஆடு மரித்துப்போன மட்டின்

விஜயவேலிவேதக்குட்டி ஐயரின் ஆசனங்களுக்கு அக்காலத்தில் யாழ்ப்பாணத்தில் செல்வாக்குள்ளவர்களாயிருந்த கூல் (Gould) அப்புக்காத்து முதலிய சிலர் பிறப்பித்த பொய் மரணசாதனமே இவ்வளசுருக்குக் காரணம். இம்மரணசாதனத்தைப்பற்றிக்கோட்டிலே பெரும் விளக்கம் நடந்தது. அன்றிரவு எதிரிபக்கத்தைச் சேர்ந்தவர்கள் யாரோகோட்டுவீட்டின் புகுந்து வளக்குக்கொப்பியைக் கவர்ந்துசென்றனர். இதனால் இவ்வளக்கு 4 வருடக்காலமாக இழுபட்டுச் சேணித்துக்கிடந்தது. துவைனம்துரை (Twynam) யாழ்ப்பாணத்துக்கு எசண்டாய்வர இவ்வழக்கைப்பற்றி அக்கறைப்பட்டு அவர் விடாமுயற்சியால் ஞெஸ்மலைக்கொக் பொலிஸ்கீதகாரனால் விளங்கப்பட்டு, சுப்பிறீம்கோட்டுக்குப் பாரப்படுத்தப்பட்டது. கொழும்புநகரிலே ஆங்கில யூரித்துரைமார்கள் சமூகத்திலே சேர்றிச்செட்மோர்க்கன் (Sir Richard Morgan) இராணியின் அத்துவக்காத்தாய் வளக்கை நடத்த எதிரிகள் குற்றவாளிகளாகக்காணப்பட்டு, கிறீசி (Creasy) அதி நீதிபதியால் மறியல்த்தண்டனை பெற்றார்கள்.—
இ. மே.

136

The Jaffna College

The Jaffna College, situated at Batticotta in North Ceylon, is, as far as we know, the first attempt of a Christian Community in a heathen land to establish a college of their own. It originated in a spontaneous effort, made by the native Christians of Jaffna in 1867, to establish a Christian College, which should give a superior education both in the English and vernacular languages. A meeting of educated Tamils was called, and was largely attended. At this meeting a scheme was adopted, and a Committee appointed to collect funds and take initiatory steps towards establishing a Christian College. Principally through the efforts of this Native Committee, £ 1,700 were raised in Ceylon –a large sum, when it is remembered that in Jaffna the wage of a labouring man is only six pence a day. The people of America, hearing of this effort on the part of the Native Christians and believing those most worthy of help who try to help themselves, contributed £ 6,000 and the American Board of Missions gave, for the use of the College land and buildings worth £ 5000. Early in 1872 the College was started under the general management and control of a Board of Directors. This Board of Directors is at present composed of the Senior Missionaries of the three Missions working in Jaffna, namely, the Church of England Mission, the Wesleyan Mission, and the American Mission, along with the Government Agent of the Northern Province, and representative native Christ ian gentlemen of the community:—*Seven Years in Ceylon by Mary and Margaret W. Leitch.*

137

Kanakasabaipillai (Alias Evarts)

இவர் அளவெட்டியிலே உ௯வருடம் மாசிமாதம் 12ந்திகதி பிறந்தவர். சமயாசாரத்தாற் புரொத்தெஸ்தன் கிறீஸ்தவர். இவர் வட்டுக்கோட்டைப் பழையசாஸ்திரசாலையிலே இங்கிலீஸ்பாஷையோடு தமிழ்க் கற்றுத்தேற்றமுற்று, அவ்விடமிருந்த உவாட் (Dr. Ward) வைத்தியரிடம் ஐரோப்பிய வைத்தியங் கற்றனராயினும், பிதாத்தமிழ் வைத்தியராய் இருந்தாராதலால் அவரிடங் கற்ற தமிழ் வைத்தியமே இவருக்கு அதி சித்தியாக அதிலே இவர் பெருங்கீர்த்தி பெற்றார். வைத்தியத்திலன்றி இலக்கண இலககியங்களில் மிக்க திறமையுள்ள புலவராதலின் "புலவர்" "புலவன் கனகசபை" என்னும் நாமங்களால் அழைக்கப்பட்டார்.

இவரது பாடல்கள் சொற்சுவை பொருட்சுவைகளாற் செறிந்தன. பற்பல தனிப்பாக்கள் அன்றித் திருவாக்குப்புராணம் எனப் பெயரியபுராணம் ஒன்றை இயற்றினர். 1873ம் ௵ தைமாதம் 4ந்தேதியில் இறந்து உடுவில் மிஷன் சவக்காலையிற் சேமிக்கப்பட்டார். யாழ்ப்பாணத்திலே மிஷனரிமார் வருவதற்குமுன்னே படித்திருந்த இரண்டு பெண்களுள் இவர் மாதா ஒருவர்.—பா. ச. தீ.

138

Rev. Levi Spaulding, D. D.

யாழ்ப்பாணத்தைச்சேர்ந்த உடுவிற் கோவில்பற்றில் அமெரிக்கன் மிஷியோனரியாகிய அர்ச்சிய கனம் லேவி ஸ்போல்டிங்பண்டிதர் 1873ம் ௵ ஆனிமாசம் 18ந்திகதி புதன்கிழமை 83வயதில் மரித்துவிட்டார். அஞ்ஞானிகளுக்குச் சேவாக்கைக்கூற 54 வருஷங்களுக்கு முன்வந்த இந்தக்குருவும் அம்மாவும் பெற்றோர் தங்கள் பிள்ளைகளை நேசிக்கிறதைப்பார்க்கிலும், தங்களிடம் கற்றுவந்த பெண் பிள்ளைகளை நேசித்துவந்தார்கள். நம்முடைய தேசத்தவரின் இகபர சலாக்கியமே இவருடைய காதலாகவிருந்தது. இவர் தமிழ்ப்பாஷையைத் திர்க்கமாய்க் கற்றுத் தமிழ அகராதி, இங்கிலீசுத் தமிழுமான அகராதி, வேறுமனேக புத்தகங்களுமியற்றினர்.—*The Christian Friend.*

139

Governor Gregory in Jaffna

His Excellency the Governor (Sir William Gregory) and suite consisting of his Private Secretary, Cockburn Stewart Esqr., Major Clay, the Hon'ble the Colonial Secretary and Dr. Charaley arrived here on the evening of the 8th instant, and took their quarters for the night at the residency of the Government Agent. The next morning His Excellency proceeded to the Queen's House, Fort, and there met the principal headmen and Kachcherri officers who had expressed their desire to see the Governor. An address was read giving His Excellency a respectful and heartfelt welcome for which he thanked the assembled concourse of people. In the evening the Government Agent Mr. Twynam, gave a grand dinner-party to His Excellency, inviting the elite of the European Community of Jaffna. On Tuesday evening the Governor visited the Convent Girls' School and there met His Lordship Dr. Bonjean. The same evening another dinner party was given to His Excellency by the District Judge, Mr. D. E. de Saram. On Wednesday morning S. Mudlr. Saverimuttu Mudaliyar, who had been invested by Sir Hercules Robinson with the title of Mudaliyar of the Governor's Gate, was presented with a gold medal and chain, all the native headmen and several others being present. His Excellency in giving the testimonials spoke in terms of praise of the ability and integrity of the Mudaliyar. The ceremony was the first of its kind witnessed in Jaffna and happy were the Jaffnese to see a very respectable fellow townsman of theirs who had served the Government well and worthily for a period of 46 years, and who had maintained a high gentlemanly character throughout, receive a distinguishing mark of honour from the highest in the land, in special recognition of his long and faithful services. In the afternoon, the Mudaliyar entertained the Vice Regal party and other important officials at his house, which was very tastefully decorated and furnished. His Lordship Dr. Bonjean also honoured the Mudaliyar with his presence on the occasion. The circumstances connected with the presentation of the gold medal and chain to the Mudaliyar were very gratifying to his friends and would doubtless serve to gladden the remaining years of his life.—*C. C. Messenger Feb. 1874.*

140

Nicholapillai Sinnatamby

Mr. Sinnatamby was a Kachcheri Officer well-known in his day. His natural aptitude for business and steady habits of life won for him fair success. Of his three sons who are all dead, the eldest Mr. J. E. Nicholas was a Proctor, another Mr. S. Bastiampillai, Mudaliyar of the Jaffna Kachcheri and the third Mr. P. E. Francis was a Landing Waiter at the Customs, Jaffna. Bastiampillai married a daughter of Chevalier Saverimuttu Mudaliyar. Mr. Sinnatamby died at Jaffna in 1874:—*J. H. Wittebron.*

141

Coomaraswamy Mudaliyar

As a lad Coomaraswamy Mudaliyar was so precocious that he is said to have "lisped in numbers, for the numbers came," as in the case of Pope, before he entered upon his teens. His easy circumstances enabled him to follow the bent of his mind and devote himself to the pursuit of poesy from first to last, as a labour of love. He died in his 83rd year on the 30th December 1874. His literary remains consist of the drama called Indra Kumara Nadakam and the encomiastic poem called Arulampala Kovai, in honour of his friend and contemporary Arulampala Mudaliyar.

Coomaraswamy Mudaliyar married Sivakamipillai (the daughter of Punniya Maniagar) who bore him two sons, the younger being the subject of this notice and the elder Sapapathy Mudaliyar of the Jaffna Fiscal's Office, who died in 1884 and whose only son Duraiswamy Maniagar passed away prematurely on the 11th February, 1904.—*The Life and Times of C W. Katiravelpillai.*

142

The Jaffna Prince of Wales' Reception Fund

The Jaffna Prince of Wales' Reception Committee has proved a complete success. The subscriptions, a very large portion of which has been received, amount, it is said, to above Rs. 10,000, by no means an inconsiderable sum in itself, and for Jaffna a remarkably high sum certainly to raise. A beautiful silver casket and a choice set of Jewels of Jaffna workmanship are in readiness for presentation. An address has also been prepared and adopted and a deputation named to proceed to Colombo to read the address and present the casket and contents to the Prince in behalf of the inhabitants of the Northern and Eastern Provinces. It is proposed to devote the remaining sum of money in the hands of the Committee to some memorial to perpetuate the great event which is to take place shortly, and signalize the future annals of Ceylon.—*C. C. Messenger, Nov. 1875.*

143

Overseer Corps

Often it is said that a great man leaves the impress of his mind upon everything he handles. The same remark also appears in another form—"Great men leave their foot-prints on the sands of time." Although the grave has closed over Ceylon's great roadmaker, Major Skinner, he still lives to us in the great works associated with his name. and we have little doubt that so long as British rule obtains in Ceylon his name will go down to the remotest posterity honoured and cherished. The formation and organisation of our overseer corps was his noblest work, not only because overseers are very useful to the public, but chiefly because in the adoption of this measure his end and aim was the promotion of native interest. Well did it become a great man to seek, call, train, and encourage native talent. The overseers trained in his time are all practical man, possessing large acquaintance with works in the Island; and in recognition of their ability and industry he raised to the office of Superintending Officers more than three gentlemen taken from the ranks.—*Ceylon Patriot 6th August 1881.*

Among those trained by Major Skinner and received government appointments as Superintending officers besides Mr. Armstrong were the late Mudaliyar Welupillai the famous builder of the Katugastotta Bridge, the late Mr. Shirman, who constructed the larger portion of the Balangoda --Haputale Road, the late Messrs Pethaperumal, Harward. and Woodall (all of them Tamils, who distinguished themselves in the Department): *Memoir of Francis Mullyah Armstrong.*

144

G S. Puvirajasinghe

The death took place on the 7th instant, at the early age of 37 of Gabriel Solomon Puvirajasinghe, Proctor of the District Court of Jaffna. The. deceased received an excellent English education and possessed all the choice qualifications necessary to render himself a distinguished member of the Legal profession. His genial disposition and winning address endeared him to all classes of the community and his premature death is the subject of general regret:—*J. C. Guardian 19th May 1877.*

145

T. Chinnatamby

இவர் கிறிஸ்தாப்தம் 1830-ம் ௵ சித்திரை ௴ 4ம் திகதி உடுப்பிட்டிக்கோவிற்பற்றைச் சேர்ந்த தனக்காரக்குறிச்சியிலே, பிறந்தவர். இலக்கண இலக்கியங்களில் மாத்திரமல்லத் தமிழ்க்கணித சாஸ்திரத்திலும் தேற்றம்பெற்று, அத்துடன் திருத்தப்பட்டிராத வட்டுநகர் சாஸ்திரசாலையிற் கற்றவரும் தமது சுற்றத்தவருமாகிய வீரகத்தி (Mr. Kopler) உடையாரிடம் இங்கிலீஸ் சில அளவைச் சாஸ்திரங்கற்று, அச்சாஸ்திரம் யாவர்க்கும் உபயோகப்படவேண்

டும் எனும் அபிப்பிராயங்கொண்டு அதனைச் செய்யுளாக்கி அதற்கு நில அளவைச் சூத்திரமென்று பெயரிட்டார். சோதிட சாஸ்திரத்தில் நிபுணத்துவம் அடைந்து சோதிடச்சுருக்கம் என்னும் ஓர் நூலையும் இயற்றினர். இவ்விரண்டோடும் நின்றுவிடாது, வீரபத்திர சதகம், வீரபத்திரர்பதகம், வீரபத்திரரூஞ்சல், புதச்சக்திமுருகையபதிகம், விக்கினேசுரர்பதிகம், வீரமாகாளியம்மன்பதிகம், சிவதோத்திரகீர்த்தனை, மதனவல்லிவிலாசம், இராமவிலாசம் என்னும் பாடல்களன்றிப் பலதனிப்பாக்களும்பாடினர். பா. ச. தீ

146

Mr. Armstrong and some Public Works of Jaffna

In 1878 Mr. Armstrong was transferred to Jaffna as District Engineer and Superintending officer. The following gentlemen were some of the illustrious sons of the North, who were Mr. Armstrong's contemporaries in the Public Service, during the time he held office in Jaffna:–The late Mr. C. W. Kathiravetpillai, the distinguished and well-known Police Magistrate of Kayts (father of the Hon'ble Mr. K. Balasingam). Mr. T. M. Tampoe, late Crown Proctor, and acting Police Magistrate Jaffna; the late Mr. Arunasalam, Sub-Collector, Kangasanturai; the late Dr. W. Paul, Medical officer in charge of the F. N. S. Hospital in Jaffna (father of Dr. Chelliah Paul, First Surgeon, General Hospital); and the late Mr. J. N. Sandrasagara, Superintendent of Minor Roads, Jaffna. While in Jaffna Mr. Armstrong was chiefly entrusted with the maintenance and up-keep of the roads, and among the construction works done by him, the most lasting and useful works carried out by him is the Punnalai Causeway, a splendid roadway over the lagoon between the Island of Karadivu or Leyden and the Peninsula. Among works carried out by Mr. Armstrong in the Jaffna District, besides the causeway, are the Kankesanturai Landing Pier and Point-Pedro Jetty and Harbour Works, Rest-House at Kankesanturai, Puloly Hospital, Point-Pedro, the Valvettyturai Customs, rebuilding of Fort Hammanheil in Kayts, rebuilding of the Jaffna Grain Shed, Customs and Overseer's Quarters, forty cells at the Jaffna Jail, the Land Registrar's office and Record Room, Jaffna. Among his trusted subordinates were, the late Mr. Morris Chellappa (the father of Mr. A Rajanayakam, the esteemed Secretary of the Jaffna District Court, and of Mrs. H. Hallock of Colombo), the late overseer Nagamuttu of Moolay, who was afterwards appointed as Head Overseer, P. W. D, and Mr. K. Kathiravelu of Puloly (father of Mr. Ratnasingham, Chief Clerk of the Jaffna District Court:—*Memoir of Francis Muttyah Armstrong.*

147

Sandrasagara Pandithar

இவர் உடுவிற்கோயிற்பற்றிலே பிறந்தவர். கிறிஸ்தவராகி நதானியேல் என்னும் நாமம்பெற்றுக் காலஞ்சென்றவரும் திகாந்தம் எட்டிய கீர்த்தி உற்றவருமாகிய, ஸ்போல்டிங் பண்டிதர்க்கு (Rev. Dr, Spaulding) ஆசிரியராகி, அநேக புத்தகங்களைமொழிபெயர்க்கவும், இயற்றவும், அப்பண்டிதருக்கு உதவிசெய்துவந்தாரன்றி, நல்லூரிலே நயிற்தேசிகர் (Rev. J. Knight) தமிழ் ஆங்கில அகராதி ஒன்று செய்யமுயன்றபோது அவர்க்கு உதவிசெய்யப்போன பல சிரேட்டருள் ஒருவராயும் இருந்தார். வயோதிகராய் 79 வயசில் 1879 ம் ௵ ஐப்பசி ௴ 26 ந் திகதி இறந்த இவர் சமஸ்கிருதபாஷையிலுஞ் சிறக்கத் தேர்ந்தவர். இவரது சிரேட்டபுத்திரர் டாக்தர் உவைமன் நதானியேல் சுவாமிநாதர் (Dr. Wyman Nathaniel) பாம்பனில் வயித்தியராகவும், மத்தியபுத்திரராகிய ஈ. ஈ. தில்லையம்பலம் நதானியேல் உவெஸ்லியமிஷன் போதனாசத்திப் பாடசாலைச் சிரேட்ட ஆசிரியராகவும், கனிட்டபுத்திரராகும் ஈ. ஈ. அம்பலவாணர் நதானியேல் யாழ்ப்பாணம் பொலிஸ் "கோட்டு" உத்தியோகத்தராவும் இருக்கிறார்கள். பா. ச. தீ.

148

Arumuga Navalar

இவர் தமிழ்வித்துவான்களின் சகாயத்தால் அரியநூல்களை உணர்ந்து பாண்டித்தியம் பெற்றாரன்றிச் சமஸ்கிருதத்திலும் பயிற்சி உடையராய் உவெஸ்லியன் மிஷன்பாடசாலையில் ஆங்கிலபாஷையுங் கற்று, 20 வயதில் அப்பாடசாலைத்தலைவரான பீற்றர் பேர்சிவல் தேசிகருக்குத் (Rev. P. Percival) தமிழ்ப்பண்டிதராகி வேதாகம மொழிபெயர்ப்பில் அவருக்கு நல்ல உபயோகியாகி அவருடன் கூடிச்சென்னைபட்டிணம்போய்த்திரும்பினவர். 1845 ம் ௵ வரையிலும் அவருக்குத் துணைசெய்து அப்பால் அவரது வேலையை விட்டுத் தம்மூரிலே சைவசமயத்தை வளர்க்கவும், பாடசாலைகளைஸ்தாபிக்கவும், பிரசங்கம் செய்யவும், கருத்துட்கொண்டாராகி, முன் பின் முப்பத்திரண்டு வருடங்களாக அம்முயற்சியிற் காலம் விட்டார். வண்ணார்பண்ணை, புலோலி முதலான இடங்களில் அன்றிச் சிதம்பரத்திலும் ஓர் பாடசாலையை ஸ்தாபித்தார். இவர் முன்னர்வண்ணார்பண்ணையிலும் பின்னர் சென்னபட்டணத்திலும் அச்சியந்திரசாலைகளை ஸ்தாபித்தார். சென்னைபட்டணத்திற்குப் பலமுறையுஞ் சென்றுதிரும்பினர். அவ்விடத்தில் இவரது அச்சுச்சாலை இப்போதும் இருக்கின்றது. சிறியவும் பெரியவுமான அறுபதுக்கு மேற்பட்ட புத்தகங்களைத் திருத்தி அச்சிட்டுப் பிரசுரித்தாரன்றி, அவ்வாறுசெய்ததற்காக வேறு சிலவுத்தலைபாதிகளையில் முடித்தும், சில

சுற்றிற்கைவிட்டுயிருக்கவே சாத்திரப்பிரகாரம் வயது ஐம்பத்தாறு, மாதம் பதினொன்றில் பிரமாதிவருஷம், அதாவது பிறவிட்ட 1879 ம் ஆண்டு தேகவியோகமாயினர். பாடும் திறமையிலும் இவர் குறைந்தவரல்லர். கீர்த்தனங்கள். அன்றித்தனிப்பாக்களும்பாடினர். சிலகாலமாக யாழ்ப்பாணத்தில் நடைபெற்றுவந்த சைவ உதயபானுப் பத்திரிகையும் இவர் செய்த முற்பிரயத்தனங்களை வித்தாய்க்கொண்டே உற்பத்திபெற்றது:—பா. ச. தீ.

149

Mr. V. Yanamuttu

Mr. Yanamuttu, Contractor and General Merchant, passed away on the 23rd February 1907. He will be long remembered as the pioneer of the Mail Coach Service from Jaffna to Point-Pedro and Kankesanturai:—*Life* of *Nicholas Puvirajasinghe Mudaliyar.*

150

Sangarapillai Mudaliyar

Don Philip Sangarapillai Mudaliyar was the scion of an old family whose ancestors did signal service to the Portuguese Government and were greatly honoured by them. One of his ancestors is said to have superintended the construction of the Jaffna Fort in 1632. Mr. Sangarapillai was born A. D. 1770, and we find him in the early days of the British accession in Ceylon, in charge of what was then designated the "Oppum" Department under the then controller of Jaffna. The function of this department was to issue "Oppums" or permits for the exercise of honorary ceremonies on occasions of marriages, births, deaths and other domestic occurrences, when the attendance of the Blacksmith, the Carpenter, the Dhoby, and the Barber were compulsory for the purpose of decorating the house with white cloth, spreading cloth on the ground for the newly-married couple to walk upon and for the temporary canopy, and for other services appropriate to their respective castes. An "Oppum" was also required for riding in a "Palanquin." It was unlawful in those days for any one to have honorary ceremonies, such as we have de-detailed above, performed or to ride in a Palanquin or to have mine without an "Oppum" under the hand of the officer of the "Oppum" Department who granted it after careful inquiries made as to the caste and social status of the applicant. —*J. H. Wittebron.*

The "oppums" were written in Tamil on slips of ola or palmirah leaf with a margin on the left on which were stamped the initials of the civil or revenue officer with whose approval and authority they were issued— A few of these "oppums" are in the possession of the compiler, of which the earliest bearing date Feb. 4. 1745, was issued during the administration of Julius Valentyn Steyn Van Gollnesse to Don Sanchuvampillai Deiogu Vas on the occasion of his being invested with the rank of Mudaliyar under the name and title of Don Dieogu Vas Puvirajasinghe Mudaliyar, allowing him at the same time the privilege of using a tusker, palanquin, cloth for the ground to walk on, white canopy, and drums by Pandarams. The latest, bearing date 24th June. 1818, was issued during the time of William H. Hooper, Collector of Jaffna, to Puvirajasinghe Mudaliyar Manualthamby, granting him the privilege of riding in a palanquin.

151

Rev. T. P. Hunt

Rev. Hunt came of a family in Chavakachcheri. He was the youngest in a family of five boys. The father consigned him in charge of the American Missionaries of the far-famed Vaddukoddai Seminary.

The boy was a poor scholar, not bright and winsome at first and was the subject of ridicule from his classmates. But he was religious, studious, patient, meek and energetic. When he was in one of the higher classes, one day he solved a problem in Higher Mathematics, which no one else in his class could do. It brought about a difference in the feeling of the class towards him. From that day he was regarded as a genius and commanded the respect of his schoolmates and Professors which he retained till his death.

The principal works of his life are the founding of Jaffna College and the Jaffna Trading Company Limited. He was the author of many religious tracts and he won a prize for his best tract in Tamil entitled 'Which is True." His Magnum opus in this line was his "Evidences of Christianity in Tamil."—*The Church of Christ in Ceylon.*

152

Saverimuttu Mudaliyar

Sandrasegra Mudaliyar Saverimuttu Mudaliyar was a son of Sandrasegra Mudaliyar of the Jaffna Customs. He was born in 1802 and entered Government Service as a Civil Storekeeper. In 1839 he succeeded Philip Muttukisna Mudaliyar as Mudaliyar of the Jaffna Kachchcheri. The work of the Native Department having gradually increased in proportion and responsibility, Aseervatha Mudaliyar was appointed assistant to Saverimuttu Mudaliyar. Saverimuttu Mudlr. was a prominent officer and was well-known and respected throughout the Island. He was esteemed and trusted by Government Agent Dyke, while Sir William Twynam who reigned in "Old Park" for over a quarter of a century had in Saverimuttu Mudaliyar his "guide, philosopher, and friend." He took a prominent part in the buildings connected with the Cathedral Church of Jaffna and was never satisfied till he saw them completed. He had the Celebration of the Festival of the "Month of May," and the devotions for the 30 days preceding the festival. He took also considerable interest in the annual Paschal Representation in the Cathedral. Upon the recommendation of the late Arch-bishop Bonjean, Saverimuttu Mudaliyar was created a Knight Chevalier of the order of St. Gregory the Great by his Holiness Pope Leo. XIII.

He had an only son who died young. He left two daughters one of whom married S. Bastiampillai Mudaliyar and died without issue. His liberality in all matters concerning the Church was so great, that almost all he possessed of was devoted to the maintenance and advancement of the Church. And up-to-date his name is remembered with gratitude by the clergy and the laity. And when one looks on that stately pile of St. Mary's Cathedral, in the building of which he had taken no inconsiderable part and within sight of which his mortal remains are laid to rest, one cannot help applying to him the memorable epitaph on Christopher Wren. "Simonumentum quaeris circumspice."—*J. H. Wittebron.*

153

Eliza Agnew

Miss Eliza Agnew has been affectionately called by the people of Jaffna "The mother of a thousand daughters."

She was born in New York City, February 2, 1807, and decided to be a Missionary when eight years of age:—"*The Church of Christ in Ceylon.*"

154

Jaffna in 1830

There were then no roads, properly so-called, beyond the Pettah. Even the Main Street from the fort terminated near the 3rd Cross Street, beyond which it was a mere sandy track. In the villages, the "Parish Roads" of the Dutch were the sole means of communication; while there were no traces of the present trunk lines to Chavakachcheri and Point Pedro, Valvettiturai and Kangesanturai, Mathakal and Punnalai. The salt lagoon running through the Peninsula, from Ariyalai to Thondamannar, was not bridged either at Puthankuli or Vallai, and the rainy season terminated all intercourse and trade between the parishes of Jaffna and those of Vadamaradchi on the North and Tenmaradchi on the East. Pachchillapally, now the cocoanut garden of the North, was comparatively little known, except as the domain of the elephant and the black bear. Elephants roamed about Kaithadi and paid surprise visits to the Town; Cheetahs committed sad havoc on cattle, and jackals in plentiful packs held their midnight concerts in close proximity to the town. The age of gang robberies, of ear-cutting, torch-light robberies and highway robberies, had not then passed, and the names of noted burglars, such as Arivan, Nenaivan and Palaivetty Kantan, continued still to exercise a terrific spell over peaceful house-holds. Travelling was beset with sure and certain danger:—*Life of Nicholas Puvirajasinghe Mudaliyar.*

155

Naganathapillai

இற்றைக்கு ஏறக்குறைய 60 வருடங்களுக்கு முன்னே சண்ணாகக்குறிச்சியிலே இவர் பிறந்தவர். வட்டுக்கோட்டைச் சாஸ்திரசாலையில் அரங்கேறியவர். அரசாட்சியாரிடம் முல்லைத்தீவிலே தலிபாஷித முதலியாராகி அங்கிருந்து கற்பிட்டிக்கோட்டிற்குச் சென்றவர். தென்மொழியிலன்றி வடமொழியாகிய சமஸ்கிருதத்திலும் மிகவல்லவர். இங்கிலிஷிலன்றிச் சிங்களத்திலுந்திறர்.—பா. சு. தீ.

156

G. P. SavundaranayagamPillai

இவர்யாழ்ப்பாணத்திலே பழையவட்டுக்கோட்டைச் சாஸ்திரசாலையில் இற்றைக்கு முன்பின் 50 வருடங்களின்முன்னே ஆசிரியராய் இருந்து பெயர்படைத்த கபிரியேல் திசேரா என்பவரது கனிட்டபுத்திரர். சமயசாரத்தில் மூர்த்திப் புரோத்தெஸ்தரும் பித்திக்கதலிகருமாகிய இவர் முதல் வட்டுக்கோட்டைச் சாஸ்திரசாலையிற் படித்து மறுபடி சென்னை இராசதானிசென்று பீ. ஏ. என்னும் பண்டிதப்பட்டமும் பெற்று, அப்பகுதியிலே பிரபலிய நியாயதுரந்தரராய் இருந்தவர். தமிழ் தெலிங்கு இரண்டிலுமன்றி இங்கிலிஷிலும் சில புஸ்தகங்களுக்கு ஆக்கியோருமாயினர்.

சிலகாலம் ஆங்கிலேய புதினப்பத்திரிகையும் ஒன்றைநடத்தி வந்தவர். நல்லவாசாலாலங்காரப்பிரசங்கியாகும் இவர் சென்னைச் சர்வகலாசாலையிலே வித்தியாபட்டம் பெறப்போகும் மாணுக்கரைப் பரீட்சிப்பாரில் ஒருவராய் அநேக ஆண்டுகளாக அரசாட்சியாரால் தெரிவுசெய்யப்பட்டிருந்தவர். புலவராய் மெய்ஞ்ஞானக்கீர்த்தனை

எனும் பாடலை இயற்றி அச்சிடுவித்தார். இவரது தாயார் யாழ்ப்பாணத்தில் இருந்த ஒந்தாச்சியோர் என்பாரது புத்திரி. தகப்பன் கொழும்பு இராசதானியிற்பிறந்தவர்— பா. ச. தீ.

157

Revd. John Hensman

I have received the news of Mr. Hensman's departure with much regret. I saw a good deal of him each time I visited Jaffna and had a very high regard for him. He was an able man I should say, as well as a good one, and had done a good day's work in the Lord's Vineyard:— *Right Revd. R. S. Copleston.*

The Revd. Mr. Hensman had a very large family. The second son having died in infancy, there were left eight sons and four daughters. Charles, Samuel, James, and Edward had proceeded to South India, one after another, and entered the Madras University. Charles passed the First-in-arts examination, and with the help of his uncle, Mr. Christian Philips, who was Government Schoolmaster, got an appointment in the Madras Educational Service. Samuel passed the First-in-arts examination and returned to Jaffna, where, after serving in the Wesleyan Mission as a teacher for some time, he was appointed Headmaster of the Jaffna College under the American Mission. James had a distinguished University career and passed the B. A., when he was 20, and was immediately taken into the Madras Educational Service. Alfred received his education in the Colombo Academy (Royal College) and afterwards passed out as a Proctor:—*The Life of Revd. John Hensman.*

158

The Cyclone of 1884

We have had a superabundance of rain in 1884. During the latter part of the year, two cyclones, one on the 16th of October, the other on the 14th of December, burst forth, causing destruction over this unfortunate district. The loss to the Peninsula has been heavy and extensive both in life and property:— *The Jaffna Catholic Guardian Jan. 10.1885.*

No atmospheric disturbance within the recollection of the oldest inhabitant, has been attended with such disastrous results, nor is there any event on record among us, or traditionally handed down to us, which can at all come into comparison with the one we have just witnessed:—"*The Ceylon Patriot.*"

159

V. Ramalingam

இவர் சுதுமலைக் குறிச்சியிலே பிறந்தவர். வழக்கமாய் ஆனைக்கோட்டை வயிரமுத்து உடையார் இராமலிங்கமென்று அழைக்கப்பட்டவர். இங்கிலிஷ் தமிழ் எனும் இருபாஷைகளுங் கற்றவர், புலவராய்ப் பற்பல தனிப்பாக்கள், பதங்கள், சிந்துகள் பாடினர். சன்கிளையந்தாதியோடு மாணிக்கவாசகர் விலாசம், தமயந்திவிலாசம் என்று பெயருள்ள இரண்டுவிலாசங்களையும் பாடினர்:— பா. ச. தீ.

160

A few words on duty

Colombo,
12th June, 85.

My Dear Sir,

Allow me to thank you for sending me the printed copy of your address on "Duty."

Much of it is particularly useful, and I am very glad to notice what you say on pages 9 and 10 against that pestilent cravdoing for a smattering of bad English which is unfortunately doing so much harm, and causing so much poverty amongst the rising generation in Ceylon. If you, and others in your position, will continue to preach the dignity of labour, and the miserable indignity of false gentility based on a belief that a little English places a young man "above'' honest labour, you will be not only greatly aiding me in an up-hill struggle against fashion and prejudice, but you will be doing real good in your generation to the people of your country.

Yours faithfully,
H. W. Green.

To,
James H. Martyn,
Sub-Inspector of the R. C. Mission Schools, Jaffna.

161

Jaffna Railway Meeting

The meeting to take steps to memorialize the Government to extend the Matale line of Railway in a Northerly direction, originally advertised to be held on the 29th ultimo, having been postponed owing to heavy rain, was held on Saturday last, the 14th instant, at the District Court House. There was, not-withstanding the heavy rain, a large and respectable attendance. Mr. Cross, the Manager of the local branch of the new O. B. C., presided. Several resolutions were moved and seconded. The principal speakers were Messrs Allagacoen, Santiagopillai, Tampoe, Nagalingam, Kanagasaby, Ilankiar, the Rev. Fr. Lytton and the Rev. Messrs Griffith, Gomes and Winston. All the speakers, without a solitary exception, concurred in the desirability and expediency of the extension of the Railway to the North:—*The Ceylon Examiner, 19th November, 1885.*

162

Ambalavana Mudaliyar

Rasakaria Sinkai Ariya Ambalavana Mudaliyar, Maniagar of Valigamam North, was the brother of the late Dr. Cleveland, and the father-in-law of the late well-known Velupillai Mudaliyar of the P. W. Department. After a service of about 40 years, during which time he had earned the confidence of Government and the good-will and esteem of the inhabitants of his district, he succumbed to some serious abdominal distemper. The Office of Maniagar of Valigamam North, was from time immemorial, in the possession of the family of the late Rajanayaga Mudaliyar Iragunatha Mudaliyar of Mallagam:—*The Ceylon Examiner, Nov. 1885.*

163

A. Eliatamby

Mr. Eliatamby, head clerk of the Jaffna Kachcheri, was appointed by the late Mr. Dyke as a clerk at Mullaitivu. He rose step by step, till he became the head clerk of the Jaffna Kachcheri. He has been in service for the last thirty-nine years. He was respected by all for his kindness, courtesy and impartiality. During the long period he had been in employment, he seldom gave offence to any of his superiors or brother clerks:—*The Ceylon Examiner, Nov. 1885.*

164

Galaxy of Tamil Poets

I have carefully read Mr. Arnolds' "Galaxy of Tamil Poets." It supplies a real deficiency in our literature and may help much in increasing a regard for the national authors. Its popular form and interesting style make it very readable. I have no doubt that both in India and Ceylon it will be universally sought after and read with avidity:—*R. O. D. Asbury.*

165

G. S. ArianayagamPillai

Mr. G. S. ArianayagamPillai, B. A., B. L., was Puisne Justice, High Court, Trevandram. The Cochin Argus writes:—

"His whole career as a Judge was not only unblemished to the utmost but unanimous public opinion ran throughout the length and breadth of the land that there was not a more honest upright and conscientious Judge. The breath of scandal, which has assailed many a Judge not only of Travancore, but of elsewhere too, never dared to approach him. The fact was he was scrupulous, just and impartial even to a fault. The proverbial sword of justice in his hands descended without the slightest regard or respect to persons."

ArianayagamPillai and SavundranayagamPillai were brothers. Mr. A. G. Tambinayagam, who is married to Mary, sister of Jos. N. Sandresegra Mudaliyar, Maniagar, and Mr. A. M. Muttunayagam, retired Puisne Justice, Trevandram, who is married to Pearl, the second daughter of the late Advocate C. Brito, are the sons of Mr. ArianayagamPillai.

166

The Jaffna Hindu College

The Jaffna Hindu College was founded in 1887 under the name of "The Native Town High School" by the late Mr. William Nevins Sithamparapillai. In 1889 the management was transferred to Mr. S. Nagalingam, Advocate, who located it at Vannarponne. In 1890 the institution was placed under the control of "The Jaffna Saiva Paripalana Sabai," a society of the leading Hindus of Jaffna, formed for the purpose of promoting the cause of Hindu religion and education. The Sabai, which had then as its president Mr. T. Chellappahpillai, B. A., B. L., retired Chief Justice of Travancore, removed the school to a temporary building on the present site and reorganised it under the name of "The Hindu High School."

In 1892, Mr. N. Selvadurai B. A., son of the late Mr. William Nevins Sithamparapillai, who founded the institution, took charge of the school as its Headmaster. The College was incorporated in 1902 by an ordinance passed by the Legislative Council of Ceylon and it is now managed by a Board of Directors, of whom the Hon'ble Mr. A. Kanagasabai B. A., Advocate, is President. The immediate management of the institution is entrusted to Mr. V. Casippillai, Supreme Court Proctor, Jaffna, and Vice-President of the Board. A large and handsome new edifice erected at a cost of upwards of Rs. 10,000, and which, with recent extensions now cost about Rs. 50,000, was occupied by the College on the 28th of September 1895. In 1897 Mr. S. Nagalingam, Vice-President of the Saiva Paripalana Sabai, and Manager of the College, passed away. He was the greatest patriot of his generation and held a unique position in the hearts of his countrymen. Another great loss, which the College sustained, was the death of Mr. S. T. M. Pasupathy Chettiar, which occurred in 1906. He was the Treasurer of the "Siva Paripalana Sabai" and of the Board of Directors of the Hindu College, and was one of the original founders of the College aud also architect of the buildings. In November 1909, Mr. N. Selvadurai B. A., Principal, severed his connection with the College to take up the Headmaster-ship of the Trinity College, Kandy. He was in charge of the institution for about 18 years. As the Principal of the College, he had played a leading part in shaping the educational history of Jaffna. His invaluable services to this College, will always be gratefully remembered by his countrymen. He has been succeeded as Principal of this College by Mr. G. Shiva Rau B. A., L. T., who has had considerable experience in teaching. There is at present attached to the College a small Library and a small Laboratory for teaching Physical Science. The College Boarding House was opened on 30th May, 1910:- *Jaffna Hindu College Calendar, 1910.*

167

Mr. J. G. Cherubim

Mr. Joseph Gabriel Cherubim, was the son of Mr. G. P. Ponniahpillai, the local agent of the B. I. Steam Navigation, Company He was about 19 years of age, and it is not 3 months yet since he was appointed to the post of Store-keeper of the Government Timber and Firewood Depot. A young man of the most affable and unassuming character and above all a model Christian he had won for himself the affection and esteem of all who came in contact with him:—*The Jaffna Catholic Guardian, May 5th, 1888.*

168

F. Mortimer

Mr. Fredrick Mortimer was once Assistant Collector of the local Customs, and latterly a cocoanut planter at Palai. He married the eldest daughter of our Government Agent and had three children. He was very much loved and esteemed by all:—*J. C. Guardian, July 28th, 1888.*

169

The Revd. Father Patrick O' Flanagan

Father Flanagan was born in the country of Limerick, Ireland, in May of the year 1842. His whole family soon after left for Ceylon, so that he was but still a child when he first touch-ed its shores. Not very long subsequently, his father died. Patrick, the future missionary, attended school at the "Jaffna Boys' Seminary, now known as St. Patrick's College, and, later on went to Pondicherry to complete his studies at the Colonial College there. Returning to Jaffna, he made up his mind to become an Oblate. Immediately after his ordination, he was placed at the head of the Jaffna Boys' Seminary. In 1874, he succeeded the late Very Revd. Father Salaun as Director of the Orphanage, and also, as Missionary at Colombogam. As Director of the Orphanage he made many improvements. Mention might be made of the Industrial School, and the Training School, of the new dwelling and the beautiful new Chapel he built, changing the old dwelling and the old Chapel into a school and dormitory for the boys of the Orphanage. The good he effected as Missionary might be inferred from the love and respect his parishioners had for him. Thanks to his energy and devotedness as Manager of Schools, Catholic education has made great advances in the diocese:—*J. C.Guardian, Feb. 2, 1889.*

170

Solomon Johnpulle

Mr. Solomon Johnpulle came of an old and respectable family. He was born in 1836. His father, the late Philip Johnpulle was the proponent at Mannar under the Church Mission Society. He was the youngest of three children. He received his first lessons in English in a Government school, and then joined the Chundiculy Seminary under the Revd. Mr. Johnstone. This was all the schooling he ever had. His real education was his own work, and of him, it may be most emphatically said that, he was a self-educated, self-made man. He early acquired a taste for reading, and having free access to the Church Mission library, he became a careful and constant reader, storing his mind with various knowledge and acquiring that exceptional and, for a Jaffna Tamil, wonderful command of English, which in after life attracted the attention and even extorted the admiration of his European superiors and of the public at large. Among his earliest contributions to the local press was a letter to the oldest Jaffna Newspaper. the "Morning Star," exposing the wholesale plagiarism of the short-lived "Literary Mirror" conducted by Mr. Crowther and others, then connected with the Wesleyan Central School. This letter gave rise to a controversy which excited much interest. The editors of the "Mirror" supported by Proctor Ball and others, denied the charge, but young Johnpulle, though single-handed, reiterated the charge and published the article in the "Mirror" side-by-side with a passage from Herschel of which it was a base copying. The editors of the "Mirror" were silenced and young Johnpulle became favourably known as a youth of great promise. From this time he wrote frequently to the Colombo papers especially to the "Ceylon Observer", whose veteran editor has truly spoken of him as "an exceptionally intelligent Tamil gentleman." In 1862, Mr. N. G. Gould, who visited India, returning with a printing press, started the "Jaffna Freeman" and Mr. Johnpulle found congenial employment in writing for it. In fact the new venture owed its popularity and power to the facile and vigorous pen of Mr. Johnpulle who exposed many a local grievance with the greatest tact and success. He always wrote with telling effect when he had to deal with public wrongs. "The Freeman" while yet in its infancy, found a rival in the "Ceylon Patriot", started and conducted by Mr. Katiravetpillai, the present Police Magistrate of Kayts. After a couple of years Mr. Kathiravetpillai gave up his connection with the "Patriot", but the "Patriot" was destined to live, and when the Free press passed into Mr. Johnpulle's hand, he preferred the title "Ceylon Patriot," amalgamating it with the "Jaffna Freeman". Mr. Johnpulle was in the Civil Engineer's Office, till 1866, when he was transferred to the Jaffna Kachcheri as Thombo-holder by Mr. Dyke. In 1867, or thereabouts when Registration was introduced. Mr. H. S. O. Russel who had succeeded Mr. Dyke, made Mr. Johnpulle the clerk to the Provincial Registrar, as well as the Registrar of the Jaffna District. Mr. Russell in common with every other European with whom Mr. Johnpulle came in contact, soon knew his value and worth and appointed him Honorary Secretary of the Jaffna Friend-in-need Society, a post hitherto filled by leading Europeans alone. Mr. Russell's successor, the present Government Agent, probably entertained a higher opinion of Mr. Johnpulle's character and abilities, and in 1875 when the Prince of Wales visited Ceylon, Mr. Twynam nominated him chief of the deputation that waited on His Royal Highness in Colombo and read the address to the august Visitor as the representative of the Tamil population of the Island. From 1862 to 1877 Mr. Johnpulle was a prominent figure in Jaffna taking a leading part in all public movements and filling a large space in the eyes of his countrymen. Writing was his forte. We know of no man in Jaffna who wrote so fast or so well without a blot or a blunder in his manuscripts and displaying an exceptional command of a foreign language and of ideas perhaps still more alien to an Oriental. Of his extraordinary promptitude as a writer, a characteristic instance is furnished by a gentleman who was on the Prince of Wales' Reception Committee which so fully represented the learning and intelligence of the Northern Province. The Committee had to consider the draft address of His Royal Highness, but the address was not forth-coming and the Committee were so pressed for time that they could not postpone the matter for another day. While everyone else was fidgetting at the difficulty before him, Mr. Johnpulle undertook to write the address then and there and in less than half an hour, produced one, which was unanimously approved and adopted. Mr. Johnpulle died in 1889:—*The Ceylon Patriot, February 15th 1889.*

The present of Tamil Jewellery to the Prince of Wales, for Her Royal Highness the Princess of Wales, is the result of a happy inspiration and stands out distinct from all the other forms of loyalty which have been evinced.

The following is the list of Jewellery:—One snake bangle set with rubies and diamonds; one lion-faced bangle set with rubies and diamonds; one elephant hair bangle set with pearls; one bracelet composed of seven elephants; one chain carved in roses; one neck-lace; one cross brooch set with pearls; one round cross brooch, and one round brooch, all of rose pattern; one cross brooch in tortoise shell; one butterfly brooch in tortoise shell; one pair earrings in rose pattern; one pair earrings (pulukkudu pattern); three bar rings; one puzzle ring of four pieces, and another of seven pieces.

These jewels (worth about 4,000 Rupees) were enclosed in a carved silver casket. The outer surface of the lid was engraved with a representation of a forest scene surrounded by a wreath of lotus flowers; on the inner surface, besides the Prince of Wales' feathers was an inscription in gold in Tamil and English indicating that the jewels came from the inhabitants of the Tamil Provinces of Ceylon. There were about twelve workmen employed, the most noted of whom was Karthikasar Supramanyar. Among the Native Chiefs who came from the North and who correspond in position to the Ratamahatmayas of the Sinhalese provinces were Maniagar Manikavasaka Mudaliyar and Maniagar Ratnasinha Mudaliyar:—*Ceylon Observer, 9th Dec. 1875.*

A magnificiently bound copy of "Rousselet's India and its native Princes," containing the Prince's autograph was presented by His Royal Highness to Sir M. Coomaraswamy. *Ibid.*

Contrary to all expectation and after the idea had been abandoned as hopeless, the Deputation from Jaffna reached Colombo on the 8th and succeeded in presenting to His Royal Highness, the Prince of Wales, the very splendid set of Jaffna jewellery, of which so much has been heard. The Deputation consisted of K. P. Kanagaratna Mudaliyar, Interpreter Mudaliyar of the Jaffna Kachcheri and Treasurer of the Reception Committee; Mr. S. Johnpulle Registrar of marriages, births and deaths and Secretary of the Reception Committee; S. Manikavasaka Mudaliyar, Maniagar of Jaffna; A. I. Irakunatha Mudaliyar, Maniagar of Valikamam West, Mr. William Paul, Surgeon F. N. S. Hospital; V. Ratnasinha Mudaliyar, Mudaliyar of Mullativu; Mr. J. Nolan, Secretary of the District Court of Jaffna; Mr. N. Visuvanathapillai, Interpreter of the Minor Courts, Chavakachcheri; Mr. S. Ramalingam, Mr. W. Somasundram. Mr. M, M. Cader Meydeen, (Moorish shop-keeper.)

There were also the following representatives from the Eastern Province, viz., M. Covington Esq., Colonial Surgeon, Ezekiel Somanader Mudaliyar, Chief Mudaliyar of the Eastern Province, W. Allagakoon Mudaliyar, Shroff of the Batticaloa Kachcheri.

The Deputation had almost despaired of meeting the Prince on account of the non-arrival of the jewellery from Jaffna, when exactly at 4 p. m. Kanagaratna Mudaliyar arrived with the jewellery almost direct from Jaffna, after two days'' continuous sailing. His Excellency Sir W. H. Gregory very graciously arranged that the Deputation should avail themselves of perhaps the last half hour available, and having seen them all arranged in regular file in the spacious hall of the Queen's House, His Excellency made the following arrangement in regard to the presentation of the jewellery and the address, viz., Kanagaratna Mudaliyar to hold the box of jewellery, supported by the chief Mudaliyar for the Eastern Province; Mr. S. Johnpulle to read the address; W. Allagakoon Mudaliyar to hold the beautiful gold casket in which the address to be presented.

Exactly at half past four p. m. His Royal Highness appeared when His Excellency the Governor introduced the Deputation and on their behalf begged permission for the address being read and the jewellery being presented. Mr. Johnpulle read the address and putting it in the casket presented it to the Prince. Kanagaratna Mudaliyar then came forward, and presented the box of jewellery for the Princess, which His Royal Highness inspected with apparent interest, asking questions. His Royal Highness then thanked the deputation for the gift and the interview ended:—*Ceylon Observer, 10th Dec. 1875.*

171

Innasitamby Parikariar

Mr. Innasitamby, the well-known native physician of Sillalai, was an exemplary Catholic, sincerely devoted to the Church, highly useful to his country, widely esteemed and respected as a gentleman and of great repute as a medical man:—*J. C. Guardian, 23-2-89.*

172

Two new Priests honoured

The relations and friends of the Rev. Father D. J. Chrysostom waited on him at St. Martin's Ecclesiastical Seminary to offer him their congratulations on his elevation to the priesthood. To mark the happy event by some tangible tokens of affection and regard, they presented him with a chalice and Mass Book. The chalice was the gift of Mr. B. Deogupillai, the father of the new priest and the Mass Book an equally estimable present from the Catholics of Trincomalee:—*J. C. Guardian, March 23rd, 1889.*

The Rev. Father A. L. Poologasingam paid his first visit as priest to his native place Ilavalai, where he was received in a beautiful pandal put up close by the church of our Lady of Dolours— The friends and relatives of the Rev. Father presented an address with a Missal, chalice, a set of breviaries and vestments :—*Ibid.*

173

William Nevins

The death of Mr. W. Nevins, a gentleman greatly admired as a scholar and particularly as a mathematician, took place on Monday night last the 18th instant. He was well versed in Tamil and Sanskrit and leaves behind him several works to tell the mastery he possessed of the former language. He counted pupils in India and Ceylon by the thousand. His demise coming so soon after his Jubilee as a teacher, which was celebrated with much pomp a few months back, has caused deep regret wherever he was known :—*Ibid.*

Nevins is a leading and respected educationalist, noted for his tenacious memory and his solid knowledge. From the Batticotta Seminary, he transferred his services to the Wesleyan Central School, Jaffna, of which he continued the Headmaster almost to the close of his life. He was the author of an English-Tamil

Dictionary, now out of print, but valuable, in view of his clever original definitions of modern scientific terms. His son Mr. Selvaduraipillai, B. A., is the Principal of the Hindu College at Vannarponnai. In his preface to his popular Tamil-English Dictionary, Mr. Miron Winslow, originally of the Jaffna and latterly of the Madras American Mission, makes mention of Carroll and Nevins, in acknowledging the assistance he received from native scholars in the compilation of his work:—*The Life and Times of Mr. C. W. Kathiravetpillai.*

Mr. Samuel Nevins, the eldest son of Mr. William Nevins, was one of the Jaffnese who had distinguished themselves in India. He was a Vakil of the Madras High Court and was connected with the Madras University, as an examiner of candidates for the B. A. Examination. He married Susan, the second daughter of the late Mr. VanVicton (Santiagopillai), originally employed at the Jaffna Customs and latterly as Kanakapillai under Mr. Dunlop, the pioneer of cocoanut cultivation in Jaffna.

174

Arulampalam, Proctor

Mr. Proctor Arulampalam was a distinguished scion of one of the best aristocratic families of Jaffna. Born in 1850, an heir to the wealth, influence and antiquity of the great Ampalavanar family, he was left fatherless at the eighth year of his age, and grew up under the care of his uncle, the late Mr. Ampalavanar of the Ceylon Civil Service, who had him taught at the Presidency College, Madras. He married in May 1880 and leaves behind an infant son of five of years of age, his young widow, aged mother, two sisters and his two brothers—Messrs Mailvaganam and Elayatamby of Copay:—*J. C Guardian, 11-5-89.*

175

The Catholic Press of Jaffna

இற்றைக்கு ஐம்பதுவருஷங்களுக்குமுன்னே யாழ்ப்பாணமேற்றிராணியாராய் இருந்த மகாமேன்மைதங்கிய பொன்சீனாண்டவர் அவர்களுக்கு பிராஞ்சிய மந்திரியொருவரால் ஒருசிறு அச்சியந்திரம் உபகரிக்கப்பட்டது. அக்காலத்திலேயாழ்ப்பாணக்கத்தோலிக்க மிஷனைச்சேர்ந்தவருள் அச்சியந்திராவப்பியாசம் மிகவும் அபூர்வமாயிருந்ததினால் அதின்தன்மை ஒருவருக்கும் புலப்படவில்லை. அதைப்பற்றிச்சிந்திப்பாருமின்றிக் கறைபிடித்துப்பாழடைவதாயிருந்தது. அப்போது மாணுக்கனுயிருந்த C. Andrew என்பவர் அதிற்சற்றேகவனஞ்செலுத்தி அதைஒருவிதமாய்ப்பாவனைப்படுத்த முயன்றார். அப்படியானமுயற்சி ஒருவாறு சித்தியானதை அறிந்த மேற்றிராணியாண்

டவர் சந்தோஷப்பட்டு அதற்குவேண்டிய உதவிகளெல்லாஞ்செய்து, 1871ம் ஆண்டு "அர்ச். சூசைமாமுனிவரின் கத்தோலிக்கு அச்சியந்திர"மென்னும் சிறந்தநாமத்துடன் பகிரங்கபாவனைக்கு ஏற்படுத்தலானார்.

அன்னாட்டொடங்கி நாளொருவண்ணம் பல இயந்திர நழபாடங்களினால் விருத்திபெற்றுப் பூரணநிலைக்கு வரலாயிற்று. மேலும் Andrew என்பவரின் விடாமுயற்சியால் அச்செழுத்துவார்த்தல், பூவேலைப்படங்கள் இயற்றுதல், அசையாவச்சிரக்கல் முதலிய பல வேலைகளும் ஏற்படுத்தப்பட்டு நடைபெற்றுவருகின்றன. அன்றியும் பாடசாலைத்தமிழ் உறுப்புக்களை மாணவர் அளவுபிரமாணத்துடன் எழுதிப்பழக்கக்கூடிய ஐங்கோட்டமைப்பும் மேற்படி Andrew என்பவராலேயே முதன்முதலாய் இயற்றப்பட்டு தற்போது எங்குமகையாடப்பட்டுவருகின்றது:— *A. M. C.*

176

The Jaffna Catholic Guardian

This paper was started as an Anglo-Tamil fortnightly in 1876. It was issued weekly from 1876 to 1893. In 1894 the paper was published in two separate sheets, the one in English appearing once a week, and the other in Tamil once in two weeks. A further enlargement of the paper took place in the beginning of 1896:—*P. M.*

177

The Hindu Organ

The Hindu Organ was founded in September 1889 by the Siva Paripalana Sabai and is still its property. Mr. T. Chellappapillai, who was not only a great jurist but also a renowned Mathematician and eminent English, Sanscrit and Tamil Scholar, undertook to edit the English pages of the fortnightly Anglo-Tamil paper, as a labour of love, without pay; and Mr. T. Kailasapillai, nephew of Srila Sri Arumuga Navalar, became unpaid Manager of the "Hindu Organ" and its Tamil Editor.

Mr. Chellappahpillai, owing to failing health, relinquished his connection with the paper in the beginning of 1891, although he retained the presidentship of the Saiva Paripalana Sabai till his death, which occurred in May 1902. At the instance of the late Mr. Advocate S. Nagalingam, who took special interest in ensuring the continued existence of the Hindu Organ, Mr. A. Cathiravelu, Proctor, and now an unofficial member of the Jaffna Local Board since its establishment, and Mr. A. Sabapathy, the present Editor, joined the staff as unpaid joint Editors.

Among those who founded the "Hindu Organ" and cordially co-operated in establishing it on a firm and successful footing, special mention should be made of Mr. V. Casippillai, the present Crown Proctor of Jaffna and Secretary of the Saiva Paripalana Sabai and of the late Mr. S. T. M. Pasupathy Chettiar, Treasurer of the Sabai.

Mr. A. Cathiravelu took a very prominent and leading part as joint Editor from the early part of 1891 to July 1892, when Mr. A. Sabapathy became sole Editor. In fact he contributed during this period of joint Editorship more articles to its columns than Mr. Sabapathy. Though Mr. Cathiravelu ceased to be joint Editor between July 1892 to July 1899, yet he very readily acted as Editor more than once during the absence of Mr. Sabapathy from Jaffna and did not lose his interest in the "Hindu Organ". The "Hindu Organ" and the Hindu Community are, under a very deep debt of gratitude to Mr. Cathiravelu for coming to the rescue of the paper soon after the death of Mr. Chellappahpillai and editing it with great public spirit, conspicuous ability and at considerable self-sacrifice, for long periods. In fact, his articles were characterised by breadth of view, vastness of informations and soundness of judgment, sustaining the reputation of the paper as a useful and impartial organ of the public.

Mr. T. Kailasapillai continued to be Manager and Tamil Editor till 25th November, 1896.

Mr. P. Kartigesapillai succeeded Mr. Kailasapillai as Manager and Tamil Editor on a nominal salary. He was, however, relieved of his duties as Manager on 1st June 1903 by Mr. S. Kandiahpillai. The gradual improvement of the "Hindu Organ," and its continued success in the realm of journalism, have been chiefly due to the indefatigable labours, organising capacity, business habits and technical skill of Mr. S. Kandiahpillai, the present Manager.

Mr. A. Sabapathy has been now connected with the "Hindu Organ" either as joint Editor or sole-Editor for the last 24 years. The Editor of the Hindu organ has been now, for the last three years, very ably and efficiently assisted by Mr. S. Sivagurunathan, the assistant Editor, who makes the work of the Editor light. He has been a valued contributor to the columns of this paper from its early days.

The Hindu Organ was started on the 11th September 1889 as a fortnightly Anglo-Tamil Newspaper, converted into an English weekly on 5th July 1899 with a separate fortnightly Tamil edition, enlarged in size and form on 11th July 1906, and published by-weekly from 10th July 1913 with the weekly Tamil edition:—*The Hindu Organ Silver Jubilee Number.*

178

Anthonipillai Rajakariar

Mr. Anthonipillai was a gentleman of position in Jaffna and widely known as a tobacco merchant. He was the second son of Saverimuttu Mudaliyar of Mantotte and brother of Mr. S. Manuelpillai Rajakariar :—*J. C. Guardian, July 26, 1890.*

Mr. A. B. Rajakariar, the present Udaiyar of Jaffna Town is the eldest son of Mr. Anthonipillai Rajakariar. He has been Udaiyar for the last 18 years. Alert and painstaking in the discharge of his duties, he is held in great esteem by the people. The late Maniagar of Jaffna, Thampapillai Adigar, wrote of him:—"Mr, Rajakariar has always maintained a high character for efficiency and uprightness. In point of intelligence and general knowledge, he is superior to the other Udaiyars of the district. His reports are always written in English, and he attends to his work very promptly and regularly. He is well qualified to do the duties of "Chief Headman". Mr. V. Muttukumaru Mudaliyar, the present Maniagar of Jaffna says:— "Mr. Rajakariar has discharged his duties to my entire satisfaction. In my opinion he is well qualified to do the duties of a Chief Headman."

179

Sandrasagra Mudlr. Nicholaspillai Mudlr.

Nicholaspillai Mudlr. was well nigh ninety years old when he died. He was one of five brothers, the most notable among the others being the late lamented Chevalier Saverimuttu Modlr. and counted among his children a Minister of the Altar, the Revd. Fr. X. N. Sandrasagra, and Mr. J. N. Sandrasagra, the Superintendent of Minor Roads. He served Government for a long time as Shroff Mudlr. and Superintendent of Customs Jaffna, the latter, an office now extinct. Endowed with a heart that knew no guile, he was beloved and respected by all, for his simple, unostentatious manner. The Church of St. James' at Klaly bears undying testimony to his devotion and liberality. Nicholaspillai Mudlr. had enjoyed excellent health up to almost the very brink of the grave. He had a great dislike for conveyances of all sorts, and a sight really touching it was to see him even so late in life as a couple of years back or so, go with tottering steps and leaning on some faithful arm:—*J. C. Guardian, August 23rd 1890.*

180

Ponniahpillai Cherubim

Mr. Ponniahpillai was for several years employed in Southern India as a Railway contractor and an engineer. During the past few years he held the post of Agent of the B. I. S. N. Company in Jaffna. In this capacity he gave the ship-owners every satisfaction and enjoyed a perfect confidence of the traders. It is chiefly to his initiative that the "Catholic Guardian" owes its origin. Although His Grace Dr. Bonjean, then Vicar Apostolic of Jaffna, had long entertained the idea of starting a journal, for the defence of the rights of the Holy Church, and the eternal principles of truth and justice, it was Mr. Ponniahpillai, who induced him to let it see the light of the day at the time it did. *J. C. Guardian, October 25th 1890.*

Mr. Ponniahpillai's eldest daughter, Anne, is married to Mr. A. D. Saverimuttu, a trusted officer of the firm of Walker Sons & Co. Ltd.

181

Palmyrah Fibre Industry

Mr. Percy V. Appleby is at present in Jaffna, representing a Colombo Firm of manufacturers and trying to introduce the manufacture of a new product from the palmyrah palm. The part of the tree to which he wants to give a new use is the stalks covering the trunk of the palmyrah, which here-to-fore used to be dried and sold only as fuel. Mr. Appleby was busy during the week explaining to visitors at Queen's House, Fort, how the stalks are to be beaten and what prices would be offered for the black and white fibres contained in them. The process is extremely simple and presents none of the hardship and unpleasantness of beating out cocoanut fibre:—*J. C. Guardian, Jan. 24th 1891.*

182

Mr. Kathiravetpillai's Fellow-teachers

Among Mr. W. Kathiravetpillai's colleagues and fellow-teachers in the Wesleyan School were Nicholas Saverimuttu and Jonathan Crowther, who belonged to the promising band of students trained by Mr. Percival, of whom the most distinguished were Henry Francis Muttukistna, Barrister-at-law, and Morgan Covington, Medical Officer of Batticaloa, whose higher education at Calcutta was generously undertaken by Sir Anthony Oliphant, Chief Justice, whose attention they had attracted on the occasion of his visit to their institution. With Saverimuttu Mr. Kathiravetpillai, formed an acquaintance, which, in after years, ripened into intimacy. Savirimuttu and Crowther, following in the wake of Mr. Kathiravetpillai, aspired to the profession of Law. Saverimuttu gave up his law studies owing to feeble health and eventually passed and practised as a Notary. Crowther was latterly well-known as the Crown Proctor and Notary of Batticaloa and as a leader and representative of the Native Community at the Eastern Capital:—*The Life of C. W. Kathiravetpillai.*

183

John Toussaint

யாழ்ப்பாணத்திலே ஒல்லாந்தர் வமிசத்தவராய், நெடுங்காலவியாபாரியாய், செல்வராய், குணசீலராய், எல்லாராலும் அறியப்பட்டவராய், எல்லாராலுஞ் சங்கிக்கப்பட்டவராயிருந்துவந்த மெஸ். ஜோண் துசேயின்ற் துரைசென்றதிங்கட்கிழமை காலஞ்சென்றனர். அவருக்குவயசு 65. காய்ச்சலுங்கிருணியுமே மரணத்தின்காரணம்:—கத்தோலிக்கப்பாதுகாவலன்.

184

Magdalene Bastiampillai

Magdalene Bastiampillai was the second daughter of the late Sandrasagra Mudlr. Saverimuttu Mudlr., Knight of the Order of St. Gregory the Great. About a fortnight ago, she caught a malignant fever, which carried her off in spite of the best medical assistance obtainable. Since the death of her lamented father in 1882, the deceased lady in conjunction with her sister, Miss Mary Saverimuttu, had continued to provide every year to the May Devotions in the Cathedral, by having its walls and roofs tastefully decorated and the altar of our Lady decked with nice flowers chiefly artificial and made by her own hand:—*J. C. Guardian, March 26th, 1892.*

185

Archbishop Bonjean

It is with deep regret that we have to announce the death of the head of the Roman Catholic Church in Ceylon, Archbishop Bonjean. On the new division of Vicariates by His Holiness the Pope, he was appointed Bishop of Colombo and as such by his example and admonition infused in the clergy under his diocese, an amount of zeal and self-denial which earned for them the admiration of all men. Among the monuments of his zealous efforts in the cause of education stand the Jaffna College and Seminary, and St. Benedict's Ecclesiastical Seminary. He was also instrumental in getting out the Franciscan Sisters for the Civil Hospital and also established the Convent at Moratuwa and the Home for the aged. Of broad views as a church dignitary, which created friends for him amongst members of other religious denominations, of an unassuming disposition which secured for him the respect of all with whom he came in contaet, given up largely to charity which extended to all irrespective of race or colour, the Archbishop of Colombo has departed this life universally regretted and deservedly respected. By the death of His Grace, the Roman Catholic denomination have sustained a very great loss, as in him they had always found a warm-hearted friend and a faithful, though at times stern adviser. His place in their affections and hearts will not be refilled, and his memory will be cherished with great devotion and affection for a long time. On the above subject a Buddhist writes as follows:—"I am grieved to hear the death of His Grace. In him Ceylon loses a clever man and a true friend of education. His manly qualities, his valiant defence of the helpless in all matters, coupled with his great love to the Sinhalese as a nation, made many others than Roman Catholics to respect, admire and love him. Truly Ceylon weeps for the loss of a good man". In taking our leave of the sad subject which has occupied the attention of the public for the last three or four days, we can only reiterate our sympathy with the Roman Catholic community in the irreparable loss they have sustained and our admiration and profound respect for the deceased prelate who by a life of zeal and devotion in his Master's cause and unostentatious charity had endeared himself not only to the members of his flock, but also to all classes of the community:—*The Times of Ceylon.*

186

Rev. W. W. Howland

The Revd. Mr. W. W. Howland was the oldest member of the American Mission. He was 75 years old, over 40 of which he spent in Jaffna chiefly in connection with the Female Boarding School at Uduvil. He was the oldest Protestant Missionary in Jaffna and was much respected:—*J. C. Guardian Sept. 3rd, 1892.*

187

Dr. Chapman

Dr. Chapman was a favourite student of Dr. Green and a very successful Medical Practitioner. He was associated with Dr.

Green in the translation of English Medical Books into Tamil and among the works which he translated are the treatises on Anatomy, Physiology and Indian Pharmacopoeia and Chemistry. When Dr. Green left Jaffna for good, Dr. Chapman was appointed his successor at the Manipay Dispensary and Medical class— an appointment which he held till his death:—*J. C. Guardian, Sept. 24, 1892.*

188

A. Paul Mudaliyar

A. Paul Mudaliyar was the Chief Mudaliyar of the Jaffna Kachcheri and as such the Chief Headman of the Northern Province. He belonged to a family well and widely known and respected. He entered the service of Government as a Postmaster in 1862. Ten years later he was transferred to the Jaffna Kachcheri. He was gentle and unobtrusive by nature. In public as well as in private life he maintained a high character as a thoroughly good man:—*J. C. Guardian, Jan. 21, 1893.*

189

L. Gasparpillai Mudaliyar

Mr. Gasparpillai Mudaliyar was Adigar of Mannar and died on 15th January 1893. He possessed one great virtue as a Headman. He did not care to make, much less to save, money after the fashion of Headmen generally. Towards the poor he was always liberal. He was an honest Headman and an exemplary Catholic. Mr. Gasparpillai is a nephew of the late Rev. Father Xavier, a step brother of Mr. Lopez Manuel, Sub-Inspector of schools, and a son-in-law of the late Mr. Patchiço, Adigar, J. P. and Mudaliyar of the Governor's Gate:—*J. C. Guardian, Jan. 28, 1893.*

190

B. Deogupillai

Mr. B. Deogupillai, Translator of the District court of Jaffna, was the father of Mr. D. Philips, Catholic Mission Inspector of schools and of the Revd. Fr. John Chrysostom, O. M. I.

The ancestral connections of Mr. Bastiampillai Deogupillai were very respectable. One of his ancestors, Don Deogu Mudaliyar who was a Respadore under the Dutch Government, is still remembered as the donor of some lands for the church of St. Mary's and as the patron at whose instance the eminent Catholic poet of Tellipalai, Don Philip, composed the Gnananantha Puranam. Another of Mr. Deogupillai's ancestors was Mr. Gabrielpillai who willed away some of his paddy fields to St. Mary's Church.

The deceased had the inestimable advantage of being brought up by a pious mother who, playing an important part in the administration of domestic medicines, made her influence for good as an earnest and zealous Catholic deeply felt in domestic circles.

Mr. Deogupillai got the appointment of an assistant master in the Government English School opened in Jaffna by the late Mr. Dyke. After some years the Government school was closed, in view of the efforts put forth by the Protestant Missionary bodies in the matter of education; and Mr. Deogupillai elected to practise as a Sworn Translator. In this capacity he was connected with the Jaffna Courts during the latter half of his life, and there is hardly a case-book, some portion of which is not in his hand-writing The atmosphere of the Courts is certainly very unfavourable to morality and honesty, but he earned a wide reputation as a strictly conscientious, perfectly trust-worthy and uniformly steady worker,—a reputation which he has well maintained to the last:—*J. C. Guardian, August, 12, 1893.*

I9I

C. Arunasalam

Mr. C. Arunasalam was sub-collector of the Kankesanturai Customs. He was a well-known and respected member of the Hindu community and an old and faithful servant of Government. *Ibid.*

192

Seemampillai Mudaliyar

Mr. Seemampillai Mudaliyar, Adigar of Musali Nanaddan commenced life as an overseer, about twenty years ago and his career has been a remarkable one. From the rank of an overseer he rose to the position of Adigar of the most important division of the Mannar District. He enjoyed the confidence of Mr. Twynam as well as of the immediate superiors under whom he had to serve. In addition to his ordinary duties he was charged during the last fifteen years with the supervision of the arrangements connected with the Pearl Fishery. Kind, genial and willing to make himself useful to others, he was the most popular Headman of the Mannar District:—*J. C. Guardian, Sept 16, 1893.*

193

Fredrick Johnpulle

Mr. Fredrick Johnpulle, one of the oldest and leading members of our community, came of an ancient and respectable family. He was born on the 10th of December 1828. His father,

Philip Johnpulle, was the Proponent at Mannar under the Government. Mr. Johnpulle received his education in the Church Mission School at Nallur and at the completion of his studies went over to the Church Mission Institution at Cotta, then under the management of the Revd. Dr. Bailey, the father of the present Government Agent of the Southern Province. There he learnt for sometime and on his return to Jaffna, received an appointment in the Chundiculy Seminary as a teacher, where he soon established a high character for efficiency and thoroughness. He made application to Mr. Dyke for a post under Government. The Revd. Mr. Johnstone backed him up and he was successful in getting the Shroffship of the Kankesanturai Customs. From Kankesanturai, he went over to Point Pedro as Shroff of the Customs. Here he remained till 1877, when he was transferred to Trincomalee, where he was entrusted with the office of Chief-clerk and Landing Waiter of the Customs. Here he continued to work till 1890, a period of 13 years maintaining his high character for efficiency and honesty. In July 1890 he sent in his papers for retirement. Almost all the superiors under whom Mr. Johnpulle worked, especially Messrs Reid and Pennyquick, have formed a high opinion of his character and qualifications :—*J. C. Guardian, 10-2-94.*

194

Nathan Strong

Mr. Nathan Strong *Alias* Ambalavanar Chittampalam, established himself in conjunction first with Mr. Ripley and then with the late Mr. R. Asbury as Printer at Manepay. Mr. Strong was one of the first among the Jaffnese to take to printing business. Mr. L. F. Leisching of the Ceylon Civil Service whose brief account of Ceylon was printed in 1861 by Strong and Ripley, Jaffna, says, in the preface to his book:—"It will not perhaps diminish any feeling of interest which may be excited by it to add that it has been printed and bound by natives of Jaffna, who for some years past, have had in their own hands, the press and binding establishment which formerly belonged to the American Mission and who carry on their business independently of foreign aid":—*J. C. Guardian, Feb. 24th 1894.*

195

Naranar Varithamby

This gentleman owned extensive property at Chavakachcheri and adjoining villages. As Udaiyar he weilded great influence. He was noted for his munificence and hospitality. Mr. T. N. Valupillai, Proctor, is one of his grandsons :—*C. N. P.*

196

An Anecdote of Mr. Dyke

A good story and a true one is told of the late Mr. Dyke, who in his passage through the Vanni came up to the ideal of an Eastern potentate in the pomp and circumstance of his retinue, consisting of horses and bullocks and carts and palanquins and tents and luggage and carters and coolies and cooks and butlers and torches and messengers and waiters, *et hoc genus omne.* With all this imposing paraphernalia of Asiatic regality, Mr. Dyke, the *facile princeps* of our Northern Rajahs, in one of his official tours through his extensive Province, encamped at Mantotte, then in the heyday of its prosperity, flowing as it did in fact and not in fiction, with milk and honey, as Canaan of old. The chief Headman of the district entertained the Rajah in right royal style. Of the various provisions sent to the encampment with munificient hospitality, the milk supplied was the most remarkable, being excellent in quality and so super-abundant in quantity as greatly to exceed the greed of the Government Agent's numerous retinue, to whom it was never before given to drink so plentifully, without let or hindrance, of the most nourishing fluid food. Mr. Dyke surprised to a degree, and staring as he never had done, in vulgar wonderment, asked the Headman whence came that truly amazing supply of milk. The Headman making the most of his opportunity to create a profound impression as to his immense wealth in cattle, told the Rajah, what amazed the Rajah the more, that if he would lay down a pipe all the way to Jaffna, he might expect an unfailing supply of, as much or even more, milk to flow daily, without any cost or difficulty, in time for his morning coffee, from the Mantotte Dairy to the Jaffna Residency:—*J. C. Guardian*, March 3rd 1894.

197

The Guardian Libel Case

This case in which the defendants, Revd. Father L. Mauroit, Proprietor, and Mr. C. Andrew printer and publisher, of the Jaffna Catholic Guardian, were charged with printing and publishing libelous articles in that paper against Mr. Arunasalam Sapapathy, Editor of the Hindu Organ, came on for trial before the Supreme Court at Jaffna, on the 26th of February 1895, the Hon. G. H. Withers, acting Senior Puisne Justice, presiding. The prosecution was conducted by Mr. Dias, the Crown Counsel, assisted by Advocates Allagakoen, Nagalingam, Kanagasabai and Muttiah and Proctors Mylvaganam and Tambiah. Mr. Advocate Dornhorst appeared for the defence, being assisted by Advocates Sampayo, Fernando,

Senathirajah and Vanniasinham and Proctors Nicholas, Johnpulle, Strantenburg and Santiagopillai. His address to the Jury was a masterpiece of forensic oratory, combining sound reasoning with satirical pleasantry. The defendants were not put into the dock but were allowed to sit at the Bar through the courtesy of the presiding Judge. The trial was one of sustained interest from first to last and the prevalent feeling was one of anxious suspense, till the Jury brought in a verdict of "Not guilty":—*J. C. Guardian, 23rd, March 1895.*

198

Chelliapillai B. A., B. L.

This gentleman was a native of Jaffna and practised his profession as a Lawyer at Cudappa. He was at the time of his death Chairman of the Municipality of that town. He was married to a niece of Mr. Proctor Carpenter of Uduvil. His death was the result of an accident caused by a fall from his horse while riding.:—*Hindu Organ, Aug. 21st, 1895.*

199

Jubilee of Sir W. C. Twynam

Mr. (now Sir) William Twynam first entered the service in May 1845. In October 1848 he was appointed Assistant Government Agent of Jaffna and in September 1869 became Government Agent of this Province. His official Jubilee, therefore, has come after he had been Government Agent of this Province for over a quarter of a century. This event is a unique one in the history of this colony. No other Civilian, since the British conquest of the Island has been spared by Providence to celebrate his official Jubilee:—*Hindu Organ, November 13th, 1895.*

Mr. Twynam was Knighted in 1896.

200

The Jaffna Commercial Corporation

On the 17th April 1896 at 4.30 p. m. was held at the office of the Ceylon Steamship Co. Jaffna, a meeting in connection with a proposed joint stock company to be started in Jaffna. A sub-committee was appointed to draft regulations of the company and 15 gentleman were appointed as the first Directors. Their names are as follows:—Messrs M. Geddes, Alex. Toussaint, A. Kanagasabai, S. Nagalingam, Wm. Mather, G. W. Toussaint, M. B. Swampillai, S. Manuelpillai, R. M. Veluppillai Mudaliyar, Cumaravelupillai, V

Casippillai, S. Venasithamby, S. Naganather, Basmanandu and Muttusamipillai of Puttoor. Mr. Alex. Toussaint has been appointed Treasurer and Mr. Proctor S. T. Arnold, Secretary. The capital of the company will be Rs. 100,000—"divided into 1000 shares of Rs. 100—" each. About 300 shares have been booked. The objects of the company are to carry on trading and general banking business:—*Hindu Organ, April 22, 1896.*

201

J. B. Sathupathy, Barrister

Mr. Sathupathy was the eldest son of Sathupathy Soosaipillai, the wealthy merchant of Jaffna. Proceeding to Colombo, he took to the study of Law; but a European friend advising him to go to England, he acted upon his advice and joined St. Catherine's College, Cambridge, in order to perfect his general knowledge, after which he kept terms at the Middle Temple and was duly called to the English Bar. He returned in 1887 as the First Jaffna Catholic Barrister. Mr. Sathupathy married a niece of Mr. Advocate Christopher Brito. He removed in 1889 to Puttalam, where he was in active practice. He was called upon to fill the post of Acting District Judge and Police Magistrate, the duties of which he discharged with credit to himself and satisfaction to the public:—*J. C. Guardian.*

202

Poologasingha Mudaliyar

தெல்லிப்பழையைச்சேர்ந்த உச்சித வித்துவானுகிய இவர், சமயசாஸ்த்திரக் கவிஞர். இவர்க்கு அருளப்பநாவலர் என்று மறுநாமமுண்டு. இவர்செய்த புராணம் திருச்செல்வராசர்காவியம்:—பா. ச. தீ.

203

Mr. Brown Sinnatamby

Mr. Brown Sinnatamby, the Father of the Jaffna Bar, was the father of the late Mr. Advocate Nagalingam and the elder brother of Mr. Eliatamby, for many years the Head clerk of the Jaffna Kachcheri:—*Ibid.*

204

J. E. Sattrukalsinghe

Mr. John Edward Sattrukalsinghe was the second son of the late Manuelpillai Sattrukalsinghe Mudaliyar, brother of the more widely known Aseervatham Mudaliyar of the Jaffna Kachcheri. The patrimony of the deceased placed him above want and his knowledge of medicine coupled with his genial disposition made him popular. Born and brought up a Protestant, he embraced the Catholic faith in 1896, when he was formally received into the Church at Madu while on pilgrimage. Edward Sattrukulasinghe married Mary Elizabeth, the eldest daughter of Proctor G. S. Puvirajasinghe and had two children, a son and a daughter. The son is E. R. T. Sattukalsinghe, who is employed as a clerk in the Excise Department:—*J. C. Guardian, Aug. 18, 1898.*

205

Tamil Shorthand

We heartily welcome the publication of a system of shorthand for the Tamil language, invented by the Rev. Father, P. Dunne, O. M. I., Principal of St. Patrick's College. The system is presented within the short compass of 16 pages and recommends itself by its conciseness as well as clearness. Explanations are given, both in English and Tamil on one page followed by illustrations on the next, thus enabling the reader at a glance to comprehend the signs employed:—*J. C. Guardian.*

206

The McLeod Hospital

The McLeod Hospital at Inuvil, Jaffna, was opened on Saturday last, the Rev. Mr. Trimmer of the Weslyan Mission presiding and Miss Howland declaring the building open. Mr. Proctor Changarapillai read a paper giving some account of the new Hospital, which is due to the collections made by the Misses Leitch, two American ladies who spent seven years in Ceylon:—*J. C. Guardian, October 1, 1898.*

207

Francis Asbury 1860—1898

Francis Asbury was born in January 1810 at Chandilipay. He received his education in the famous Batticotta Seminary during the time of Dr. Poor. He was sent as a teacher, by the native Evangelical Society, to Valvetty, where Mr. Wyman Kathiravatpillai (afterwards Police Magistrate) was one of his first students. In 1834 when permission was granted by the Madras Governor, Dr. Spaulding with three Missionaries and three Tamils including Mr. Asbury went to Madura to commence the work of evangelization. Mr. Asbury remained there, for about 25 years. In 1859 he returned to Jaffna :—*The Church of Christ in Ceylon.*

208

W. M. S. Twynam

Mr. William Moir Sommerfield Twynam, was the eldest son of Sir William Twynam. While in his estate at Pachchillapalli, the malarial fever of which he complained, took a sudden and serious turn and he was removed in a semi-comatose state to his residence in Jaffna where he expired:—*J. C. Guardian, Dec. 3, 1898.*

209

G. N. Puvirajasinghe

Mr. Nicholas Puvirajasinghe was a very popular and promising young man employed as second clerk of the Mannar Kachcheri. He was the eldest son of the late Mr. Gabriel Puvirajasinghe, Proctor of Jaffna, and the son-in-law of Mr. Joseph Manuel, Udaiyar of Mannar West:—*J. C. Guardian, February 11, 1899.*

210

Dr. A. C. Evarts

Dr. Alfred C. Evarts is the youngest son of the late Dr. J. Evarts, originally Resident Surgeon of the Jaffna F. N. S. Hospital, under the late Mr. Dyke, and the brother of a more brilliant and talented scholar, the late Dr. J. C. T. Evarts, who while in Calcutta, won the gold medal awarded by His Royal Highness the Duke of Edinburgh for obtaining double honours in Surgery, and whose career in Colombo as a rising Surgeon working his way manfully up to eminence and command like Drs. Koch and Rockwood, was abruptly terminated by a fatal accident in the practice of the art in which he excelled. Dr. A. C. Evarts, devoted himself so zealously and successfully to his duties as to secure the good will and approbation of his superiors, Drs. Keyt, Attygalle, Dias and Thornhill. He is a son-in-law of Mr. S. Pedrupillai, one of our popular and well-known townsmen:—*J. C. Guardian, April 29, 1899.*

211

The Jaffna Clock Tower

The Jaffna Clock Tower commemorates the visit in 1875 of His Royal Highness the Prince of Wales to Ceylon and perhaps also Sir James Longden's administration of the Island from 1877 to 1884. The tower was designed by Mr. Smither, the Government architect. The cost was met partly by the balance of the Jaffna Prince of Wales' Reception Fund amounting to Rs. 6000—

and partly by further local contributions amounting to Rs. 4000— The clock was the gift of the late Sir James Longden:—*J. C. Guardian, Novr. 26, 1892.*

212

Suppramania Mudr. Philippupillai

Mr. Philippupillai was a brother of Mr. S. Deogupillai, Udaiyar of Jaffna. His father Suppramania Mudaliyar popularly known in Jaffna as Arachy Muttar was the Udaiyar of Jaffna and was subsequently appointed Maniagar of Jaffna. Mr. Philippupillai went to Mannar in 1855 where he married the daughter of the late Gasparpillai Philippupillai. He entered Government service as native writer of the Kachcheri there in 1858. He was appointed Police Assessment clerk in 1864 and Registration clerk in 1877. He was promoted to an Adigarship in 1884:—*J. C. Guardian, April 14, 1894.*

213

The Centenary of St. Mary's Cathedral

The 25th of December 1894 will be a red letter day in the annals of Jaffna. That day witnessed a triumph of unity and fervour and zeal by the Catholics of Jaffna, who vied with each other in celebrating the first centenary of the dedication of their Cathedral. The evening devotions in the church on the 25th instant began at 3 o'clock. The Very Revd. Fr. Mauroit, as celebrant, blessed the new Gold Crown specially made to commemorate the occasion and placed it on the statue of our Lady of Assumption. It is fairly worth about Rs. 1000. The sketch of the history of the Cathedral during the past hundred years compiled by Mr. John H. Martyn from the Chronological Notes by the late lamented Dr. Bonjean and from old documents was read by him in the Cathedral. After Vespers the procession which then started was of a truth, the largest and grandest ever witnessed in Jaffna:—*J. C. Guardian, December, 29, 1894.*

214

J. I. Pieris

Mr. J. I. Pieris of Tuticorin had established himself as a merchant of our town during the last fourteen years. In him we lose one who, by his intelligence, his social and agreeable qualities, his skilful and successful dealings as a merchant and above all, by his exemplary life as a Catholic, had made himself a personal friend. He was indeed so well-known to high and low, rich and poor, that not to have known him would have in fact argued oneself unknown, and the good-will and popularity which he enjoyed have been evidenced by the general sympathy, which his unexpected death has evoked. His faith and his zeal as a Catholic were put to proof whenever the conversation turned upon religious doctrine or practice; he was always equal to the occasion and he silenced his non-Catholic adversaries by the force and acuteness of his reasoning. In the devotions in our churches he took a prominent part and his familiar form and penetrating voice will now be much missed on occasions of great festivals. He belonged to a leading family of Tuticorin Catholics:—*J. C. Guardian, May 20, 1899.*

215

Miss Mary Saverimuttu

By the very sad and quite unexpected death of this well-known and highly respected native lady, a prominent figure has been removed from the Catholic circles which she had long adorned by her intelligence and guided by her personal inflnence. Miss Mary Saverimuttu was the eldest daughter of the late Chevalier Saverimuttu Mudaliyar, who as Chief Mudaliyar of the Jaffna Kachcheri and Chief Headman of the Northern Province, was long regarded as a fitting sample and representative of the Tamils. She received an excellent Catholic training under the late Mrs. O. Flanagan and her father spared nothing to give her a good English education, so much so that, in after life she came to be acknowledged as the most educated, refined and accomplished lady of our town. She was Catholic to the backbone from first to last, playing her part as an exemplary Christian, always loyal to the Church and to the clergy with whom she heartily co-operated in every good work, and always generous in her expenditure for religious and charitable purposes. Since her father's death in 1882, she carried on the celebration of the Month of May and it must be said to her infinite credit that the celebration, year after year, during the last 17 years, lost none of the splendour and grandeur it had attained under her father. Following in his footsteps, she also took a great interest in the annual representation of the Passion during Holy Week on the Cathedral grounds. She also continued to be the leading and most active member, since its foundation by Dr. Bonjean, of the Congregation of St. Anne for promoting piety and charity among Catholics. To her dying day she maintained the dignity and prestige of her father's household. In fine, though not a religious, she devoted her whole life and all her means to the service of religion with all the zeal of a religious. In her lamented death the Catholic community loses a most exemplary and influential member, and the Catholic clergy one of its most steadfast friends and warmest supporters:—*J. C. Guardian, June 3rd 1899.*

216

C. Thiagar

Mr. Thiagar was well-known as a Tamil Scholar and Pundit. He started in life as a clerk under the late Mr. Bastiampillai, the well known Supreme Court Proctor. Mr. Thiagar then served for a short time as sworn Translator in the Courts. The Colombogam Orphanage was about this time started by the late Dr. Bonjean, and as a competent Tamil Pundit, was required there as well as at the Jaffna Boys' Seminary (now St. Patrick's College.) Mr. Thiagar offered his services which were accepted and thus began a career of usefulness which lasted forty years and during which he served as the fountain-head of Tamil to the great body of Catholic youths pursuing their studies whether at the Orphanage or at the College. He was so kind and amiable so genial and endearing and so ready and willing to impart what he knew that the four generations of pupils with whom he had to do and who are now to be found in all parts of the Island and in many parts of India and the Straits, will receive the announcement of his demise with unfeigned regret. In addition to his work as teacher, he was associated with others under the Mission as a translator and compiler of school books:—*J. C. Guardian, August 12, 1899.*

217

A. Philipiah

Mr. A. Philipiah was the grandson of the late Mr, Soosai pillai, a District Court Proctor and son of the late Mr. Philipiah, also a Proctor. Sir William Twynam first employed him as a third clerk in the Kachcherri Post Office in which post he displayed his business habits, regularity, punctuality and great carefulness so much, that he was soon made second clerk and afterwards Postmaster. He leaves behind a widow, three sons and a daughter. Messrs J. E. Philipiah, Inspector of Police, presently at Batticaloa, George Philipiah, Assistant Inspector of Schools, and R. S. Philipiah of the Road Committee, Jaffna Kachcherri, are the sons of Postmaster Philipiah:—*The Ceylon Patriot, Oct. 6th 1899.*

218

S. Ramupillai

Mr, Ramupillai was a successful and skilful medical practitioner and his reputation was not confined to Jaffna alone but known in other parts of the Island and South India also. Mr. Rampillai was a philanthropist in the true sense of the word. His long and useful life was spent in the service of his countrymen in affording medical aid daily to hundreds of the poor and helpless. His patience and equanimity of temper were very remarkable. He was never known to have lost his temper or entertained even professional jealousy. His nephew and son-in-law Mr. Sittampalam Kandapillai, on whom the public had great confidence as a physician, had predeceased his uncle about two years ago:—*The Hindu Organ, 17th Oct. 1899.*

219

Don H. Appuhamy

It was in 1888 that Mr. Don Hendrick Appuhamy first bought the arrack rents of the Northern Province. His business capabilities and spirit of enterprise and above all his unceasing energy are well-known. The generosity that he displayed towards his friends and relations and the pleasure that he took in allowing as many of his countrymen as possible to profit by the affluent circumstances in which it had pleased God to place him, are facts that speak volumes of his kindly disposition. Mr. Appuhamy had always been an exemplary Catholic and distinguished himself by his ready and liberal donations for religious and charitable purposes:—*J. C. Guardian, Dec. 2nd 1899.*

220

Imperium in imperio for Jaffna first mooted

It was in 1864 that the question of an *imperium in imperio* for Jaffna was first mooted. There was no Police Force then. Mr. Percival Ackland Dyke was everything and did everything and none of his acts ever roused public opposition, as none ever caused public dissatisfaction. Mr. Henry Francis Muttukisna, the most fluent Tamil speaker or rather English speaker, just then fresh from a visit to Europe and smitten perhaps with an ardent love for the progressive institutions of the West, called a public meeting and harangued with all his eloquence, the burden of his song being that the time had come for Jaffna to set about to take upon herself the direction and Government of her own internal affairs. In the discussion that followed, Advocate Gould, Proctors Puvirajasinghe and Santiagopillai, Mr. S. Johnpulle, the journalist, Mr. R. Williams, the schoolmaster, and others took a leading part.

The majority of the speakers scouted the idea of a Municipality for Jaffna and the motion fell through completely; nor was it revived during the decade in which it was started:—*J. C. Guardian March 17th, 1894.*

221

Revd. Robert Pargiter

Mr. Pargiter was Principal of St John's School, Chundiculy; for 26 years. He retired in 1866. Mr. Pargiter is regarded as the builder, if not the founder, of St. John's College. He was born in the year of the battle of Waterloo. His eldest son is a lecturer on Sanskrit at the University of Oxford:—*P. M.*

222

Proportion of male and female Births

Is the number of male births equal to female births—is it greater, or is it less? These are questions to which all the resources of physiologists from Aristotle down to our own time, afford no means of reply. And yet at the present day, we by the employment of what now seems a very natural method, are possessed of a truth which the united abilities of a long series of eminent men failed to discover. By a simple experiment of registering the number of births and their sexes, by extending this registration over several years in different countries, we have been able to eliminate all causal disturbances, and ascertain the existence of a law which, expressed in round numbers, is, that for every twenty girls there are born twenty-one boys: and we may confidently say, that although the operations of this law are of course liable to constant aberrations, the law itself is so powerful that we know of no country in which during a single year the male births have not been greater than the female ones:—*H. T. Buckle.*

223

Holy Family Convent English School, Jaffna

The above institution situated in the Main Street and almost hidden from view by wide-spreading trees and bright shrubs, is a magnificient edifice, the main building being about 150 feet by 40 and the two side-wings, 115 feet by 40. All round runs a broad shady verandah supported by massive columns some 14 feet high. These latter are apt to strike a visitor with admiration. The foundation stone of the convent was laid in June 1864, two years after the arrival of the sisters of the Holy Family—the first nuns who trod the soil of Ceylon. It is worthy of note that the Holy

Family Convent was the first establishment of education in the North to send in pupils for the Trinity College musical examination:—*Amicus Special Edition, April 17th, 1914.*

224

Wesleyan Mission Buildings

The Wesleyan premises at Jaffna, our principal station, are situated near the esplanade. At the Northern end, the Chairman and General Superintendent of the District lives in what was the residence of the Dutch Commandant. A lengthy suite of rooms with venetian doors and windows, runs back from the Southern side of the main building. These communicate with one another and are used as class-rooms for the boys' school. Continuous with them is a respectable dwelling-house, the boarding-school for girls. At a distance stands the old Methodist place of worship altered into a school, and called St. Paul's. It looks across to the new Chapel, which gives it the cold shoulder, facing the esplanade, at the opposite corner. This chapel, was opened in 1823:—*Hindu Pastors by the Rev. E. J. Robinson, Late Wesleyan Missionary in Ceylon, 1867.*

225

Louis Nell

Mr. Nell had a long and honourable career. During his stay in Jaffna early in the sixties, he displayed considerable literary activity, while steadily pursuing his professional duties. At the request of the Revd. J. C. Mola, the then principal of the Jaffna Boys' Seminary, (now St. Patricks' College) he delivered a course of lectures on English Literature to the senior students of that institution. An interesting and exhaustive essay on Adam's Peak, printed in pamphlet form at the Manepay Press, was from his facile pen. In view of an out-break of cholera, he published in the local Patriot, a series of informing articles on "cholera, its causes and the means of its prevention and cure", written at the instance and with the assistance of Mr. Benjamin Santiagopillai, the veteran Proctor. Retiring at length from the Public Service of his own Island, Mr. Nell has sought and found a permanent home in Switzerland, so health giving and delightful indeed as to make him almost forget the "patriot's boast" that "His first, best country ever is at home":—*The Life and Times of C. W. Kathiravetpillai.*

226

The Old Teachers of the Chundicully Seminary

I may begin by paying my small tribute to the memory of

267

some of my early school-masters, who helped in the shaping and moulding of the infant mind at the Chundicully Seminary. There was Mr. Cleveland—no relation of the ex-president of the U. S. A.—but a gentleman, very likely a graduate of the Vaddukoddai Seminary, who hailed from Nallur. He was in charge of the lower school, a stalwart man with a stern look, a good disciplinarian, rather partial to the betel leaf like many a Government officer of his time. Mr. Joseph Canagasabai, a shrewd man, rather erratic in his ways, clever at finding short methods to solve intricacies in grammar and arithmetic and in unlocking the springs of knowledge in dull-headed boys. Mr. Beadle Suppramaniam, an excellent teacher, of rather quick temper and often venting his energy on the unfortunate palms of delinquents: guava sticks were constantly in requisition. Mr. Nicholas who was always in spotless, white "angarka and taru". I once examined him more closely while he was hard at work, explaining to us some difficult lessons, my improvised telescope of an exercise book suddenly flew through the window in shreds. He was a conscientious man and it was a pity he left the school abruptly. Mr. P. Vannitamby, a very useful and handy man, teacher, stage manager, secular agent etc. His great infirmity was to suddenly fall into the arms of Morpheus when not in a state of locomotion. He held on to the school through its many vicissitudes. Mr. Aseervatham, a teacher of considerable experiences, patient, gentle and reserved in his manners, always in restful repose in his chair which he rarely vacated. All good men and true. But the man who greatly contributed to the formation of my character in after years was Mr. Jeremiah Evarts. In the annals of the St. John's College, his name must rank high and his niche must be side bv side with that of the other great headmaster, Mr. Robert Williams:—*R. H. Hoole Mudaliyar.*

227

Madu

A famous place of pilgrimage attracting about 50,000 people annually. Under the Goanese Fathers the Church was a mere mud hut said to have been erected by a certain Moyes of Mannar about the year 1823. The corner-stone to the present magnificient Church, towering above the giants of the forest, was laid by Dr. Bonjean on the 8th of August 1872. His immediate successor continued the building but the major part of the work was accomplished under Dr. Joulain. A grotto of Our Lady of Lourdes adorns one end of the Tank bund. Madam Louis of Negombo made a contribution of one thousand rupees towards the work:—*J. C. Guardian, Jan. 31st 1920.*

228

Puthumadam or Pullavely

The first report on the vicariate of Jaffna says; "The Church of St. Sèbastian belonging to the Mission of Pachillaipaly is a famous one in the vicariate, several thousand people resort there every year to fulfil their vows on the festival day, which happens on the 5th July. From 1896 the date has been changed to 8th July to suit the convenience of pilgrims returning from Madu:—*Ibid*-

229

Sangara Pandithar

இவர் யாழ்ப்பாணம் உடுவிற் கோவிற்பற்றைச் சேர்ந்த சுன்னாகத்தில் விரோதி வருஷம் சித்திரை மீ 21ந் திகதி பிறந்தவர். நீர்வேலியே இவர் வசித்த ஊர். இவர் இங்கிலிஷ் பாஷையுஞ் சற்றே அறிந்தவர். இவர் தமிழிலே சைவப்பிரகாசனம் என்னும் ஓர் நூல் செய்திருக்கின்றார். இஃதன்றிச் சமஸ்கிருத பாலபாடம், சமஸ்கிருத இலக்கணம் ஆதியாம் வேறுசில நூல்களோடு சிலவற்றுக்கு உரையுஞ் செய்தனர். வடதேசயாத்திரைசெய்துதிரும்பும்போது புதுச்சேரியிலே, பிரமோதூதவருஷம் புரட்டாசி மீ 12ந் திகதி 42 வயசளவையில் வைசூரிகண்டு தேகவியோகமாயினர். இவர் புத்திரர் சிவப்பிரகாச பண்டிதர் வல்லகல்விமானாய்ப் பலமாணாக்கருக்குப் பாடஞ்சொல்லி வருகின்றார்:—பா. ச. தீ.

230

Sinna Madu

Monseigneur Vistarini when in charge of the Islands baptised some people in the village of Saravanai. These soon fell back. Fr. Sandrasagra first put up a school and then founded a Church for the scattered flock. On the 4th of July 1895 the first mass was said in the new cadjan structure. From 1896, the feast has been celebrated on the 5th of August every year:—*J. C.. Guardian,*

231

T. Mudaliyar Abraham

On the 1st January 1900, on the dawn of a new year, and of a new century, Mr. Abraham received his children, grand-children and great grand-children, gave them appropriate advice, the last, as he thought, he was destined to give and then dismissed them with his blessing. Retaining his consciousness almost to the end, he expired peacefully, after receiving the last sacraments, on the 5th January, 1900, in his 92nd year:—*J. A. T.*

Mr. G. N. Tisseverasinghe, who is practising as a Proctor in the Jaffna Courts, is a grand-son of Mr. Abraham.

232

The Northern Railway

This Railway holds pride of place not only on account of the long period of agitation which preceded its sanction, but also by reason of its length and cost.

The construction of the Railway at the Kurunegala extremity was begun in April, 1900 and at the Jaffna extremity in July of the same year, under Mr. Oliver as Chief Resident Engineer. The Kankesanturai—Chavakachcheri section, consisting of the 21 miles of the line which include Jaffna itself, was opened by me for public traffic in March, 1902, and the Chavakachcheri—Pallai section, 14 miles in length, was opened in the following September. In little more than a year from now it will be possible to leave Jaffna in the early morning and be in Colombo in the evening of the same day:—*Sir J. W. Ridgeway.*

233

V. S. Mariampillai

Mr. Venus S. Mariampillai belonged to a respectable family of Karampan, Kayts. Proceeding to Colombo when young, he took to the cigar trade. His steady habits and natural aptitude for business won for him considerable success. Mr. Mariampillai married Gertrude Chellamma, the eldest daughter of Mr. S. S. Annasamypillai, the well known merchant of Jaffna:—*C. S.*

234

The Pearl Fishery

The pearl fisheries in the Gulf of Mannar have been for centuries a lucrative source of revenue to the Government of this Island. During the one hundred and seven years of British rule over £1,000,000 net revenue has accrued to the colony from these fisheries, representing an average annual income of some Rs. 150,000. But the income is precarious; for instance, during the period named there have been three long gaps, viz., from 1837 to 1855, from 1864 to 1873 and from 1891 till the present year.

On the recommendation of Professor E. Ray Lankester, F. R. S., the distinguished Director of the Natural History Department of the British Museum, Professor Herdman, F. R. S., of the University of Liverpool, was approached, and eventually agreed to devote his energies to the task of discovering this dicontinuity.

This gentleman, who is acknowledged as one of the greatest authorities upon the economic development of the food resources of the sea, was to formulate a scheme which should mininize or neutralize as far as possible the inimical agencies at work, and thereby induce some degree of regularity in future in the fishery returns.

In January, 1902, Professor Herdman, accompanied by his assistant, Mr. J. Hornell, arrived in Colombo. Some three months were devoted to a personal investigation of many phases of the problem, and before his departure, in the following April, Professor Herdman arranged for the installation of his colleague in a temporary marine laboratory at Galle, to continue there further experimental work:—*Ibid.*

235.

The Vanni

The greatest need of the people of the Vanni is a supply of good food and water, and for this village tanks are absolutely necessary. In 1896 the provisions of Sir Henry Ward's minute were extended to Mannar and the Vanni. The restoration of larger tanks has also been going on. Kanukkani is still under restoration in the Mullaitivu District, and the Giant's tank, Mannar, has been completed. A very important irrigation work to aid Jaffna cultivators was sanctioned at Karachchi on the south side of the Jaffna Lagoon, and its construction has already begun. This will eventually irrigate 20,000 acres. Progress has also been made in opening up new roads in the Vanni, and in improving those already existing:—*R. W. Ievers.*

236

R. H. Leembruggen

Mr. Leembruggen was in Government service for 37 years. His first appointment was as Headmaster of the Matara Boys' English School. Thirteen years after, he was appointed Principal of the Colombo Female Seminary, which was a leading institution for girls in Colombo and was abolished twenty years ago. He was then appointed as clerk, first in the Attorney-General's Office, and afterwards in the Secretariate. In 1892, he was appointed Inspector of Schools:—*Hindu Organ, 9th Decr. 1903.*

237

Rev. E. P. Hastings

The Jaffna College opened on the 3rd of July 1872 under the presidency of Rev. E. P. Hastings, D. D., and under the control of a Board of Directors chosen from the three missions in Jaffna. Dr. Hastings presided over the College with great ability and success for seventeen years and it was well that in the providence of God he was the first President. His missionary zeal, his connection for some years with the Seminary and above all the personal magnetism of his character, gave him a unique influence in the community. He was a fine English Scholar and a born ruler of men and boys in the sphere of work that fell to him. In power of organization and at the some time in attention to the minutest details he had few equals. Work to him was a pleasure. Above all, the leading of young men to Christ was the one object he kept steadily in view. No wonder that under him the foundations of the College were so well and truly laid that if his successors did no more than follow in the lines marked out by him, the work was bound to advance:—*The Jaffna College Miscellany.*

238

Rev. S. W. Howland

The Rev. S. W. Howland, D. D., succeeded Rev. E. P. Hastings in 1889. He was a man of saintly character, a profound scholar of such rare abilities that one wondered that he should have been content to remain in such a limited field of work as Jaffna. The affectionate regard in which he was held will best appear from the familiar name by which he is known among the churches here. Every one calls him here "Samuel Ayyar". Under his influence the reputation of the College grew beyond expectation. This growing prosperity however received a check when Dr. Howland went on furlough to America owing to ill-health and severe blow when he went home for good in consequence of the illness of Mrs. Howland. But Mr. W. E. Hitchcock, M. A. Vice Principal, by his ability and devotion, filled up the vacancy, very ably till the appointment of the Rev. R. C. Hastings, M. A., to the Presidency of the College in 1899:—*Ibid.*

239

S. Duraisamy, Maniagar

Mr. Duraisamy was an able and conscientious officer, and was much respected both by the people and the Government. He belonged to an old and respected family at Uduppiddy. Mr. C. W. Kathiravetpillai, the retired Police Magistrate of Kayts, is his father's brother:—*Hindu Organ, 24th Feb. 1904.*

240

Dr. M. Candiah

Dr. Candiah was a Licentiate of the Ceylon Medical College

and was employed in the planting districts. On retiring from Government service, he settled down in Jaffna. When the new Registration Ordinance was brought into operation, he was appointed Registrar of Births and Deaths for the town of Jaffna:—*Hindu Organ, 6th April, 1904.*

241

New Advocates

Mr. Abdulcader is the first Moorish gentleman in Ceylon who has passed as an advocate. Mr. Niles is the son of the Rev. D. P. Niles, a well-known Wesleyan Minister. Mr. Culanthaivelu hails from Valvedditurai and is a gentleman of high connection there:—*Hindu Organ, 6th April 1904.*

The Rev. Mr. D. P. Niles was blessed with a good ancestry. His father, Nathaniel Niles, was one of the first converts among the Tamils in Jaffna, and the first Licensed Preacher in the American Mission:—*G. J. Trimmer.*

A memorial tablet to the Rev. D. P. Niles has been placed in St. Peter's Wesleyan Church, Jaffna. It is of pure white marble, on a black back-ground. The epitaph reads thus:—

In Loving Memory
of the
Rev. Daniel Poor Niles

Born 30th April 1836, Died 10th December, 1915, in the 79th year of his age, and the 45th of his Ministry.

A loving father, an erudite scholar, a skilful translator, an eloquent orator, a persuasive preacher, a zealous evangelist, a far-seeing counsellor, a wise administrator, a loyal colleague, a faithful friend:—*G. J. T.*

The Rev. Mr. D. P. Niles was one of the most illustrious sons of Jaffna and the most talented of the Wesleyan Tamil Ministers of this Island:—*L. P. S.*

The Protestant Tamil community in particular and the Tamils of Ceylon in general, have lost a good and great man, an erudite scholar, a deep thinker, a sage adviser and gentleman of unblemished character and spotless integrity .... He was always considered an ideal native minister—learned, pious, sagacious, dignified, and withal tolerant towards other faiths as much as his position as a minister of Christ would permit:—*A. Sapapathy.*

242

Thirunelvely Well

Pumping operations under the supervision of Mr. R. W. Smith of the Public Works Department were resumed in August at the

273

well at Tirunelvely, three miles from Jaffna, selected by the Director of Public Works, a steam pump being used. The well was deepened' to 40 ft, two tunnels opened at the bottom level from opposite sides of the well. The quantity of flow increased daily and uniformly as the excavation proceeded until a point was reached when the pumping machinery was unable to deal with the flow of water and reduce the level sufficiently to allow the men to work in the headings. On the data obtained final plans and estimate are now being framed. The water has been found to be of excellent quality:—*Administration Report on the Northern Province.*

243

W. N. S. Aserappa

Mr. Aserappa is a gentleman of high social position, unimpeachable character, liberal views and independent means. He has enjoyed the confidence of the Government, as his appointmen more than once to act as Crown Counsel, Deputy Fiscal of Colombo and Municipal Magistrate, would show. Mr. Aserappa is a liberal minded gentleman:—*Hindu Organ, 27th April, 1904.*

244

C. W. Kathiravetpillai

Mr. Kathiravetpillai combined in himself qualities which could rarely be found in one individual. He was not only a person of very high social position, but was also a gentleman of unblemished character, spotless integrity and vast erudition. Neither calumny nor jealously could point to one incident in his private or public life, as a lawyer or a Government Official, which could be considered unworthy of the eminent position which he held among his countrymen. He was one of whom his countrymen were justly and truly proud, and was an ornament to the Tamil Community. He was a man of serene temper, calm judgment and unruffled patience. Nothing could disturb the equanimity of his mind, even on occasions of the sorest trial or the greatest excitement. Although he has died full of years—he was about 80 years of age at the time of his death—and full of honours, yet his death is a great loss to the community.

Having retired a few years ago, he was fully occupied till a few days before his death in the preparation of a Dictionary of the Tamil language. This work, though incomplete, will be a standing monument to his scholarship and persevering industry.

The magnitude of the work will be seen from the fact that its first volume which is just out deals with only words beginning with "அ", the first letter of the Tamil alphabet. He leaves behind a widow, an only son and two daughters, who are married to his nephews, Proctors Sivapragasam and Katiresu :—*Hindu Organ, 20th April, 1904.*

Mr. Katiresu is the author of a Notary's Manual and other works. His brother, Mr. Rajaretnam, who is an Advocate, practising in Jaffna, has compiled and published a "Digest of Ceylon Law".

245

N. Ponniahpillai

Mr. Ponniahpillai was the eldest son of the late Dr. Nallathamby, Assistant Colonial Surgeon, Ceylon Medical Department, and nephew of the late Canapathipillai Mudaliyar, Maniagar of Jaffna. He was himself an amiable and popular Chief Headman. He leaves behind a widow, an only son, Mr. Rajagopal of the Jaffna Fiscal's Office, and an only daughter, who is married to Mr. Kantyah, Secretary of the Jaffna District Court:—*Hindu Organ, 11th May, 1904.*

246

Anuradhapura Riots

Anuradhapura, up to 1873, when the North-Central Province was created by Sir William Gregory, was indeed a buried city. It was a mass of entangled jungle up to the very doors of the few Government buildings then existing. There was no town, hardly a bazaar, and the only access for pilgrims was along the main road whence they had to grope their way as best as they could by narrow and devious paths to the sacred shrines buried in thick jungles. The British Government have changed all that. The jungle has been driven further and further back, the shrines have been disinterred and exposed to the light of the day, a town has been built and wide roads constructed. Gratitude has not been the reward of the Government. A local branch of the body known as the Maha Bodhi Society has sprung into existence, some of the members of which, have put forward on behalf of the Buddhists the most extravagant claims to Crown lands in Anuradhapura, and whose ultimate object, there is unmistakable evidence to prove, is the total exclusion from the town and its environs of all persons not of their persuasion. The claims advanced were refused by Government, and when an appeal was made to the Secretary of State, he also rejected them.

There was then a lull, and believing the society to have withdrawn its extravagant pretensions, I proceeded to negotiate a settlement which would concede the reasonable requirements of the Buddhist Community. I was prepared, for instance, to grant land round the principal dagobas sufficient for the erection of pansalas and seminaries. The negotiations, which were carried on through the medium of the Honourable Member who represents the Kandyan Singhalese in the Legislative Council, were indeed on the eve of a satisfactory conclusion, when some of the agitators thought they would extort by violence, concessions which had been refused to constitutional agitation. Advantage was accordingly taken of the great annual gathering of pilgrims in June to excite and inflame the crowd, and (although the respectable pilgrims for the most part held aloof) certain buildings to which the agitators had objected and also the Roman Catholic School and Church were soon wrecked and destroyed by fire. Stern measures were promptly taken for the restoration of order and the punishment of the rioters who have received a lesson which will, I hope, make them pause before they again attempt to force the hand of Government by violence:—*Sir J. West Ridgeway.*

247

Saravanamuttu Mudaliyar

This gentleman, the Maniagar of Tenmaradchi, was highly respected by the people for his good and amiable qualities. Successive Government Agents held him in the highest esteem and treated him with marked deference. He held the office of Maniagar for 20 years and was a Mudaliyar of the Governor's Gate and a gold medalist in connection with Queen Victoria's Golden Jubilee:—*Hindu Organ, 22nd June, 1904.*

248

Mrs. Ramanathan

This eminent Tamil lady, who was highly educated and accomplished, was a daughter of Mr. E. Nannithamby Mudaliyar of Colombo. Her eldest son, Mr. Rajendram, is now in England studying law and the eldest daughter is married to Mr. Muttukumaraswamy, a son of the late Thambiah Mudaliyar. She was the leader of the Tamil Society in Colombo and was much esteemed and respected by all who knew her on account of her kind and gentle nature :—*Hindu Organ, 6th July, 1904.*

249

S. Canter

Mr. S. Canter was about 70 years of age at the time of his death. Being very pious and learned and having had no worldly cares or anxieties, he spent the evening of his life in the service of God. He had every reason to be a happy man. Of his two sons, the eldest, Mr. Periathamby is now acting Sub-Collector of Valvettiturai. and his youngest son is Mr. Sundram, the popular and rising officer of the Colombo Customs. Of his three daughters, the eldest is married to Mr. M. Sapapathy, the Interpreter of the Jaffna Police Court, the second daughter to Mr. M. Kanagasabai, Sub-Collector, Kayts, and the youngest to Mr. M. Kanagasabai, Preventive Officer at Mandativu:—*Hindu Organ, 3rd Aug. 1904.*

250

Dr. Paul

Dr. William Paul was a graduate of the Manepay Medical School established by the American Mission. He was first employed as Preventive Officer at Paumban. In 1874 he was appointed Resident Surgeon of the F. N. S. Hospital. He had an extensive practice and was very successful. Dr. S. C. Paul of the General Hospital, Colombo, who is regarded as one of the ablest Surgeons of the present day, is his eldest son. Mr. T. Sanmugam, B. A., Headmaster of the Central College, Mr. Edward Mather, Agent of the Ceylon Steamship Company, and Mr. M. Rajasuriar, District Engineer, are his sons-in-law. The late Dr. Nicholas and the late Mr. D. A. Tambiah, Surveyor, were also his sons-in-law:—*C. N. P.*

251

Material Improvement

The Province and especially the Jaffna District, shows evident signs of material improvement, and there is a marked contrast between the Northern Province of 1903 and that of 1873, thirty years ago. Mud huts are being replaced by stone houses, more jewellery is worn and there are more vehicles of all kinds in use and money generally is more plentiful. The improvements may be attributed to the opening of roads all through the Peninsula and to the spread of education for which greater facilities are afforded in the peninsula than in many other parts of the Island. Jaffnese now are in more frequent communication with the other parts of the Island and with India and the Straits Settlements and if one can judge from the money order payments made in the local Post Office, there are ample grounds for believing that a very large amount of money finds its way into Jaffna from outside:—*Administration Report on the Northern Province for 1903 by Mr. J. P. Lewis, Acting G. A.*

252

A. Naganather

Mr. Naganather was the only son of the late Mr. Arumugam, who was broker first in the firm of Aston Scot & Co., and afterwards in the employment of Messrs Bois Brothers. Mr. Naganather was part proprietor of the Orient Boat Company and was possessed of immense property in Colombo. He was an estimable gentleman and died of pneumonia at the early age of 31 years: *—Hindu Organ, 19th October, 1904.*

253

William Digby

Mr. William Digby, was in the seventies connected with the Ceylon Observer as its Sub-Editor. He subsequently became Editor of the Madras Times and of some Provincial Dailies in England. He was also the Author of the "Life of Sir Richard Morgan". Mr. Digby was made a C. I. E. for his philanthropic labours in connection with the Indian famine of 1878. He was also the author of several works on Indian topics and the Indians had no greater Champion of their rights in England than Mr. Digby. His death is a great loss to all Eastern subjects of His Majesty:— *Hindu Organ, 26th Oct 1904.*

254

I. Velupillai

Mr. Velupillai was the brother of the late Mr. Ilanthalaivasingha Ragunatha Mudaliyar, Maniagar of Valigamam West and uncle of the present Maniagar Mr. I. Mudaliyar Tillainathar. Mr. Velupillai acted as Maniagar of Valigamam West during the illness of his brother. He was a quiet and unassuming gentleman.*—Hindu Organ, 26th Oct. 1904.*

255

S. Sapapathipillai

Mr. Sapapathipillai was the second son of the late Mr. A. Sinnathamby, who was Crown Proctor of Jaffna, and a brother of the late Mr. Advocate Nagalingam. He was a gentleman of ample means. He donated to the Jaffna Hindu College a room of his go-down in the Grand Bazaar valued at Rs. 2000 as his father had previously donated to the same institution Rs. 1000 in cash to found a mathematical scholarship —an institution of which his brother, Mr. Nagalingam, was the chief founder:*—Hindu Organ, 2nd Nov. 1904,*

256

N. Ford

Mr. Iampillai Vytialingampillai alias N. Ford was the father of Mr. Advocate Duraiswamy and was a gentleman of vast experience, keen intelligence and scientific knowledge. He had held high and responsible offices first in the state of Travancore and subsequently in the Straits Settlements:—*Hindu Organ, 14th Dec. 1904.*

257

S. Kantappasakarar

Mr. Kantappasakarar was a brother of the late Manikavasaka Mudaliyar, Maniagar of Jaffna, of Vytilingam Mudaliyar, Maniagar of Vadamaradchy and of Mr. Mailvaganam, Government Storekeeper. The present Maniagar of Vadamaradchy West, Sivasithampara Mudaliyar is his nephew and Mr. Narayanasamy, Proctor, Colombo, is married to one of his daughters:—*Hindu Organ, 14th Dec. 1904.*

258

Gold Medal for Jaffna Cigars

Mr. M. B. Swampillai, the well-known Jaffna merchant, is the recipient of a gold medal at the St. Louis Exhibition for the cigars and tobacco sent out by him from here to that great Exhibition. He is to be congratulated on the distinction he has achieved. He has proved that, under improved methods of curing and manufacture, Jaffna tobacco and cigar can hold their own with the products of any part of the world:—*Hindu Organ, 14th Dec. 1904.*

259

S. Ponnampalam

Mr. Ponnampalam was an ideal clerk and was employed in the Land Registrar's Office Batticaloa, but having resigned that office owing to ill-health, he was employed as a clerk for a long time under Messrs Casipillai & Cathiravelu, Proctors, and continued to be so till his death:—*Hindu Organ, 1st Feby. 1905.*

260

Mrs. Senathi Rajah

Mrs. Senathi Rajah, wife of Advocate E. S. W. Senathi Rajah and the eldest daughter of Advocate C. Brito was a highly educated and enlightened Tamil lady and had the honour of being presented to the late Queen Victoria, when she visited England with her husband on the occasion of the diamond Jubilee of Her Majesty:—*Ibid.*

261

The Northern Railway

The iron horse has begun to run between Colombo and Jaffna. The first August 1905, will be ever remembered in the annals of Jaffna as the day on which the distance between Colombo and Jaffna was reduced to a run of 13 hours and 20 minutes. The gift of the railway to Jaffna is chiefly due to our late Governor, Sir J. West Ridgeway. The Tamils of Ceylon owe a deep debt of gratitude to Sir Ridgeway, Mr. Chamberlain and others out of Ceylon, who have been instrumental in securing the Railway between Colombo and Jaffna. Among gentlemen who bore the brunt of the agitation in Ceylon, particular mention must be made of Mr. Ramanathan, Father Lytton and the late Mr. Advocate Nagalingam. The Hon. Mr. Ferguson and Mr. Capper also threw the weight of their influence on the side of the Jaffna agitators soon after the agitation was set on foot in Jaffna and the support which distant Jaffna received from many leading Europeans was due to Mr. Ferguson and Mr. Capper.

Though it will be invidious to mention names, we are tempted to make mention of one name—that of Mr. Charles Strantenberg the veteran Proctor, who was for 20 years from 1885 till the 31st July 1905, the Honorary Secretary of the Jaffna Railway Committee. There had been several changes in the Chairmanship and Membership of the Committee either owing to the death, ill health or removal from the station, of its members. But the people of Jaffna were fortunate enough to have had all along one good working Secretary.

How busy death has been in our midst may be judged from the fact that about half the members of the Committee, as it originally stood are not alive to witness the running of the great Northern Railway, to secure which they worked so hard:—*Hindu Organ, 26th Aug. 1905*.

262

V. Sinnappa Mudaliyar

This gentleman, the retired Maniagar of Valigamam North, served the Government for a long time, first as an Udaiyar, and then as a Maniagar with much acceptance. He was educated at the now defunct Batticotta Seminary, where by his industry and assiduity he won the esteem and even the affection of his masters and superiors. His retirement took place in 1900 after a meritorious service of 43 years under Government. He was one of the recipients of the Diamond Jubilee medal awarded to old and faithful servants. He leaves behind a widow and three sons to bemoan his loss. The sons are Mr. Mootatamby, Medical Practitioner, Mr. Visuvappa, Registrar of marriages and Mr. Appadurai, District Engineer's Clerk, Jaffna:—*Hindu Organ, 23rd Aug. 1905.*

263

Sir H. Blake in Jaffna

The first Governor who visited Jaffna with his lady was the father of the present Inspector of Police, Sir James Longden, who visited Jaffna about the end of the seventies. After Sir James Longden, Sir Arthur Gordon, Sir Arthur Havelock, and Sir West Ridgeway visited Jaffna, but none of them was accompanied by his lady, A special interest attaches, therefore, to the present visit of Sir Henry Blake, which had been marked by much enthusiasm among the people, This enthusiasm is also due to His Excellency beihg the first Governor who has travelled by the Railway itself, which has once for all put an end to the isolation of Jaffna:—*Ibid.*

264

Representatives of the Colombo Press

Among visitors to Jaffna during the Gubernatorial visit were Mr. Coates of the "Ceylon Independent," Mr. Ferguson of the "Ceylon Observer," Mr. Jones of the "Times of Ceylon," and Mr. J. G. C. Mendis, Proprietor of the "Ceylon Standard". During their stay in Jaffna they were most busy seeing as much as possible of men and things and the knowledge and information thus gathered will stand them in good stead in conducting their respective papers:—*Ibid.*

265

Dr. Pararajasingham

Dr. Pararajasingham alias Appapillai was stationed in several parts of the Island as Government Medical Officer including Anuradhapura, Kalmunai, Point Pedro, and Kankesanturai. He was always held in the highest esteem by Government and the public on account of his sterling qualities, high character and abilities as a Medical Officer. The late Sir William Gregory liked him so much while the Doctor was stationed at Anuradhapura that he bestowed on him the rank of Mudaliyar which has seldom been conferred on a Medical Officer:—*Hindu Organ, 22nd Nov. 1905.*

266

An Agricultural Company

A company was started on the day Governor Sir West Ridgeway opened the Northern Railway. Lands were applied for. But Sir Henry Blake's Government proposed such terms that the company was unable to accept them. It has been since wound up:—*Hindu Organ, 14th August, 1901.*

267

James Hensman

In the retirement of Mr. James Hensman, B. A., Fellow of the Madras University and Principal of the Kumbaconum College, after 35 years service, the Educational Department of the Madras Presidency loses one of the most distinguished officers, who has been rendering valuable service in the cause of Education. He is one of the sons of Jaffna who have distinguished themselves in India:—*Hindu Organ, 5th Oct. 1904.*

268

Mrs. M. Covington

Mrs. M. Covington, widow of the late Dr. Covington, Senior medical officer, Eastern Province, came of an ancient and illustrious family in the Eastern Province and was the most prominent and most respectable Tamil lady in the Province. She leaves behind five daughters and an only son, the youngest of her children. Her eldest daughter is married to Mr. C. C. Krishnapillai, second clerk of the Batticaloa Kachcheri. Her second daughter is the wife of Mr. R. W. Allegacoon, Police Magistrate of Chilaw; the third daughter is married to Dr. A. Chinniah of Batticaloa, the fourth daughter to Mr. C. Ponniah, late salt storkeeper, Batticaloa and the fifth daughter to Mr. W. Ollegasekaram of the Batticaloa Kachcheri. Her only son, Mr. Victor Covington, is a planter, and the member of the Local Board, Batticaloa. Her grand-children number thirty five, and great grand children two:—*Hindu Organ, 9th Nov, 1904.*

269

Wiseborn Volk

Mr. Volk was one of the educational pioneers of Jaffna, long and honourably connected with the Batticotta seminary. He is the grand-father of Mr. C. Perumalpillai of the firm of Perumalpillai and Chelliah, Proctors.

270

Bucket Pump

Mr. S. T. Thomas of Vayavilan who has recently returned from the Straits on leave, has, with a view of reducing labour and facilitating irrigation, imported into Jaffna from London a new type of Pump called "Noria" or Bucket Pump. The Pump is adapted for well irrigation in the Peninsula:—*Hindu Organ, Jan. 18th, 1905.*

271

R. W. Ievers, C. M. G.

This gentleman joined the Ceylon Civil Service in 1872, and after serving in various parts of the Island in different capacities, became Government Agent of this province in 1896, succeeding Sir William Twynam. Everybody admitted Mr. Ievers' great abilities as an administrator, and his keen intelligence to understand men and things. But the expectations, formed of him by the public at the time he assumed the Government Agency of of this Province, were not fully realized, and the general verdict has been that he was not a great success as the head of this Province. His hobby was the horse-breeding experiment in the Island of Delft, which has been the means of causing immense injury to the interests of the poor people of that Island. It must be said to his credit that he was a warm advocate of Irrigation in the Vannies, where he spent the greater part of his time on circuit. The Karachi works and others which are being restored or completed in the Province during the last few years, are the fruits of Mr. Ievers' strenuous advocacy in the cause of Irrigation in the Province:—*Hindu Organ, 22nd Feb. 1905.*

272

Alfred. C. Tampoe

Mr. Alfred Tampoe, the youngest son of Mr. T. M. Tampoe, retired Police Magistrate of Jaffna, proceeded to England in 1898 as University scholar from St. Thomas College and had a brilliant University career, having passed the Mathematical Tripos of Cambridge with credit. He is the first Ceylonese who has achieved success in the Indian Civil Service Examination:—*Hindu Organ, 5th Oct. 1904.*

273

Salt Manufacture

Salt has been manufactured at the salt-pans at Uppar from time immemorial. We do not know if any historical record exists to show when and under what circumstances the manufacture commenced. But there is no doubt that it was going on under the Dutch. From time immemorial, a section of the people of Chiviateru has been the manufacturers and they are of the Chivia caste, with a sprinkling of people from other castes.—Kovia and Vellale. The Government have a monopoly of the salt. The manufacturers are bound to sell the salt to Government at prices fixed by Government. But before Government made it a monopoly the manufactures used to take and sell the salt in different villages in the District. In the year 1885 the manufacturers were made to take out licences before entering upon their operations:—*Hindu Organ, 25th, Sept. 1907.*

274

N. Edirvirasinghe

Mr. S. Nicholas Edirvirasinghe, was the popular Postmaster of Vannarponne. His amiable disposition and punctuality in the discharge of his duties have won for him great esteem and much regard in Vannarponne:—*Hindu Organ, 28th Feb. 1906.*

275

Dr. Thomson. M. B. etc. (Ed).

This eminent Doctor was attached to the Manipay hospital for the last six months. During his stay here, he has effected radical cures in several complicated cases which were pronounced as hopeless. By his transfer, Jaffna loses one of the best doctors that it has ever seen:—*The Hindu Organ, 28th Feb. 1906.*

276

Dr. C. T. Mills

This gentleman, who was a very popular Doctor in this peninsula, was for some years connected with the Jaffna F. N. S. Hospital as its first Dispenser or Resident Surgeon. Resigning this position, he took service under the American Mission and was the means of training hundreds of medical students for service as medical Practitioners throughout the Island and in the Straits:—*Hindu Organ, 2nd May, 1906.*

277

P. Coomaraswamy

In the death of Mr. P. Coomaraswamy, late member of the Legislative Council of Ceylon, the Ceylonese have lost one of their most trusted leaders, and the Tamils of Ceylon, a foremost member of their community. The Ceylon Observer has truly said in its obituary notice of this gentleman that "not for several years has the Tamil community suffered such heavy blow as that which has just befallen them in the death of Mr. Ponnampalam Coomaraswamy." Mr. Coomaraswamy was born on the 7th Dec. 1849. He was the eldest of the well known and distinguished three brothers. His father was the late Ponnampala Mudaliyar who, in his day, commanded great influence in Colombo, having been one of the earliest Tamil settlers in the metropolis and having been once assistant to the Government Agent at the Colombo Kachcheri. Mr. Coomaraswamy's mother was the only sister of the late distinguished Tamil Knight, Sir M. Coomaraswamy and daughter of Coomaraswamy Mudaliyar who was the first Tamil member of the Legislative Council. "The three brothers," as Mr. Coomaraswamy and his brothers were called, occupied a unique position in Ceylon. They were each and all admittedly head and shoulders above their compeers among the Tamils, and even in the case of the other communities in Ceylon, no three brothers ever rose to such eminent and commanding position as occupied by Messrs Coomaraswamy, Ramanathan and Arunachalam :—*Hindu Organ, 13th June, 1906.*

278

S. Pedropillai

Born in April 1836, Mr. Pedropillai was a little over seventy when he died. After studying in the Jaffna Boys' Seminary, now St. Patrick's College, Mr. Pedropillai became a member of the teaching staff along with the late Bros. Byrne and Brown and Mr. W. Santhiagopillai. He was next employed by the late Father Bonjean, late Archibishop Metropolitan of Colombo, as one of his secretaries. He was subsequently employed as a clerk in the Civil Medical Department, Matale. The chief occupation of his life, since then, was the management of a Bakery, the oldest and most successful enterprise of the kind in Jaffna which he started soon after his marriage with the daughter of Mr. Anthony Tiru-Chelvam. Mr. Pedropillai took a lively interest in all public movements and contributed liberally to all enterprises that called for assistance and support. He also took a keen interest in St. Joseph's Catholic Library and was a member of the Friend-in-need Society's Hospital Committee. Mr. Pedropillai was a prominent figure in all social gatherings and there was perhaps no one that honoured invitations with such scrupulous care as Mr. Pedropillai, and visiting the sick was a duty of love that he never missed:—*St. Patrick's Annual.*

Mr. Pedrupillai was granted a Silver Medal at the Agricultural and Industrial exhibition held in Jaffna in 1889 under the Presidency of Sir William Twynam for the excellent bread and biscuits turned out by his bakery which is now managed by his son, Mr. P. Christopher, who is held in great esteem by the public of Jaffna for his honesty, punctuality and fair dealing.

279

Dr. A. B. Santiago

Dr. Santiago was the son of the late A. Mudaliyâr Santiago-pillai, Maniagar of Jaffna, and received his early education in the Jaffna Boys' Seminary. He then proceeded to India where he joined the Madras Presidency College. In 1873 he joined the Ceylon Medical College, and won a Government Scholarship. Dr. Santiago's first appointment was to the Kandy Hospital in 1877.

He was acting Colonial surgeon of Jaffna when cholera broke out at Point Pedro, and he took such effective measures to check the spread of the epidemic, that he received a letter from His Excellency the Governor, thanking him for his services on the occasion. His services, while in charge of the Convict Establishment, were so much appreciated by Government, that he was sent on a special mission to South India to study the medical system obtaining in the prisons there. Dr. Santiago paid two visits to England, and availed himself of his two trips to Europe to see men and things. At the Capital of Christendom, he had the rare privilege of an audience with his Holiness Pope Pius IX. On the previous occasion. he had been to Rome and seen His Holiness Pope Leo xiii :—*St. Patrick's Annual.*

280

K. Balasingham

Mr. Balasingam is the only son of the late Mr. Kathiravetpillai, Police Magistrate of Kayts. He is of quiet and unobtrusive habits, well conversant with law and highly popular. He is possessed of great abilities and high character:—*Hindu Organ, July 24, 1907.*

281

James H. Martyn

Mr. James Martyn, the well-known townsman, was, for several years, Editor of the Jaffna Catholic Guardian. He was of a retiring disposition and did not therefore figure so prominently before the general public as his great talents entitled him to do. He was one of the best products of the English education in the East and in him was found a happy combination of the West and the East. He was a most versatile writer of English and his style was always admired. He was at the same a great admirer of Tamil literature and always tried to promote its study. It is not easy to replace a man of Mr. Martyn's intelligence, intellect and research, and Jaffna is much the poorer for the loss of such a distinguished citizen. He was the eldest son of the late Mr. Henry Martyn, well-known in his day as a scholar and literary man:—*Hindu Organ, October 2, 1907.*

Mr. James Henry. Martyn was the elder son of the late Mr Henry Martyn, the distinguished scholar and tutor who for many years held with great acceptance and efficiency the post of General Storekeeper, Jaffna. Young Martyn received his first lessons in English from the late Mrs. O. Flanagan, mother of the late lamented Father P. O. Flanagan, O. M. I., Director of St. Joseph's Orphanage and Manager of Schools. He was next a pupil of the late Mr. William Nevins, whose scholarly attainments are too well known to need comment. On the death of his father he joined St. John's Chundikuly, where he was a class-mate of that other distinguished scholar, Mr. Lewis Williams, Inspector of schools, India. His subsequent scholastic career was confined to the Jaffna Boys' Seminary, now St. Patrick's College, which Institution was then in charge of those illustrious pioneers of Catholic Education in Jaffna, the Rev. Brothers Conway and Dowling, the latter of whom the deceased has so faithfully and effectually portrayed in the admirable sketch published in the St. Patrick's annual of 1906. Among his class-mates were Mr. L. Manuel, our much respected Assistant Inspector of schools, Mr. S. Abraham, retired Headmaster of St. Patrick's College, now being seriously ill at Narantanai, Kayts, Mr. C. Kavanagh, Mr. Ribeira and the late Mr. Joseph Muttutamby, Headmaster, St James' School, Karayoor, Mr. Francis Boudewyn, Record-keeper, District Court, Jaffna, and Mr. B. J. Tisseverasinghe Interpreter, Police Court, Chavakachcheri. In 1868, Mr. Martyn was appointed a teacher in St. Joseph's Orphanage when this Institution was under the management of the late illustrious Dr. Christopher Earnest Bonjean O. M. I., then a priest, who was not slow to discover Mr. Martyn's rare capabilities, and did not fail in time to give tangible proof of his regard and affection. For some seven years Mr. Martyn was a teacher at St. Patrick's College and such of his pupils as are yet living can testify to the thorough grasp he had of every subject that he taught, and the tact and skill with which he instilled knowledge into the minds of his youthful charge. In the early seventies he was an Inspector of schools under the Catholic Mission. In 1877 he was placed on the staff of the "Jaffna Catholic Guardian" which was then being edited by the late lamented Father M. A. Murphy. Some few years later he was sent as a teacher to St. Michael's School, Batticaloa, but he did not remain there long. On his return to Jaffna, he resumed connection with this paper which he had, however, subsequently to give up owing to certain untoward circumstances. He then took up the management of the "Ceylon Patriot", which paper he edited for nearly five years. His last connection with the "Catholic Guardian" was the longest unbroken period in his journalistic career, which illness forced him to close about a year ago. Mr. Martyn enjoyed a well-merited reputation as a writer of English. He had a remarkable command of the language and wrote with great facility and precision. He was a devourer of books, and a close student of contemporary history. He had a most capacious memory and might well be called an Encyclopedia of information of all sorts of subjects. The public know better than we can tell with what ability Mr. Martyn conducted this paper while he was its sole Editor. One great achievement that must be laid to the credit of his able pen was the abolition of the horse-breeding establishment at Delft. Mr. Martyn was of an extremely retiring disposition, but his services were in such great demand for drafting petitions, memorials and addresses that he was in constant touch with all sorts and conditions of people. Two interesting publications brimming over with valuable information regarding men and things are his Life of the late Mr. C. Kathiravetpillai, Police Magistrate of Kayts, published some time ago, and a Biography of his own distinguished father, printed at this press and distributed among his close relations and friends shortly before his death. Mr. Martyn was, besides, a ready speaker and had always a deal to say that was new and interesting. He was also a good Tamil scholar able to speak and write the language with elegance and accuracy. An important lecture delivered by Mr. Martyn was one on "Duty," a copy of which was sent to the then Director of Public Instruction and elicited high encomium. The disease which cut off a most precious life in the midst of an exceptionally useful career was a pulmonary disorder contracted some two years ago :—*J. C. Guardian, Oct. 5th 1907.*

282

C. Tirunavakarasu, Advocate

Mr. Tirunavakarasu was the son of Mr. Cartikesar, employed for many years in the minor Courts at Jaffna. He was educated at the Wesleyan Central College, Jaffna, and at the Royal College, Colombo, where his class-mates were Mr. B. W. Bawa and Mr. C. M. Fernando of the Metropolitan Bar and Dr. H. M. Fernando of the Civil Medical Department. He passed as an Advocate in 1892. For a few years he practised at the Colombo Bar. In 1896, he married the eldest daughter of Dr. W. G. Rockwood, and one or two years afterwards removed to Jaffna with Mrs. Tirunavakarasu. Mr. Tirunavakarasu had a good practice at Jaffna, took a leading part in public movements, and in various ways endeared himself to the people:—*Hindu Organ, Oct. 20th 1907.*

283

Samarasinghe Mudaliyar

This gentleman, the Superintendent of Post Offices, Jaffna, was undoubtedly one of the ablest and most popular of the heads of the local Post and Telegraph Offices. Being a most capable and conscientous officer and endowed with great qualities of head and heart, he was deservedly held in high esteem by the Government and loved and respected by the public:—*Hindu Organ, Nov. 13th 1907.*

284

Ceylon Dinner in England

The Ceylon dinner in England brings together all Ceylonese young men who are at that time residents in the British Isles as also such Britishers, retired officials and others, as have the welfare of the Ceylonese at heart and sympathise with their aspirations. The function affords an opportunity for the sons of Ceylon scattered over in different parts of Great Britain and Ireland not only to become acquainted with each other but also to ventilate the grievances of their country in England before the British public:—*Hindu Organ, 29th Jan. 1908.*

285

Avirampillai Parikariar

Avirampillai (as well as his brother Parikari Vythimuttu of Piravukalkudiyiruppu) commanded a very lucrative practice in Jaffna Town. His services were in such demand that at all hours of the day and night, his house would be besieged by patients. As a physician, he was very successful. He had an only daughter, who married the late Mr. John Nicholas, chief clerk of the District Court of Jaffna:—*J. G.*

286

Thambapillai Pulaver

Philip Thambapillai was a popular native physician and poet. He was in great demand by the poor who had great confidence in him. He was an expert in diagnosing cases by the pulse. As a poet, he was the author of the "Kanagasabai Nadagam," a popular drama; and he composed various other poems and contributed to other Nadagams especially the "Padai Veddu". He was known as a man of ready wit; and though not a great scholar, he was able to produce pieces of cutting sarcasm or ready wit on the spur of the moment. The late Messrs J. P. and F. P. Vannitamby were his step-brothers:—*J. G.*

287

Artists and Artisans of Jaffna

யாழ்ப்பாணத்திலே சித்திரங்கள் இயற்றுவதில் திறமைவாய்ந்த ஐரோப்பியராலும் பாராட்டப்பட்டவர் பலர். மேஸ்திரி சந்தியோகு சிற்பத் தொழிலில் தேர்ந்தவர். இவரால் இயற்றப்பட்ட சந்தியோகுமையோர் ஆலயத்தின் தூபி மிகவும் வியப்புக்குரியது. லேம்ஸ்டினில் என்பவர் சித்திரப்படங்கள் வரைவதில் முதன்மைபெற்றவர்.

289

அவுரம்பிள்ளை யோசேப்பு இரும்புக் கம்மியத்திற் கனிசித்திபெற்று ஐரோப்பியராலுங் கணிக்கப்பட்டவர். காதர் மம்மது சருமவேலை யிற் றீரர். சின்னத்தம்பி தாமோதரம்பிள்ளை பொன்னுபரணங்கள் செ ய்வதில் நிகாந்தம் பேரெடுப்புற்றவர். தச்சத்தொழிலில் வண்ணார் பண்ணையில் வசித்த காத்தியென்பவர் பெரும்புகழ் படைத்தவர்:—
M. F.

288

Atthothayam

அருத்தோதயம் ஒரு விசேடகாலம். இது அறுபது வருஷத் துக்கொருதரம் தைமாசத்தில் ஒருஞாயிற்றுக்கிழமையில் சூரியன் மகரத்திலும் சந்திரன் வியதீபாதயோககூடின திருவோண நட்சத் திரத்திலும் இவையொன்றாக உதயமாதல். இந்நாளில் ஸ்நானம் தருமம் முதலியன செய்தால் விசேடமென்பது திண்ணம்:—
The Coronation Dictionary.

289

Dr. S. Sinnappoo

Dr. S. Sinnappoo, grandson of the late Mandalanayaka Mudaliyar of Chunnakam, was a favourite student of Dr. Green. He was by his profession and other ways very serviceable to his friends and relations. His eldest son, Dr. Manikam is holding a high appointment under Government in Perak :—*Hindu Organ, March, 18th, 1908.*

290

S. Sidamparapillai

Mr. Sidamparapillai was the only son of the late Mr. S. Saravanamuttu, who was Udaiyar of Vannarponne East, and was also Acting Maniagar of Jaffna at the time of his death. He was brother-in-law of Mr. A. Chelliah, the present Udaiyar of Vannurponne East. Mr. Sidamparapillai received a good education and was married to a sister of Mr. A. Sabapathy, Member Local Board, Jaffna: –*Hindu Organ, March 25th, 1908.*

291

The Jaffna Catholic Club

This Club--the Home of the Old Boys of St. Patrick's College--is the development and perfection of St. Joseph's Catholic Library. The object of the Club is to bring the former students of the College into closer touch with one another and stimulate them to Catholic endeavour and offer them all the advantages of a refined social as well as intellectual life on Catholic principles and in a Catholic atmosphere:—*Amicus, Special Edition, April 17, 1914.*

292

A. Kingsbury

Mr. Appukutty Kingsbury, late Professor of Mathematics in the Jaffna College, was the father of Mr. T. K. Sinnatamby, B. A., Asst. Professor of Mathematics, Jaffna College. He was the father-in-law of Mr. S. Veeraswamypillai, B. A., Professor of Mathhematics in the Jaffna Hindu College and a brother of the late Rao Bahadur C. W. Thamotharampillai, B. A., B. L., and Mr. C. W. Chinnappapillai, retired P. W. Supervisor:—*Hindu Organ, April, 22, 1908.*

293

C. Coomariah Mudaliyar

Mr. Coomariah, the retired Registrar of Lands, Jaffna, was a very capable and conscientious officer. He belonged to an influential family in Mannar:—*Hindu Organ, June 10th, 1908.*

294

B. Santiagopillai, Proctor

By the death of Mr. Benjamin Santiagopillai, a land mark has been removed. Mr. Santiagopillai will be best remembered as the Nestor of the Jaffna Bar and a most capable and successful criminal lawyer. As a mark of respect to the memory of the deceased, who had practised as a lawyer in the local courts for forty-five years, the District Court and the Police Court were closed for half a day. He was the eldest son of the late Arasnilaiyidda Mudaliyar Santiagopillai, and brother of Mr. A. S. Nicholas, retired chief clerk of the minor Courts, Point Pedro and of the late Dr. A. B. Santiago, Assistant Colonial Surgeon. Born on Feb. 17th, 1837, young Santiagopillai received his early education at the Chundicully Seminary and then joined St. Thomas College, Colombo, from which Institution he graduated, during the time of Mr. J. Bailey. In 1861, he articled himself under Barrister, Mr. C. Stewart. He passed his examination as a Proctor and returned to Jaffna in 1863. In 1865 he married Muttamma, the only daughter of the late Aseerwatham Mudaliyar and Interpreter of the Jaffna Kachcheri, the largest landed proprietor in Jaffna. Mr. Santiagopillai was a prominent member of the Jaffna Railway Committee and was one of those who formed the memorable deputation headed by the very Revd. Father C. H. Lytton, which waited on His Excellency Sir Arthur Havelock in Colombo, to pray

291

for the extension of the Railway to Jaffna. Mr. Santiagopillai leaves behind five sons and two daughters, among the former being Dr. Richard S. Santiago, Medical Officer, Mantota:—*J. C. Guardian, Sept. 8th 1908.*

295

S. M. Rajakariar

Mr. Saverimuttu Manuelpillai Rajakariar, a leading merchant and landed proprietor of the Town, was engaged largely in the tobacco trade and also took part in the salt and arrack rents and had risen to great eminence and position. He was well-known in Colombo as the proprietor of the charity box cigar boutique at Kayman's Gate. He was a member of the Catholic Church and always took a prominent part in all functions of the Church:—*Ceylon Patriot, Oct. 16th 1908.*

296

A. Hoisington

Mr. Hoisington was the last Gilcherist scholar of Ceylon, who travelled in Europe and America and spent 8 years in practical Engineering in the latter country. He is possessed of rare qualifications in the science of engineering:—*J. C. Guardian, March 20, 1909.*

297

Dr. Rockwood

Dr. Rockwood was a most skilful and distinguished physician and had by rare ability proved himself "the greatest surgeon in the East." His reputation was not confined to Ceylon or the adjacent continent, but had extended far beyond the seas to Great Britain, where he won the esteem of such eminent members of the medical profession as Dr. Marcus Beck, Dr. Charles Stonham. Dr. J. Bland Sutton, Sir Thomas Barlow, Lord Lister, and Sir Frederick Treves. Dr. Rockwood had also done good service as a member of the Legislative Council. William Gabriel Rockwood was born in Jaffna on March 16th 1843. He was the second of the four children of the late Mr. Elisha Rockwood, Sub-Collector of Customs and a well-known mathematician. On his obtaining the degree of Dr. of Medicine of the University of Madras, a member of the Board of examiners paid him the following rare compliment:—I have lately had on behalf of the Madras University to examine a man of the name of Rockwood, from Ceylon, for the Degree of Dr. of medicine, and certainly was quite unprepared to meet a candidate for medical honours of this country so remarkably proficient. I fully believe that in any English or

Scotch University he would have carried the highest honours:—*J. C. Guardian, April 3rd, 1909.*

298

M. Nalliah

Mr. M. Nalliah was the son of Muthalitamby Hay, who was the chief Government Surveyor of the Northern Province during the time of Mr. Dyke. Mr. Nalliah was educated in the Chundicully Seminary and passed out as a licensed surveyor 35 years ago. Following surveying as a private practitioner, he set himself up in business and became the prince of paper merchants in Jaffna. Mr. Nalliah was happy in his children and had the pleasure of seeing his two elder sons, T. R. and R. R. Nalliah and his son in-law practising as lawyers with acceptance to the public. *Ibid.* Mr. Nalliah's third son, Dr. N. R. Nalliah, M. R. C. S., L. R. C. P., and S. London was appointed Resident Surgeon, Western General Dispensary, London, in March, 1916.

299

A. Mailvaganam

Mr. Mailvaganam was rightly styled "the Laird of Copay" on account of his high connection and the possession of extensive landed properties in Jaffna. His father was at one time offered a seat in the Legislative Council of Ceylon, the highest honour a man of his position could aspire to. Mr. Mailvaganam was a J. P. and Unofficial Police Magistrate. He was one of the Champions of the Railway to the North and of the agitation for the better management of the Jaffna F. N. S. He possessed amiable qualities which endeared him to every one:—*J. C. Guardian, Sept. 11th 1909.*

300

S. Chinniah

Mr. Supramaniar Chinniah, Maniagar of Jaffna, was originally employed in the Public Works' Department and subsequently joined the Colombo Municipality, as an assessor. He was Maniagar of Jaffna for two years.

301

C. Strantenburgh

Mr. Charles Strantenburgh was well and widely known as a Proctor of the District Court of Jaffna and a Notary Public. He was remarkably successful in the practice of both professions. He was the leader of the Catholic Burgher Community. He was one of the Members of the Committee appointed to organize the Jaffna Catholic Library and it was certainly a strange coincidence, that he departed this life the very day that the Catholic Library celebrated its twenty fifth anniversary. He was associated with the late Mr. Adv. Mutukistna, in the compilation of the Tesawalamai and was for many years a Member of the Provincial Road Committee and of the F. N. Society and Secretary of the Jaffna Railway Committe:—*J. C. Guardian, 18 Sept. 1909.*

302

K. Sivasamboo

Mr. Sivasamboo was a son of Kathirithamby Mudaliyar, Maniagar of Valigamam North in the nineties, a nephew of the late Proctor Mailvaganam and a son-in-law of Dr. Harward Sinnatamby and a brother-in-law of Mr. S. Thuraiappah, Notary Public:—*J. C. Guardian, 30th Oct. 1909.*

303

T. Nagalinga Mudaliyar

Taivar Nagalingam was well known as one of the wealthiest merchants, shipowners and landed proprietors of Point Pedro. It was his public spirit and munificence that determined Government to honour him with the title of Mudaliyar:—*J. C. Guardian, Dec. 4th, 1909.*

304

Jaffna Local Board Election, 1909

The contesting candidates in this election were Messrs A. Cathiravelu, Proctor, S. C., A. Sapapathy, Editor, Hindu Organ, S. Thambiahpillai, Proctor. S. C., and Joseph Cherubim, Steamer Agent. Fr. Boury's vote being rejected by Mr F. H. Price on the decision of Mr. V. Casipillai, the legal adviser of the Board, Mr. Cherubim gave up his candidature as advised by his agent, Adv. H. A. P. Sandrasagara. The three sitting members were then declared duly elected:—*J. C. G.*

305

B. M. Selvatambo

Mr. Selvatambo belongs to a respectable and well-known family of Mullaitivu. Some of his relations have held and are holding the post of minor headman in the District. The father and grand-father of Mr. Selvatambo were land owners and farmers. Mr. Selvatambo himself is one of the largest landed proprietors, owning estates, fields, gardens and houses at Mullaitivu and Jaffna, and rubber and coffee estates in the F. M. S. He is at present employed in the P. W. Department under the Government of the Straits, where he is held in great esteem as a steady and efficient officer. He takes a keen interest in all social movements and has contributed largely to charitable and philanthropic objects. In 1904 Mr. Selvatambo married Mary Beatrice, the eldest daughter of Mr. M. M. Puvirajasinghe:—*M. S.*

306

Lopez Manuel

Mr. Manuel was born in 1849 and received his education at the Jaffna Boys' Seminary. He passed the Cambridge Examination in 1866, topping the list of candidates in the whole Island. He was appointed teacher at his Alma Mater in 1867 and in 1881 became Government Sub-Inspector of schools:—*St. Patrick's Annual.*

307

S. Bastiampillai

Mr. Saverimuttu Bastiampillai of Karampen, more familiarly known as Sivalaiyar from his fair complexion, came of an influential family of Karampen and maintained to the last a name and prestige that pointed him out as the foremost man in the place. A typical specimen of the old time land-lord, his residence was always a scene of contentment and cheerfulness and no one called on him but felt it a pleasure to partake of his hospitality. He married twice. By his second bed, he had five daughters, the eldest of whom married the late Mr. P. Amedius, Chief Clerk, Land Office, Parit Buntar, Perak:—*J. C. G.*

308

G. Puvirajasinghe

Mr. Gabriel Robert Puvirajasinghe, Clerk, Irrigation Department, Anuradhapura, took to his bed with a stroke of paralysis and in five days was no more. He was a very capable officer and throughout his whole term of office enjoyed the regard and confidence of all his superiors. He was specially commended for work done in connection with the Maha Illupalama scheme. He took the keenest interest in all Catholic movements and especially the Catholic Mission at Anuradhapura. Mr. Robert was a scion of one of the most respectable families of the town of Jaffna, being the second son of the late Mr. Proctor Gabriel Puvirajasinghe. In July 1903 Mr. Puvirajasinghe married Rebecca, a grand-daughter of the late Markupillai Gnanapragasam, the influential and popular Moopu of St. Mary's Cathedral, Jaffna:—*J. C. Guardian, 25th June, 1910.*

309

Casket presented to Sir Henry McCallum

The casket in which the address of the Jaffna public was

presented to H. E. Sir Henry Mc Callum was a fine specimen of artistic workmanship. It was made of silver, cylindrical in form with a golden lotus flower in each end. In the centre, was embossed in gold plate an adaptation of the Royal Coat-of-arms to suit the general significance of the occasion—a Purana Kumba, the Hindu symbol of prosperity being prominent in its centre. The body of the casket, on each side of the central design, was engraved in dull glow with four tobacco leaves. It is a lofty idea most happily conceived by its author, to depict the great advantage to our prosperity (symbolised by the Purana Kumba, accruing solely by our connection with the Great British Empire) symbolised by the coat-of-arms in the centre, as instanced in the recent release of the Jaffna Tobacco industry from a catastrophe. Mr. A. Mootootambipillai of Navalar Kotam, the author of this design, is to be congratulated and great credit is also due to Mr. Suppiah Patter, the skilful goldsmith of Vannarponne, who most faithfully and with rare artistic ability executed it:—*Hindu Organ, Aug. 10th 1910.*

310

V. Arumugam

Mr. Arumugam is the elder brother of Mr. V. Casipillai, Crown Proctor of Jaffna, and father of Mr. A. Cathiravelu, Proctor, Supreme Court, and member, Local Board, and of Mr. A. Canagaratnam, Proctor, S. C., and Editor and Proprietor of the "Ceylon Patriot." The late Dr. A. Ponnampalam, M. B. C. M., also was one of the sons of the deceased gentleman:--*Hindu Organ, Oct. 19th 1910.*

311

Joachim N. Sandrasegra

Mr. J. N. Sandrasegra was the son of Nicholas Mudlr., and nephew of Chevalier Saverimuttu Mudlr. After graduating from the Jaffna Boys' seminary he joined the Government Factory. In 1869 he was appointed superintendent of Minor Works, Jaffna. He did very valuable Service for the Road Committee and built several of the Rest-houses and public markets of the Province:—*St. Patrick's Annual.*

H. A. P. and J. N. Sandrasagara, Advocates, are his sons and his only daughter, Gertrude, is the wife of Mr. J. H. Vanniasingam, Barrister, the leader of the Jaffna Bar.

312

Dr. Kailasapillai

Dr. Kailasapillai served Government for upwards of 33 years

in Jaffna, Chavagachcheri, Mullaitivu and Kangasanturai. He was Asst. Col. Surgeon for some years in Jaffna. Mr. Proctor C. Perumalpillai, of Colombo, Drs. S. Thuraiappa, L. M. S. and C. Sivasithamparam, L. M. S. are his sons-in-law:—*H. O.*

313

Dr. V. Muttukumaru

Dr. Muttukumaru was the son of the late Mr. Vytianather, Udaiyar of Anaicottai. C. M. Sinniah Mudlr. Shroff of the Jaffna Kachcheri, is a cousin of the deceased gentleman. Dr. Muttukumaru was employed as a Government Medical Officer. His eldest son, Mr. V. S. Muttukumaru is Head Clerk of the Matala Kachcheri and Mr. V. M. Muttukumaru is the energetic Secretary of the Jaffna Local Board:—*Hindu Organ, Nov. 9th 1910.*

314

C. Brito

Mr. Brito was a prominent figure in Ceylon till he retired into private life some years ago, having been leader of the Bar and acted as Deputy Queen's Advocate and District Judge of Batticalao. Mr. Brito was a great Tamil Scholar:—*Hindu Organ December 1910.*

315

J. M. Varanakulasinghe.

Mr. Varanakulasinghe was the son of Manuel Varanakulasinghe, shipping Agent, Pesalai and Vangalai—He was Adigar of Manthai for many years and commanded the greatest respect:—*St. Patrick's Ammal.*

316

M. N. Sinnappah

Mr. M. N. Sinnappah belonged to a respectable family at Moolai, his uncle being the late Mr. S. Canagaretne Mudaliyar, the founder of the Chulipuram English school, and one of his cousins being Mr. C. M. Chellappah, the manager of the Victoria College. He was a very successful contractor of Works in the Straits Settlements. He was equally enterprising in Kurunegala and Jaffna. In Jaffna he was able to leave behind him the Inuvil Hosipal and the Ridgeway Memorial Hall as monuments of his skill and energy. Mr. Sinnappah also interested himself in the agitation for the Northern Railway. In 1908 H. E. the Governor McCallum was invited by Mr. Sinnappah to Moolai where specimens of Jaffna workmanship, art and industry were exhibited:— *Hindu Organ February, 15, 1911.*

317

Dr. Nallamma Murugasan

Dr. Nallamma Murugasan returned to Jaffna from England on the 31st May, 1911, after obtaining the degrees of L. R. C. P. and S. (Edin.) L. F. P. and S. (Glas) and L. M. (Dublin). She was given a brilliant and unique reception at the Railway station, and an address was read to her by Mrs. Evarts, wife of Dr. Evarts, at her family residence and a purse presented in token of public regard.—*Hindu Organ.*

318

S. Ponnampalam. Proctor:—

This veteran Proctor was the son of the late Mr. Sinnakuddy, one of the earliest and richest Proctors of Jaffna. Having been stricken blind, Mr. Ponnampalam was obliged to give up his extensive practice ;—*Hindu Organ, June 21, 1911*-

319

R. W. Allagacoen

Mr. R. Allagacoen began official life as a minor clerk in the Batticaloa Kachcheri with a salay of Rs. 15. per mensem. He passed the clerical examination in 1879. He was next appointed Kachcheri Mudaliyar of Trincomalie. Sir West Ridgeway selected him for the subordinate Civil Service, now called its Local Division. He was Police Magistrate of Kaltura, Chilaw, Kayts and Point Pedro and Chavakachcheri. At the time of his death, he was in the receipt of Rs. 7,500, per annum. He was conferred the rank of Mudaliyar of the Governor's Gate on the occasion of His Majesty's Coronation:—*Hindu Organ.*

320

Coronation Celebration in Jaffna

The celebration in Jaffna of the Coronation of His Most Gracious Majesty George V was the heartiest and the most enthusiastic function ever known here. Every house was decorated and illuminated in the best possible manner. The distribution of unboiled rice supplied by Mr. K. Vytilingam, the arrack renter, to the poor numbering over 5000 persons at the District Court premises, was a sight worthy of the occasion. The Government Agent, Mr. Freeman, started the distribution by serving, with his own hand, one measure of rice and five cents to the first pauper. Cloth also was given at the Ridgeway Hall to about 1000 persons. Coronation Honors were conferred on Thambapillai Mudaliyar and Mr. R. W Allagcoen, P. M, of Pt. Pedro and Chavakachcheri:—*Hindu Organ.*

321

A. N. Tiruchelvam

Mr. A. N. Tiruchelvam was one of the best known business men of his day and keenly interested in all public movements. The eldest son of Mr. Anthony Tiruchelvam, a flourishing Timber Merchant of the early forties, young Tiruchelvam received his early education in the Old Jaffna Boy's Seminary, now St Patrick's College, and then proceeded to St. Joseph's College, Negapatam, since transferred to Trichinopoli. On his return to Jaffna, he joined his father in business and after his father's, death greatly enlarged his activities, adding to the timber trade extensive business in copra, cigars, beche-de-mer etc. and even going in for planting, in which he enjoyed much success:—*St. Patrick's annual.*

322

Vallipuram, Tea Shop-keeper

Mr. Vallipuram is well-known on account of his public benefactions. The Ganga Chattram in the Grand Bazaar, the Bathing Ghat at Keerimalai and several costly wells in important centres, are monuments to Mr. Vallipuram's munificence and generosity. It was he who first started tea and confectionery shops on a grand scale in Jaffna and his wealth was mainly acquired by this enterprise:—*Hindu Organ, September 20, 1911.*

323

Rao Bahadur L. C. WilliamsPillai

Rao Bahadur L. C. WilliamsPillai, B. A. was a distinguished Tamil gentleman who by his brilliant scholastic career, his conspicuous official position in India, and the exemplary life he led, has brought honour and fame to his mother country of Jaffna. The following is abridged from an account by Mr. J. M. Hensman, which appeared in the "Morning Star" of the 22nd November, 1911.

In Mr Williams was centred a combination of qualities which have not been found in any one man in the past history of Jaffna. He was naturally very highly gifted. That he was learned goes without saying. His literary gifts were splendid. He was a mathematician of no mean order. He was professor of Philosophy and Ethics. In the Madras Educational Department he rose to one of the highest positions open to a native of India or Ceylon. But what are any or all of these marks of distinction to compare with his open and generous nature, his kindness and consideration for all alike irrespective of rank or station, his untiring willingness to help, his wonderful patience and forbearance, his tolerance of human weakness and frailties, his ten-fold return in kind of the love of those who loved him, his ready forgiveness of even meanness and ingratitude and his deep self-sacrificing and abiding interest in the welfare of those beloved. He was the eldest son of the late Robert Williams, Headmaster of the Chundiculi Seminary, now St. John's College. He was born on the 27th February, 1853 and was 58 years and 9 months old. He was married in June 1879, to a daughter of the late Rev. B. H. Rice. His eldest son, Dr. R. R. Williams M. R. C. S. and M. B. and C. M. (Madras) is Assistant Surgeon and Port Medical officer, at Tuticorin. His son-in-law, Mr. W. R. Watson, B. A. and B. Sc. is Professor of Science and Mathematics in Trinity College, Kandy.

324

V. Kanagasabai

Mr. Kanagasabai was a very popular and able native physician. He came of a skilled medical family, being the grandson of the well-known native physician of Tinnavely, Mr. Chanmugam, and uncle of the late Mr. Muttutamby, who died recently in the Straits Settlements:—*H. O.*

325

M. Coomarasurier

Belonging to one of the highest and most illustrious Tamil families in Ceylon, possessed of independent means as one of the largest landed proprietors in the Province, and endowed with great qualities of head and heart, Mr. Coomarasurier not only maintained worthily the traditions and dignity of his family but also enjoyed in an eminent degree the esteem and regard of the authorities and the general public. Successive Government Agents from the time of Mr. P. A. Dyke to Mr. H. R. Freeman deservedly held Mr. Coomarasurier in the highest respect. Mr Coomarasurier married the elder daughter of the late Mr. S. Ambalavanar, Police Magistrate of Kayts, and sister-in-law of the late Mr. A. Mailvaganam J. P., U. P. M. of Copay, and leaves behind, besides his widow, three sons and a daughter. His eldest son is Mr. MuttuCoomarasurier, the Maniagar of Vadamaradchy West, his second son is SivaCoomarasurier, Landed Proprietor, and the third son is Mr. Sathasiva Coomarasurier, student at law:—*Hindu Organ, December, 27, 1911.*

326

Dr. V. Saravanamuttu

Dr. Saravanamuttu began his English Alphabet at the age of 16 and in 5 years was fit to commence his studies in the Ceylon Medical College. Another five years saw him a licentiate of the Medical College. At the age of 40 he had the courage to submit to an examination in Latin at the University of Durham, where a few months later, he graduated as M. D. No other Ceylon man has yet taken the Degree of M. D. of Durham. Dr. Saravanamuttu had served Government in all parts of the Island. To the poor he was as kind and attentive as to their wealthier neighbours. He was never influenced in his treatment of cases by a consideration of fees. His eldest son, Dr. R. Saravanamuttu, who is an M. B. C. M. of Madras and is seeking further qualifications in England, will arrive here shortly to take up his father s practice:—*Ceylon Independent, January, 1912.*

327

M. B. Swampillai

Mr. Swampillai was one of the most popular and esteemed citizens of Jaffna. He had the advantage of a sound education. At an early age circumstances necessitated his taking charge of the business carried on by his father. He married Helen Rasammah, a sister of Mr. P. S. J. Chrysostom, Proctor S. C., by whom he had two children, a son and a daughter. Mr. Alfred Swampillai is his son. *Hindu Organ, Feb. 21, 1912.*

Mr. Swampillai's only daughter, Regina Stella Chellammah is married to Mr. Paul Rajaretnam, District Munsiff.

328

Allen Abraham

Mr. Allen Abraham is a well-known professor of mathematics in the Jaffna College. His attainments in the vernacular are equally high. He has also attained to great proficiency in Astronomy. In 1912 he was elected a Fellow of the Royal Astronomical Society and he is the first Ceylonese to obtain this distinction. He is an example of humility to the cultivated classes of our community:—*A. B.*

329

The Titanic

The "Titanic" struck an iceberg in the Atlantic and sank down. Mr. W. T. Stead, the eminent English journalist and the Editor of Review of Reviews, and Colonel Astor, the most prominent

American financier were among those who lost their lives in the calamity:—*Hindu Organ.*

330

J. P. Cooke

The connection of Mr. Cooke with the Seminary College and High School has been almost continuous of nearly seventy years. He graduated in the class of 1852. His life record is one of great earnestness and untiring activity in advancing the interests of Christian education and progress in the country:—*Jaffnal College Miscellany.*

331

Ramanathan's College

The Hon. Mr. P. Ramanathan's College in Jaffna for the Hindu girls accommodates 200 boarders. Day scholars are also admitted. The buildings are arranged round an open courtyard 150 feet square. A verandah skirts the square on all sides making a very pretty promenade within the College for the girls. It contains spacious dormitories and classrooms. The lavatory arrangements in the Northern and Southern wings are excellent. The dining rooms and kitchens are spacious. The grounds consist of 25 acres situated in Uduvil, about a mile from the Chunnakam Railway Station. It is considered to be one of the finest buildings in North Ceylon:—*Amicus, Special Edition, April 17, 1912.*

332

Dr. C. Dutton

Dr. C. Dutton was connected with the Jaffna Friend-In-Need Society for many years. He was one of the ablest and most successful physicians and surgeons in Jaffna. He did service that was greatly appreciated by the public:—*Jaffna Catholic Guardian.*

333

Brownrigg Sattrukalsinghe

Mr. Sattrukalsinghe was the elder son of the late Sattrukalsinghe Mudaliyar Manuelpillai and a nephew of the late S. Mudaliyar Aseervatha Mudaliyar of the Jaffna Kachcheri. His grand father was the late Don Gaspar Sattrukalsinghe Mudaliyar, who during the last days of the Dutch rule in Ceylon, held the high office of Chief Registrar for Jaffnapatam. His great grandfather, was Don Diogo Paramanatha Mudaliyar, a noteworthy chieftain and the younger brother of Don Diogo S. Mudaliyar Kathirkama Pulavar, an exceptionally gifted physician and poet of his day. Mr. Sattrukalsinghe qualified himself as a Proctor in 1876, and practised his profession in Jaffna:—*J. C. Guardian, Feb. 1. 1913.*

334

A. Mudaliyar Sinnatamber

Mr. Sinnatamber was a leading and influential landed proprietor of Alavetty. He was the father in-law of W. Mudaliyar Muttuvelupillai of Kanderodai and the only son of Rajakaria Sinkai Ariya Ambalavana Mudaliyar, Mudaliyar of the Governor's Gate:—*J. C. Guardian.*

335

J. N. Saverimuttu

Mr. James Nicholas Saverimuttu came of an ancient and highly respected Tamil family of Jaffna, the members of which have held offices of trust and responsibility under the Portuguese Dutch and English rulers of Ceylon, and discharged their duties with such distinction as to receive various titles of honour and enjoy the esteem and confidence of the general public. From generation to generation their leaders and representatives have filled a large space in the eyes of their countrymen, partly by reason of their official position and influence and partly by the distinction they won in the field of literature as its professors and patrons. His grandfather, late Mr. Henry Martyn, the leading land-owner and resident of the town of Jaffna, was a tutor, artist, preacher, journalist and Government storekeeper under the worthy Government Agent, Mr. Dyke. Moreover he was readily accepted as a member of the Royal Society of Great Britain and Ireland for constructing two wonderful Terrestrial Globes in 1835. His uncle, the late Mr. James H. Martyn, the Editor of the "Jaffna Catholic Guardian", was considered as one of the cleverest writers of idomatic English among his distinguished countrymen. Late Mr. Saverimuttu left no stone unturned to follow the foot prints which his ancestors have left on the sands of time. He received his education at St. Patrick's College, Jaffna. In 1897 he was attached as an assistant clerk in the Central Irrigation Board and purely through meritorious service, when the Irrigation Department moved to Trincomalee, he rose as the chief correspondence clerk of the Department. At the time of his death he was holding an enviable and responsible position at the Jaffna Kachcheri. He succumbed to the dire malady of pneumonia:—*Ceylon Morning Leader.*

336

A. Saverimuttu

Mr. A. Saverimuttu was Editor of the Jaffna Catholic Guardian from 1905. He had received an excellent classical formation at St. Martin's Seminary and St. Patrick's College. His English style was very chaste. Mr. Saverimuttu taught English and Latin classes at St. Patrick's College, till he took up the post of Editor of the Guardian, after Mr. James Martyn's demise:—*J. C. Guardian, Feb. 7, 1914.*

337

F. X. Nicholas

Mr. Nicholas was the only son of the late Mr. James E. Nicholas, a well-known member of the legal profession and a grandson of the late Proctor Velichorpillai Bastiampillai. Mr. Nicholas married Gertrude, the eldest daughter of Mr. S. M. Vanderkoen, Office Assistant and Salt Inspector, Puttalam:—*J. C. Guardian July, 11, 1914.*

338

C. S. Vaughan

Mr. Vaughan was such an efficient officer—gentlemanly, sympathetic and firm withal—he had begun to do excellent work—no less a work indeed than the proverbial cleansing of the augean stables—and his rule gave promise of a thorough improvement in the administration of the Province:—*J. C. Guardian, Dec. 19, 1914.*

339

K. Chinnatamby

Mr. Chinnatamby was at one time responsible for the reorganisation of the Irrigation Revenue System in the North-Central Province. Transferred from that district to Mullaitivu as head clerk of the Kachcheri there for a short time, he was thence on the recommendation of Mr. Horsburgh transferred to Kaltura, to organise the distillery work. It is there he came under the notice of the Hon'ble the Colonial Secretary, the Colonial Auditor and the Excise Commissioner; all of whom praised Mr. Chinnatamby for the originality and the talents displayed in his work:—*J. C. Guardian, Feb. 27, 1915.*

340

Reclamation, Work Karayoor

The number of prisoners employed on the reclamation work was nearly 400. An area of about 14,800 square yards had been reclaimed during the year 1914, bringing the total reclaimed area to about 54,800 square yards, which is over 11 acres in extent:—*Report of Major A. De Wilson.*

341

T. C. ChangaraPillai

Mr. ChangaraPillai was a man who never shirked his duties and kept up the dignity of his profession. He was 84 years old and practised his profession for 51 years. He was Crown Proctor for a considerable number of years and acted as Police Magistrate many times:—*J. C. Guardian, June 10, 1916.*

342

Ratna Mailvaganam

Mr. Mailvaganam, advocate, has been appointed Maniagar of Valigamam East. This is the second time, in the annals of this island, that a member of the learned profession has been appointed Chief Headman. The post of a Mudaliyar, Maniagar or an R. M., is a unique one in Ceylon, from which one could render real service to his country.:—*The People's Magazine, December 17, 1916.*

343

J. A. Tisseverasinghe

Mr. Joseph Abraham Tisseverasinghe took a keen interest in all Church matters and the new church at Mandativu will ever stand as a living monument to his untiring labours in the Lord's vineyard. He was a gentleman highly esteemed for his honest and upright habits, loved for his charitable and loving disposition and respected for his paternal and friendly advice. He was 74 years old and leaves behind a son, Mr. J. A. J. Tisseverasinghe, Proctor S. C. and a daughter who is married to Mr. G. W. Tamber, a Teacher in the Wesleyan Central College. —*The Morning Star, January 10, 1917.*

Mr. Tisseverasinghe joined the Customs Department in which he served as Sub-Collector at Mullaitivu, Point Pedro and Mannar, till he retired as Chief clerk of the Galle Customs in 1902:—*The Ceylon Independent, January 9, 1917.*

344

The Great War and its Causes

As we look right across the history of man through all recorded time there is no moment that stands as peer to that in which the clock struck on August 4th, 1914, and the twelve days of fate ended. In that hour the old world was broken up and melted down. From the Orkneys across Europe and Asia to New Guinea and Samoa, from the Yangtse across two oceans through America to the Zambesi and the Tigris, every land and people saw their familiar life shattered. For each a new epoch had opened. All future human life—labour, capital, commerce; government, social life, national being; our inter-racial relations—all date a new world from that midnight. Time itself was in

305

travail. The world-fire was kindled by three shots from a Browning pistol. In that sense the right hand of Prinzip (the Serb student of Austrian nationality, who on June 28th, 1914, assassinated the Archduke Francis Ferdinand, heir to the Throne of the Austrian Empire, with his wife, when at Serajevo visiting the newly annexed provinces of Bosnia and Herzegovina) has already slain its million men. But this murder, though it was made the immediate occasion of the War, was not its cause. The causes of the War were political, racial, diplomatic, and intellectual. If any one political event above another led the Central Empires to precipitate war at that time it was that the Balkan War, by reviving a free Serbia, had thrown a mighty dam across the Eastward movement of the Germanic race. Serbia cut the Berlin-to-Bagdad line. She strangled the Hamburg-to-Basra land route to the East. Politically, then, this baulked passion of Germany for dominion in the Near East, as a decisive step in a struggle for world empire, was the cause of the War. If we seek its racial origin we find that in the antagonism of Slav and Teuton. Diplomatically, as Sir Edward Grey said, war became inevitable through "the absence of good-will in Berlin." But in the last resort, as Lord Acton declared, "Ideas are the cause and not the result of public events." In that ultimate sense the cause of war was a philosophy of force and of "will-to-power," issuing in an ethic of savagery. That philosophy became incarnate in a centralised, despotic Government in which the army is supreme, and was propagated through a splendid educational system. It created as its tool a mighty scientific war-machine which, in the hand of the General Staff, is the true master of Germany. Its exponent of supreme power was Nietzsche. The historian who applied its principles to the State was Treitschke. It was reduced to military theory by men like von Bernhardi. Its origin was in Germany. But its missionaries were everywhere:—*Basil Mathews.*

345

The Emden

A number of vessels, with a speed of 25 knots and an armament of 4 inch guns, was built by Germany to raid the commerce of Great Britain, if ever hostilities should arise between the two nations. One of these vessels was the Emden. She is said to have caused as much damage as that of the Alabama. Hunted by the navies of four nations, she eluded their vigilance and succeeded in rounding up some thirty vessels and sending them to Davy Jones' Locker. Her captain, Karl von Muller, proved one

306

of the most resourceful and chivalrous naval commanders of Germany. He threaded the Eastern waters and whenever he captured an enemy, he took in whatever was required, and sank the vessel, while seeing to the safe landing of the crew and passengers at the nearest shore. At one time he paid a flying visit to Madras and dropped a few shells among the oil tanks of the city. At another time he put into the port of Penang, torpedoed a Russian cruiser, sank a French torpedo boat, and steamed away, before she was known or noticed. The Emden is said to have perpetrated altogether a loss said to vary between £ 2,000,000 and £ 4,000,000. She was at last caught by the Sydney, one of the fast cruisers of the Australian Navy, and on being reduced to the last extremity, hoisted the white flag. The captain was accorded the full honours of war upon his surrender. The Emden was destroyed on November 8th near the Cocos Keeling Islands, where the Commander intended to put the British telegraph station out of action:—*M. J. P.*

346

Mudaliyar R. C. Kailasapillai

Mudaliyar Kailasapillai was the son of the late Mr. Sittampalam of the Government Service. He was a distinguished student of the Jaffna Boys' Seminary and later on became a reputed Tamil Scholar. His Government Service began in the Public Works Department. Then he became Interpreter of the Supreme Court. In 1901, he was the Chief Kachcheri Mudaliyar of Jaffna and a year later he was made Chief Mudaliyar, Eastern Province. He was next transferred to the Secretariat as Tamil Interpreter to His Excellency the Governor. He had the privilege of accompanying the Embassy to the Sultan of the Maldives in 1912 with Sir John Keane and Mr. E. B. Denham, when the state sword was presented to the new Sultan, the present ruler of that Dependency:—*J. C. Guardian, Feb. 24, 1917.*

347

Birth-Day Honours, 1917

In this investiture held by His Excellency Sir John Anderson in Queen's House, Colombo, on the 6th instant seven Tamil gentlemen were the recipients of honours.

Mr. C. Namasivayam is well-known for his munificence and philanthropy. He is a very popular and an esteemed member of the Tamil Community.

307

A. Naganatha Mudaliyar is another gentleman unconnected with the Government. His sphere of activity has been mostly connected with the Central Province.

Mr. S. Ramalinga Mudaliyar, Chief Mudaliyar of the Jaffna Kachcheri, is one of the most popular, straight forward and highly esteemed officers of the Government. As Tamil Interpreter Mudaliyar of the Supreme Court, and now as Chief Mudaliyar of the Jaffna Kachcheri, he has enjoyed the confidence and esteem of the Government Agents of the Northern Province.

Mr. G. Rasiah Vallipuram is the Superintendent of Minor Roads, Batticaloa, and is an officer of great efficiency and exceptional worth.

Mr. S. M. P. Vanderkoen rendered meritorious service to Government in various capacities in the Puttalam District.

Mr. J. D. Philips is an officer of the Land Settlement Department and those who know him speak highly of him.

The rank of Vannianar conferred on the Octogenarian, Mr. S. Asaipillai, is a novel one, and is a fitting recognition by Government of his enterprise in connection with the development of the Vannies. He started a mail coach service in 1880 between Jaffna and Matale which continued to run till the opening of the railway. He was in fact the pioneer of every movement in the Vannies:—*The Hindu Organ, June 11, 1917.*

348

St. Martin's Seminary

In the report of the Vicariate Apostolic of Jaffna for the year 1850 reference was made to a "Seminary to form an indegenous clergy." What Dr. Bettachini contemplated in 1850, Dr. Bonjean was enabled to carry out in 1869. On the 12th November 1874, the Seminary was placed under the patronage of St. Martin of Tours. The students and professors of the Seminary had to be housed in a portion of the Mission building till the 11th November 1878, on which date—by a happy coincidence the feast of St. Martin of Tours—the large walled premises known as Mooyaart's garden were purchased for Rs. 21,000. The old building in the "garden" served as the residence of the students till 1884, when it was pulled down. The splendid new building where they are now comfortably located, was completed in 1889, costing about Rs. 40,000:—*J. C Guardian, August, 12. 1893.*

This Seminary has already given to the Catholic Church in Jaffna 25 zealous native priests. It was shorn of its higher classee in 1905, the students being sent to St. Bernard's Seminary, Colombo, to prosecute their studies in divinity. The building is in the pure Gothic style and would be an ornament to any large city. Its architect was the Revd. Fr Meary, now archpriest of the Colombo Cathedral:—"*Amicus,*" *Special Edition, April, 17th 1914.*

349

Isaac Tambyah

Mr. Tambyah is a well-known Jaffna gentleman of exceptional intelligence and superior attainments. He is an Advocate and practised his profession in Jaffna for some years. He is a frequent contributor to newspapers and magazines. He edited the Ceylon Law Review and in 1904 started the Christian Review He also edited the St. John's College magazine for some time. In 1912 Mr. Tambyah went to England and was admitted to the English Bar. He was also elected a Member of the Incorporated Society of authors and he is the first Ceylonese to be admitted to this honour. Mr. Tambyah is now practising his profession in Penang. He married Mankala Nayagam, an educated and accomplished lady, and the authoress of a novel in Tamil, entitled "The Broken Heart." She is the youngest daughter of the late J. W. B. Kumarakulasinghe Mudaliyar, Chief Clerk and Interpreter of the Minor Courts of Jaffna, well-known as a scholar and author. Her brother was the late K. C. B. Kumarakulasinghe Mudaliyar, who was Chief Translator and Interpreter to H. E. the Governor, and of him Sir West Ridgeway wrote in the Review of his administration of Ceylon from 1896 to 1903 as follows:—

"Mudaliyar K. C. Bar Kumarakulasinghe whose death occurred in June of this year, was a Tamil gentleman of high personal character consistently loyal to the Government he served during his 17 years in the Secretariat". Mr. R. R. B. Kumarakulasinghe, the present Maniagar of Valikamam North, is another of her brothers:—*C. N. P.*

350

Sergeant Kandasamy

Sergeant Kandasamy possesses some testimonials from the Superintendent of Police and one or more from the present Inspector-General of Police. They speak highly of his character, his aptitude for work and above all his tact and of the number of rewards received by him:—*Hindu Organ, Sept. 17, 1917.*

351

Jaffna Cathedral Repair

St. Mary's Cathedral begun in 1789 was made ready for use in 1794. Between 1837 and 1852 a Committee sitting for the purpose extended and completed the building with new wooden pillars giving away the old ones to the Church of our Lady of Miracles. Between 1868 and 1882 Chevalier Saverimuttu Mudaliyar built the terraced porticos of the Church and the greater part of the enclosure wall which was completed by Mr. M. M. Edirmanasinghe in 1883. The marble tabernacle and exposition of the high altar were got down from Europe at the cost of a thousand Rupees in 1875. Later improvements include the renewing and adorning of the altar. The high altar to the present day recalls a touch of Father Chunavel's pencil in the two adoring angels on its either side. The altar of the Holy Face on a side wall in the nave containing the Christ of the Crucifixion—a statue much venerated by the older type of Christians—is also a later addition. Under Dr. Joulain a niche and altar to St. Anthony were added on the same wall in 1895 when the new devotion known as the Bread of St. Anthony was started in the Cathedral. In 1899 the roof of the edifice threatening to fall down, a thorough repair was undertaken, trusses of strong Palai wood being introduced and about half of the rafters renewed. Mr. M. M. Edirmanasinghe gave all the trusses while Bastiampillai Mudaliyar supplied the new rafters. The Sanctuary floor also was raised. Dr. Joulain presented his Cathedral (1901-4) with a splendid Chime of Bells, the first of its kind in the North, ordered from Messrs Paccard & Co. France, at the aggregate cost of 9862 rupees, the scaffolding for the basse bell costing 1240 rupees. The four units forming the Chime were named after the Christian names of the four Oblate Prelates of Jaffna, viz., Stephana (Semeria) Christopher (Bonjean) Andrea (Melizan) and Henrica (Joulain). The bigger of the two old bells that had been presented by the Oblates to the Cathedral in 1861 was removed to Madhu, while the smaller one was given away to the newly founded Nallur Mission:—*I. C. Guardian, December 7, 1918.*

352

A. Paramanathan

Mr. Paramanathan is a brother of Messrs A. Canagaratnam, Assistant Shroff of the Hong Kong and Shanghai Bank, Colombo, and of A. Velupillai, Treasury Officer, Kachcheri, Chilaw. Mr. Paramanathan was an old boy of Central College, Jaffna, and latterly of Trinity College, Kandy. He went to England to study engineering in London. He enlisted at the outbreak of War in the Royal Bucks Hussars as a trooper and left England in August 1915 for Egypt, and was stationed at Cairo for eight weeks, till he was sent to their first battalion then fighting at the Dardanelles. He was at the front for about 10 months and saw a good deal of fighting till he was invalided to England from Egypt in May last year:—*Ceylon Observer, July 30, 1917.*

353

A. MootootambyPillai

A well-known Tamil Scholar and a Registered Medical Practitioner, Mr. MootootambyPillai was a prominent figure in Jaffna and his name as "Ward and Davy Mootootamby" is a familiar one throughout the District. As an author he is well-known throughout the Tamil world, having edited and published several valuable books:—*Hindu Organ, Nov. 5, 1915.*

354

Local Board Election, 1917

In this election there being no contest for ward No. 3, Mr. C. Arulampalam, the only candidate, was declared duly elected. The result of the contest for wards 1 and 2 was as follows:—Mr. R. R. Nalliah elected for Ward No. 1 by a majority of 91 votes (399 to 208) over his rival candidate, Mr. Regis Rajakariar and Mr. K. Kanagasabai for Ward No. 2 by a majority of 41 votes over Mr. M. Asaipillai, the opposing candidate:—*J. C. Guardian, Jan. 12, 1918.*

355

S. Cathiravelpillai

This gentleman was Shroff of the now defunct Oriental Bank Colombo. On retiring he returned to Jaffna and spent the evening of his life at Keerimalai. He was largely instrumental in getting the Keerimalai Sivan Temple rebuilt. His Keerimalai madam stands as an enduring monument to his philanthropy. He spent the long life and large fortune with which God blessed him in doing good to his fellow countrymen. Mr. C. Namasivayam J. P. and Mr. C. Gnanasekaram J. P., are his distinguished sons:—*Hindu Organ, Jan. 10, 1918.*

356

P, J. Rajah

Mr. Philipupillai John Rajah is a grandson of Mr. Markupillai Gnanapragasam. the well-known and widely respected Moopu of the Jaffna St. Mary's Cathedral. His appointment as President of the Village Tribunal and Maniagar of Delft, has proved a blessing to the poor and neglected population of that remote and ocean-bound isle. While endearing himself by his large-hearted sympa thy and munficience to the indignent and distressed, he has by his steady and earnest devotion to duty maintained a high character for efficiency and integrity as a public officer. The Ceylon Patriot wrote of him:—Mr. Rajah is an officer combining in himself both ability and integrity among other desirable qualifications and we are sure that his appointment will be fruitful of good results in Delft. His long and faithful service to Government, his unblemished character as well as his family connections fully entitle him to such a responsible office. Mr. Rajah has held various offices of trust and responsibility, at Vavuniya, Mullaitivu, Jaffna and Tondaimannar, in the Judicial and Revenue branches of the service, There is no doubt that like those of his ancestors who were Maniagars and Adigars at Jaffna and Mannar, he will discharge his new duties so as to win the approbation and good-will of the Government and the public.

357

M. Somasundram

Mr. Somasundram, son of the late Mr. Muttiahpillai, Maniagar of the Islands, succeeds his father as Maniagar. The appointment is a popular one:—*J. C. Guardian.*

358

S. M. Rasiah

Mr. Rasiah is a grandson of the well-known Appa Vidhan of Karampan, who was an extensive land-owner and commanded considerable influence. He was educated at St Patrick's College, and was first employed at the Colombo Oil Mills under Messrs Leechman & Co., and afterwards under E. B. Creasy & Co. By devotion to duty, honesty and regular attendance, he gained the approbation and good-will of his employers and bade fare to rise high in the estimation of the Company, but circumstances compelled him to return to Jaffna where he was fortunate to obtain an appointment under Government. He is at present the Salt Storekeeper at Thondaimannar, a very responsible office, the duties of which he discharges in a way highly satisfactory to the Government and the public. Mr. Rasiah is a cousin-german of P. C. Nicholas Mudaliyar, Office Assistant:—*C. N. P.*

359

William Wadsworth

In addition to being a sound lawyer, Mr. Wadsworth, who has been acting in a Judicial Capacity, gained the reputation of being a fast worker, his knowledge of the law enabling him speedily to settle points arising in trials, which is a great factor in expedition. His appointment will for this reason considerably strengthen the District Court Bench:—*The Times of Ceylon.*

The present appointment indicates the desire of the Executive Government to avail itself of the best talent of the sons of the soil in filling high positions. We understand that the Judges of the Supreme Court and the Crown Law Officers had formed a high opinion of the marked ability and sound judgments of the new Judge, Mr William Wadsworth. The present appointment is also unique in the Colombo District Court Bench, this being the first time that a member of the community, to which the new Judge belongs, has been appointed to a permanent place on it, an honour being thereby conferred on that community:— *The Ceylon Observer.*

Mr. William Wadsworth is the son of the late Charles Wadsworth, who was Headmaster of the C. M. S. Training School at Copay.

360

The American Mission of Jaffna

அமெரிக்கமிஷன் சங்கத்தவர் இத்தேசத்தவரின் இகபரநன்மைகளுக்காக ஊழியஞ்செய்யும்பொருட்டு அனுப்பியமிஷனரிமார் ஆண்கள் அறுபது, பெண்கள் எழுபத்தைந்து, மொத்தம் நூற்றுமுப்பத்தைந்து. இவர்களால் யாழ்ப்பாணம் அடைந்த நன்மைகளோ அனந்தம். இச்சங்கத்தவர் இத்தேசத்தவரை நன்னிலைப்படுத்த ஏராளமானபணத்தைத் தாராளமாக இறைத்து, தங்கள் காலங்களையும் இங்குள்ளவர்களுக்குவழங்கித், தேவையான யாவற்றையும் உபகரித்து தமதுமெய்யன்பை விளக்கினர். அக்காலத்தில் இக்குடிகளின் கல்விவிருத்திக்காக அரசினர்செய்தமுயற்சி மிகக்குறைவு. சுதேசிகள் செய்தமுயற்சியோ அதினுங்குறைவு. அமெரிக்கமிஷனரியாரும் மற்றும்பிறமிஷனரிமாருமே அங்கில சுதேசபாஷைகளைக் கற்பித்துக் கல்வியை விருத்தியாக்கப் பிரயாசப்பட்டுவந்தனர். அமெரிக்கமிஷனரிமார் வந்த ஒரு வருடத்தில் இவர்கள் ஸ்தாபித்த பாடசாலைகள் ஐந்து. அப்பாடசாலை

களில் படித்தமாணுக்கர் தொகை இருநூறு. இருபதுவருடங்களுக்கிடையில் 1836 ல் பாடசாலைகளின் தொகை 155. மாணுக்கரின் தொகை ஆறாயிரம். 1915 ம் ஆண்டில் இம்மிஷனுக்குட்பட்ட பாடசாலைகளில் படித்த மாணுக்கர் தொகை பதினாயிரத்துக்குமேலாம். இவர்கள் முதல் தெல்லிப்பழையிலும் பின்னர் தாமதெரிந்துகொண்ட மற்றைய இடங்களிலும் தருமப்பள்ளிக்கூடங்களை ஸ்தாபித்து, மாணுக்கரைச் சேர்த்து அவர்களுக்கு ஊண் உடை கல்வி முதலியவற்றை உபகரித்துமவந்தனர். இவ்வகையாக இவர்கள் வந்த ஏழாம் வருடம் 1823 ல் அவர்கள் ஸ்தாபித்த ஆங்கிலபாடசாலைகளில் கல்விபயின்றோர் தொகை 118. அக்காலத்தில் இத்தேசத்தார் ஆங்கில கல்விகற்பதில் விருப்புக்காட்டவில்லை. மிஷனரிமார்பிரயாசத்தால் அப்பாஷையை ஆரம்பத்தில் கற்றவர்கள் உத்தியோகம் பெற்று பணமுழைப்பதைக் கண்டபின்னரே பலருந்தங்கள் பிள்ளைகளுக்கு அதைக்கற்பிக்க ஆசித்தனர். இம்மிஷனரிமார் இவற்றோடு நில்லாது இங்கிலாந்து அமெரிக்காவிலுள்ள சர்வகலாசாலைகளுக்கு நிகராய், செமினரி எனனும் பெயருடன் ஓர் சர்வசாத்திரசாலையை 1823 ம ஆண்டு வட்டுக்கோட்டையில் ஸ்தாபித்தனர். இச்சாத்திரசாலையோ திசை எங்கும் இசைபரப்பி 1855 ம் ஆண்டுவரையும நிலைத்து 700 பேருக்கு மேற்பட்ட மாணுக்கருக்கு உயர்தரக்கல்விகற்பித்து யாழ்ப்பாணம கல்வி செல்வம மற்றும சிறப்புகளில் மேனிலையடையவுஞ்செய்தது. இவ்வித்தியாசாலைக்காக செலவிடப்பட்டபணம மூன்றுலட்சம் ரூபா. 1855 ம் ஆண்டு வட்டுக்கோட்டைச் செமினரி நிறுத்தப்பட்டதன்மேல் இம்மிஷனரிமார் அங்கே ஓர் போதனவித்தியாசாலையை ஸ்தாபித்தனர். 1872 ம் ஆண்டு ஸ்தாபிக்கப்பட்ட யாழ்ப்பாணக் கல்லூரியானது ஆங்கில பாஷையை விருத்தியாக்கி வருகின்றது. இன்னும் இம்மிஷனரிமார் உடுவில் உடுப்பிட்டி சிலகாலம் வராணி என்னுமிடங்களில் விடுதிப்பெண்பாடசாலைகளை ஆரம்பித்தனர். 1824 ம் ஆண்டு உடுவிலிலும் 1868 ம் ஆண்டு உடுப்பிட்டியிலும் ஏற்படுத்தப்பட்டபாடசாலைகளில் இதுவரையில் ஈராயிரத்து ஐஞ்ஞூற்றுக்கு மேற்பட்ட பெண்பிள்ளைகள் சேர்ந்து படித்து அறிவொளியைப் பெறுவாராயினர். இன்னும் இம் மிஷனைச் சேர்ந்த வைத்திய மிஷனரிமார் வழியாக யாழ்ப்பாணமஅடைந்தநன்மைகளோ அளவிடற்கரியன. இத்தேசத்தில் நூற்றிருபது மாணுக்கருக்கு, ஆங்கில, தமிழ்ப்பாஷைகளில் ஆங்கில வைத்தியத்தை நன்குகற்பித்து, அவர்களைத தேர்ந்தவைத்தியர்களாக்கி, ஆங்கிலவைத்திய அபிமானம பெருகச் செய்தனர். மிதிமைஐயரின் பின் இருபது வருடங்களாக வைத்திய மிஷனரிமார் யாழ்ப்பாணத்துக்குக்கிடையாதுபோகப் பின்னர் வந்த மிஸ. லீற்ஸ் அம்மாமார்களின் அருமுயற்சியால் மானிப்பாயில் ஓர் வைத்தியசாலையும் பெண்பிள்ளைகளுக்கும, பிள்ளைகளுக்குமாக இணுவிலில் ஓர் வைத்திய சாலையும் ஸ்தாபிக்கப்படலாயின. இவ்வைத்தியசாலைகளில் சதே

314

சபெண்கள் பலர் உத்தமசேஷ்மாராகப் பயிற்றப்பட்டிருக்கின்றனர். இம்மிஷனரிமார் வட இலங்கையில் முதன் முதல் அச்சியந்திரத்தை ஆரம்பித்து கல்விவிருத்தி மார்க்கவிருத்திக்கேதுவான பலபுத்தகங்களையும், இலங்கையில், சுதேச ஆங்கிலோபாஷைகளில்நடைபெறும் புதினப்பத்திரிகைகளுள் முதலாவதான உதயதாரகைப்பத்திரிகையையும் அச்சிட்டுப்பரப்பிவருகின்றனர். இவ்வகையாக அமெரிக்கமிஷன் மூலமாக யாழ்ப்பாணம் பெற்றுவருகின்ற நன்மைகளோ அநேகம்:—1916 ம் வருஷம் ஐப்பசி மாசம் 4 ந் திகதி வெளிப்பட்ட உதயதாரகைப்பத்திரிகையில் இருந்து சுருக்கி எடுக்கப்பட்டது.

361

Kathirkama Pulavar

Kathirkama Pulavar was the grandfather of the wealthy and well-known Aseervatha Mudaliyar of the Jaffna Kachcheri, who figured so prominently during the early period of Mr. Dyke's administration. Of his eventful life, Arumuga Navalar contributed an appreciative sketch to the defunct "Lanka Snakan" newspaper, while one phase of it was notioed by Mr. Gunetileke, the accomplished editor of the Orientalist, in a paper on "Folklore" giving an entertaining account of how the poet, in the exercise of his magical art, placed a band of robbers in an almighty fix, while in the act of rifling his house. Nallathamby Pulavar was a great devotee as well as a large land-owner of his time, who made poetry his pastime and whose grave, according to a prediction of his, has become the site of the present Treasury of the Jaffna Kachcheri. To a later generation belong Parimalam and Vairamuttu, the authors of Dramatic compositions of a high order, besides many excellent fugitive pieces:—*B. S.*

362

Mary Annamuttu

Mary Annamuttu, relict of the late Mr. S. Pedropillai, was the only daughter of the late Anthonypillai Tiruchelvam, and grand-daughter of Manueltamby Mudaliyar Tiruchelvam, Udaiyar of Kayts. She was gifted in many ways; she had a clear, keen perception, which made her equally successful in business and a valued friend in trouble. She fulfilled the duties of a Christian wife and mother with calm and edifying dignity:—*J. C. Guardian, 9th March, 1918.*

363

The Twynam Museum

The site of the building is set in a grove of Mahogany trees between St. John's College Hall and the Main Road. The building will, for the present, consist of three rooms, an octagonal entrance hall and two wings. The stone was laid on the 22nd March 1918, by Miss Nora Twynam on the 91st birthday of her father, Sir William Crofton Twynam, K. C. M. G., who retired from the Civil Service of Ceylon in 1896, after having served the Government and the public for a period of 50 years:—*The Ceylon Morning Leader.*

364

Sir John Anderson

Not many people in the North knew our late Governor by sight, yet when it was known that he had passed away from their midst, a sombre gloom entered their several homes. Sir John Anderson was a typical administrator of the Colony, anxious and sympathetic and brought the judgment of a broad and critical mind to bear on public questions. That such a ruler possessing the soul of a gentleman should have been removed from our midst at a very needful time is indeed our misfortune;—*St John's College Magazine:*

No nobler exponent of the ideal of justice which governs the British race, has yet arrived in our country:—*Dr. P. E. Pieris*

365

P. S. J. Chrysostom

Mr. P. S. J. Chrysostom, Proctor, Supreme Court, was the eldest son of the late Mr. S. Pedropillai. In 1901, Mr. Chrysostom passed as a Proctor and practised his profession in Jaffna. He acted on two occasions as Police Magistrate and Commissioner of Requests, Kayts, and proved himself a capable magistrate:—*J. C. Guardian, 27th April, 1918.*

In October 1901, Mr. Chrysostom married Josephine Lizzie Alagamma, a daughter of Esakial Rogers Arasaretnam Mudaliyar, Secretary of the District Court of Mannar.

366

A. N. Santiago, Barrister

Young, talented and possessed of a fair competence, Barrister Santiago was unassuming in his ways. His disposition was gentle and genial, his manners polished and affable. His principles were strict. In his dealings with his neighbours and others, he was fair, sincere and honest. He said "no" with decision, and "yes" with caution. Everybody who came in contact with him, held him in real esteem and affection. So polite, so humble, and so considerate was he in his behaviour. The deceased's father was the late Dr. A. B. Santiago, F. R. C. S. and L. R. C. P:—*J. C. Guardian, 18th May, 1918.*

367

The Kandy Papal Seminary

The 18th May 1918 was the Silver Jubilee of the Papal Seminary at Kandy. The first student arrived on the 18th of May 1893. The first rector was the late Rev. Fr. Grosjean S J. By the 1st of August 1893, the students numbered eleven. Towards the end of the year 1897, the number of students rose to 60 with a staff of six professors. The first priest ordained was Fr. Vincent Fernando of Galle, 1898. Since then, about 183 priests are reckoned among the former pupils of the seminary, of whom six have gone to their eternal reward. In 1889, on the establishment of the hierarchy in India, Pope Leo XIII decided to found a general seminary for the formation of an indigenous clergy for securing the stability and progress of the church in that country and in pursuance of that decision, the Papal Seminary was established in Kandy. It occupies a secluded plot of ground at a distance of two miles from the mountain capital:—*Summarised from The Madras Catholic Watchman.*

368

Jos. N. Sandrasagara, Maniagar

By family prestige, by education, by his character and sterling qualities – not to speak of his spotless career in the public service for the last twenty-five years—Mr. Sandrasagara eminently merits the honour of J. P. conferred on him by Government-*Ceylon Patriot, June, 1918.*

369

George Daniel

After 35 years as a faithful servant of God in the C. M. S., and after a happy period of retirement among his own people, able to relate with tears of joy the story of God's gracious providence towards him, the Revd George Daniel passed away to his Heavenly Home. From his family have gradually sprung up twenty or more families who are a great strength to the Copay Church:—*Life of Revd. John Hensman.*

370

S. T. Carthigasen

A memorial has been erected at Ratnapura in memory of the late Mr. S. T. Carthigasen. It bears the inscription:—"In memory of S. T. Carthigasen, D. E., P. W. D., who in the floods of 1913, near the spot gave up his life in rescuing others." A photograph of the memorial was sent to Mr. Carthigasen's father, Mr. K. Sinnathamby.

371

Fr. S. Marian

The Rev. Fr. S. Marian is the first Tamil in Ceylon to join the celebrated order of St. Ignatius. He is a native of Batticaloa and received his early training at the Kandy Papal Seminary. He is now on the staff of St. Michael's College, Batticaloa:—*J. C. Guardian July, 1918.*

372

B. Francis Mudaliyar:—

As Registrar of Lands, Jaffna, Mudaliyar Francis was the head of an important and responsible office and the marked ability and tact he displayed in the discharge of his onerous duties was often complimented by successive Registrar Generals, foremost among whom is Sir P. Arunachalam, who on receiving intimation of the Mudaliyar's death wired his regret to the bereaved widow, referring at the same time to the deceased's abilities and deploring his death as a great loss to the public service. The present Registrar General Mr. W. L. Kindersley writing to Mrs. Francis on the 9th instant says:—

Registrar General's Office
Colombo, 9th October 1918

Madam,

I have the honour to acknowledge with regret, the receipt of your telegram of the 8th instant intimating the death of your husband and to convey to you my sympathy in your bereavement. Mr. Francis has held several important appointments in this Department and by his death I lose a capable and thoroughly reliable officer who was devoted to his work. He had an exceptionally meritorious record of service. I am, madam, your obedient servant. Sgd. W. L. Kindersley, Registrar General.

Mudlr. Francis received his education at St Patrick's College and he was one of the brightest among the distinguished band of students trained by the late able and learned Principal, Rev. Father Dunne in Shorthand and Book-keeping—two subjects newly introduced into the curriculum of school studies. Mudaliyar Francis was the first to obtain distinction in Short-hand in 1896. He passed the Government Clerical Examination and entered the Public Service as a clerk in the Registrar General's Office, Colombo, where his efficiency and ability were soon recognised. Mudaliyar Francis was in Jaffna for a period of ten years, during which time the tact and expeditiousness he displayed in the discharge of his duties, the courtesy shown to all those who had to approach him on business and the uniform kindness shown to the officers under him, were such that the public began to recognise him as a model Officer. In 1916 Mudaliyar Francis was appointed Senior Relieving officer and Inspector of Registrars of Marriages, Births and Deaths. In July last he was again sent to Jaffna as Registrar of Lands at his own request. Mudaliyar Francis married in 1904 Mary Beatrice, the eldest daughter of the late Mr. John Philips, originally of the Registrar's office, at Kandy:—*J. C Guardian, 12th October, 1918.*

Mr. A. S. Johnpillai, a brother-in-law of Mudaliyar Francis, is a careful and energetic officer of the Postal Department with which he has been connected for the last 25 years. He has served at Hambantota, Jaffna, Kandapola, Batticaloa and other places and has gained the reputation of a painstaking and obliging officer.

373

Soosaipillai Innasitamby

Mr. Soosaipillai Innasitamby popularly known as "Pariaryar," belonged to the family of Culatunga Mudaliyar of Mathagal, whose father was the late Anthukuddi Innasitamby, Pariaryar of Chillalai. The poor and needy found in him a warm friend and sympathiser. The Church of St. Mary's, the Holy Family Convent, and the Mortuary Chapel, where his remains lie in rest are standing memorials of the faith of Mr. Soosaipillai Innasitamby:—*J. C. Guardian, 9th Nov. 1918.*

374

Looting in Jaffna

On the 10th November, 1918 a riot occurred in Jaffna resulting in the looting of several cloth boutiques. The police promptly quelled the riot. Eight rioters were injured, one fatally. Representations were received from the traders, whose property had been stolen by the rioters, praying for compensation. These traders were partly Tamils and partly Moormen. The damage as originally stated amounted to Rs. 35,169; but it was eventually reduced to Rs. 22,132, which is the assessment by the Government Agent. It was decided to recover this amount under Ordinance No. 23 of 1915:—*Precis of Government Correspondence.*

375

The Armistice

After 51 months of horrible blood-shed and unspeakable suffering, the war has come to an end. November 11th 1918 will mark one of the most important epochs in the world's history. This date will go down as the day in which not simply the Great European War, but all wars came to an end:—*The Morning Star, 18th Nov. 1918.*

376

Flood Relief

On Sunday the 17th instant the Peninsula of Jaffna was visited by a storm of wind and rain, I believe, unprecedented in its history. During 24 hours of that day, not less than 25 inches of rain fell in Jaffna. Heavy rain had also fallen on the previous Friday and Saturday, so that the soil was completely saturated, and there was general flooding in many places to a very serious extent. Great damage has been done. A large number of houses has been destroyed and their contents including food stuffs damaged. Thousands of cattle and sheep have died, seriously crippling the agricultural resources of the country. Many cocoanut and other trees have fallen and much damage has been done to plantations and crops. Hardship and distress are prevalent over large areas. An appeal is therefore made to the sympathy of the public for funds to afford immediate relief and to enable the sufferers who are in destitute circumstances to rebuild their houses and to resume their normal daily lives. A strong relief Committee has been working in the Jaffna Manlagar's Division (including Jaffna Town) since Tuesday, and the Chief Headmen are also organising and affording local relief, but outside assistance is also urgently required. I am prepared to receive any remittances.

Jaffna Kachcheri, B. S. Horsburgh,
22nd Nov. 1918. Govt. Agent, N. P.,

A sum of Rs. 100 was advanced to each of the unofficial members of the Local Board from the L. B. Funds for immediate relief work This amount was refunded. Arrangements were made with Government for the free supply of jungle timber from Pooneryn for rebuilding the fallen houses of the distressed. The boatmen of Jaffna, Kayts, Mandativu and Colombuturai agreed to make one trip free to bring the timber to Jaffna. H. E. the Governor was pleased to send Rs. 300 in aid of the Relief Fund and authorized the Government Agent to spend up to Rs. 2000 in providing relief. The Straits Government contributed 5000 dollars to the relief fund. A large number of gentlemen in the island as well as in the F. M. S., both European and Native, generously responded to the appeal of the Govt Agent. The second memorandum on the relief measures issued in March 1919 by Mr. B. Horsburgh, Chairman, Flood Relief Committee, has the following: The subscriptions received up to date in aid of the Flood Relief Fund amounts to Rs. 46,358.23 of which 29,228.87 have been spent. The receipts include the very generous contributions made by the Government of the Straits Settlements and Federated Malay States, each Government contributing 5000 dollars.

377

William Adam Clough

Mr. William Adam Clough retired Surveyor of the F. M. S., was presented by H. E. the Governor at the Garden Party at the Old Park on the 16th instant with the I. S. O., medal granted to him for his efficient and faithful services in the F. M. S. His Excellency conversed with Mr. Clough for some time and then said that it gave him great pleasure to present the medal granted by His Majesty the King. Mr. Clough is an old boy of Jaffna College, and a native of Karadivu:—*Morning Star, January 1919.*

378

Dr. Henry Joulain, O. M. I.,

It is with deep regret that we have to record the death last Friday night at Jaffna of His Lordship the Right Rev. Dr. Henry Joulain, O. M. I., who was Bishop of Jaffna for 25 years. His Lordship's devotion to the cause of religion as the leader and head of the Roman Catholic Church in this District is well known and the generous aid he was always giving to educational and social progress in Jaffna won for him the affection of not only his own flock but of the entire community of Jaffna:—*Ceylon Patriot, 12, Feb. 1919.*

379

William Black

Mr. William Black served in the Public Works Department for forty years and has done good and efficient work. Most of his superiors have testified to the zeal and energy with which he has performed his duties throughout.

380

B. Loppupillai

Mr. Bastiampillai Loppupillai was a well known and wealthy resident of Mathakal and a prominent member of the Catholic Community of the place. In spite of the great influènce he commanded, he led an unostentatious, humble life. He was a merchant, did a thriving business and had a large circle of friends both in India and Ceylon. To the end of his long life, he took great pleasure in helping the needy and distressed. He died in the hundredth year of his age on the 6th October 1913. The following is from an obituary notice that appeared of him :—

இவர் வல்லுவெட்டித்துறையிலே ஜெனனமானவர். அவ்விடத்தே திசையெலாமிசைபரப்பிய திருமேனியார் வெங்கடாசலமெனும் பெரியதம்பியாரின் நெருங்கிய பெந்துவானவர். இற்றைக்கு 64 வருடங்களுக்குமுன்னே மாதகலிலே அவ்வூராரான மகா ஸ்ரீ. ஸ்ரீ. சிறி அந்தோனிப்பிள்ளையின் புத்திரி மதலேனம்மாளை விவாகம்புரிந்து ஐந்து புத்திரிகளையும் மூன்று புத்திரரையும் பெற்றுக் குன்றாத வாழ்வும் குறையாத செல்வமுமுடையவராயிருந்தார். மெஸ் ஞானப்பிரகாசபிள்ளையும் மெஸ் சூசைமுத்துவும் தைரியநாத அச்சியந்திரசாலைத்தலைவர் மெஸ் வ. லோ. அமிர்தநாதபிள்ளையும் இவருடைய புத்திரர்.

381

Industrial and Artistic Work in Jaffna

An effort is being made to rekindle into life the ancient artistic craftsmanship which Jaffna was noted for. The number of craftsmen in the filigree and granulated art has dwindled down to two. Unless some effort is made the art is in danger of dying out. The Government has come to the assistance of the people and will erect a school if the people will provide the site. All that remains is to collect Rs. 3000, which is the price of the land. Mr. N. Sivakolundu, Proctor, President, and Treasurer of the Jaffna Co-operative and Credit Society, is interesting himself in the matter:—*Morning Star, Aug. 16, 1919*.

382

Mrs. Parker

Mrs. Parker, widow of the late Dr. Parker, is a sister of Revds. Champion and Rice. She was educated at the Uduvil Boarding School and spoke English remarkably well. Her memory for facts and dates was extraordinary. The deceased leaves behind her a son, Mr. Parker, retired Interpreter, Supreme Court, and two daughters, Mrs. Worthington of Vaddukoddai and Mrs, Chellappah, wife of Dr. Chellappah:—*Morning Star, March, 15th 1919.*

383

M. M. Thurai Rajasingham

Mr. Thurai Rajasingham is the fourth son of the late Mudaliyar J. T. Muttiah, Chief Interpreter, Supreme Court. He was, only 17 years old and had a brilliant career at St. Benedict's College. In his 13th year he passed the Junior Cambridge Examination, obtaining first class honours and distinction in Mathematics and Science. The following year he passed the Cambridge Junior School Leaving Certificate Examination with first class honours and distinctions in Mathematics, Science, History and Religious knowledge, and won the Hewavitarne Science prize and Doctor Muttucumaru's scholarship, having come out first in Ceylon in the examination. In his 15th year he passed his Cambridge Senior School Leaving Certificate Examination with second class honours and in the following June he passed the London Matriculation Examination:—*M. S. April, 26th, 1919.*

384

S, Thampiahpillai

Mr. Thampiahpillai is the eldest son of Dr. T. Sivapragasampillai of Vannarponnai and is a gentleman of independent means. He is a Director of the Hindu College and of the Jaffna Commercial Corporation:—*Hindu Organ, Dec, 18, 1907.*

385

Rao Bahadur C. Murugasampillai

Mr. Murugasampillai was in the Madras Government Service and held the position of Deputy Collector, Tanjore. Dr. M. Coomarasamy, the well-known medical practitioner of Colombo, is his son. Mrs. Arumugam, the wife of Dr. S. Arumugam, and Mrs. Vytialingam, the wife of Proctor Vytialingam, are his daughters:—*Morning Star, May 17th, 1919.*

386

S. T. Spencer

Mr. Samuel Thurairetnam Spencer was the scion of an old and distinguished family. His ancestors were men of note, who owned extensive lands in Changuvely and commanded influence for several generations. His grand-father, the late Thomas Spencer, was one of the first batch of distinguished students trained at the famous Batticotta Seminary. Young Spencer was born in Jaffna on the 9th of Dec. 1892. His father is Mr. Levi Ponniah Spencer, B. A. of the Central College. His mother, Emily Rasamma, is the only daughter of Mr. Arumugam Newton Sabapathypillai of Arali East, who for over half a century since 1870 was a well-known and familiar figure in Jaffna. Young Spencer had a brilliant career at the Jaffna Wesleyan Central College, studied Law and at 21 set himself up in practice as a Proctor and Notary in the metropolis. He had established so high a character as a steady, earnest and conscientious worker, that it is certain, that had his life been extended to full manhood, he would have risen to greater eminence and added greatly to the honour and prestige of the family:—*H. P. S.*

387

V. N. Sivaya

Mr. V. N. Sivaya was a leading figure among the Hindu Community in Rangoon for many years. A native of Jaffna, he graduated at Calcutta, and as a Barrister-at-Law he set up practice in Rangoon in the early eighties and had been a Municipal Commissioner for many years. He was associated with the Congress party:—*Madras Mail.*

388

Peace Celebrations in Jaffna

The celebrations in connection with the signing of peace with Germany were had with great eclat in Jaffna. At day-break the bells in Churches and temples were rung and services held. Several streets in the town were beflagged. Private residences and public buildings were well decorated. At noon there was distribution of rice at the District Court premises, to more than 1,700 persons. The Government Agent was present. In the afternoon there was a Police and School parade in the Esplanade. Three salvos were fired by the Police in honour of the occasion. At the school parade thousands of children of both English and Vernacular schools were present. It was a fine sight to see the school children and several companies of scouts, march past, with flags and banners of variegated colours, saluting the Union Jack and the Government Agent, the local representative of His Excellency the Governor, who stood on a raised platform. At the close of the parade, War certificates were distributed to the Police. Following the parade, a memorial tree was planted in the green opposite the Ridgeway Hall by the Government Agent. The Hon. Sir A. Kanagasabai gave a short address, the substance of which was given in Tamil by M. S. Ramalinga Mudaliyar. At dusk there were general illuminations in the town. The function closed with a fine display of fireworks in the Esplanade:—*M. S. July 26th, 1919.*

389

Arrival of the new Bishop of Jaffna

His Lordship the Right Revd. Dr. Jules Andrew Brault, O. M. I., the new Bishop of Jaffna, travelled by the night mail train on the 24th instant, attended by Revd. Fr. Charles Boury, O. M. I. The following morning he was met at Elephant Pass by the Revd. Fr. E. Desloges. who took His Lordship in a car to the rest-house hard by. Later, Fathers Matthews and Francis motored down to the rest-house. About 3.45 in the afternoon the Episcopal party left for Jaffna in two cars. Facing the Ridgeway Hall a spacious pandal had been erected in the form of a Greek cross and beautifully adorned. Seats had been provided for the clergy and the ladies and gentlemen of Jaffna Society. The Band got down from sea-street, Negombo, by Messrs J. and S. Machado, struck up a lively air as the car came in sight and the Bishop was received by the Very Revd. Father the Administrator, the Vicar of Missions, and the members of the Reception Committee. He was garlanded by Mr. Joseph Cherubim and conducted to the dais in the pandal where Mr. Philip Moses Secretary, Reception Committee, garlanded His Lordship and Mr. J. H. Vanniasingham, Barrister-at-Law, read an address on behalf of the Catholics of the Diocese of Jaffna:—*J. C. Guardian, Feb. 28th 1920.*

390

S. K. Lawton

Mr. Lawton was a self-made man and rose to eminence through indefatigable energy, pluck and industry. Devoting special attention to photography he acquired great skill and proficiency in it and excelled as a photographer and photo artist. Being a deep thinker, he invented certain photographic processes which were well recommended in British photographic journals. He also invented a recipe for the manufacture of insect proof materials and obtained a British patent for it. He had a command of English and acquired an easy fluency of style, and was a contributor to papers and magazines. He took a great interest in the cause of education and was the manager of a number of schools. He also took part in all movements calculated to benefit the people in general·—*Morning Star, Sept. 20th, 1919.*

391

Gabriel C. Patrick

Mr. Patrick is a well-known townsman of Jaffna, loved and respected for his genial and amiable disposition. He was originally employed in Negombo as a teacher in St. Mary's School, where he secured the good-will and esteem of the educated community of that town by the efficient and thorough manner in which he discharged his duties. In 1898 he came to Jaffna and joined the staff of St. Patrick's College where he is at present headmaster. Mr. S. C. Patrick who is employed in the Government Analyst's Office, Colombo, and Mr. M. Patrick who had a distinguished career at St. Patrick's College and afterwards at St. Joseph's College, are his sons:—*A. E.*

392

M. Thambapillai, Adigar, J. P.

Thambapillai Adigar entered Government Service as Native Writer in the Mallakam Courts and was subsequently tranferred to Jaffna. His next appointment was as Tamil Interpreter of the Police Court, Kandy. He was soon transferred to the Police Court of Jaffna. Sir William Twynam then appointed him Maniagar of Tenmaradchi and in 1884 made him Maniagar of Jaffna, which office he held till his retirement in 1907. He was successively made a Mudaliyar, Mudaliyar of the Governor's Gate, Adigar of the Tamils, and Justice of the Peace for the Island. He was also presented by the Government with long service medal before his retirement:—*Hindu Organ, 13th Oct, 1919.*

393

Don Philip

இவர் யாழ்ப்பாணத்தைச் சேர்ந்த தெல்லிப்பழையிலே வசித்தவர். சமயாசாரத்தாற் கதலிக் கிறிஸ்தவராம். இவர் தொம்பியோகு முதலியின் விருப்பப்படி விசுவாசவிளக்கமாகிய ஞானானந்த புராணமெனும் ஒருகாவியத்தை 1104 விருத்தப்பாவில் அதிக வியப்புப் பெற இயற்றினர். இக்காவியத்தைச் சென்னைபுரியை அடுத்த இராயபுரம் அ. சவிரியப்பமுதலியார் குமாரராகிய ஜெகராவு முதலியார் பலபிரதிகளைக்கொண்டு குரு. சங். தே. மரி. ஞானப்பிரகாசநாத சுவாமிகள் முன்னிலையிற் பரிசோதித்து அவர் உத்தரவுப்படி 1874ம் வருஷம் அச்சிடுவித்தார். இதற்கு இயற்றமிழ் ஆசிரியராம். தி. விசாகப்பெருமாள் ஐயர் முதற் பல புலவர்கள் சாற்றுகவி சொற்றிருக்கிறார்கள். இப்புராணப்பாக்கள் மற்றைய தமிழ்ப்புராணப் பாக்களுக்கு எவ்வகையேனும் தோல்விபோகா:—பா. சு. தீ.

394

B. Bell

Mr. Bell died in Burmah. He was first employed in the Ceylon Government Railway Department and was one of the Engineers who traced the Jaffna Railway route from Kankesanturai to Anuradhapura, About 11 years ago, he married the only daughter of the Rev. G. J. Trimmer, Superintendent of the North Ceylon Wesleyan Mission.

395

Freeman Memorial

The Freeman Memorial Ward attached to the Inuvil Hospital and founded in memory of our late sympathetic Government Agent, Mr. F. R. Freeman, was opened on the 28th ultimo at 5 p. m. Among those present at the function were the Hon. Mr. A. Sapapathy, Mr. M. S. Ramalinga Mudaliyar and Mr. S. Asaipillai, who represented the Freeman Memorial Committee. Mr. Sapapathy after speaking a few words in appreciation of the signal services done by Mr. Freeman, opened the Ward, which is exclusively intended for the poor:—*J. C, Guardian, 6th Dec. 1919.*

396

The Jaffna Historical Society

We learn from the Hindu Organ that a Society under the above name has been formed with a view to encouraging the study of the History of Ceylon in general and of Jaffna in particular:—*J. C. Guardian, 20th Dec. 1919.*

397

Rev. E. Groussault, O. M. I.,

The Rev. Bro. Groussault has rendered good social and public services. His devotion to the social amelioration of the people of this district is well known. Many a cause of public charity not only among members of his own Church, but among our varied community, has found in him a warm supporter and active promoter. He is a keen worker in the Temperance cause and is a great force in Local Option Campaign. His varied activities for the public welfare have endeared him to the Jaffna Community. —*Ceylon Patriot.*

398

Victory Column

Mr. Ernest Abraham, Draughtsman, P. W. D., Colombo, has won the 1st prize awarded in the All-Ceylon competition for the best design of the proposed Victory Column to be erected shortly in Colombo. For this competition several famous artists from all parts of Ceylon competed. The prize offered is Rs. 200 in cash:—*J. C. G.*

399

Local Board Election, 1919

This election came off on the 31st ultimo. For the Eastern Ward Mr. C. Arulampalam, the sitting member, was returned unopposed. For the Western Ward, Mr. M. Asaipillai opposed Mr. K. Kanagasabai, the sitting member. Mr. Kanagasabai after putting in a few votes in his favour, retired. When the votes were finally counted the figures were for Mr. Kanagasabai—12, for Mr. Asaipillai—132, spoiled 8. In regard to the Central Ward, the contest, which created great stir, was between R. R. Nalliah, the sitting member, and Mr. S. Katiresu. At the close of the polling when the votes were counted the figures were for Mr. Nalliah—266, for Mr. Katiresu—107 and spoiled 7. Mr. Asaipillai was elected for the Western Ward and Mr. Nalliah for the Central Ward. The mode of voting was by secret ballot, this being the first time, this system was tried in the Local Board Election in Jaffna:—*Ceylon Patriot. Jan. 14, 1920.*

400

Tambiah S. Cooke

Mr. Thambiah was a prominent and leading member of the Local Bar. His father was the late Mr. J. P. Cooke, head-master of the Vaddukoddai English High School and the Manager and Proprietor of the "Morning Star" and his mother was the daughter of the late N. S. Strong. He was Proctor of the District Court of Jaffna for the last 30 years. He had a very large and lucrative practice at the Bar, and was held in high esteem by the many District Judges before whom he practised. His eldest son is Dr. Gunaratnam Cooke, M. B., B. S. (London). His second son, Mr. T. C. S. Jayaratnam is in the Indian Civil Service:—*The Morning Star, Feb. 21st 1920*

Mr. Chelliah H. Cooke. who was on the Teaching Staff of the Jaffna College and who is at present connected with the "Morning Star" as its Tamil Editor is a brother of Mr. Proctor Thambiah Cooke.

401

Tuition Scholarship

I am glad to announce that one tuition scholarship was founded in the course of the year by Mr. Samuel. F. Johnpulle, Head Clerk of the Loan Board Office, Colombo, in commemoration of the consecration of His Lordship Dr. Jules Brault, as Bishop of Jaffna, and a tuition-half scholarship by Mr. V. Murugasapillai of Vannarponnai in memory of his late wife, Mrs. SelvaKanmany Ammal:—*Report of the Rector of St. Patrick's College for 1920.*

Mr. Samuel F. Johnpulle is the only surviving son of the late Mr. Fredrick Johnpulle. Young Johnpulle after a very successful career in St. Patrick's College received his first appointment under Government in the P. W. D. Colombo, in 1890. He passed the Government Clerical Examination in 1893, and was employed at Kurunegala, Negombo, Colombo and Kandy till January 1904, when he was transferred to the General Treasury. In 1907 he was specially selected to the office of Chief Clerk of the Trincomalee Kachcheri to introduce the new system of accounts which was then being adopted throughout the Island. In 1911 he was transfered to the NuwaraEliya Kachcheri as Chief Clerk and was next promoted to the present post of Chief Clerk, Loan Board. He was promoted to Class I Grade I from 1st February 1920. In all the stations he served, he has established a high character as a throughly upright, straight-forward and efficient officer, enjoying the confidence of the Government and the goodwill of the people. Mr. Johnpulle has always been willing and ready to help those who deserved help and his generosity has been directed towards the relief of needy orphans, some of whom he has fed, clothed, educated and settled in life. His latest act or philanthropy is the founding of a scholarship of Rs. 1000 in connection with St. Patrick's College. This scholarship is intended to commemorate the consecration of Dr. J. A. Brault, O. M. I., as Bishop of Jaffna. By the terms of the endowment provision is made for the support and education of an intelligent Catholic pupil whose parents are too poor to defray the expenses of his higher education. It may be noted that this is the first regular scholarship founded in St. Patrick's College since it came into being seventy years ago:—*D. A. P.*

402

Miss (Dr.) H. R. Williams

This distinguished young lady has taken up duties in the Inuvil Hospital as Assistant to Dr. Curr. She took up the four year's course of the Madras Medical College, and was registered by the College in 1918 as a Medical Practitioner, "legally qualified for the practice of Medicine, Surgery and Midwifery." Her connection with the Government Maternity Hospital, Madras, gave her oppportunities for special training in midwifery and diseases of women and children:—*The Morning Star.*

403

George Stanhope Aseervatham

Mr. Stanhope was a grandson of the late well-known and wealthy Aseervatha Mudaliyar. He was educated at St. Patrick's College and afterwards at the Jaffna Central College where he had a distinguished career, passing the Calcutta Entrance Examination. On the completion of school studies, he proceeded to Colombo and took up law. On the sudden death of his father he had to come to Jaffna. He was for some years teaching at St. Patrick's College and latterly at the Hindu College:—*J. C. Guardian, March 13, 1920.*

404

Rev. G. G. Brown

Giles Gorton Brown was born April, 9, 1869, in Bellwood, Ontario, Canada. His father, Rev. Robert Brown, was of Scotch parentage. In September 1899, he was married to Miss Clara Pendleton, with whom he became acquainted in Oberlin College, and they sailed for Ceylon, October 7th, arriving in Jaffna, December 11th, 1899. His life here is an open book. There have been some who did not fully understand the meaning of that book. But to uncounted hundreds, his life as Station Missionary, Principal of Jaffna College, and Evangelistic Missionary has brought blessing and comfort and strength. With him there was neither high nor low. His heart went out to those who were in need, either physical or spiritual:--*Morning Star, March 20th, 1920*.

405

Very Rev. Fr. Charles Beaud

Fr. Beaud was connected with St. Patrick's College for many years as Principal and Professor. He was on the missions and then in the Seminary as Superior and Professor of Theology. When Fr. Beaud took charge of the College, he started a class of Surveying and Levelling and taught those subjects successfully. He was at the same time Professor of Mathematics and Science. He designed and built the Science Laboratory of St. Patrick's College. This is one of the best laboratories and is built on the most modern lines:—*J, C. Guardian,*

406

Birthday Honours, 1920

Justice of the Peace, Jaffna District.

Mr. Philip Moses, retired Chief Clerk, Minor Courts. Jaffna. Retired last April, after 37 years highly meritorious service. Is much respected by the general public of Jaffna.

Adigar.

Mr. Cadirgamar Murukesar Sinniah, Mudaliyar of the Governor's Gate, retired Shroff, Jaffna Kachcheri. Has rendered long and faithful services to the Government. Is a member of the District Road Committee and a member of other local bodies and institutions in Jaffna. Is the manager of certain educational institutions and author of a Tamil Work on Agriculture. Is greatly respected by the people of Jaffna.

Mudaliyars of the Governor's Gate,

Mr. Paul Chinnadurai Nicholas, Mudaliyar, Extra Office Assistant, Jaffna Kachcheri. Has rendered 32 years valuable and faithful service to the Government. Has recently been appointed to class V of the Civil Service.

Mr. Mangaperumal Sinnatamby Ramalingam, Chief Mudaliyar, Jaffna Kachcheri. Has done excellent work as Chief Mudaliyar Jaffna Kachcheri, 30 years service.

Mudaliyars

Mr. Iru Marapu Tiyya Chellappa Rasanayagam, Secretary, District Court, Jaffna, 30 years service. Has done excellent work as Secretary for the last 7 years. Has an unblemished record. Took a keen interest in agriculture in Dumbara District, where he was instrumental in establishing the first Co-operative credit Society in the Island. He is a Tamil Scholar of great repute and takes a special interest in all literary and social matters.

Mr. Saravanamuttu Vythianathar Wickremasinga, Tamil Interpreter to the Governor and chief Translator, 23 years service. Strongly recommended by the Principal Assistant Colonial Secretary, in view of the position which Mr. Wickremasingha holds and has held with great acceptance for the last five years:—*J. C. Guardian June, 5, 1920.*

While the recipients of Birth Day honours, the list of whose names appears above, have all our congratulations, we must, knowing, as we do so intimately his merits, offer our hearty felicitations to Mr. P. Moses on his well-deserved distinction. "Justice of the Peace," is a fitting title to one who has throughout his long years of service been endeavouring to promote peace and concord among all classes of people. We regretted his recent retirement from Public Service not so much for his own sake as that of the poor and the helpless whom his official position enabled him to befriend. The official remark which is in itself a fine testimony says that Mr. Moses is much respected by the Jaffna Public and that is literally true. It is a compliment to him as well as to the people of Jaffna who know how to appreciate a man's true worth. We wish that God may grant Mr. Moses a long life to enjoy the honour so deservedly won:—*Ibid.*

In 1903, Mr. Moses married Rebecca, the youngest daughter of the late Solomon Gabriel Puvirajasinghe, Proctor.

407

William Mather

Mr. Mather was the managing Director of the Jaffna Commercial Corporation and head of the firm of Messrs, Wm. Mather & Sons Ltd. He was possessed of untiring energy and enormous business talents. He was the life and soul of the Jaffna Commercial Corporation, which is the only Banking Institution in Jaffna and has been of much use to the public:—*The Ceylon Patriot.*

Mr. Edward Mather, who succeeds his father as Managing Director of the Jaffna Commercial Corporation and head of the firm of Messrs. William Mather & Sons Ltd., Solomon Mather, Inspector of the Stores of the Commercial Corporation Branches, Dr. George Mather, M R. C. S., L. R. C. P, who is in extensive practice in Jaffna, Rev. James. S. Mather, Pastor, Alfred Mather, Agent, Ceylon Steam Ship Company, and William A. Mather, Broker, are the sons of the deceased gentleman.

408

B. Joachimpillai

Mr. Bernard Joachimpillai is a well-known and popular Notary of Jaffna, practising in the English and Tamil languages. He had a distinguished career in St. Patrick's College where he received his education and where he was employed as a teacher for some years. Some fifteen years ago he passed as a notary and is practising his profession ever since. He is prompt and expeditious in the discharge of his duties—qualities which have secured for him an extensive practice:—*A. E.*

409

Tamil Training Schools

தற்காலம் யாழ்ப்பாணத்திலுள்ள போதனாசிரியப் பயிற்சிக் கலாசாலை

கன் ஆறு. கோப்பாயிலுள்ளது சேர்ச்மிஷனைச் சேர்ந்தது. இப்பாடசாலை தொடக்கந்தொட்டு நன்குகற்றவர்கள் தலைமையாயிருந்து நடத்தப்பட்டுவருகின்றது. டிஸ்திரிக்நீதவான் மெஸ். உவில்லியம் உவாட்ஸவோர்தின் பிதாவும் இப்பாடசாலையிலே தலைமையுபாத்தியாயராயிருந்தவர். தற்கால உபாத்திமார் மெஸ். இளையதம்பி உபாத்தியார், மெஸ. முருகேசு, மெஸ். வ. குமாரசாமிப்பண்டிதர். இவர் வடமொழி தென் மொழி இரண்டையும் பூரணமாய்க் கற்றநீரர். நல்லூர் பெண்பாடசாலையும் சேர்ச் மிஷனைச்சேர்ந்தது. தலைமை உபாத்தியாயர் மெஸ். குணநாயகம். கொளும்புத்துறைப்பாடசாலை கதலிக்மிஷனைச்சேர்ந்தது. இதிலேபடிப்பிக்கும் உபாத்திமாருள் விற. சவிரிமுத்து, விற. பிலிப்பு இருவர். இவர்களில் முந்தியவர் இலக்கண இலக்கியங்களிலும் கணிதத்திலும் வல்லவராய் சில புத்தகங்களுக்கு ஆக்கியோனுமாயிருக்கின்றார். பிந்தியவர் ஆங்கில தமிழ் இரண்டிலும் தேர்ந்தவராய் இலங்கைச் சரித்திரம், பூமிசாஸ்திரம், அளவைநூல் முதலிய புஸ்தகங்கள் இயற்றி இருக்கின்றார். மேற்கூறியவர்களோடு இப்பாடசாலையில் உடன் உபாத்திமாராயிருப்பவர் மெஸ். அ. தோமஸ், மெஸ். மூ. பிரான்சிஸ்பிள்ளை என்பவர்கள். இவருள் முதல்வர் கதலிக்மிஷன் பொறுப்பில் அடிபடும் பூமிசாஸ்திரங்கள், பாலபாட புஸ்தகங்களுக்கும் ஆக்கியோனும் துணைவருமாயிருக்கிறார். தற்போது, யாழ்ப்பாணம் கன்னியாஸ்திரி மடத்துப்போதனுசத்தி வித்தியாசாலைக்கு தலைமை உபாத்தியாயருமாயிருக்கிறார். இரண்டாமவரானவர் வித்தியாபகுதிக் கோட்டேச்சைய முதலாந்தரந் தொடக்கம் ஆறாந்தரமட்டுமுள்ள கணிதபுத்தகங்களுக்கு ஆக்கியோன். வேம்படிப்பாடசாலை உவெஸ்லியன் மிஷனைச்சார்ந்தது. மெஸ். சாள்ஸ் தலைமை உபாத்தியாயர். உடுவிலுள்ளது பெண்பாடசாலை. இது அமெரிக்கன்மிஷனைச்சார்ந்தது. தலைமை உபாத்தியாயர் மெஸ். லேமன்:—A T.

410

C. Sittampalam

News received that Mr. C. Sittampalam of St. Peter's College, Cambridge, son of Mr. A. Cathiravelu, Crown Proctor, Jaffna, has got through Part II, Mathematical Tripos. Mr. Sittampalam did not attend the examination having sustained an accident and broken his right arm, but in view of his past work, the University has granted him what is called aegrotat Tripos, the degree granted to persons who are sick or indisposed and cannot take up the examination:—*Hindu Organ.*

411

A New Pump

A Jaffna Tamil gentleman has invented a new pump for baling large volumes of water. A demonstration of the working of the new pump was given at the Office of the Provincial Engineer, W. P., Mr. W. C. Price, when Mr. A. E. Caldicott, the Deputy Director of Public Works was also present. It is claimed for the invention that water could be baled out of streams or wells with a minimum expenditure of labour, besides having the added advantage of being able to pump water to very high levels. The demonstration was highly successful. The inventor (Veeragati Arumugam) is now applying for a patent to the Registrar of Patents:—*Ceylon Observer, July 16th 1920.*

The patent has since been granted.

412

C. Namasivayam

Mr. Namasivayam was a much respected member of the commercial life of the Colony in addition to being a prominent figure in financial circles. He was an ex-chairman of the Low Country Products Association, and owned cocoant estates at Kalutara and Kurnegalla, and rubber plantations at Chilaw and Ratnapura. It was in philanthropic work, however, that Mr. Namasivayam was best known to the general public. He had been looking forward keenly to laying in August the foundation stone of the new library he has given in connection with the proposed new University. He has also offered an art gallery to the city. At Keerimalai in Jaffna, he conducted and financed a charitable institution, to which he attached a Reading Room. He was a member of the Royal Asiatic Society. Mr. Namasivayam leaves behind him a widow, a daughter (Mrs. J. Thiyagaraja) and a fourteen year old son and a brother:—*Ceylon Observer, July, 29.*

413

Dr. M. Sinnatamby

Dr. M. Sinnatamby, M. D., F. R. C. S., who only lately retired from the post of Superintendent, Colombo lying-in-home, held a high position in the Medical Profession in Ceylon. He was esteemed as a citizen of sterling qualities. He was philanthropic and had a great pleasure in serving his countrymen in various ways. He was one of those whose names were suggested for the Tamil seat in Council when the last term of the Hon. Mr. K. Balasingham expired last year:—*Ceylon Patriot, Aug. 28, 1920.*

414

Annapuranie (Mrs. S. Hallock)

This lady was the daughter of Veerasingham Chellappah of Navaly and a sister of C. Rajanayagam Mudaliyar, late Secretary of the District Court of Jaffna. She married the late Dr. S. Hallock and leaves behind five sons and four daughters:—*Hindu Organ.*

415

The Tellipallai Training School

When the American Deputation of 1855 decided to abolish the Batticotta Seminary, this institution served to fill the gap, which it did admirably till the Jaffna College was established in 1872. Looking over the long period in which this institution has flourished, first at Vaddukoddai, and then at Tellipallai, we may notice three outstanding points of usefulness in its career. The first is the high grade Christian training given to the pupils which enabled the Christian Community to be supplied with well-equipped pastors and numerous teachers for the vernacular schools throughout Jaffna. The second direction in which this institution has served the public is its work in fostering the Tamil language and literature. The third point of its usefulness is the industrial department started by Rev. T. S. Smith:—*The Morning Star, August, 28th 1920.*

Among those who were connected with the Tellipallai Training School as headmasters, Mr. S. S. Jeremiah was one of the most prominent and distinguished. He was a sound Tamil Scholar, gifted with good poetical talents. He has written some popular school books of which the Tamil Readers for the senior classes, have been pronounced excellent:—*K. V.*

416

M. Arumuga Upathiyayar

This scholar is well-known and respected among Ceylon Tamils. For more than 40 years he has continuously worked for Tamil literature as a teacher, as the publisher of about eight Tamil works, and as public reader and expounder of the Puranas, the Ramayana and Mahabharatha in temples and popular assemblies:—*The Hindu Organ. July, 29. 1920.*

417

Dr. Gunam F. Cooke, M. B., B. S., L. R. C. P., M. R. C. S.,

Dr. Cooke received his early education at the Jaffna Central College and finished his College course at the Royal College. Arriving in England in 1912 he joined St. Bartholomew's Hospital London, and had a distinguished career having held the appointments, Resident Midwifery Surgeon, Senior House Surgeon and Opthalmic House Surgeon. Latterly he held an important post at Shoreditch Infirmary:—*Hindu Organ, May. 27. 1920.*

418

American Medical Mission Work

One hundred years ago, Dr. John Scudder took up his work as Missionary Physician at Pandateruppu, where can still be seen the building erected by Dr. Scudder and used by him as a small hospital and dispensary. In 1833 Dr. Nathan Ward took up medical work at Vaddukoddai. When Dr. Scudder was transferred to Madras in 1837 to found the famous Arcot Mission, Dr. Ward fitted up a small hospital in the Seminary buildings and began the training of Tamil physicians. To Dr. Fisk Green belongs the honour of developing an institution for medical service to the whole country. Dr. Green was the pioneer of an organized department of Medical Work in the Mission. The work so well begun was again taken up by Dr. and Mrs. Scott in 1893 and in 1898 another important addition took place in the establishment of the Medical Work for women at Inuvil in charge of Dr. Curr. The building of the Manipay Hospital, the opening of the Green Dispensary at Karadivu, the remarkable development in buildings and extent of the McLeod Hospital at Inuvil are quite recent. *The M. S. Oct. 16th 1920*

One hundred years of American Medical Mission Work.

1820—Dr. John Scudder, the first Medical Missionary to the East, began his labours at Pandateruppu and Chavakachcheri. A few young men trained to practise Western Medicine.

1833—Dr, Ward opened Medical Work at Vaddukoddai.

1847—Dr. Green assumed charge of the Medical Department. Removed to Manipay and enlarged.

1847-73—Expansion of Medical Work under Dr. Green. 60 native physicians trained. 4,000 pages of standard medical books translated into Tamil.

1886—1376 patients registered at Station Dispensary.

1873-1880—Medical classes continued under native instructors. Dispensary work done under trained native physicians.

1893—Dr. T. B. Scott and Mrs. Mary E. M. Scott reopened the Medical Work at Manipay.

1893-1913—Period of large growth and service of Hospital and Dispensary at Manipay under Dr. and Mrs. Scott. Growth from 35 inpatients in 1894 to 1,166 in 1911. Dispensary patients 3,670. Work largely self supporting.

1893-98—Women's Medical Mission projected and brought to fruition in McLeod Hospital at Inuvil, by the Misses Leitch.

1898—S. F. Green Memorial Hospital opened at Karadivu.

1898—24th September McLeod Hospital formally opened in charge of Dr. J. H, Curr,

1900—Branch Dispensary opened at Chavakachcheri and continued for two years. New surgical Ward opened at Inuvil.

1911—New Maternity Ward, Mcleod Hospital completed. Entire cost, (Rs. 10,000) met by gift of grateful patients and their friends.

1913—Medical work at Manipay placed temporarily in charge of a Tamil physician.

1916—Formal opening of "Centennial Cottage" for private patients, Inuvil.

1918—Somervile Ward opened at Inuvil.

1919—Freeman Memorial Ward dedicated for the use of poor patients at Inuvil Hospital.

Statistics:—	1908	1919
In-patients	882	2041
Dispensary Patients	1905	3848
Maternity Cases	141	488

The Morning Star, Oct. 23rd, 1920.

419

Ponnampalam Ramalingam

Mr. Ramalingam is the son of the late Mr. Ponnampalam of Nallur, who was a member of the Clerical Service. Mr. Ramalingam's elder brother, Mr. Villavarayan, Barrister-at-Law, was a University Scholar from Ceylon. Mr. Suntheralingam, another Jaffna young man, passed the Indian Civil Service Examination last year. Mr. Ramalingam is the fourth young man from Jaffna to pass this very difficult competitive Examination:—*The M. S. Oct. 16th 1920.*

420

Rao Sahib Chelliah Christmaspillai

Mr. Chelliah was educated in the Jaffna College. He taught at the Tellippallai school for a time, and then entered the Madras University where he took his B. A degree. He then joined the Government Service in which he rose. to the position of Tashildar, and on his retirement was made a Rao Sahib. After his retirement, he accepted the position of Dewanship in a Zemindeari in Singampatti, Trinnevely District. He leaves behind his widow, six children, an aged mother, and two brothers, Messrs. S. C. K. Rutnam and J. C. V. Rutnam of Colombo and two sisters:—*The M. S., Oct. 30th, 1920.*

421

Rev. C. D. Velupillai

Rev. C. D. Velupillai was born in 1861 and was 59 years of age at the time of his death. He belonged to a Hindu family, and came under Christian influence in the Tellippalai Training School which he entered in 1873, and from which he graduated in 1877. He was one of the best products of the Training School, and was one of the splendid men whom that institution has given to the Christian Ministry in Jaffna. He had an aptitude for historical studies, and his work on the history of the American Mission is at present in the press, and is expected to be a full account of the work of the American Mission churches for a century. Mr. Veluppillai had a reputation of being a good Tamil scholar, and his regular contributions to the "Morning Star" were highly appreciated:—*The Morning Star, Nov., 13th 1920*

422

Dr. J. M. Handy. M. D.

Dr. Handy was the youngest son of the late Rev. T. P. Handy, Incumbent of the C. M. S. Church at Nallur. After serving for a few years in the Ceylon Medical Department, Dr. Handy proceeded to Singapore and started private practice. He made a great reputation as a medical practitioner and had till his death the leading practice in Singapore. He was the family physician to His Highness the Sultan of Johore. In 1917 Dr. Handy went to England and obtained the M. D. degree at the University of Durham. Dr. Handy was also a great philanthropist. He built and furnished at his expense "The Handy's Library" attached to St. John's College in memory of his late brother, the Rev. Charles Handy, B. A., Headmaster of St. John's College. The "Fall Dormitory" attached to St. John's College was also built by him in memory of Revd. Fall, who was Dr. Handy's tutor. His philanthropy extended far beyond the circle of his early career. The big response from the Straits and F. M. S. in connection with the relief of distress caused by the floods in Jaffna in 1918 was due in a large measure to the example set by Dr. Handy and the prompt measures he took on a telegram from the Editor of this paper:—*Ceylon Patriot, Nov. 10th, 1920.*

423

The Jaffna Inthirai Oil Mills

The installation of the oil engine and mill which has cost over Rs. 60,000 to erect, is due to the enterprise of Mr. C. S. Kandiah Chetty. At the opening of the Mill, Sir William Twynam, K. C. M. G., who may well be considered the G. O. M. of Jaffna, presided:—*The Ceylon Patriot, Dec. 15th 1920.*

424

Joel Fitch

Mr. Fitch was educated at the Batticotta Seminary and belonged to the last class of that institution. He served as personal assistant to Father Smith and Father Hastings for a time, and then was appointed Headmaster of the Udupiddi Girl's School. He was then employed under the Misses Leitch at Manipay and subsequently appointed Evangelist of the Manipay Hospital, from which position he retired some years ago. He leaves behind his two sons, Rev. Edwin Fitch, Missionary in North India and Robert Fitch, Broker in Colombo, and one daughter, Mrs. J. V. Chellappah. Mrs. C. H. Cooke, his eldest daughter, died some years ago:—*The M. S. Jan. 8th 1921.*

425

M. Ayniahpillai

The deceased was a gentleman of high and stern principles, well cultured and possessing great influence among all communities. He was much respected for his upright character. He was 67 years old and leaves behind a widow, one daughter and three sons, one of whom, Mr. A. C. Mohideen, succeeds him as manager of the Abdul Cader & Co. Store in Main Street, Jaffna:— *The M. S. Jan. 24th, 1920.*

426

The Golden Jubilee Celebration of St. Patrick's College

The 26th day of December 1900 will ever be remembered by the people of Jaffna as a day of great rejoicing. On the morning of the day Mass of Thanksgiving was celebrated by the Bishop. Te Deum was chanted and the service was brought to a close with the Benediction of the Blessed Sacrament. The Gymkhana meet came off the next day. This over, His Lordship Dr. Joulain, the Rev. Fathers and the gentlemen present entered the College Hall. Father Dunne, the Principal, said that, as the Secretary of the Jubilee Celebration Committee who had undertaken to write out the History of the College, was still indisposed, he had to introduce to the audience his brother, Mr. John H. Martyn, to read the account, the latter had prepared. Mr. Martyn then read out the History of the College. This over Mr. P. E. Francis, stepped forward and read a beautifully illuminated address. Mr. M. B. Swampillai, the Hon'ry Secretary of the Jubilee Committee, presented to His Lordship a purse of over Rs. 800, contributed to in aid of the Golden Jubilee of St. Patrick's College. The Bishop then left the Hall. Light refreshments were served round in abundance.

The next day came off the cricket match between the past and present pupils of the College. In the evening the annual Prize-giving function took place. A Drama entitled "Malediction" was put on the boards and the grand celebrations came to a very successful and happy close:—*J. C. Guardian, 12th January 1901.*

427

Sir Ambalavanar Kanagasabai

The Hon. Mr. Ambalavanar Kanagasabai was born at Tellippalai in Jaffna district in 1856, and educated first privately and afterwards at the Madras University, where he graduated in arts in 1878 in the Christian College. He then studied Law under the late Mr. C. L. Ferdinands, Deputy Queen's Advocate, and was called to the Bar in August, 1882. He practised at Jaffna, where he became the leader of the Bar. In that capacity he identified himself with various movements for the welfare of the people of the North, and took a prominent part in the agitation for the Northern Railway, making a telling speech in favour of it, when Sir West Ridgeway first visited Jaffna in 1897. Nine years later his appointment as Tamil member of the Legislative Council was generally welcomed and he held that position for ten years. Mr. Kanagasabai did good work in Council and though he was never aggressive, he showed an amount of firmness when he advocated any particular cause, while his tact and good sense won for him the esteem and respect of the officials. Mr. Kanasabai is a member of the Royal Asiatic Society and the Agricultural Society; and has been on the Board of Education, President of the Board of Directors of the Hindu College, and a member of the Committee of the Victoria Home for Incurables. It may be mentioned that he is the third Tamil gentleman to be Knighted, the late Sir M. Coomaraswamy having been the first and Sir Ponnampalam Arunachalum the second:—*The J. C. Guardian.*

428

Hudson Paramaswamy

Mr. Hudson was a distinguished Professor of the Jaffna College. He took great interest in the Jaffna Association, in the North Ceylon Educational Association and in all Christian and Temperance movements. His scholarship in Latin and Tamil was so high that he was selected by the Madras University as a competent scholar to collaborate in the compilation of the Tamil Lexicon to be published under the auspices of that University:—*H. O.*

429

Rev. Joseph Benjamin

Mr. Benjamin belonged to a respectable family of Columbuturai and was born in 1831. His parents were rigid Hindus. His father Kuncher Kanapathipillai was manager of the Pillaiyar Temple at Ilanthaikulam in Columbuturai. Young Benjamin was sent to the Chundicully Seminary where he came under Christian influence. Rev. O'neill then in charge of the Church Mission found him to be a lad of parts and promise. On his graduation along with the late Solomon JohnPulle and other distinguished students he was appointed a teacher in the Chundicully Seminary. In course of time Mr. Benjamin became a Christian and was the means of converting the other members of his family. Mr. Benjamin studied for the ministry and worked as a pastor under the Wesleyan Mission at Point-Pedro, Jaffna, Trincomalee and Batticaloa. He was a good Tamil scholar and has written some religious works. Rev. J. V. Benjamin, the retired Pastor of the Wesleyan Mission and Dr. Richard Benjamin, who is well-known and popular with all classes of the Jaffna community, are his brothers:—*P. H. B.*

430

Lance Corporal R. Aiyadurai

Whilst firing at the enemy, Lance Corporal Aiyadurai was sniped through the head and killed instantly. He was a very gallant man. He set a fine example to all ranks on account of his cleanliness, smartness and cheeriness. I felt his loss very keenly as I had grown very fond of him. He died the death of a brave soldier. He was buried on the battle field:—*Letter received by Mr. C. J. Aiyadurai, father of the deceased, from E. R. Freeman, Lt. Col. 23rd Royal Fusiliers, B. E. F. England.*

431

F. N. S. Hospital

The most important conditions on which the transfer of the Friend-in-need Society's Hospital was made were that the Government should appoint two unofficial visitors; that they should name two wards, one after the late Mr. P. A. Dyke, and the other after Sir William Twynam: that they should complete the half-finished Victoria Lying-in-Ward, and call it the Victoria Jubilee Ward; and that they should respect the caste and religious feelings of the patients in the Hospital. by making provision for food being prepared and served by such cooks as would suit all castes:—*Hindu Organ, Nov. 27th 1907.*

432

Kumaraswamy Pulavar

Chunnakam Kumaraswamy Pulavar is widely known and respected among the Tamils for his deep learning. He is one of the founders and a leading member of the Jaffna Tamil Sangam, and the Jaffna ChenTamil Sangam, is the head-master of the classical section of the Jaffna Saiva PragasaVidyasalai, and has brought out new editions and annotations of several classical works. He is also a good Sanscrit scholar::—*Hindu Organ, June, 28th 1920.*

433

Rev. G. J. Trimmer

Mr. Trimmer was Chairman of the North Ceylon District of the Wesleyan Mission. He was a zealous missionary, an able administrator, and an impressive preacher. The following particulars are gathered from the "Batticaloa Lamp" of the 24th July 1920:—Mr. Trimmer came to Ceylon in 1877. His first appointment was to Batticaloa, as principal of the Boys' Central School. One of his colleagues on the staff was the Rev. R. N. Sethukavalar, M. A., Vice-Principal, whose death occured the day before that of Mr. Trimmer. Two years after, Mr. Trimmer went as Superintendent of Kalmunai Station, where in 1881, he was married to Miss Caroline Bestall. From 1882 to 1884 he was in Point Pedro. He took charge of the Batticaloa station again in 1884. In 1889 he went to England. In 1891 the Revd. Edmund Rigg who was chairman of the District, retired and Mr. Trimmer succeeded him. For a period of 30 years—a record in the Methodist connection—Mr. Trimmer has held that important post.

434

Paul Chinnadurai Nicholas Mudaliyar, C. C. S.

Nicholas Mudaliyar, who counts large experience in Provincial Administration, having been chief clerk in various Kachcheries and Extra Office Assistant at Jaffna Kachcheri, will prove an acquistion to Batticaloa:—*Ceylon Patriot, Aug. 11-1920.*

Mudaliyar Nicholas is an intelligent and capable officer held in great esteem by successive Government Agents of the Northern and Eastern Provinces, where his official career is being mostly spent. Mudaliyar Nicholas is a great agriculturist and during his term of office at Tricomalie he assisted Mr. E. B. Denham, then Secretary of the Ceylon Agricultural Society, in organising shows and promoting agriculture. He contributed a useful brochere on "Agricuture in Tamil Districts," which was generally accepted as a very useful compilation:—*C. M. Leader June, 4-1920.*

Mudaliyar Nicholas' eldest son Joseph S. Nicholas, is employed in the Excise Department as Superintendent, and his second son, Dominic V. Nicholas, F. C. L. (B'gham), M. B. T. (Lnd.) A. C. R. A. (Glasgow) who was employed under the Ceylon Government, is now in the Straits, having married a daughter of Mr. M. Cathiravalu, a distinguished Jaffna man widely known as the Penang Milionaire. Mr. C. Canagaretnam, Lecturer, Tropical School of Agriculture, and Mr. W. Sinnatamby, Superintendent of works of the Jaffna Local Board, are his sons-in-law. The Mudaliyar's present wife, Kanmanipillai, is a grand daughter of the late Ethirveerasingha Nitsingha Talaivasingha Mudaliyar, Maniagar of Welikamam West, who did yeoman Service to the Government, in that, as stated by the Ceylon Patriot of 30th January 1891, "he had, at a time when the idea of a journey to Kandy was appaling to the Tamils of the North, the pluck and promptitude to lead a corps of 600 men in order to help Colonel Hardy in the subjugation of the Kandian kingdom, by opening roads, carrying baggages, clearing the jungle for military operations, and by conveying copper coins from outstation treasuries to the mountain capital—services which he performed fearelssly though at great personal risk."

435

Sabaratna Mudaliyar

S. Sabaratna Mudaliyar is one of the most prominent and leading members of the Hindu community of Jaffna. He is a sound English and Tamil scholar and is a frequent contributor to newspapers and magazines and his contributions are always appreciated. He is also well-versed in Siddanta Philosophy. He is a government officer and has served over thirty years in various capacities, and in various districts, as clerk, Interpreter Mudaliyar, Kachcheri Mudaliyar and Fiscal and has rendered effiicient and meritorious service:—*M. C.*

436

J. V. Chelliah

Mr. John Vetivelu Chelliah is the Professor of English Literture and Latin at the Jaffna College. He is an M. A. of the Calcutta University. He is also the present English Editor of the "Morning Star." His brother, J. V. Chinniah, is a Proctor practising in the Jaffna Courts:—*P. J,*

437

The Jaffna Apothecaries' Company

This is one of the leading and popular houses in Jaffna for European Medicines of all kinds. Commenced early in 1890 as a small dispensary at "JayaVasa" in grand Bazaar, it has, by the subsequent addition of Oilmanstores, Wines, Spirits and Malt Liquors, Drapery and other Departments, secured the support and patronage of the general public, and developed into one of the most flourishing establishments. Its success is due to the untiring energy and strong common sense of the proprietor, Dr. S. Ponnusamy, who, it must be said to his credit, takes a keen interest in all social and philanthropic movements:—*C. P. M.*

438

James Lawson

Mr. Lawson James is well-known in Jaffna as a Photographer. He has been practising the art for the last twenty years and more. He is prompt and expeditious in his work and the public patronise him. Some of the Photos executed by him are pronounced by competent judges as excellent:—*C. P. M.*

439

Parikariar Palany

Mr. Palany was a noted native physician of Nallur. He had a good knowledge of Indian Pharmacopoeia and commanded an extensive and lucrative practice. He was very successful in the treatment of cases of snake-bite. He was a contemporary of Avurampillai, Thambapillai, Kanagasabai and other native physicians of Jaffna. His son, Sinnadurai, is also a good native physician and is now in active practice at Nallur.

Of the present day native physicians of Jaffna the most noteworthy are Mutttukumaru of Vannarponne and Kandiah of Kanthermadam. They are both very skilful men and command a large practice:—*C. P. M.*

440

Archbishop Bonjean

That Archbishop Bonjean was in no manner a Ceylonese is well-known, yet he was long identified with us as to be one of us. He was born the same year as James de Alwis and died the same year as Sir Samuel Grenier. He was meant to be a lawyer by his father, the councillor of the High Court of Riom, who desired that his son, Christopher Bonjean, should adopt the profession of which he himself was a distinguished member. But he who was purposed into higher ends was called from the probability of becoming his own people's law-giver, to be not only the Moses, but the Aaron of a chosen nation, far away from his country and kindred. The wisdom that blessed him with the best and beautifullest of the blessings of time—to minister to others and not to be ministered unto—dimmed his eyes to the kingdoms of the world and the glory of them, and showed him in the last days only from the Pisgah of his Archiepiscopal labours a view of Canaan of Earth's passing greatness, as the earnest of the more abiding glories of a better Land. Thus from the Nazareth of the Northern Province out of which, I am told, no good or greatness comes, Bonjean came. The Boake controversy is well-known about certain Latin words. If the reported result of the controversy is to be relied upon, Father Bonjean had certainly emerged victorious. In 1868 he wrote on the Inopportunists' Theory of Papal infallibility, an invaluable contribution commended by 42 Archbishops and Bishops as the most conclusive testimony in favour. Should through any unforeseen circumstance the memory of Archbishop Bonjean die out in Ceylon, it will still live for ever in the Annals of the Eccumenical Council of the Vatican. In the year 1878-79 during the epidemic of cholera, Father Bonjean rendered great service going about doing good. His name is remembered with esteem and reverence by all classes of people. He was a great educationist. He contended for the Board of Education in 1864 and we today have the Board an accomplished fact. Ceylon may come to forget the name of

345

Christopher Bonjean, the echoes of his voice may grow fainter, the fiery glow of his language may burn itself out in the course of ages, and the halo of thunder and earthquake that circles his individuality may fade away from the recollection of posterity, but neither time, nor the infinite beyond, can blot out the work and life of one who content "to be poured out as a libation" strove to live up to his own motto "Impendar et Superimpendar": — *Isaac Thambyah.*

441

Jaffna and its Administrators

The Northern Province was one of the earliest to be formed and the largest in extent till the year 1873 when Sir William Gregory dismembered it by erecting the Nuwarakalawiya District into a separate province called the North Central. From the thirties to the sixties of the last century, a period of about 38 years, the late Mr. P. A. Dyke was the Government Agent of the Northern Province and on his death Mr. (now Sir) William Crofton Twynam, K. C. M. G., who was then in charge of the North Western Province and who had long been associated with Mr. Dyke as his trusty henchman, first as office assistant and then assistant Government Agent at Mannar, secured the appointment after a short interval during which the affairs in the North were administered by the late Mr. H. S. O. Russel. Mr. Twynam who was born on the 22nd March 1827 entered the Ceylon Civil Service on the 23rd May 1845 at the age of 18, assumed charge of the Northern Agency about half a century later and inaugurated his administration on the lines of his illustrious predecessor. Thus another long reign was ushered in and for fully 27 years Sir William was 'The Raja of the North,' serving under a dozen Governors and administrators. It would be difficult to enumerate the many and various directions in which his beneficient activities have been exercised during his administration. They are many and well-known to the people. It is sufficient to say that to his ability as an administrator he joined a rare sympathy with the needs and aspirations of the people. His sympathy was felt not only by the educated classes but by the poorest and most ignorant section of the people. He knew the whole of Jaffna in a way in which very few Jaffnese themselves know it.

Sir William strenuously opposed the introduction of both a Railway and a Local Board into Jaffna during the 27 years of his administration. But things have changed, The first erection of the Northern Railway so long the subject of agitation and pooh-poohed by the first Railway Commission as 'A Railway to the Moon' and by Sir Arthur Gordon (afterwards Lord Stanmore) as a tantalizing vision, was declared open by Sir West Ridgeway in Jaffna on 11th March 1902 and the Local Board was established in 1906 with Mr. F. H. Price as its first chairman. It may not be known to many that Sir William Twynam took an absorbing interest in the, management of the Jaffna Friend-in-need Society which was established by the late Mr. Dyke in 1841 and he handed over to it the sum of Rs. 10,000.00 which had been collected by his friends and admirers and presented to him on the occasion of the celebration of his official jubilee, on the distinct understanding that the society should utilize these funds for the completion of the building known as the Victoria Lying-in-ward. The society had spent up to the time of Sir William Twynam's retirement and handing over the Hospital to Government in 1907, about Rs.. 20,000 on the buildings connected with the ward. But they remained incomplete owing to want of funds. It will be seen that the Hospital was in charge of the society for nearly 66 years.

Sir William Twynam's indefinite continuance in the Northern Agency was a matter of frequent complaint both on the part of the people and of the civilians who looked to the post as one of the plums of the Ceylon Civil Service, and strong representations were made to the Governor as well as to the Secretary of State for the Colonies regarding the manifest inexpediency of allowing him to retain his post beyond the age limit, in contravention of recognised rules, when the agent of every other Province was frequently changed or transferred, At length Mr. Twynam was knighted and asked to retire on first January 1896 with a service of 50 years, exceeding even that of his former venerated chief. Between them they administered the province for 66 years. The Patriarchal Government of Jaffna came to a close with the retirement of Sir William Twynam and the late Mr. R. W. Ievers, C. M. G. promoted over the heads of a dozen seniors, was specially sent to Jaffna by Sir West Ridgeway to inaugurate a new and vigorous policy as a desirable departure from what was regarded in certain quarters as the hum-drum administration to which the people in the North had long been accustomed. Mr. Ievers was certainly not a civilian of the old school. As a genial and cultured Irishman he did inaugurate a new policy in the North.

Mr. Ievers was succeeded by a dozen Government Agents, namely, Messrs F. C. Fisher, E. T. Noryes, G. S. Saxton, H. H.

Cameron, J. P. Lewis, F. H. Price, H. R. Freeman, C. P. Vaughan C. R. Cumberland, R. A. G. Festing and Mr. Benjamin Horsburgh, M. A. (Edinburgh). Mr. Horsburgh who joined the Ceylon Civil Service on the 19th October 1889 has been working in different capacities in the North, first as Cadet, Office Assistant and Police Magistrate, Jaffna, Assistant Government Agent and District, Judge, Mullaitivu and Mannar respectively. The unrivalled knowledge Mr. Horsburgh has acquired of the Northern Province in his capacity as a Revenue and Judicial Officer and his appointment as an Assistant Superintendent in connection with two of the most successful Fisheries on record, preminently entitle him to be its permanent Government Agent.

Sir William Twynam's interest in the welfare of the North even after his retirement is as great as that of any native of the country. He is the President of the Jaffna Y. M. C. A. and continues to be the President of the Jaffna Public Library established in 1848, in the fourth year of his administration. He is also the President of the Ceylon Agricultural Society started by Sir Henry Blake, and a member of the Plant-Pest Board for the Revenue District of Jaffna.

Sir William Twynam headed the deputation that waited on Sir Henry Mac-Callum at Queen's Cottage, NuwaraEliya, in 1913, travelling all the way from Jaffna, when the prospects of the tobacco trade in Jaffna with the native States of Travancore were imperilled by the increase in Customs duty levied, and the restrictions placed on tobacco imported into the States, he was able to obtain the Governor's help to set back a course of action that threatened the ruin of the entire tobacco industry in the North.

Sir William Twynam who was drawing a salary of Rs. 18,000 per annum at the time of his retirement was granted a pension of Rs. 12,333.33cts. per annum with effect from 16th January 1896 for his long, faithful and meritorious service, and is residing at "Alfred Villa", a fine commodious bungalow on the Beach Road, and the people trust that the G. O. M. of Jaffna will be spared for the enjoyment of his "otium cum dignitate" for many years to come:—*Jaffna Catholic Guardian, Dec. 31st 1915.*

442

HENRY MARTYN (என்றி மாட்டீன்)

எர்பெறுமிலங்கைப்—பேர்பெறுதீவின்
வடதிசைக்கண்ணே—தடம்பெறவமைந்து
சிருஞ்சிறப்பு—மாரவேகொண்ட
யாழெனுங்குடாநா—டாளுமன்னவர்
இருப்பிடமாகும்—பொருப்பினைநிகர்த்த
தலைநகர்தன்னை—நிலைமையாய்க்கொண்ட
சுண்டிக்குழிப்பெயர்—கொண்டகுறிச்சியில்
ஆயிரத்தெண்ணூறு—மேயபன்னொன்றில்
வந்தவதரித்தொரு—சுந்தரனென்ன
இருந்திடொளில்—பெருந்தயைபொழியும்
பெரியமாதா—அரியவாலயத்தில்
எழுந்திராநின்ற—செழுந்தகைபூண்ட
விக்கார்ஜெனறல்—தக்கோனென
சொயிசி—டி—சிக்குரு—செயிரறுகோவைக்
குரவனின்கரத்தாற்—பரமனருளிய
ஞானஸ்நான—மானதுபெற்று
கிறிஸ்தோப்பரெனுஞ்—சிறப்புறுநாமம்
பேறுறத்தாங்கிப்—பிறங்கியிருக்கையில்
எழாம்வயசில்—வாழுமூரிலே
அமிழ்தெனவளங்குந்—தமிழதுகற்க
அனுப்பவதனை—மனங்கொளக்கற்று
வந்திடொளி—லந்தமில்கீர்த்தி
சுமந்துவிளங்கிய—அமரிக்கமிஷனரி
மார்பலர்வந்து—காரிருள்மொய்த்துப்
பாழுறக்கிடந்த—யாழ்ப்பதிவாழ்வுற
அங்கங்குபற்பல—துங்கமாவித்தியா
சாலைகளமைத்துச்—சீலமாயவற்றில்
அங்கிலபாஷை—மங்கிடாதொளிர
வூட்டினரவற்றுட்—சேட்டமானது
துல்லிபம்படைத்த—தெல்லிமாநகரில்
பூரெனுமையர்—பேருறத்தந்த
வித்தியாபீடமே—யுத்தமமென்று
கேட்டவரெவரும்—கூட்டமாயோடி
வந்துதம்மக்களை—யந்தமகானிடம்
எற்குமாறு—தோற்றிவேண்டினர்.
இத்தகச்செய்தி—மைந்தன்கிறிஸ்தோப்பர்
தந்தையின்காதில்—வந்துதொனித்திட
காற்றுள்ளபோதே—தூற்றிடவேண்டுமென்

துன்னினராகத்—தென்னுமணிநிகர்
தன்மகன்றன்னை—அன்னாநற்சாலையில்
நற்பருவத்தே—கற்பிக்கவெண்ணி
தெல்லியம்பதிக்கு—நல்லநாளொன்றில்
கொண்டுசென்று—கண்டுபூரையரைச்
சேர்க்குமாறு—நேர்ந்துகேட்க
ஐயரென்செய்வோம்—பையனையேற்க
இடமினியில்லை—நடவுமினென்றிட
வாட்டமுற்றே—வீட்டினுக்கேக
வாமகனென்றே—தாவியழைக்க
கூர்மதிபடைத்த—வேருறுபாலன்
ஐயபொறுக்க—பையப்போகுவம்
என்றுமறுத்து—நின்றுகொண்டனன்.
ஐந்துமணியில்—வந்துகூடிய
கற்போரெல்லாம்—விற்பனமாக
ஆடலயர்வதை—நாடியேபார்க்க
ஐயர்வருவதைப்—பையனார்கண்டு
ஓடிமுன்மறித்து—வாடியமுகத்துடன்
ஐய! கேளொன்று—பையனுன்சொல்ல.
நானுமேயுமும்—பேருனபட்டியில்
இடம்பிமடியுமோ—ராடுமேய்ந்திட
இடம்பெறுதென்று—தடங்கல்செய்வீரோ
என்றுதுணிவொடு—நின்றுமொழிந்திட
பையனுத்திரத்தை—ஐயருணர்ந்து
கண்ணியபையன்—துன்னியமதியை
வியந்துதம்முன்னே—நயந்துமகிழ்ந்து
இப்பயல்பின்னால்—ஒப்பறுவிளக்காய்
விளங்குவானென்றே—களங்கறமதித்து
தன்னளிசார்ந்து—கன்னியவாயிரத்
தெண்ணூற்றிருபத்—திரண்டினிற்றமது
பாடசாலையிற்—பட்சமாயேற்றனர்.
பாங்குடனிருந்து—ஆங்குறுகலையெலாம்
பருகுவனன்ன—வார்வத்தனாக
கேட்பவைகேட்டுளத்—திட்பமாயமைத்துத்
தலைமாணாக்கனாய்—நிலவியகாலை
நன்மனவிருப்புற்—றுன்னியபரோப
காரசிந்தையு—மாரவிளங்கிய
எண்ணரும்பணத்தொகை—பண்ணியஅமரிக்க
தனவந்தர்கூடிக்—கனபணமுதவி
எம்பதிசிறக்கத்—தம்பொறுப்பாலே
நல்லிடத்திலோர்—பல்லதிநூட்டுஞ்
சாத்திரசாலை—காத்திரமாகத்

தாபிக்கவென்று—தயாளமாய்க்கேட்க
மாண்டகுகுணத்தோ—டண்டெபாதிரி
மார்பலர்கூடித்—தேர்ந்துதம்முன்னே
வட்டுநகரையே—இட்டமாய்த்தெரிந்து
கட்டடமொன்றைச்—சட்டமாயமைத்துத்
தெல்லியுடுவில் — நல்லமானிப்பதி
பண்டையவட்டு—பண்டத்தெருப்பு
என்னுமைந்திடங்களில்—துன்னியிருந்த
அங்லோசுதேச—விங்கிதவிடுதிப்
பாடசாலையிற்—கூடியிருந்த
மாணவர்தம்முட்—டூணெனவிளங்கிய
வித்தியார்த்திகளைப் புத்தியாய்த்தெரிகையில்
சாத்திரசாலையி—னேத்திரமாமென
முன்னமேமதித்த—மன்னுபூரையர்
கிறிஸ்தோப்பரையுங்—குறிப்பாயெடுத்து
என்ரிறிமாட்டி—னெனும்பெயர்தந்து
அன்னசாலையில்—மின்னவைத்தனர்.
சாத்திரசாலையின்—காத்திரந்தன்னை
ஜெமிஸ்எமெர்சன்—ரெனன்ற்துரையானவர்
சாலப்பெருத்த—மேலத்தேசத்துள
சர்வகலாசாலைக்குச்—சரியெனவிதந்தன
றென்றாலதன்மே—வியம்புவதென்ன.
அன்னசற்சாலை—யுன்னதமுறையாய்க்
கடன்மடைதிறந்து—இடமெலாந்தேங்க
விட்டதுபோலவும்—விலைமதியாத
பொன்மலைமுரிந்து—கன்மனங்கொள்ளப்
பொழிவதுபோலவும்—புகலரும்விதத்தொடு
பலசாகையாக—நிலவியிருந்த
சாத்திரமெல்லாஞ்—சூத்திரமாக
விற்பனபண்டிதர்—கற்பனைசெய்ய
மாட்டினென்னுந்—தாட்டிகமுடையான்
கடித்ததெல்லாங்—கரும்புபோலவும்
பிடித்ததெல்லா—மிரும்புபோலவும்
ஞாபகசத்துத்—தாபகமுடையனாய்
ஒருகாற்கற்றது—இருகாற்கற்றிடா
இயல்பினனாகலின்—எவற்றையும்விடாது
அங்கிலங்கணிதந்—துங்கசோதிடங்கள்
அங்காதிபாதம்—மங்காதபூவகம்
தத்துவமுதலா—மெத்தகைக்கலையும்
ஐயந்திரிபறக்—கைவரக்கண்டவன்.
வித்தைத்தமிழொடு—ஐந்திலக்கணங்களும்
சந்தமிகுந்த—சமஸ்கிருதமுதலாம்

வடமொழிதென்மொழி—திடமுறக்கற்றனன்.
கைத்தொழில்சித்திர மெத்தவுங்கற்றவன்
சிற்பங்கம்மியம்—நற்றச்சுவேலை
தையல்வேலை—துய்யநற்சாயம்
ஊட்டுவேலையும்—நாட்டமாய்க்கற்றவன்
கட்டுவேலை—திட்டமாய்ப்பயின்றவன்
விளையாட்டிலுங்—களையாத்தீரன்
தேகசவுரியம்—வாகாயுடையவன்
செப்படிவித்தையு—மொப்பவேசெய்வான்
சர்வபண்டித—சாகரமாமிவர்
கண்ணியந்தன்னை—மண்ணினிலுள்ள
மாந்தர்களெல்லா—மாந்தருமுறையாய்
நயப்புறச்செய்த—வியப்புறுகலைஞன்.
இத்தகையாளன்—சித்திரமாக
எழுதியபடங்கள்—பழுதிலச்சாலையில்
தூக்கியும்வைத்ததைத்—துதிப்பர்பலரும்.
அவ்வாறுகையி—லழகுறுமிலங்கையை
ஆண்டுவந்த—மாண்டகுகுணத்தான்
ஹெருப்பெட்கோட்டன்—மறப்பருமன்னரிச்
சாஸ்திரசாலையிற்—சமுகமாயிருக்க
எண்ணூற்றுமுப்பத்—திரண்டினிலங்கொரு
பகிரங்கசோதனை—நயம்பெறவைத்தனர்.
அச்சோதனையில்—அதுல்லியமாக
மாட்டின்வள்ளல்—கோட்டியில்முதல்வனாய்
அரங்கேறிநின்று—ரவரையுடனே
அந்தஆண்டிலே—அந்தக்கல்லூரியில்
மைந்தனேதந்தையாய்—வந்ததுபோல
ஆசிரியராக—நேசபாதிரிமார்
அமர்த்தினரிவர்பெருஞ்—சமர்த்துகள்காட்டி
நல்லிசையோடு—பல்வகைச்சாஸ்திர
அறிவைப்புகட்டச்—செறிபலமாணவர்
வந்துகூடி—யந்தமில்மகிழ்வொடு
கேட்டவையெல்லாங்—கோட்டமில்லாது
வணங்குமியல்புள—வணங்கொள்தேவுலகப்
பைந்தருவென்ன—நந்தவில்லாமல்
அள்ளியிறைக்க—வுள்ளமகிழ்ந்து
கற்றனர்வல்ல—விற்பனமாணவர்.
அவரவர்நாம—மாங்காங்குபுலப்படும்.
ஆதனிலதனை—ஈங்குநிறுத்தி
அப்பாணடக்த—வொப்பருஞ்செயல்களைச்
செப்புவமெடுத்துத்—தப்பிதமின்றி.

பதிசாஸ்திரமும்—பலதர்க்கநூலும்
விதியொடுகற்று—மதமதுமாறி
அமரிக்கசபையி—லார்வமாய்ச்சேர்ந்து
உத்தமபோதக—உத்தியோகத்தினில்
வைத்திடமிக்க—வாய்ச்சாலகமாய்
வேதம்போதித்து—விளங்கியுமிருக்கையில்
உதயதாரகை—யுதயமாம்பொழுததன்
அதிபராகவும்—இதம்பெறவிருந்தனர்.
நாற்பத்துமூன்றில்—நல்லயாழ்நகரில்
குத்தகைக்காரனும்—குவலயப்பரப்பும்
மெத்தவுமுடைய—உத்தமனான
சந்தியாப்பிள்ளை—தந்தநன்மதலை
மரியைப்பிள்ளையை—உரியநற்பாரியாய்
முடித்துவாழ்ந்து—நடக்குங்காலையில்
கல்லூரித்தொடர்பை—மெல்லநழுவி
அரசினர்பகுதியி—லமர்ந்திடவெண்ணி
உப்புக்கந்தோரி—னுயரியபதவி
காலியாயிருத்தல்—கண்டுகருத்துடன்
விண்ணப்பஞ்செய்ய—வண்ணல்டைக்துரை
சித்தமிசைந்து—அத்தகைப்பதவியை
அருளவேற்றுப்—பழுதறநடத்தையில்
சாராயக்காரிய—வாராய்வுமதனோ
டடர்வனமரங்களின்—கடமையுமாபத்துக்
குதவிவைத்திய—பதவியின்பொறுப்பும்
இட்டமாயிவரிடம்—விட்டனரவற்றைத்
தக்கமாதிரியாய்—மிக்கசாக்கிரதையாய்
நடத்தினதன்றி—நலிவுறுபிணியரைத்
தண்ணளியொடு—தாபரித்திருந்தனர்.
சுப்பிரீங்கோட்டுத்—துவிபாஷிகராயும்
வைத்திடப்பெற்றுச்—சித்திரவிதமாய்ப்
பாஷாந்தரப்—படுத்தியதிறமையை
நீதியரசர்கள்—போதவேமெச்சினர்.
இத்தனைப்பொறுப்பெலாம்—வித்தகன்சரிவர
முடித்தநேரமே—படிப்பையும்விடாது
இடைநேரங்களி—லின்பமாய்ப்படிப்பார்.
கம்மியங்கைத்தொழில்—பம்மியயாவினும்
தமதுநேரத்தைச்—சரிவரச்செலுத்தி
நாழிகைவட்டம்—நவமாயியற்றவும்
திருத்தவும்புதுக்கவும்—தெளிந்துங்கொண்டனர்.
நற்குணன்மாணவர்க்—குற்றநற்றுணையாய்
இருக்கவெப்போதும்—கருத்தாயிருப்பவர்.

பிரங்கமான—பள்ளியினிகழும்
பரீட்சைத்தினங்களிற்—பங்கும்பற்றுவார்.
வில்லங்கங்களினு—லல்வற்படுவோர்
ஆங்காங்கிருந்து—ஈங்குவந்தெய்தி
ஆலோசனைகேட்—டாறுதலடைவார்.
இளமைதொட்டே—இனியகானரசக்
கடலின்மூழ்குங்—கரிசனையுடையராய்
பாடுவராடுவர்—பரதசாஸ்திரங்களை
நாடுவர்கற்பர்—நவீனகவிகளை
ஆக்கவும்வல்ல—அருமைப்புலவன்.
அன்னைமரியா—யன்றுசிலுவையில்
அறையுண்டிறந்த—அருமைமகனின்
பாடுநினைந்து—படுபிரலாபத்தை
ஒப்புயர்வில்லா—ஒப்பாரியாகப்
பாடியெவரும்—படிக்கவுஞ்செய்தனர்.
அப்பிரலாபம்—அவனியிலின்றும்
செப்பரும்விதமாய்—சிந்திக்கப்படுவது.
நாடகங்களுள்—நன்றெனப்புகழ்பெறும்
சகுந்தலைவிலாசஞ்—சரியெனத்தக்க
எஸ்தேர்விலாசமு—மின்புறப்பாடினன்.
நாற்பத்தொன்பதில்—நண்ணுதம்வயலில்
முட்டைக்கிணைறென—மொழியுமோர்கூடம்
ஆழமாய்த்தோண்டி—அதற்கொருசூத்திரம்
தாமாயியற்றித்—தண்ணீரிறைத்தனர்.
சூத்திரகல்ல—சாத்திரமாயினும்
தண்ணீர்நிறையத்—தக்கிடாததினால்
அந்தமுயற்சியை—யம்மட்டினிறுத்தினர்.
பிரதிமைப்படங்களைத்—திரமுறுவகையாய்
நடத்தியவற்றிலும்—நனிசித்தியடைந்தனர்.
ஐம்பத்துநாலி—லணுகியகொள்ளை
நோயால்வாடிய—நோயாளருக்கு
பால்பெருந்தொகையாய்ப்—பருகக்கொடுக்க
வேண்டியபடியால்—வெகுசெலவுடனே
வாங்கிவருகையில்—வளமைக்காரர்
பாலினீர்கலந்து—பணவாசையாலே
விற்பதுகண்ட—விற்பன்னமாட்டின்
பாலையுநீரையும்—பகுத்துவெவ்வேறு
பகுதியாய்க்காட்டிப்—படிறர்தங்களை
வெட்கப்படுத்தி—யுட்கவுஞ்செய்தனர்.
ஐம்பத்தைந்தி—லழகியமூன்று

சூரியகடிகை—யேருந்ச்செய்து
ஒன்றுகந்தோரிலும்—ஒன்றுதம்வீட்டிலும்
ஒன்றையாபீசிலு—மொப்பமாய்வைத்தனர்.
ஐம்பத்தாறி—லரசனும் டைக்கு
காத்திராவகையாய்க்—கந்தோரில்வந்து
கந்தோரிற்குவித்துள—காட்டுமரங்கள்
ஒவ்வொன்றிற்கு—முரியபெயரைக்
கேட்டுவருகையில்—கெட்டித்தனமாய்
மறுமொழிசொல்லி—வருகிறபோது
ஒன்றன்பெயரை—யுரைக்கவறியா
திதுவுமோர்மரந்தா—னென்றவர்கூறிய
குத்திரவிடையைச்—குறிப்பாயறிந்த
டைக்குமன்னவர்—மிக்ககெதியாய்
வீறுகொண்டெழுந்து—எறிவண்டியில்
விரைந்துவெறுப்பொடு—வீடுபோவதை
மாட்டீன்கண்டு—மறுபடியவரைச்
சாந்தியாக்கத்—தக்கவிதமாய்
வனத்தருத்தொகுதியை—வகைவகைநிரைத்து
இடாப்பொன்றெழுதி—யெல்லாவகைக்கும்
பெயர்களுந்தீட்டி—பிழையறவனுப்பினர்.
மன்னவரதனை—மனத்திடைமதித்து
திருப்தியடைந்து—தெளிந்துகொண்டனர்.
ஐம்பத்தெட்டி—லழகிடகரிடை
பம்மியஆடவர்—பலரையுமழைத்துச்
சபையொன்றுகூட்டிச்—சான்றோருமவர்
ஆண்பாலார்கள்—அழகுறுபெண்கள்போல்
கொண்டைவளர்த்தக்—குடுமிகட்டுதல்
அழகலவென்று—ஐரோப்பியர்போல்
சிதீல்விடும்வழக்கைக்—கேடறவைத்தனர்.
தம்முடைமகார்க்குத்—தையலும்பழக்கி
சட்டைகளணியவும்—சரிவரப்பழக்கினர்.
சுதேசவுடைகளைச்—சொற்பஞ்சொற்பமாய்
சற்றேதிருத்தமாய்ச்—சார்த்திடச்செய்தனர்
ஐம்பத்தொன்பதி—லவன்முன்விடுத்த
சத்தசத்திய—கத்தோலிக்கமே
உத்தமமறையெனச்—சித்தத்துணர்ந்து
தாமாயதிலே—சார்ந்தனருடனே
அமித்தவாண்டி—லாசனக்கோவிலின்
அகன்றவீதியி—லமைக்கப்பெற்ற
சிறந்தமண்டபத்தி—னிறைந்தகுருளன்
சமேரியாவிசப்பின்—சம்மதப்படியே

பதிசாஸ்திரத்திற்—பழுத்தபழமாய்
விளங்கியவொஞ்சின்—வித்தகக்குரவர்
அக்கிராசனரா—யாசனத்தமர
அங்கிளவெஸ்லிய—னுங்கக்தோலிக்க
சமயசாரியத்தார்—அமர்வுடன்கூடி
வாதிக்கும்விதமாய்—வனைந்தாமெழுதிய
சமயதர்க்க—சல்லாபமொன்றை
சோதிவிளங்கு—மாதிவாரந்
தோறும்வாசிக்கத்—தொடக்கியும்விட்டனர்.
மேல்வீட்டுமெரியாம்—பின்னைகத்தோலிக்கனும்
சேவியர்ச்சுவாமியின்—சேட்டதமையனூர்
தம்பிமுத்து—தான்வெஸ்லியனும்
'ஆசனக்கோயிலி—னமருபதேசியார்
பேருனமைந்தன்—பிறன்சிஸங்கிளனும்
ஆய்கின்றுதத்தம்—அனுசாரப்படியே
வாதித்துவந்தனர்—வாய்ச்சாலமாக.
இந்தநல்வாதை—யின்பமாய்க்கேட்க
வாரந்தோறும்—வந்துகூடிய
பேர்கள்தொகையும்—பெருக்கமுற்றது.
அடுத்தமார்கழியில்—முடிந்ததுதர்க்கமும்.
இவ்வாறிருக்கையில்—டைக்குமன்னவர்
உப்புக்குதத்தி—லொருதொகையுப்பு
குறைந்ததுகண்டு—சிறந்திடுமிவரைக்
குறைந்தநினியாயங்—கொடுவெனக்கேட்க
பற்பலநியாயம்—பகர்ந்ததுமன்றி
சாஸ்திரமுறையினுந்—தக்கநியாயங்
கொடுக்கவதனைத்—தடுத்துமன்னவர்
அங்கீகரியா—தவரையக்கணமே
வேலையாணிறுத்தினர்—வித்தகன்வெகுண்டு
அந்நியாயங்க—ளமைந்திடப்பெற்ற
விண்ணப்பமொன்றை—விரைவுடனெழுதி
அப்பொழுதிலங்கையை—யாளுகைசெய்த
சான்ஸ்மெக்கார்திக்குச்—சமர்ப்பிக்கவதனை
ஒப்புக்கொள்ளாம—லுள்ளதீர்வையைப்
பெலப்பித்தனுப்பினர்—பின்னருமதனை
அம்பலவாணர்தம்—மனுமதிப்படியே
சென்னைக்கவனர்—தன்னிடஞ்சென்று
தன்னுடைமனுவைத்—தாழ்ச்சியாய்க்காட்ட
அவரதையேற்று—அன்பொடுபோர்த்து
தாயரசாட்சிக்குத்—தந்தனருடனே.
மன்னுயிம்மாட்டின்—சென்னையைவிட்டு

அறுபத்தொன்றை—யுறுபங்குனியில்
ஜென்மநாடணுகிச்—சிலதினப்போதில்
முழுதினரொருநாள்—முடிவுறவந்த
சுவாதநோயது—சோவிகள்செய்வதை
குருமனை தன்னிற்—பெருமையோடிருந்து
வைத்தியஞ்செய்த—வணக்கத்துக்குரிய
மோலாச்சுவாமிகேட்—டேலவேவந்து
மருந்துகளூட்டி—வருத்தியநோயைச்
சற்றேதணித்துச்—சாந்திசெய்திட
பொஞ்சின்சுவாமியார்—அஞ்சிவருந்தி
அவஸ்தைச்சடங்கை—யாவலாய்ச்செய்ய
முழுவதுங்குணமாய்ப்—பழுதறநிற்கையில்
தன்னருமக்களைத்—தய்வுடனழைத்து
தக்கநன்மதிகள்—சாற்றினரவர்க்கு.
ஆதனமுழுமையு—மவர்தமதன்புடை
மனைவியின்பேரில்—மரணசாதனம்
செய்துமுடித்துச்—சிந்தையுவப்பொடு
பூரணபெலன்பெற—காரணமாக
ஆபத்துக்குதவி—யாகுமாஸ்பத்திரி
போயவணிருந்து—நேயதன்மாணவ
வைத்தியர்கையால்—வைத்தியம்பெற்று
வருகையில்வியாதி—ஒருவிதமாக
சொஸ்தமானதென்—றுத்தமனறிந்து
அறுபத்தொன்றி—லாகியதபசு
காலமதனின்—கடைசிவாரம்
ஒன்றியமுப்பத்—தோராந்திகதி
பெரியசனியெனு—முரியதினத்தில்
கேடிலாத்தமது—வீடுசேர்ந்திட
வேண்டுமென்ற—விருப்பங்கொண்டு
வைத்தியர்தம்மை—வரவழைத்தவர்க்கு
பிரியாவிடைகள்—பிரியமாய்ச்சொல்லி
புறப்படும்வேளையில்—மறப்பருவைத்தியர்
ஒருதரமருந்தை—யுட்கொள்ளுமாறு
நெருக்கிடைசெய்ய—நிபுணராதலின்
ஐயங்கொண்டு—கையைநீட்டி
சோந்தப்பி—நீயிம்மருந்தைத்
தருவதேதென்று—தர்க்கமிட்டபின்
என்மாணவனீ—யுன்னிலேநம்பிக்கை
வைக்கிறேனென்று—வாங்கியுட்கொண்டதும்
பக்கத்திருந்தோர்—பார்த்துளம்பதற
மருந்தையுட்கொண்ட—இரண்டொருகணத்துட்

பேச்சுமூச்சின்றிப்—பிரிந்தவராவி
ஆதிபரப்பொரு—ளீதமாயருளும்
ஒப்பில்லாவின்பஞ்—செப்பமாய்த்துய்க்க
அந்தமிலமரர்—தம்பதிநாடி
அவனியைவிட்டு—அகன்றதுடனே.
அவரொடுநின்ற—அன்பர்கள்பலரும்
பிரலாபத்தோடு—பிரிந்தசடத்தைத்
தூக்கிவந்தனர்— துய்யவன்மனைக்கு.
கண்டதேயேங்கி—மாண்டனரோவென
மக்களுமொக்கலும்—மாய்ந்துமாய்ந்தழுதிட
கர்த்தருயிர்த்த—கருதருகாளா
மாதிவாரத்—தனைவருங்கூடி
அன்னைமரியாயின்—ஆசனக்கோவிலுள்
பூமதானம்—புலம்பலோடு
செய்துசென்றனர்—சிந்தைகலங்கவே.
ஈங்கிவர்பாடுகே —ளிவ்வாறாக
அங்கேபிங்கிலந்துக்—கனுப்பியிருந்த
மனுவைத்திறந்து—மந்திரத்தலைவர்
நியாயத்தோரணிகளை—நேரிலேபார்த்து
சரியெனத்தேர்ந்து—தவறிலனாக்கி
முந்தியபதவியில்—முறையொடுவைத்து
வேலையினின்று—விலக்கினகால
முழுதுக்குஞ்சம்பழம்—வழுவறக்கொடுக்க
ஆஞ்ஞாபித்தே—யனுப்பினர்கடிதம்.
இந்தகற்கட்டளை—இங்குருமுன்னரே
மாட்டீனிறந்து—மறைந்தனராதலின்
மன்னவர்டைக்கு—மனமிகநொந்து
இவருடைஞாபக—மென்றுமிருக்க
எண்ணியோர்தெருவை—யிவர்மனைக்கருகால்
புதிதாய்த்திறந்து—புகழுறவதற்கு
மாட்டீன்றோட்டென—வழங்குநற்பெயரை
இட்டுவைத்தனர்.—இன்றுமப்பெயர்
நன்றுவழங்குதல்—நல்லாயறியலாம்.
றெயிலாவிறங்கி—யித்தெருவழியே
நேர்தெற்கேபோனால்—நெடுந்தெருவந்திடும்.
மாட்டீன்பெற்ற—மக்களீரேழு
இறந்தோரெழுவ—ரெஞ்சினோரெழுபேர்
எஞ்சியபேரில்—இருவராண்பிள்ளைகள்
ஜேம்ஸ்-எச்-மாட்டீன்—இவருட்சிரேட்டர்
தந்தையைப்போன்ற—தக்கறிவுடையவர்.
ஜே.பி.செமினறி—யென்றுமுன்வழங்கிய

சென்பத்திரிசியார்—சிறந்தகல்லூரியில்
ஆசிரியராக—அநேகவாண்டுகள்
போக்கியபின்னர்—பொலிவுறுகதலிக்
பள்ளிக்கூடப்—பரீட்சகராகச்
சின்னாளிருந்து—சிறந்துதுலங்கினர்.
பற்பலவின்ப—பாஷிகமுரைப்பார்
நெடுந்தீவார்செய்த—நிறைந்தவிளைவில்.
மண்ணெண்ணெயூற்றி—மாரணஞ்செய்து
குதிரைமேய்நிலமா—யதிகரிப்பித்த
புண்ணியன்செயலை—யுண்மையாயெழுதிய
ஒருகண்டனத்தால்—விருதுபடைத்தவர்.
ஒப்புயர்வில்லா—மெய்ப்பொருட்கல்வி
தப்பறக்கற்று—விற்பனராகி
தமிழகராதி—தகவுறச்செய்தும்
ஊர்காவற்றுறையி—லொப்பறுநீதி
பதியாயிருந்த—பண்டித ருவைமன்
துரையின்சரிதையை—உயர்ந்தோர்வியக்க
சொற்சுவைபொருட்சுவை—துலங்கவெழுதி
இப்புவிதன்னி—விலங்கவும்வைத்தனர்.
பல்லாண்டுகளாய்ப்—பாங்குறுமங்கிள
பாதுகாவலன்—பத்திரஅதிபராய்
வாகுறநடத்தி—வருகிறபோது
நவயசதிலே—நாதனழைக்க
விண்ணுலகெய்தும்—விருப்பமோடு
மண்ணுலகொருவி—மறைந்தனர்விரைந்தே.
கனிட்டபுத்திரன்—யோண்.எச்.மாட்டின்
அங்கிளத்தமிழெனு—மிங்கிதபாஷைகள்
செவ்விதிற்கற்று—தேர்ந்தவாசிரியரும்
பத்திராதிபருமாய்ப்—பல்லாண்டிருந்து
பற்பலவினோத—பாஷிக்கமுரைக்கவும்
சித்திரவிதமனுப்—பத்திரமெழுதவும்
வல்லபம்படைத்துத்—தெள்ளியவிதமாய்
ஆசனக்கோவிலி—னாதிசகாப்த
சரித்திரத்தமிழில்—சுருக்கியுமெழுதினர்.
சம்பத்திரிசியார்—விம்பகல்லூரியின்
வைபவந்தன்னை—வகையுறவங்கிள
பாஷையிலெழுதிப்—படிக்கவுந்தந்தனர்.
யாணகர்வாசிகள்—யாவரும்பயன்பெற
இச்சிறுநூலையு—மியற்றினரிவரே.
இத்தமகாரின்—மைந்தர்மாத்திரமோ
விண்மணியொத்த—பெண்மணிமக்களும்

கூர்மையுங்குணமு—மோர்மமுங்கொண்டு
கல்வியில்மிக்க—செல்வியராயினர்.
ஜூனியர்ஸீனியர்—சோதனையிரண்டிலும்
தனிதிறங்காட்டி—கண்ணியத்தோடு
அரங்கேறினதன்றி—உரங்கொடுமீண்டும்
மாண்புறுயாணகர்—மாதுகளுள்ளே
கன்னிகாமடக்—கல்விச்சாலையில்
முயற்சியோடு—முதன்முதலாக
லண்டன்மற்றிக்—கெனும்பெரும்பரீட்சையில்
சித்தியும்பெற்ற—வுத்தமியான
மேரியோசேப்பெனுஞ் —சீரியசிறுமியும்
மாட்டீன்வன்னல்—மகண்மகள்புத்திரி.
இந்நூலியற்றிடும்—இந்தநல்வேளையில்
அரிசனையாகக்—கைப்பிரதிபலவும்
பிழையறவெழுதி—வழுவறவிலக்கக்
குறிப்புகளோடு—குலவுமேற்கோள்களும்
சரியொத்துப்பார்த்து—நிரைபெறவைத்து
புறூவ்ஷீற்பிழைகளும்—முறைமுறை
திருத்தவுதவியுஞ்—செய்தனராமே.

List of Collectors and Government Agents of the Northern Province

Name	Month	Day	Year
John Jarvis	Dec.	3,	1795
Burton Gage Barbut	Dec.	27,	1797
George Lusignan	Jan.		1803
A. Cadell	Dec.	21,	1805
W. Montgomery	Nov.	5,	1806
J. W. Carrington	June	27,	1808
John Deane (acting)	Aug.		1810
Thomas Eden	Jan.	29,	1811
J. W. Carrington	Sept.	16,	1811
Thomas Eden	Mar.		1813
W. H. Hooper	Mar.		1815
Charles Scott	Feb.	6,	1822
C. Brownrigg	Dec.	30,	1825
William Gisborne	May	17,	1827
Joseph Price	July	12,	1828
P. A Dyke	Oct.	1.	1829
H. S. O. Russel	Oct.	23,	1867
W. C. Twynam	Sept.	15,	1869
R. W. Ievers	Jan.	16.	1896
F. C. Fisher (acting)	April	10,	1897
R. W. Ievers	Dec.	15,	1897
E. T. Noyes (acting)	June	10,	1900
R. W. Ievers	Nov.	23,	1900
G. S. Saxton (acting)	Nov.	10,	1901
R. W. Ievers	Jan.	5,	1902
J. P. Lewis	June	3,	1903
F. H. Price	April	14,	1906
H. R. Freeman	Mar.	30,	1910
C. P. Vaughan	Aug.	11,	1913
C. R. Cumberland	Feb.	29,	1914
B. Horsburgh	Jan.	1,	1915
B. Constantine	Mar.	1,	1919
H. W. Codrington (acting)	Oct.	27,	1919
B. Constantine	Feb.	27,	1920

Captains-General and Governors of Ceylon

Whilst in possession of the Portuguese

Pedro Lopez de Souza
Jerome de Azevedo
Francois de Menezes
Manuel Mascarenhas Homen
Nanha Alvares Pereira
Constantin de Say Noranha
George d'Albuque
Constantin de Say Noranha
D. George d'Almeida
Diego de Melho
Antoine Mascarenhas
Philippe Mascarenhas
Manuel Mascarenhas Homen
Francois de Mello Castro
Antoine de Sousa Continho { under whose administration Colombo was surrendered to the Dutch
A. D. Merely Menezes,
Last Captain General in Command of Jaffna and Mannar.

Ceylon Almanac.

Governors of Ceylon

With the dates when their administration commenced
Whilst in possession of the Dutch

Willem Jacobszen Coster, Commander at the surrender of Galle	13th	Mar.	1640
Jan Thuysz, President and Governor at Galle	21st	Aug.	1640
Joan Matsuyker, Ordinary Councillor and Governor at Galle	24th	May	1641
Jacob Van Kittenstein, Governor at Galle	25th	Feb.	1650
Adrian Van Der Meyden, Governor at Galle	11th	Oct.	1653
Adrian Van Der Meyden, Governor at Colombo	12th	May	1656
Ryklof Van Goens, Governor—Administration Commenced	12th	May	1663
Jacob Hustar, Extraordinary Councillor of India and Governor	27th	Dec.	1663
Ryklof Van Goens, administered the Government from	19th	Nov.	1664
Lourens Van Peil, Commander, President Governor and Extraordinary Councillor of India	3rd	Dec.	1680

Thomas Van Rhee, Governor and Extraordinary Councillor of India	10th	Jan.	1693
Paulus de Rhoo, appointed Governor and Director of Ceylon	29th	Jan.	1695
Gerrit De Heer Governor	22nd	Feb.	1697
The Members of Council	26th	Nov.	1702
Mr. Cornelis Johannes Simonsz., Governor	11th	May.	1703
Hendrick Becker, Governor, and Extraordinary Councillor	22nd	Dec.	1707
Mr. Isaak Augustin Rumph, Governor and Extraordinary Councillor of India	7th	Dec.	1716
Arnold Moll, Commander at Galle	11th	June	1723
Johannes Hertenberg, Governor	12th	Jan.	1724
Jan Paulus Schagen, Commander at Galle	19th	Oct.	1725
Petrus Vuyst, Governor and Extraordinary Councillor of India	16th	Sept.	1726
Stephanus Versluys, Governor and Extraordinary Councillor of India	27th	Aug.	1729
Gualterus Woutersz, Commander of Jaffnapatam	25th	Aug.	1732
Jacob Christian Pielaat, Extraordinary Councillor of India and Commissary	21st	Dec.	1732
Diederic Van Donburg, Governor	21st	Jan.	1734
Jan Maccara, Commander of Galle	7th	June	1736
Gustaff Willem Baron Van Imhoff, Extraordinary Councillor of India and Governor	23rd	July	1736
Willem Maurits Bruininck Governor	12th	Mar.	1740
Daniel Overbeek, Governor and Extraordinary Councillor of India	3rd	Jan.	1742
Julius Valentyn Stein Van Gollnesse, Extraordinary Councillor of India and Governor	11th	May	1743
Gerard Van Vreeland, Extraordinary Councillor of India and Governor	6th	Mar.	1751
Jacob De Jong, Commander of Jaffnapatam	26th	Feb.	1752
Joan Gideon Loten, Extraordinary Councillor of India and Governor	30th	Sept.	1752
Jan Schreuder, Extraordinary Councillor of India and Governor	17th	Mar.	1757
Lubbert Jan Baron Van Eck, Governor under whose administration Kandy was taken on the 19th February 1763	11th	Nov.	1762
Anthony Mooyaart, Commander of Jaffnapatam	13th	May	1765
Iman Willem Falck, Governor and Director of India	9th	Aug.	1765

Willem Jacob Van De Graaf, Extraordinary Councillor of India and Governor	7th	Feb.	1785
Joan Gerard Van Angelbeek, Ordinary Councillor of India and Governor, under whose administration Colombo surrendered to the arms of His Britannic Majesty, on the	16th	Feb.	1796

Ibid

British Governors of Ceylon

The Hon. the Governor of Madras in Council	Feb.	16.	1796
The Hon. Fredrick North (afterwards Earl of Guildford)	Oct.	12.	1798
Lieut-General the Right Hon. Sir Thomas Maitland, G. C. B.	July	19.	1805
General Sir Robert Brownrigg, Bart, G. C. B.	Mar.	11.	1812
Lieut-General the Hon. Sir Edward Paget, K. C. B.	Feb.	22.	1822
Lieut-General Sir Edward Barnes, K. C. B.	Jan.	18.	1824
The Right Hon. Sir Robert Wilmot Horton, Bart, G. C. B.	Oct.	23.	1831
The Right Hon. James Alexander Stewart Mackenzie	Nov.	7.	1837
Lieut-General Sir Colin Campbell, K. C. B.	April	5.	1841
The Right Hon. Viscount Torrington	May	20.	1847
Sir George William Anderson, K. C. B.	Nov.	27.	1850
Sir Henry George Ward, K. C. M. G.	May	11.	1855
Sir Charles Justin McCarthy. KT.	Oct.	22.	1860
Sir Hercules George Robert Robinson, K. C. M. G. (Lord Rosemead)	May	26.	1865
The Right Hon. Sir William Gregory, K. C. M. G.	Mar.	4.	1872
Sir James Robert Longden, K. C. M. G.	Sept.	4.	1877
Hon. Sir Arthur Hamilton Gordon, G. C. M. G. (afterwards Lord Stanmore)	Dec.	3.	1883
Sir Arthur Elibank Havelock, G. C. M. G.	May	28.	1890
The Right Hon. Sir J. West Ridgeway, G. C. M. G. K. C. B., K. C. S. I.	Feb.	10.	1896
Sir Henry Arthur Blake, G. C. M. G.	Dec.	3.	1903
Sir Henry Edward McCallum, G. C. M. G.	Aug.	24.	1907
Sir Robert Chalmers, G. C. B.	Oct.	18.	1913
Sir John Anderson G. C. M. G., K. C. B., L. L. D.	April	15.	1916
Sir William Henry Manning, C. M. G., K. B. E. C. B.	Sept.	11.	1918

APPENDIX

(A Disputed Point of Local Historv)

THE ANDRADO–PUTHATHAMBY STORY

Dryden has observed that "truth is required as the foundation of history to inform us." This is the first and most important property—the necessity of which cannot be gainsaid—to keep our understanding from the impositions of falsehood. Nevertheless, close students of history not uncommonly find the narrative of realities disfigured by their being mixed up with fables and figments. Very often facts are misrepresented, documents are garbled, and important questions and particular portions of history so treated by partisan writers as to become coloured with their passions and prejudices. This is particularly the case with regard to that portion of local history in which the two personages, whose story forms the subject of this review, played a part in the revolution that followed the Dutch occupation of the Jaffna Peninsula.

Andrado and Puthathamby are representatives of two rival sections of the Singhalese and Tamil Communities. The members of each section are to be found all over the island, dwelling side by side, in town and country. They hold important and responsible offices in every Department of the Public Service under Government. In the learned professions, and in the educational, mercantile and industrial lines, they take equal rank. As capitalists and large landed proprietors too, they are, in general, pretty well matched.

But the great disparity is in their numbers. The 'Puthathamby' section is by far the larger one. Here lies the true secret of the advantage that this section possesses over the other. Every intelligent man is aware that in most departments of life, where sectional interests come into question, numerical superiority is a potent factor in helping a party to have its own way and carry its point. In public meetings, the majority gets the day in all questions, that come up for discussion. The same principle obtains in the case of parliamentary, municipal and other elections; and the candid reader knows how often racial prejudices, caste feelings and personal dislikes have operated against the election of the fittest and most eligible candidate. In like manner, in a community, the section, which is numerically weak, is always at a disadvantage; and when the sense of rivalry between it and the stronger section becomes accentuated, the position of the former becomes one of embarrassment. An unfounded story or a silly canard respecting the weaker section finds a large circle in the stronger one, to accept it without proof, add to it without scruple, spread it without hesitation, and comment on it without charity. When to the advantage which numerical strength confers on the larger section is added the power that it derives from its influence with high functionaries, local magnates and the dispensers of power and patronage, the facility and the success with which it can bring discredit on the weaker, by magnifying its faults and making light of its virtues, can better be imagined than described.

The story in question affords a striking instance of the artful tactics, which designing individuals of the Puthathamby section, confiding in the numerical strength of their party for the promotion of their interests, have invariably employed in order to belittle the Andrado section and raise themselves and their clan in public estimation. The careful, unbiased student of history will surely be shocked to find how the stern facts of the story have been suppressed and ingenious interpolations so cleverly foisted in, as to make a real culprit an unsuspecting and harmless victim. I will not take upon myself the invidious task of narrating the story, the incidents of which occurred more than two centuries and a half ago. I shall just quote the story as told by different writers at different times and leave the reader to discern the truth and form his own judgment, adding only such remarks as are justified by the circumstances of the case.

References to the story are met with in the following works :—

No. 1

Beschryving van het Machtige Eyland, Ceylon.
Don Philippus Baldaeus, Amsterdam 1672, fol: ch: XLIV (Page 159.)

No. 2

The Yalpana—Vaipava Malai ; or The History of the Kingdom of Jaffna, Translated from the Tamil by C. Brito. (P. 52.)

No. 3

The Ceylon Almanac and Compendium of Useful Information for the year MDCCCXLIX. (P. 94).

No. 4

The Vinea Taprobanea by Philip Canjamanadan. (p. 94.)

No. 1—This is a work by a well-known historian. The Rev. Dr. Philip Baldaeus was the Dutch Chaplain during the early Dutch rule in Jaffna. The Reformed religion was first introduced by him into Jaffna, (1658-August) He was present at Jaffna during the occurrence of the incidents which he relates. It is needless for me to add that he is one of the early writers on Ceylon and his work is recognised as one of great authority.

He says :—

"Shortly after the conquest our army removed to the coast of Coromandal in order to overwin Nagapatam, but Jaffnapatam was provided with a few soldiers only, and of these, almost the greater part were Portuguese, who forgetting their allegiance to the King of Portugal, had put themselves under the obedience of the noble company. It must also be noted that there were in the castle a large number of prisoners of war."

"All these gathered together and made a conspiracy with the natives even not without the knowledge of Rajasinghe. Their intention was, while I was preaching outside the Fort in the Town, to kill all the head officers present at the sermon, whilst at the same time their accomplices in the Fort would do away with the first guard and then master the Fort, and this had not been difficult to do, if Almighty God had not been pleased to destroy their plans."

"It so happened that during the sermon Don Manual Andrado, a Singhalese, a Captain, and a Mudaliyar in the service of the noble company, together with a troop of 17 or 18 men, his ordinary attendants, stopped before the entrance of the Church, without entering, as he and his companions, were able to hear and to understand. He got as I heard it later on from himself, a peculiar insight concerning the Portuguese barbarity, the more so, because he saw, those who were around him, and they were Portuguese, constantly manipulating their rifles or Cinco—Palmas. However, as Don Andrado with his retinue did not enter, they remained also outside, and did not enter into the Church."

"This evil deed remained unknown for a few days until at last Andrado discovered the whole conspiracy to Sir Jacob Van Rhee. He at once, ordered a strong watch, closed the Fort, secured the conspirators and called me home in haste (as I was in the country to reform and visit the Churches;) as soon as I received his letter I went to the Fort and heard at once the whole treachery, how by God's Grace it had been discovered and how the conspirators were strictly kept to meet in time the due punishment. We had great reason to thank God for this gracious deliverance, as I did publicly in the presence of our Dutchmen on 15th September, 1658, taking for text Esther, Chapter 9, verses 20, 21, 22, 23, 24."

"Shortly after (after they had been carefully examined and the truth had been heard from their own mouths) they were condemned to be hanged, beheaded and put on crosses. The leader of this impious conspiracy was a native of Mannar, together with a Don Louis Puthathamby and five Portuguese. They were bound on a cross and were struck with a hatchet first in their throat and then in the chest, their hearts were pulled out and flung in their treacherous faces. A Cleric named Calderoe being a Jesuit born in Malacca was beheaded. This man had been prevented through sickness and debility to depart with the clergy and he remained for his misfortune (perdition). He was really to be pitied for the lonely part he had in the shameful affair, was a letter written to him by these rascals in which they declared to him their purpose, addressing him Padre detuas almas, the father of their souls. He did not approve their impious purpose, his heart did not allow him to betray his own countrymen, but then he had to pay for his silence with his death. The other eleven in number were hanged on a triple gallows receiving a fitting reward for their deeds. Shortly after the other prisoners were dismissed so as not to be further annoyed with these treacherous vermin. The corpses were hung on trees as food for the birds, the heads of the chief instigators of this awful proceeding were put on posts in the markets for all the passers-by to note."

The above is a full and circumstantial account, It is the first and most authoritative on record. It is both genuine and authentic. The intelligent and inquiring reader will see that no attempt is made to gloss over or disguise facts. The story is told in a matter-of-fact way, and in matter-of-fact language. The character and nationality of the writer entitle him to freedom from any imputations of partiality or prejudice.

No. 2—This is a work in Tamil prose by a Mr. Mailvaganam. All the information, which the author gives his readers in his preface, is that the work was undertaken at the request of 'the illustrious Dutch Governor Maccara,' and that he (the author) is a descendant of the celebrated Vaiya, who wrote the poem "Para—Rasa—Sekaran Ula" and the chronicle "Rasa—Murai." The late Mr. Advocate Brito, who translated the work into English, says in his preface :—

"All that is known of the author is what he says of himself in his preface. The Governor Maccara, of whom he speaks, was Jan. Maccara, who was Governor of the Dutch possessions of Ceylon in 1736. And there is sufficient internal evidence to show that the author lived about that time, but the bold language in which the policy of the Dutch is described and the prophecies which the work contains, relating to the English, must be regarded as interpolations of a later date."

It is a pity that the author has not given the exact date of the request or of the composition of the work. Nor has he told us what object the Governor had in view in making the request. It may be that the author himself was not informed of it. But if at all the request was made, it must have been made either directly by letter, or indirectly through some high Dutch Government Official at Jaffna. The publication of the letter in the former case, or the mention of the name of the official in the latter, would have enhanced the value of the book, and saved much of the doubt and disappointment which readers and writers now feel regarding the same.

The Governor to whom the author refers as 'the illustrious Dutch Governor Maccara,' and whom the translator takes care to specify as "Jan. Maccara who was Governor of the Dutch possessions of Ceylon in 1736,' commenced his administration of the island on the 7th June 1736.* He was succeeded by Gustaff Willem Baron Van Imhoff, extraordinary Councillor of India, and Governor, on the 23rd July 1736.† Thus practically Governor Maccara was Governor of Ceylon for 46 days only. The curious reader is puzzled as to what extraordinary deed Governor Maccara could have done during his administration of 46 days to entitle him to the flattering epithet of 'illustrious,' which the author confers on him. The period is too short to enable even the most talented administrator to become acquainted with the working of the different departments of the administration of a colony, to which he had just come and to which he was quite new. Indeed there was hardly time for the Governor, considering the scanty and tardy means of communication that existed then, to have visited at least the most important towns and districts and taken any intelligent interest in them. It is therefore, passing strange that no sooner had the new Governor arrived and settled down to the onerous duties of administrator of this important colonial possession than he thought of, and took an interest in, remote Jaffna, which was more isolated than now and separated from the seat of Government by nearly two hundred miles of thick and dreary jungle, and cultivating a valuable acquaintance with Mr. Mylvaganam, requested him to undertake its history, over the early part of which an impenetrable darkness hangs. Another point strikes me as singularly curious. If the Governor had requested such a work to be written, why did he not order it to be translated into the Dutch language? Or why was it not at least printed in the language in which it was written? It cannot be said there was then no establishment for printing Tamil books; for in the

---

*Of the two "commandements," Jaffnapatam and Galle, the former always took precedence, so that, whenever a sudden vacancy occurred in the Governorship of the Island, it was the Commandeur of Jaffnapatam usually, as the highest in rank after the Governor, who was called upon to temporarily administer the Government. This rule was in a few instances departed from for special reasons, as in the cases of Commandeur Arnold Mol in 1723, of Jan Paul Schagen in 1725, and Jan Maccara in 1736, who as Commandeurs of Galle had to take up the reins of Government on the sudden death of the Governor. And there was the case of Commandeur Gerrard Joan Vrelandt of Galle, who, from that post, permanently succeeded Stein van Gollenese as Governor of the island. But these were exceptional cases, because it was the practice for the Commandeur of Galle to go on promotion to Jaffna, but never the contrary—*Report on the Dutch Records— By. R. G. Anthonisz, Government Archivist.*

† See List of Dutch Governors.

year 1736, "a printing office for printing books in the native languages was established by the Dutch Government and brought into active operation." The New Testament translated from the Greek into Tamil by the Rev. Philip De Melho, Clergyman at Jaffna, was printed and published by the Dutch Government. These observations lead me to conclude that the preface to the Vai-pava-Malai is an interpolation, as certain other passages in the book are regarded as interpolations by the Translator.

Mr. L. E. Blaze, B. A., in his excellent History of Ceylon, which is used as a text-book in many of the schools of the island, gives a list of the Dutch Governors (Page 197) but omits four Governors including J. Maccara and dismisses them with the curt remark that "after he (Stephanus Versluys A. D. 1729-1732) left Ceylon, four Dutch Governors ruled in succession, but about them little is known."

The account in No. 2 relating to Andrado and Puthathamby, as translated by Mr. Brito, runs thus :—

"In respect of the Civil Government, they (the Ulanthesar) appointed Puthaththampi, a Velalan, to be Muthali for the revenue branch of the Government and Manuel Anthirasu, a man of the kuru-kula caste, to be Muthali for the writing branch. An intimacy sprung up between the two Muthalimar, and Anthirasu, being one day at Puthaththampi's house on an invitation to dinner, happened to have a sight of his host's wife, a woman of transcendent beauty, and was inflamed with a violent passion for her. She was a sister of Kayilasa Vannian and had inherited the haughty spirit and stern morality, by which her ancestors were distinguished among the nobility. She received Anthirasu's wicked proposal with indignation and displayed her resentment by subjecting his messenger to the ignominious punishment of being lashed with a broom. The spurned suitor meditated revenge and planned a diabolical one. He procured Puthaththampi's signature to a sheet of blank paper, pretending that it was to be filled up with an order for the removal of Government timber from Kachchaiththurai. But the paper was actually filled up with treasonable matters, couched in the form of a letter from Puthaththampi to the Parangkis, offering to assist them to recover the kingdom, if they would but make the attempt. A messenger, who was found carrying the letter, was seized and brought before the Governor. And witnesses were not wanting to fill up the details of the wicked farce. However, a strict investigation having been instituted, Puthaththampi's innocence was completely established. But the Governor of Yalpanam, who was a friend of Anthirasu, allowed himself to be influenced by Anthirasu's arguments and entreaties, and Puthaththampi was sentenced to death. The sentence was executed in a great hurry, before news could reach the Governor's brother, Puthaththampi's most powerful and intimate friend, who was then absent at Urkavatturai, building the Kadat-Koddai there. On the representation of Kayilaya-Vannian, who went to Kolompu for the purpose, the Governor of Yalpanam and his friend, Anthirasu, were, in the month of Puraddasi, in the year Vilampi, ordered to proceed to Kolumpu. On their way thither, the former suffered ship-wreck and was drowned, the latter was crushed to death by a wild elephant."

The above account differs greatly from that given by Baldaeus. Indeed it is quite opposed to it. Baldaeus wrote his account shortly after the occurrence of the incidents, which took place in 1658. Mylvaganam's account was written about the year 1736. Full three quarters of a century had intervened between the date of the incidents and the date of the Vaipava, Malai. It was incumbent on Mylvaganam, who undertook to write the history of an event which had taken place two generations previously, to have given the credentials of his own version, especially when there had already been left an account of the same event by a competent, disinterested, and well recognised writer, who was an eye-witness and contemporary historian, and whose description of the incidents is minute even to tediousness. The previous account, if found incorrect or untrue, should have been contradicted and proofs furnished for the correction. The author of the Vaipava-Malai has done nothing of the kind. He has not even given the source of his information. His failure to refer to Baldaeus only shows that he was ignorant of the existence of that historian's work. He appears to have written from hearsay. Baldaeus is an European, a minister of the Gospel, an alien in race and language to both Puthathamby and Andrado. What motive could he have had in hiding or misrepresenting the truth in connection with an incident touching them? On the other hand, is not Mylvaganam a partisan writer claiming Puthathamby as the representative of his section?

I shall now proceed to examine the account itself as quoted from the Vaipava-Malai. Though at first perusal, it appears to be a plain and plausible story, it cannot bear the test of a strict and searching analysis. Read in the light of historical records and local conditions, it turns out to be false and absurd. The appointment of the two men for the revenue and clerical branches of the Government, the intimacy that sprung up between them, the invitation to dinner, the sight obtained by one of the other's wife, the procuring of the signature to the blank paper, the building of the Kadat-Koddai at Urkavatturai, the ordering of the Governor of Jaffnapatam and his friend Andrado to proceed to Colombo,—the former going by sea and the latter by land—seem to be clever and ingenious devices trumped up to give an air of truth and reality to a fabrication. Considerable doubt is thrown on each of the above points by the following reasons and considerations.

The passage under review on first reading produces the impression that a settled and systematic form of Government and administration prevailed during the period in question and that the period was one of peace and prosperity. Is the fact really and historically so? Decidedly not. Let us look up history. Quite a different picture confronts us there. We find that the period was one of trouble and excitement. Force, fear, pain, anxiety ruled the land. Two great European powers were at war in the Peninsula. The town was besieged for three and a half months and it surrendered on the 22nd June 1658. With the surrender came a change—a change of rule and administration. The old Government and the old order of things passed away. A new Government and a new order of things came in. The different departments of the public service were unhinged. The heads of departments and other high officials, who were Portuguese, had to leave. Some Portuguese, however, remained and continued to give trouble till the middle of the ensuing September, when the conspiracy came to light and Puthathamby and his confederates suffered the extreme penalty of the law. From the surrender of Jaffnapatam to the Dutch, 22nd June, 1658—to the execution of Puthathamby, 15th September, 1658—there was only an interval of about three months. Was this period sufficient for a new Government, which had just obtained the ascendency, to have organised and brought into full working order, a system of administration of the perfection, indicated by the author of the Vaipava-Malai. Let the candid, impartial and judicious reader pause, consult history and pronounce his verdict.

The truth of the above picture is fully borne out by the following extract from Rebeiro's History of Ceilao (p. 387, second edition) by P. E. Pieris Esquire, M. A., L. L. M. (Cantab), and of the Civil Service of Ceylon, presently District Judge of Jaffna.

The siege of our fort was vigorously maintained and after two months' bombardment in view of the misery we endured and the lack of provisions and other necessaries, the enemy sent us a summons and offered us reasonable terms, which we declined and insisted on maintaining our defence from the 20th of March, when we first retired there till the 22nd of June; but as we saw that we had no powder, rice, or any other kind of provisions, the majority of our men killed, our bastions in ruins, and that there was no possibility of help reaching us; and as for some time the firing from the other fort had ceased—a sure sign that it had fallen—and in view of the great sickness which prevailed, we held a meeting and agreed to surrender the place. We invited the enemy for a parley, but as they saw that we were acting through necessity and that there was no possibility of help reaching us so long as they held Mannar and the fort in the harbour where they kept five ships, they would not give us any honourable terms. They would not rob us of the honour of our arms, but in every other particular we had to submit to their mercy.

Henry Charles Sirr, M. A., once "Deputy Queen's Advocate for the Southern circuit in the Island of Ceylon," in his "Ceylon and the Cingalese," describes the situation even in stronger language. He says:—

"It is at all times fearful to contemplate the horrors of war, and its attendant misery to individuals, even of the victorious nation; but how much greater to meditate on the sufferings of those attached to the conquered country? But in no history do we find greater atrocities recorded than those laid to the charge of the Dutch after the surrender of Jaffnapatam in 1658 and which terminated Portugese dominion in Ceylon". (Vol. 1. p. 250).

The evils and miseries of war and siege are well-known, and the state of Jaffna after the surrender may be easily imagined. Trade would have been paralysed. Industries would have been suspended. Their suspension would have caused want. Want would have led to criminal modes of subsistence. To repair the waste, to revive the trade, to restore industries, to re-establish order, would have been the anxious concern of the government and the people. The time would have been devoted in paying the best attention to, and employing the most active energies in, repairing fallen fortunes and setting to rights damaged property. Considering the circumstances of the time, and the straitened resources of the people, it is difficult to believe that social amenities were observed by the sons of the soil by cultivating friendship with strangers and giving and eating dinners. To take a modern illustration, could we conceive that within a few months after the reduction of Belgium, a true and patriotic son of its soil, forgetting the recent calamities of his country, forgetting the havoc and destruction done to life and property, could entertain a member of that military organisation, which had contributed to the general loot, wreck and ruin, at a dinner of which the style, extent and varicty were so grand as to find a place in the pages of history.

Let us view this question of 'the intimacy and the dinner' a little more closely. Andrado was a Singhalese and hailed from the South of the Island. He was an adherent of the Dutch and came to Jaffna as a military captain, probably in company with the armed force that besieged the town. Puthathamby was a Tamil and a resident of the North. He was then a subject of the Portuguese, though the position, if any, he held under them, is not certainly known. During the progress of the struggle between the two European powers for the mastery of the Peninsula, Puthathamby as a loyal subject of the Portuguese, would have looked upon Andrado as a bitter enemy, who had come with the Dutch to wrest his dear country from a Government, under whom he was enjoying the blessings of peace and prosperity, holding perhaps a comfortable sinecure, lording it over his countrymen, indulging hopes of preferment, and forming plans of self-aggrandisement. The defeat of the Portuguese, the surrender of Jaffnapatam and the accession to power of the Dutch, would have been a blow to his position and propects, and would have led to the destruction of his hopes. He would have been brooding over his disappointment and writhing with indignation. It was natural to expect that Andrado and the Dutch would have been from that time objects of intense hatred to him. It was more probable that he would have employed the time in devising schemes for the subversion of his enemies, as on unimpeachable testimony he has actually done, by planning the conspiracy, which culminated in his execution, than in forming an intimacy with an ostensible enemy.

The facts about the supposed intimacy and the dinner rest on the same basis and must stand or fall together. We have just seen that the conditions were opposed to the growth of friendship between the parties, and without friendship there could have been no dinner given. Nevertheless, let me consider the obstacles that might have been in the way of a dinner.

The Tamils of the North are very fastidious in the matter of where, and with whom, they eat, the Singhalese being not less so.* The community in Jaffna is in general split up into several classes, clans or castes. A man of one caste naturally feels a reluctance to eat in the house of another man of a different caste. Among the respectable classes, among families that are raised by position, wealth and influence, the feeling is stronger still. Indeed they positively abstain from all such social interdining. Well did our late governor (Sir R. Chalmers) observe that, in Jaffna, family pride and family dignity were raised to the level of a religion. Even at the present day, after more than a century of English education and christian civilization—two great and powerful solvents of caste—these notions and prejudices are as strong as ever. How much stronger would they have been two hundred and fifty years ago, when education and civilization were in a backward state? Puthathamby was a Tamil and a Sivite in his habits, notwithstanding the Christian name he bore. Jaffna was then as now the stronghold of Hinduism;

* Simon Casie Chitty in his Gazeteer (p. 52) says;—Though the Singhalese are professors of the tenets of Buddha (which recognise no distinction of caste) yet caste is observed among them with the nicest punctilliousness.

and Puthathamby could not but have been influenced by the ancient beliefs and practices of his country, environed as he was by an atmosphere of conservative habits and conventional surroundings. Would he not have thought it unorthodox under the circumstances, to invite a Singhalese, who was a man of an opposite caste, to be entertained at his table. Likewise, would not Andrado, a Singhalese, a man of a different caste, and one holding an important position in the locality, have thought it prudent to have so acted as to have evaded compliance with such an invitation.

The story of Andrado having a sight of Puthathamby's wife, and getting passionately enamoured of her, looks like a page of romance. In the case of a wild and wilful youth, brought up in indulgence and given to intemperate habits, it is possible that the sight of a beautiful woman might inflame his passion to a Vesuvian heat. But that an elderly man, a captain, one trained to military discipline and military control, and habituated to keep his passions under perfect restraint, inured to the gruesome sights of war, and accustomed to look on in cold blood on the bombardment of fine fortresses, and on the slaughter of men, women and children, was carried away by the passing sight of beauty, surpasses belief. There is, however, the doubt whether even this evanescent vision was vouchsafed to Andrado. Lord Macaulay has described in his usual graphic style how Eastern jealousy keeps watch over female beauty. The inner arrangements of the dwelling house of a respectable and rigid Hindu may not be unknown to the reader. The portion allotted to the females is quite separate. In this they generally live and move about. Even the purlieus of this portion are carefully enclosed and all intrusion on the part of strangers is vigilantly guarded against. The arrival of a male visitor is the signal for silence and retreat to the inner chambers. All talk, all motion, all noise, is hushed. The women confine themselves to their *sanctum sanctorum* till the visitor leaves. Under such conditions, as would have existed at the period of which I am writing, with all the strictness of a religious observance, how could Andrado have had a sight of the beauty? Even granting he had a sight, it was a sight and no more. The words of the Vaipava-Malai expressly are :—"Anthirasu, being one day at Puthaththampi's house ...... happened to have a sight of his host's wife." Clearly then Andrado had a sight and sight alone and that once and once alone. That is all. Not a word passed. Not a nod, not a beck, not a smile, not a "speechless message from the eyes;" no, not even the slightest sign was there at the moment of any approach to a reciprocal feeling or recognition,

But this sight only, nothing more, nothing less, can be gathered from the whole account in the Vaipava-Malai, read it and read it over, as you may. And be it noted that only the man saw the woman, not the woman the man. Her strength or her weakness, her virtues or her vices, were totally unknown to him. In such a case could we believe that the man would have attempted to offer the woman a rude shock by sending her his messenger with an ugly proposal? For that matter we might as well imagine a man meeting a beautiful woman on the highway, getting inflamed with a violent passion for her, and sending a messenger to her with a wicked proposal! But is such a thing ordinarily possible in real life? Are we in dreamland, or are we in a concrete world of sane beings, calm villains and calculating plotters, who bide their time in devising ways and means, and gaining a knowledge of the "ins and outs", for compassing their evil purposes?

As the Mudaliyar of the Revenue Branch, Puthathamby was evidently the custodian of all the cash collected by way of taxes, rents, etc., on behalf of the Government. His duties would clearly be to keep an account of the receipts and disbursements; while all orders, notices, directions or commissions, to supply goods, would issue from Andrado as the Mudaliyar of the clerical branch. Government timber had to be removed from Kachchaithurai. An order for the same was required. Who should issue the order? Evidently the officer at the head of the clerical branch. Why then should that officer go about, seeking to procure a signature to a sheet of blank paper, pretending to fill it up afterwards with the necessary details? On the other hand, Puthathamby would have grown cautious and suspicious by the time. The affair of the wicked proposal, which his wife could not have failed to apprise him of, would be fresh in his memory. He would be boiling with indignation. He would under the circumstances have insisted upon the order being filled up then and there, which in the case of officers accustomed to official routine, would not have occupied five minutes. In the then state of their feelings, both the men would fight shy of each other. Puthathamby would be loth to sign a blank paper as that would afford Andrado some chance for gratifying his malignity for the ill-treatment accorded to his trusty messenger. Andrado would as stoutly have declined to approach Puthathamby with an absurd request after the stern repulse he had already met with. After all, does it not strike the reader that an easier and more expeditious course was open to Andrado to take sweet revenge, if he was so inclined. A man who would not scruple to fill up a whole sheet of paper with treasonable matters, would certainly not have hesitated to forge a single name with every character, stroke, dot and dash of which he was daily familiar.

"A strict investigation having been instituted," says the Vaipava-Malai, "Puthathamby's innocence was completely established." Now, we are not told by whom this investigation was held. Was there a higher local tribunal than that of the Governor of Jaffna who originally sat in judgment on Puthathamby and found him guilty? Who were the officers who composed this appellate tribunal? How was his innocence established? Of the friendship and the dinner, of the vision and the wicked proposal, of the messenger's errand and the degrading punishment, of the blank paper and the signature, our author is particular enough. But on the nature of the strict investigation on the position of those who held it, on how it was brought about, on the character of the evidence by which the innocence of the accused was established —on these points, our author maintains an ominous silence.

The Vaipava-Malai proceeds to tell us that Puthathamby had "a most powerful and intimate friend" and that "the sentence passed on him was executed in a great hurry before news could reach" this friend. Of course the inference is natural that this powerful and intimate friend, who, according to the author, was the Governor's brother, might have prevented or even delayed the execution of the sentence. Now, we have nowhere found mention made, by any recognised writer or historian, that the Dutch Governor of Jaffna referred to here, had a brother. Only the author of the Vaipava-Malai and those who follow him in their versions of this preposterous story, refer to the Governor's brother, who, it is stated, "was then absent at Urkavaturai, building the Kaddat-Koddai there." This is an anachronism for which there can be no excuse. The Kaddat-Koddai, mentioned in the Vaipava Malai as then building, can refer to no other than Fort Hammenheil, which fell into the hands of the Dutch on the tenth April, 1658, and to which reference is made twice, in the extract given above from Rebeiro's Ceilao, as (a) "For some time the firing from the other fort had ceased," and (b) "The fort in the harbour." I give below two other extracts from the same eminent authority, which will show conclusively that the Kaddat-Koddai referred to by the author of the Vaipava-Malai as having been then building by the Governor's brother, who was reported as Puthathamby's most powerful and intimate friend, had been built, completed and possessed by the Portuguese long before the Dutch entered the Indian Seas in their career of conquest.

"Jaffnapatao, a quadrangular fortress, had four bastions and four half-moons or cobelos in the middle of the line of ramparts, all of which were built of pumice* stone. Here was kept the necessary artillery, and it was also the residence of the Governor of that kingdom. On one side outside the walls stretched the town, where resided three hundred families of Portuguese, and seven hundred of service-holders, with the Convents of St. Francisco and St. Domingos, the College of the Society, the Mother Church, the House of Santa Misericordia and the Hospital. Two leagues from the mouth of the harbour was a fort similar to the one of Buglo† with good artillery and garrisoned by a Company of infantry. The full number of men of war for the defence of this kingdom was two hundred Portuguese forming six companies, with some native Lascarins." (Page 130. Second Edition)

"We made some sorties to stop the works the enemy had begun and so prevented their continuing them. We had a fort at the entrance to the harbour, a little more than two leagues from the town, similar to the one *do Bogio*; this was held by a company of infantry with fourteen pieces of artillery, a constable, and two artillery men. The enemy set up their batteries at the point of the Elephant's Quay, as this was where that fort approached the land nearest; and as it was built of pumice stone they easily broke it down; and in little more than a month it was compelled to surrender from want of food and ammunition." (Page 387. Sec. Edition.)

There can be no doubt now that the statement in the Vaipava-Malai regarding the Kadat-koddai is a glaring historical blunder. It affords a clear proof that the author had written his work without proper research and without taking particular care about facts and figures. The whole story must therefore be rejected as utterly false and unfounded.

It has been suggested to me that the reference in the Vaipava-Malai may be to a fort which was built on land close to the entrance of the harbour and of which the traces are to be seen to the present day. But the reference to the *Kadat-koddai* or sea fortress is quite clear. Mr. Brito, in the Glossary appended to his translation of the "Vaipava-Malai", explains *Kaddat-koddai* as Fort Hammenheil at Kayts. Besides, the following extract from the "Colombo Journal", as quoted by Casie Chitty in his "Ceylon Gazetteer' (p. 108) should clear any doubt:—"There are the remains of a fort, said to have been erected by the Portuguese, to command the entrance to this harbour, and by a cross fire with Fort Hammenheil, to check the advance of any invading enemy." It is also a fact that the Dutch never built a fort at Kayts.

Lastly the Vaipava-Malai says that "on the representation of one Kayilaya-Vannian who went to Kolompu for the purpose,

* De pedra pomes: Coral Stone?

† Opposite Lisbon.

the Governor and his friend Anthirasu, were ordered to proceed to Colombo, and that on the way thither the former suffered shipwreck and was drowned, and the latter was crushed to death by a wild elephant." Now it is not stated why they were ordered to proceed to Colombo. Of course the inference is natural that the object of the order was to make them answer for the execution of Puthathamby. If so, they were alleged to be guilty. They stood charged of the same offence. They were accomplices. They were to appear before a higher authority to be condemned as vindictive miscreants or acquitted as honest officials who had fearlessly performed an unpleasant duty towards maintaining the safety of the state. In such a case, would they have kept together, or separated and gone, one by sea, and the other by land, thereby losing the benefit of each other's company and the only chance there was for them of comparing notes and exchanging confidences and of otherwise preparing their defence for the dreaded inquiry that would take place immediately on their arrival in the city? Suppose—and I beg pardon for putting such a supposition even for the sake of argument—that two of the writers, Mr. S. Katiresu, the Proctor and Notary, Jaffna, and Mr. A MootootambyPillai, the Tamil Scholar and Author, Navalar Kotam, both of whom have, the former in his "Hand Book to the Jaffna Peninsula," the latter in his "Jaffna History," given currency to this obviously improbable and false story, were similarly summoned to Colombo, would they elect to separate and go respectively by land and sea, and that at a time when the land journey especially was attended with perils, peculiarly great and certain by reason of the absence of proper communication, and the path lying through a wilderness infested with ferocious animals and venomous reptiles, without halting places at convenient distances to take rest and refreshment and pass off the night?

I have quoted the remark made by the Translator of of the Vaipava-Malai, that the bold language in which the policy of the Dutch is described by the author must be regarded as an interpolation. It should be noted that this story comes in just where the author commences to speak of that policy. The story should therefore share the fate of that remark. It must have been smuggled in, in the course of transcriptions which the work, having been extant in manuscript copies for years, had undergone.

It is significant that so enlightened and liberal minded a gentleman as Mr. Brito, appears to have been influenced by sectional feelings or caste prejudices. To his translation of the work which consists of 58 pages only, he adds an exhaustive appendix, extending to CXII pages and printed more closely, for the purpose of assisting the reader towards a right understanding of the author. This appendix consists mostly of translations and extracts from various books, and documents. Even Indian Mythology has been laid under contribution and an obscure Nadakam by an insignificant poet who, Mr. Brito himself admits, was a very ignorant man, had been studied and summarised with a view to illustrate the Puthathamby story. But all reference to the story as given by Baldaeus is carefully eschewed, though mention is made of that historian in the appendix.

No. 3.—This is an official publication of the Government of Ceylon, annually compiled by the officers of the Secretariat and printed. The present work was compiled, when the Right Hon. Viscount Torrington was Governor of Ceylon, and Sir J. E. Tennent, the eminent writer and historian, Colonial Secretary, and printed at the Government Press by J. Gilgot. It contains full and detailed information on the Civil, Judicial and Military establishments of the Island for the year 1849 and on other miscellaneous matters. It is now superseded by the Blue-Book. In the Chronological Table of Events connected with Ceylon given in the work, the following item is recorded:—

> 1658. Sept. A conspiracy formed against the Dutch at Jaffna by Don Louis PoodaTamby and some Portuguese is discovered by Don Manuel de Andrado, Modliar, and the conspirators executed.

The Chronological Table of events given in No 3, from which the above is quoted, was compiled by British Government officials from original documents kept in the Colonial Archives.

No. 4—.Of this work Mr. Brito writes:—

> "This is a very accurate and interesting compilation, giving an account of Christianity in Ceylon from the beginning of the 16th to the end of the 18th century. It was made by the late Philip Canjamanadan, Shroff Muthaliar of the Colombo customs, from, as he explains in his preface, Cosmas, Nicephoras, Dorothaus, Ribeiro, Baldeus, Knox, Cordiner, Hardward, Philalethes, Bohours, Dorego, and other early writers. He has also added a few well established traditions collected by himself. The work was published in 1855. Notwithstanding the Latin name it bears, it is written in Tamil prose, and the compact terseness of its style renders a summary impossible."

True to the terseness of its style, the Vinea Taprobanea refers to Puthathamby's treachery in a few words, which are rendered into English by Mr. Brito thus:—

"Rev. Caldero was decapitated in the year 1658 by the Dutch on a charge of his having concealed his knowledge of the treasonable correspondence which Don Louis Puthaththampi had with the Portuguese."

It is clear from the above that the author of the Vinea Taprobanea admits that Puthathamby was a traitor, and what other death could have any Government imposed on him than the one which he met with at the hands of the Dutch, whereas his clan ignorantly and maliciously attributed it to the Dutch Captain Andrado?

Was Puthathamby an officer under the Dutch Government? Was he a Modliar? Of the four works already noticed, two are of European Authorship. Both works describe Andrado as a Modliar, while Puthathamby is mentioned simply as a Don Louis Puthathamby. Of the office he held or of the title with which he was decorated, they tell us nothing. The compiler of the Vinea Taprobanea is in perfect accord with the European authors in what he says about Puthathamby. Andrado was a Singhalese, a Modliar, and a Captain in the service of the Noble Dutch company. We have the authority of the Revd. Dr. Baldaeus, the Dutch historian, for this statement. Did Puthathamby hold any position similar or even equal to that of Andrado? If so, the apologists of Puthathamby would do well to mention one single European historian or any other disinterested and competent writer in support of their statement. The testimony of Mr. Mylyaganam cannot be accepted as genuine. He is a partisan writer. His account is unsubstantiated by any recognised authority, opposed to chronology and history, and his statements, when put to the test, fall to the ground.

From certain facts mentioned by Portuguese, Dutch and British historians, in their accounts of the siege and surrender of Jaffnapatam, the conviction is forced irresistibly on the mind that Puthathamby was a prisoner of war from June, 1658, when the town was captured, to the following September, when he received capital punishment. Henry Charles Sirr, in his "Ceylon and the Cingalese," says:—

"Not content with the victory they had already obtained, the Dutch pursued the Portuguese to Jaffnapatam; thereby violating the articles of the capitulation, and after a siege of four months, it was surrendered, and the inhabitants were made prisoners of war." (Vol. 1 Page 250.)

Ribeiro says:—

"After fighting with them (the Dutch) we had to retire to the first street of the village where we threw up barricades. Three days later they advanced on that position, and as we found it difficult to maintain it, we retired by night to the furthest which was nearer to the fort. There we sheltered ourselves and remained for four days, but they attacked us in the flank with their artillery, and compelled us to retire by night within the fort, where also all the residents and others from the town had assembled. And as this contained only the houses of the Governor, the hospital, and a convent of St. Francisco, they all took refuge in the church and its cloisters, packed together as best they could." (Page 386.)

When active hostilities commenced in Jaffna, people began to take refuge in the fort; and as the news of one reverse after another inflicted on the Portuguese spread, it caused panic among the inhabitants, and made them seek shelter and safety within the fort. In this manner the folk of the town far and near found their way into the fort which got filled up within seven days. When the fort surrendered, they became prisoners of war. Thus the statement of the English writer is fully borne out by the Portuguese historian, who moreover declares that owing to the lack of provisions "we all underwent great misery and several of our people were consequently attacked with disease and died."

In the extract already given, the Revd. Dr Baldaeus, the Dutch historian says:—

"There were in the castle a large number of prisoners of war. All these gathered together and made a conspiracy...... The leader of this impious conspiracy was a native of Mannar, together with a Don Louis Puthathamby and five Portuguese."

There could not be the shadow of a doubt from what is stated above that Puthathamby and his accomplices were in the fort and that they were retained there as prisoners of war. How and when did Puthathamby get into the fort? It could not have been after the fort surrendered and came into the hands of the Dutch. He must have gone in before the investment of the fort, along with "the residents and others from the town," who took refuge there. The native of Mannar alluded to by Baldaeus was one of those who after the surrender of the fort of Mannar "started on the march of eighteen leagues to Jaffnapatao dead of hunger." (Ribeiro P. 385.)

It will thus be seen that during the period in which the author of the Vaipava-Malai represents Puthathamby as exercising the office of the Revenue Modliar of the Dutch, he was virtually a prisoner of war under them.

On a review of what has been already said, it does not appear that Puthathamby ever had anything to do with the Government of the Dutch. Nothing is certainly known of him except that he was a traitor and that he suffered the death of a traitor.

Several works have subsequently appeared in which the story is referred to. Most of these are written in Tamil prose and follow in the main the account as given in the Vaipava-Malai, with curious alterations and modifications. The remarks already made apply to these also. The chief works are:—

No. 5—"Puthaththampi Nadakam" by Davidu.

No. 6—"Yalpana Chariththiram or the history of Jaffna" by S. John (Page 58) 1882.

No. 7—"A Hand Book to the Jaffna Peninsula" by S. Katiresu, Proctor, District Court, Jaffna (P. 10) 1905.

No. 8 -"Jaffna History" by A. MootootambyPillai. (P, 77) 1912.

No. 5. Writes Mr. Brito:—

"Nadakam is drama. The distinction into comedies and tragedies does not obtain in Tamil. Generally speaking, in all dramatical compositions, there are a birth, marriage and death. But there is no drama without a scene of the endurance of unmerited evil or a scene of female devotion. Nor is there one which ends without poetical justice being done to all parties. The author of the present Nadakam is, as is stated in it, one Davidu, son of Juvan Costan of Mantotte. But he gives us neither the date of his work; nor that of the events which he dramatises."

The events of the drama as summarised by Mr. Brito are as follows:—

"The Dutch Viceroy of Colombo sent Anthony Amral as Governor of Jaffna and one Andirado, a man of the Kurukula caste, as Amral's Muthaliyar. Amral appointed Puthaththampi a Velalan of the Karala section, as second Muthaliyar, and one Sinne Ulanthes as Captain of the fort. Andirado made improper advances to Puthaththampi's wife, which she not merely rejected, but subjected Andirado's messengers to a degrading punishment. In order to avenge himself, Andrado had a letter framed purporting to have been written by Puthaththampi and Sinne Ulanthes and directed to Kirthi-singkan, King of Kandy, offering to betray the country to him. The letter was, of course, intercepted and its bearer acted his part exactly as had been arranged. Puthaththampi was condemned on the strength of this letter and was, by the procurance of Andirado, executed without a moment's respite. Sinne Ulanthes was then absent at Kayts building the sea-fortress. On his return he learnt the fate of Puthaththampi and, for fear of falling by an unjust sentence, committed suicide. But Puthaththampi's brother-in-law Kayilayappillai, Vanniyan of Kachchaiturai, went to Colombo and made a representation to the Viceroy, upon which both Anthony Amral and Andirado were ordered to go to Colombo to defend themselves. On the way, Amral wilfully threw himself into the sea and was drowned. Andirado was killed by an elephant at Musali or Pandaraththarthoppu. Puthaththampi left behind a widow, and a son named Sothinathan. The widow committed suicide through grief."

The discrepancies in this account as compared with that given in the Vaipava-Malai are apparent enough. The latter work is silent as to the names of the Governor of Jaffnapatam and of his brother, and says nothing of the King of Kandy. The names given in the Nadakam seem to be creations of the poet. In the list of Dutch Governors given in Histories of Ceylon, there is not one bearing the name of Anthony Amral. Ribeiro makes mention of a Portuguese Governor of the name of Anthonio de Amral C. Menezes, who was in command of Jaffnapatam and Mannar in 1658. Sinne Ulanthes is not a name. It is only a combination of two Tamil words, sinne, little or young, and Ulanthes Dutch. To a simple, soft-brained man, the younger brother of a Dutch Magnate would certainly be 'Sinne Ulanthes' or young Dutch. Our author was composing a Nadakam, in which fiction plays an important part, and what cared he about correct names? Sinna Ulanthes was in keeping with his ignorance and suited his intelligence. So he coined the name. Kirthi-Singkan or more properly Kirtisree-Raja-Singhe, king of Kandy, came to the throne in 1747. Just fancy a man living in Jaffna in 1658, offering to betray his country to a King of Kandy living in 1747. It is doubtful if so egregious a mistake was ever made by an historical tiro. But it is useless and tedious to inquire into the blunders of ignorance. Mr. Brito himself has said of the author of this Nadagam:—"Our author seems to be so ignorant a man that he uses the name Amral probably on the principle that all steamers are known to the vulgar in Ceylon by the name "Pearl", as "Pearl" was the name of the first steamer they were acquainted with". But as Mr. Brito notwithstanding his scathing condemnation of the author, has summarised the work for illustrating the Vaipava-Malai, let us at least note the main points of difference between the two accounts. The Vaipava-Malai says that Andrado and Puthathamby were Co Modliars. The Nadagam states that Puthathamby was only Second Modliar and says nothing about the dinner, the blank paper and the signature. The Vaipava-Malai represents Puthathamby alone as offering assistance to the Portuguese, while the Nadagam associates Sinne Ulanthes in framing the treasonable letter to the king of Kandy. In the Vaipava-Malai Sinne Ulanthes is the intimate and powerful friend, who might have saved Puththamby from execution. In the Nadagam he is a poltroon committing suicide through fear. Finally the Vaipava Malai says that the death of the Governor of Jaffnapatam was accidental, while the Nadagam makes it wilful. Let the reader judge between the two accounts and form his opinion.

No. 6. The second edition of this work by Mr. S. John, a native pastor of the American Mission of Jaffna, was published in 1882. To avoid tedious repetitions, which a translation will inflict upon the reader, I may say that this work gives practically the same version of the story as the Vaipava-Malai, with this difference only: that Kayilaya-Vanniyan, the brother-in-law of Puthathamby, went to Colombo, instituted legal proceedings against Andrado and the Governor of Jaffnapatam and had them summoned to Colombo.

No. 7. This work was compiled by Mr. S. Katiresu, a popular Proctor of the District Court of Jaffna, as "a Souvenir of the opening of the Railway to the North," and published in 1905. The Northern Railway—probably the longest line in Ceylon—is a great work. Indeed no greater work was ever undertaken, in or for Jaffna, by any government, Native or European. The introduction of this great civilising agent of modern times, bridging the wilderness that separates our isolated country from the metropolis, marks a new era in the history of the peninsula. The event is surely worthy of being commemorated—Mr. Katiresu is therefore to be cordially congratulated on the happy idea suggested to him by his esteemed friend, Mr. Drieberg, "of proparing a little hand book and issuing it to the public on the occasion of the opening of the Railway to through traffic."

It is a pity that the compiler had not had the like luck of being assisted by a friend in Jaffna, whose suggestions would have rendered the contents of the work equally happy. Mr. Katiresu's Hand-book professes to be a souvenir of the Jaffna Railway. But it is sadly disappointing that not a single word is said of this railway. Even the date of its opening—an event so important and unique in the annals of the North—is passed over in silence. This is a serious omission. It will, I think, be generally admitted, that a rapid but spirited account,

(*a*). of the efforts of the people of Jaffna to secure railway extension to the North, from the first meeting held for the purpose in the District Court house of Jaffna on the 14th November 1885, when Father Lytton in a lucid speech bristling with facts and figures brought the scheme from the field of visionary speculation into the region of practical politics, till its final sanction in 1889, when work commenced at both ends, or better still, till the 11th March, 1902, when Sir West Ridgeway opened the section of 21 miles from Kangasanturai through Jaffna to Chavakachcherri,

(*b*). of the stern and influential opposition it had to face, both here and in England, during the whole period of preliminary inquiry and discussion, (*c*). of those eminent and disinterested men of Jaffna and Colombo who had laboured zealously and strenuously to promote the good cause, but the majority of whom have since been gathered to their fathers,

(*d.*) of the movement that was set on foot in 1902 by a grateful people for collecting funds for the purpose of erecting a permanent memorial as a tangible and graceful recognition of the invaluable boon conferred on them by the distinguished governor, who has given them this great railway,

should have found a prominent place in the Hand-Book.

Such an account would have been more in keeping with the object with which the compiler had issued the work, and would have been of more interest than the dull paragraphs devoted to the description of the antiquated and obsolete games of Padyoddam, Kiddyadi, Kenthy, Chinky, Pasuvum Pulium,, &c; or many of the items of commonplace information, which are given in the Hand-Book, to wit:—

"Bats live in the roofs of bungalows and in the ruins of every building."

"There are no wild buffaloes in Jaffna."
"Cows are very small in size,"
"Crows are glossy black."
"Fleas are a pest."
"Frogs frequent wells."
"Hawks and kites carry away chickens.'
"Monkeys are becoming rare."

"Ticks annoy cattle and dogs." "Wasps build their nests on the rafters of houses and on trees." &c. &c, &c.,

The above quotations lead me naturally to make a few remarks on the fauna of Jaffna to which the compiler devotes a whole chapter, but of which the enumeration and description are neither full nor satisfactory. A list is given, alphabetically arranged, of the "animals, birds and insects," that are found here. Each kind of most of the species of these fauna is described in a small paragraph. The ant, that busy, interesting little creature, which moralists and philosophers hold up as an example against sloth and indolence, receives the second longest. But of several species common here, the compiler names that neuropterous kind commonly called white ants and confines his description of them to their destructive propensities only. These insects possess certain peculiarities which are well worth noticing. At certain seasons they acquire wings, and possibly, to the dismay of the inmates, fill every nook and corner of the house. Pavunanthy, the great Tamil grammarian, says in his Nannul that ants are endowed with only the three senses of touch, taste and smell. Consequently they have no eyes or ears. "A difference of opinion exists," writes H. C. Sirr, the writer whom I have elsewhere quoted, "as to whether white ants sting or bite; we know not what means they employ but we do know they can draw blood in one instant, and cause extreme pain when inflicting the wound." The same writer continues:—"The Cingalese call their nests heaps of old boiled rice," and they are composed of various substances, so amalgamated as to bear a strong resemblance to a fine white honey-comb and grains of rice. These nests are eagerly sought out by those who rear poultry; they say that chickens when fed with them thrive and fatten well. It is needless to tell the local reader that the Tamil name is Putaam Palam Choru.

Of several animals enumerated in his list, the compiler does not say a word beyond merely giving their names. Of these I may instance in particular rats and mongooses. The former are the greatest domestic pests not only here but the world over. Innumerable legions of rats abound in every part of Jaffna and infest every building; 'and the audacious boldness of these destructive vermin can hardly be credited'. They are considered the agents of dissemination of the plague and other pestilential diseases and the Government offered rewards for their distruction. As a result large numbers of rats were caught and killed. But the race cannot be wholly annihilated or extirpated; so great is the fecundity with which it multiplies.

The beautiful little creature the ichneumon or mongoose is found in every part of Jaffna. Its antipathy to snakes is well-known. But it is "the declared foe to the cobra-de-capello, and is invariably the assailant: the animal springs upon the back of the snake and seizes the nape of the neck and never uncloses its teeth until the snake is lifeless." It is also stated "that before commencing to fight, the ichneumon runs to a particular plant and eats a portion and this serves as an antidote to the reptile's poison." The mongoose is destructive to poultry. Some people bring it up in houses, but it is dangerous. The following anecdote related by Ribeiro should serve as a warning:- "The soldiers used to bring up mongoose as a protection against snakes, but they are dangerous; I knew a man who brought up one from its infancy and used to sleep with it, but one midnight he commenced shouting lustily, whereon every one hastened to see what was the matter and they found that the mongoose was attacking a portion of his body in such a fashion as almost qualified him for entering a seraglio to serve the Sultanas, and though assistance was given him at once he was compelled to trust himself to the hands of a surgeon for some time." It is ununderstandable why the compiler has excluded from his list the following specimens of the Animal Kingdom of Jaffna:—Ass, cat, civet, goat, mole, } pig, pole-cat, sheep, shrew-mouse, squirrel, duck, goose, maina, raven, snipe, teal, turkey, bug, centipede, guana, scolopendra, tadpole, tarantula, caterpillar, cockroach, cricket, earthworm, glow-worm, gnat, grasshopper, snail, spider, stag-beetle &c. &c.,

The historical sketch of Jaffna, which the compiler provides for the information and delectation of the stranger and visitor to the North, is dry and jejune. The early portion appears to have been summarised from Mr. Brito's translation of the Vaipava-Malai, passages of which have been garbled. Of the three European Governments who have successively subjugated and ruled Jaffna, the Portuguese period was the shortest. To this shortest period, the compiler allots the longest account. The Portuguese Government of Jaffna lasted nearly forty years, (1617-1658). To describing the Government of this period, the compiler devotes a little over two pages. The Dutch rule in Jaffna extended from 1658 to 1795—a period of 137 years, nearly three times as long as that of the Portuguese. But the events of this period the compiler compresses and condenses into a little over a single page. In speaking of the policy of the Portuguese Government, the compiler says that it was "governed by religious proselytism. The Roman Catholic form of Christianity was forced on the people." This is opposed to what is stated in the work, "Christianity in Ceylon," by Sir Emerson Tennent, who says:—"There is no proof that compulsion was resorted to by the Portuguese for the extension of their own faith, or violence employed for the extinction of national superstitions." It was the Dutch Government that inaugurated religious persecution in Ceylon. Catholic priests were expelled. "Proclamation was issued forbidding the harbouring and concealing of Roman Catholic priests." Even a law was enacted prohibiting Hindu ceremonies. As a lawyer and notary, Mr. Katiresu cannot be unaware of the following regulation in Thesawalame:—

"If either the inhabitants of this country within the limit of the Government, or those who are detained for some days or permanently, or Christians, shall practise any worship of gods or ceremonies of devils, such ceremonies of whatever kind in whatever place, and do honour to any idol by such ceremonies, or any Hindu ceremonies shall be discovered, they shall without mercy and regard to persons, be put in fetters. If any of those who are registered as true Christians having received true teaching shall be present, where any of their relatives, friends, acquaintances, or neighbours, practised such rites of the gods and worship of devils, and have thus done wrong associating with them, and if they shall practise such things by way of ornament and arrangement, as serve to enhance the splendor of temples, and honor false gods and devils in their houses or out, in any place through others, they shall receive as the matter may be ascertained and have happened, severe corporal punishment. The priests and all those who perform the religious ceremonies of the temples as soon as they hear this our order read, shall no longer remain, but leave the limits of the Government, and never again appear in these parts. Those who disregard this, and are discovered, shall be publicly whipped, put in fetters, and committed to labour for the space of one year. If this happen a second time, they shall be subject to severe corporal punishment.

If the compiler will take pains to study the history of the Dutch Government a little more closely, I am sure, he shall become convinced that their policy was harsher and more violent than that of Christianising through a Staff of Dutch Chaplains and of employing only Protestant Christians to Government offices."

In the version of the Andrado-Puthathamby story which the compiler gives and in the abrupt manner in which he inducts it, he shows a want of felicity and discreetness. I shall first quote the story as given in the Hand Book. It runs as follows:—

"The Governor in Jaffna had two Mudaliyars by the names of Anthirasy and Poothatamby. An untoward incident in their families has been the subject of a drama. Anthirasy being taken by the beauty of Poothatamby's wife sent word to her to pay him a private visit. In reply the lady sent a broom-stick and an old pair of slippers which made Anthirasy very indignant. He waited for an opportunity to revenge this insult. He, as co-Mudaliyar, asked Poothatamby to sign a blank paper which he did in a weak moment. Then Anthirasy wrote out a letter on this blank paper offering help to the Portuguese. Anthirasy was in high favour with the Governor and brought about a trial by night (which was against the rule) and had Poothatamby sentenced to death. Before any appeal could be made against the hasty sentence to the authorities in Colombo, poor Poothatamby was put to death. The Governor and Anthirasy however were at length summoned to Colombo. Anthirasy who went by land was killed by an elephant and the Governor who went by sea threw himself overboard."

The incidents of the story took place at the commencement of the Dutch occupation of Jaffna but the compiler regardless of the order of chronology relates it at the close of his review of the Dutch regime. It would appear that the compiler attaches great importance to this story from the amount of the space which he devotes to it. I have just said above that the history of the Dutch rule in Jaffna extending to 137 years is told in little over a single page of the Hand-book. The story in question is included in it and occupies more than one-third of the space. To be more precise I shall say that the compiler's review of the Dutch Government of Jaffna including this story occupies exactly 50 lines. Of these 50 lines the story takes up 22 lines. So that only 28 lines remain as the record of the history of the Dutch regime of 137 years. This is on an average an allotment of a single line for the events of every quinquennial period—an unparalleled example of condensation and laconism.

On examining the version of the story as given by Mr. Katiresu, the reader will easily observe that he omits what preceding writers have mentioned, and mentions what no preceding writer has said. In the versions I have quoted, the building of the Kadatkoddai at Kayts by the supposed brother of the Dutch Governor of Jaffnapatam, forms a material part of the story. This part Mr. Katiresu carefully eschews. It is not without reason that he has done so. In the Hand-Book on the very same page in which this story begins, the compiler makes mention of the historical fact that Fort Hammenheil, (the Kadatkoddai of the story) "at the entrance to the Kayts harbour had fallen to the Dutch on the 10th April 1658." Being a cute lawyer, the compiler could not but be aware that by inserting this statement, he would lay himself open to the charge of inconsistency and historical inaccuracy. For the Dutch cannot be said to build a fort which had already been built and which they had taken in fair fight. Suppressing this part of the story therefore, and by way of adding variety and novelty to his version, the compiler smuggles in the "broomstick and an old pair of slippers," forgetting that Puthathamby's wife lived at a time, when the use of slippers by Hindu ladies of Jaffna, had not come into vogue, and consequently would have possessed no old pair "to be sent in reply" to the man who had the temerity to presume to be her paramour.

What is the compiler's object in presenting this story to the intelligent and educated visitor to the North? In the first place the story is nothing more than a miserable fabrication. Even if it were true, what interest could it afford to the foreign traveller, who is aware of many cases of treason and treachery among people of all lands, races and creeds. Carefully examined, the version of the story as given by the compiler, concerns two men, one of whom, in order to pay off his grudge for some supposed insult, seeks to bring about the ruin and destruction of the other. The inevitable result of such a story on the educated foreigner is generally a scornful smile or a passing word of slighting comment on the author or compiler. If the compiler's object was to hold up the one to public execration and enlist public sympathy for the other, were there not true examples of treason and treachery, which he could have easily cited. In preparing the historical summary for the hand book intended to cater to the new-comer to Jaffna, Mr. Katiresu could not have failed to have come across many such authenticated instances. Why had he not put forward one of these? Was it not to his interest to have done so? or did the actors and personages happen to be men whom he regarded as his prototypes? The Vaipava-Malai records the case, of one Ulaguhavala Muthali, who fled from his country because of being implicated in treasonable transactions. Let the reader see how Mr. Katiresu glosses over such foul conduct. I give below in parallel columns what the Vaipava Malai and the Hand-Book say about this Muthali.

VAIPAVA-MALAI	HAND-BOOK
About the end of that month, one Ulaku-kavala Muthali of Karathivu came to their (Dutch) aid. He was a considerable Velalan of Chola-nadu, and, having been implicated in his own country in treasonable transactions against his king, he had been obliged to save his life by flight. He founded a settlement which he named Kalapumi in the Island of Karathivu.	A certain Ulagunata-Muthaly from the Chola country also came to Kala-poomy in Karativu.

Some time after the appearance of the Hand-Book, an experienced writer took up the story as given by Mr. Katiresu and published a small brochure, in which its weak points were so well and ably exposed that I cannot resist the temptation to quote it here in full.

XXX

The True Story of POOTHATAMBY'S TREASON

The Nadagam or Drama of which Poothatamby is made the hero was composed about the year 1830 by Pareemalam, a Tamil poet of Chundicully, several of whose decendants are living there as well as at Ponaryn. If those—and there are many—who have read the drama themselves and heard it sung by others—would compare it with certain incidents related by the Rev. Philip Baldaeus, the Dutch Chaplain, in connection with the early Dutch rule in Jaffna, they would presume, reasonably enough, that the only source of information open to the poet was tradition, which represents Poothatamby as having been executed for treason brought to light by Andrado (with all the zeal and promptitude of a loyal servant and citizen.) Such was the slender foundation upon which the poet had to construct the drama. He drew largely from his own fertile imagination, keeping steadily in view the class of Tamil readers and hearers whose sympathies he had to enlist and whose tastes he had to gratify. Briefly told, the tragedy transmitted by tradition, and transformed by the poet was this, that Andrado being struck with the beauty of Poothatamby's wife made advances to her, but as these advances were rejected in a haughty spirit by the woman, Andrado became so enraged as to procure the execution of her husband.

The fact however was that Poothatamby was executed and rightly so, for high treason clearly proved against him, and not because Andrado failed in his amorous advances to Poothatamby's wife. The circumstance which Pareemalam puts forward as the cause of Poothatamby's execution is a pure fabrication calculated to glorify one section and to vilify another section of the community. No serious notice however was taken of this huge fabrication for the simple reason that it was confined to the lips of Pandarams or Mendicants roving about the peninsula on festive occasions and singing portions of the drama to the accompaniment of their small drums as a means of securing small presents. What was hitherto confined to the realms of pure fiction has now taken its station as a historical fact in a Hand-Book to the Jaffna peninsula compiled by a young Proctor of the District Court, who professes to furnish trustworthy information to all new comers concerning the hitherto isolated country now opened up by the Northern Railway. This is how Pareemalam's fiction is put before the visitor to Jaffna, seeking correct information about the place and the people.

(Here follows the story as given in the Hand-book)

The latitude or licence which the poet exercised in attributing to amorous intrigue what was really the outcome of the grossest disloyalty and perfidy has been exceeded by the compiler of the recent Hand-Book in presenting to the inquiring visitor a poetical fiction as a historical fact.

The compiler's information about the Mudaliyars under the Dutch rule in Jaffna, is of the meagrest description possible. He makes mention of only two Mudaliyars in a place where under the whole period of European occupation, the securing of Mudaliarships has been the great ambition of the people.

It seems to be for a very definite purpose that the compiler has given prominence in his Hand-Book to the two Mudaliyars, Andrado and Poothatamby viz. to hold up the one to public execration as a treacherous villain, and the other to public sympathy as the confiding and innocent victim of a false friend and colleague. And this is brought about by the most impudent misrepresentation imaginable. Pareemalam in his drama does not make Andrado half so infamous as the compiler in his professedly historical sketch. Pareemalam's drama differs materially from Katiresu's Hand-Book in the narration of the principal incident. The drama says that Andrado being taken with the beauty of Poothatamby's wife sent two of his trusty messengers to her, offering her a box containing money and jewels and telling her, that if she would accept the present, he would come to her that evening. The Hand-Book says that Andrado being taken with the beauty of Poothatamby's wife sent word to her to pay him a private visit, but that she sent him a broomstick and an old pair of slippers. In the dramatic account, Andrado is made to observe the etiquette still obtaining in India in the matter of courtship, whereas, in the would—be historical account, Andrado is represented as a barbarian, offering a rude shock to a woman's modesty. Again the Hand-Book says that Andrado having got Poothatamby in a weak moment to sign a blank paper wrote out on it a letter offering help to the Portuguese. The drama, on the other hand, is silent as to the blank paper, Poothatamby's signature and the letter offering help to the Portuguese. What the drama says is that Andrado intercepted a letter addressed to Poothatamby in which it was found that Poothatamby had offered his help to the Portuguese. Finally, the Hand-Book says that in just punishment for their crimes on their way to Colombo, Andrado was killed by an elephant and the Governor threw himself overboard. The drama, it is worthy of note, makes no mention of the suicide of the Governor or of the fate of Andrado.

There is not to be found in the whole range of historical writing a grosser or bolder piece of historical misrepresentation or perversion than is found within the compass of the small paragraph quoted above from the Hand Book. Artfully and astutely enough are the broomstick, the old pair of slippers and above all the blank paper made to play a very plausible and prominent part in the tragedy which culminated in the execution of Poothatamby. From his very housetop does the compiler of the Hand-Book now proclaim the innocence of his great hero, Poothathamby, whom he would perhaps fain call the great, the good. What is the compiler's authority for what he says? He has given none, simply because he has none to give. He cannot derive much support even from the poetical exaggeration of Pareemalam. His historical summary compiled for the special information of the unsuspecting inquirer and stranger is worse than the worst piece of fiction and rests on no better foundation than for the purpose of blackening the character of the loyal Andrado and exalting that of the treacherous Poothathamby.

There is excellent, disinterested, unimpeachable testimony to oppose to Katiresu's version of the story regarding Andrado and Poothatamby. It is furnished by the Rev. Philippus Baldaeus, Dutch chaplain, in his account of the surrender of Jaffnapatam, June 21, 1658.

(Here follows the extract from Baldaeus.)

Whom are we to believe? Baldaeus, the contemporary historian and the eyewitness to the shocking incidents of which he has left a full and circumstantial record, or Katiresu, the youthful Proctor, who from his reckless version shews that he has much to learn and unlearn before he can be accepted as a safe guide by travellers and visitors seeking information about Jaffna and its people. We must under the circumstances reject Katiresu's version and we feel sure that no man in his senses will give any credence to Katiresu's extravaganza.

Andrado and Poothatamby were the representatives of two rival sections of the community. Don Manuel Andrado is described by Baldaeus as a Singhalese, a Mudaliyar and a Captain in the service of the noble Dutch Company. Don *Lewis* Poothatamby was a native of Jaffna; but there is no better or higher authority available than that of Katiresu for dubbing him a Mudaliyar. He certainly held no position similar or equal to that of Andrado. He was evidently a man, who, as the fitting sample and representative of his class, was playing a double part in his day, just in the same fashion as the bat in Aesop's fable of the battle between the birds and the beasts. His sole aim seems to have been to curry favour with the Portuguese as well as with the Dutch, unmindful of the fact of their being belligerents and enemies, as the means of finding his way to some object of self-aggrandisement. He however stood neither by the Dutch nor by the Portuguese as the firm friend of either and his treachery which finally revealed his dangerous and despicable character met with the awful punishment it fully deserved, serving as a warning to all his descendants and admirers. But have his descendants and admirers profited by the warning? * *

* * * * * * *

* * * * * * *

No. 8. This is a work written in Tamil prose by Mr. A. Mootootamby Pillai of Navalar-kotam, popularly known as "Ward and Davy." The first edition of the work appeared in 1912, and the second in 1915. In both editions, the version of the story given is the same.

Mr. M's version differs materially from all previous versions in many points. It is by far the longest. I may state that the story as told by Mr. M. occupies five pages of his "Jaffna history". In reading it, one cannot but feel that it is on a par with the most extravagant of old women's fables.

Mr. M. seems to follow the Vaipava-malai, though he does not acknowledge it, in stating that the Dutch appointed Puthathampy and Andrado as chief officers, respectively of the Revenue and the Writing branches of the Government. But he insinuates that the title of Modliar was conferred on the latter, when the appointment was conferred on him. This is not so. All previous writers, whom I have quoted, tell a different tale. Will Mr. M be able to cite one writer who is not a partisan, to show that Puthathampy was ever a Modliar? Recognized, impartial history states that Andrado came to Jaffna as a Modliar.

In describing the dinner and other parts of this story, Mr. M. relinquishes the duty, incumbent on him as an historian, of recording stern facts, and arrogates to himself the privilege, which 'Artists of fiction" use, of invisible ubiquity to enter their hero's habitation and observe inner arrangements. In the several accounts already quoted, we have seen that the dinner given to Andrado was a private one, to which he alone was invited. But Mr. M. makes his readers understand that it was a large social function to which a large number of persons were invited, including Andrado. Writes Mr. M:—One day Puthathampy invited Andrado also to a dinner party he had in his mansion. When Andrado came, Puthathampy received him, took him to a private room, had the meal served, made him dine, left two servants to wait on him, and returned to attend to the other guests.

The intelligent reader knows that, if ever there was a dinner at all, the record of facts given is as it should have been, not as it was. The statement made is in contravention of all known local customs, practices and usages of the people. Invitations to convivial gatherings are sent with caution and circumspection. Even among people of the same caste, those only are invited, who are connected with the host in some way or other. Under such circumstances, is it credible, that Puthathampy would have invited a man of a different nationality, nay of a different caste, to the family dinner he gave. It is equally incredible that Andrado, a man occupying an enviable, official and social position in the locality, would have so far lost all sense of self-respect as to attend a public banquet of which the host and guests were aliens to him not only in race but in caste. Mr. M. has undoubtedly made a statement as reckless as it is highly improbable.

What follows is a still more improbable statement and hardly complimentary to his hero. Says Mr. M:—Puthathampy's wife, while doing the round of personally attending tc the guests, entered the room, where Andrado was dining and urged the attendants to serve him with the desired viands without stint.

The entrance of Puthathampy's wife into the guest room, during the repast, is opposed to all our known notions of Hindu modes of female social etiquette and behaviour. In Hindu banquets, it is not the custom locally of the hostess to attend to male guests. Of the large company, who as Mr. M. says, came to partake of the good cheer provided by Puthathampy, a good many could not but have been strangers to his wife. Would she, whom Mr. M. and preceding writers extol as a paragon of chastity and modesty, throw away all sense of female propriety, appear before strangers, while they are eating, and attend to them?

What is Mr. M's object in introducing Puthathampy's wife into the room, where and while Andrado was dining. Mr. M. has already told the reader that Puthathampy had done the needful towards Andrado as his guest. There was absolutely nothing left undone that a host should do to a guest. Why then should the woman be made to obtrude her presence on the man, under pretence of giving an uncalled for and unnecessary order to the attendants? Did Mr. M. think or feel that the chance sight, which, as represented by the author of the Vaipava malai, Andrado had of the woman, was not enough to produce irresistible passion, and that the woman should be made to appear before the full gaze of the man to display her attractions. Mr. M. appears to have had such a notion or feeling, for he says:—Andrado saw her face, which was beautiful, heard her voice, which was sweet and observed her gait, which was elegant. The *tout ensemble*, Mr. M. avers, constituted a charm as to have made him "as dead as wood."

On what authority does Mr. M. make these statements? The reader feels that one who had ensconced himself in the room on the occasion in question could not have given a better or more minute description of the happenings there. To describe as accurately and as authoritatively, as Mr. M. has done, the tones of the voice and the mode of gait of a particular person, the writer should have heard that person speak and seen that person walk. It does not follow that a mellow voice and a dainty gait are the necessary or consequent concomitants of beauty.

Writes Mr. M:—Andrado having dined, stepped into the outer hall, talked with Puthathampy, and while his thoughts were otherwise bent, took a chew of betel and went away home.

Mr. M. writes as things would have been, as he thinks, not as things actually were. This is not history, but pure fiction; and Mr. M. would do well to remember that history is a faithful record of facts and incidents that have taken place in real life. Now, how does Mr. M. know that Andrado was in the habit of chewing betel? Who the deuce told him this? What proof or authority has he to substantiate the statement? The descendants of Andrado say that to his credit, it is still remembered, and sometimes talked about, that though a military man and in close and frequent touch with European officials of high standing, he had never used any strong drink, and that he was besides a perfect stranger to the habit of smoking tobacco and chewing betel.

As soon as Andrado reached home, continues Mr. M., he put gold coins, sweet-perfumes, and a silk cloth into a sandal-wood box, and sent the box to Puthathampy's wife through a messenger, with a wicked proposal. The messenger went, and watching an opportunity for the absence of Puthathampy, delivered the box into the hands of his wife and made known to her the proposal. When she heard it, she felt as if molten lead was poured into her ears. She got enraged, took a leathern sandal, tied it to the box and chastising the man, told him to return the same to the villain, his master.

Mr. Katiresu, who gave out his version of the story in 1905 introduced for the first time into the story an old pair of slippers and Mr. M. in 1912 came out with a paraphernalia of complimentary presents and a leathern sandal—What other new and curious things will be introduced next, time alone will show.

Mr. M. says, Andrado sent the presents immediately on his return home from Puthathampy's dinner. Had Andrado the articles ready? Was he prepared for the same before-hand? Two of the articles mentioned were rare at the time of which we are speaking. It was not everybody that would have them, much less Andrado under the circumstances. He came to Jaffna, according to reliable contemporary history, as a Captain of the army, and he would not have cared to incommode himself with sandal-wood boxes, silk cloths and gold coins, when going out on a military expedition.

What were the gold coins of which Mr. M. speaks. He would have done well, had he specified them. Andrado was a servant of the Dutch and he would have been paid in the Dutch currency. The ducat, the gold coin of the Netherlands, was not then put in circulation. The Dutch currency of Ceylon was the rix-dollar, and this was a silver coin. How came Andrado by the gold coins in question?

Such are the statements which in the name of history, Mr. Mootootamby Pillai, the Lexicographer and Historiographer of Navalar kotam, lays before an enlightened public. In this connection the remarks made by the "Ceylon Morning Leader" of 3rd April 1916, comes in extremely apropos:—

"History is not studied but misrepresented in deference to tradition. Incidents known to be false are repeated although they contradict the real historical character. The manners of the period are not understood."

With regard to the blank paper, the signature, and the execution of Puthathampy, Mr. M. follows the Vaipava-malai, but adds—Kayilaya Vannian, the brother-in-law of Puthathampy, went to Colombo and made a representation of this matter to the Dutch Viceroy of the city, who at once despatched officers to arrest the Governor of Jaffnapatam and Andrado and bring them to Colombo. These officers took the Governor by sea, and Andrado by land. On the way the Governor threw himself over-board, Andrado was killed by an elephant in the forest called Pandaraththarthopu near Musali.

The above statement is as thoughtless and indiscriminate as those already noticed. If any representation was made at all, and if it was found worthy of being entertained, the Viceroy would, in the course of his official proceedure, have called upon the Governor of Jaffnapatam for an explanation; or he may have directed an enquiry. But to be told deliberately that he sent the myrmidons of the law for the arrest and escort of a high European official merely on the representation of an interested and insignificant individual takes away one's breath. If, as Mr. M. says, the officers had the Governor and Andrado in their custody, how came they to lose their charges? Was no enquiry held on what happened to them? Were not the custodians taken to task for remissness of duty? Why is Mr. M. silent on these points?

Mr. M. expresses his regret in very effective language that neither the Portuguese nor Dutch historians have given a satisfactory account of this incident. It would have been very interesting if Mr. M. had defined the essential marks of a satisfactory account of a particular point or period of history. What does Mr. M. mean by a satisfactory account? Are details of betel-chewing, of females attending to males, while the latter are dining on a convivial occasion, and of the hostess appearing before strange and unknown guests, form necessary parts of such an account? If so, Mr. M. would do well to frame a new canon for writing history, and publish the same for the benefit and guidance of future historians.

As an historian, Mr. M. should have known that the incident in question did not occur during the Portuguese period. With the surrender of Jaffnapatam to the Dutch, the Portuguese dominion in Ceylon had terminated. The Portuguese officers and others from Jaffna to the number of one hundred and forty had been sent away to Batavia. There was no competent Portuguese writer in the place to undertake the history. Even if there were any, he could have had no interest in writing it after the evacuation of the place by his countrymen.

The incident, in due chronological order, took place during the early Dutch rule in Jaffna. The Rev. Dr. Baldaeus, the Dutch historian, has given a pretty good account of the same. A fuller and more detailed account of an event, comparatively unimportant and insignificant, is rarely met with. But the account in Baldaeus does not satisfy Mr. M., who says that Baldaeus wrote his account on the strength of the verbal testimony of Andrado. This is not so. Mr. M. does not seem to have read the account in Baldaeus fully or understood it clearly. The account from Baldaeus is extracted elsewhere, and the reader may read it and judge for himself. Baldaeus was present at the trial and execution of the conspirators and he writes :—"After they (conspirators) had been fully examined, and the truth had been heard from their own mouths, they were condemned to be hanged, beheaded and put on crosses." The authority of Baldaeus has never before been questioned. Let Mr. M. bear in mind that the Dutch historian did not write his history from the indefinite statements of a Thampupillai, or the anonymous ola book of a Maniaratnam.

Lastly in winding up the story Mr. M. says:—There is no difficulty in concluding that as Davidu, the son of Juvan Costan of Mantotte and the author of Puthathampy Nadakam, lived at a time near to the occurrence of these incidents, he must have ascertained the truth of the events he has dramatised; and as the author was a Christian, his religious promptings would not have led him to cast slur or reproach on a fellow Christian like Andrado.

How inconsistent the above statements are with the fine asseverations which Mr. M. makes in the preface to his "Jaffna History"? There he assures the reader that he has written his work with all possible care, after diligent and painstaking research, and that no statement is there made that is not supported by history, tradition or by his own personal knowledge.

Now what history, what tradition or what portion of Mr. Mootootamby Pillai's personal knowledge and erudition, support the statements in the above passage, the reader fails to see. On the contrary, the statements are made in defiance of known facts. It is clear that Mr. M. has only made an unsuccessful attempt, by a process of subtle but fallacious reasoning, to establish a substantial faith in this absurd and extravagant story.

In the first place, Davidu, the author of Poothathampy Nadakam was not a Christian. Mr. Brito, a no mean Tamil scholar, has studied and summarised the events of the Nadakam, and what Mr. Brito says of the religious persuasion of the author must carry more weight with the intelligent reader, than the indiscreet and unsupported statements of Mr. M. Writes Mr. Brito : –"Poothaththampi and his dramatist appear from this work to have been Saivites notwithstanding the Christian names they bore. For the dramatist invokes on his work the favour of his usual Hindu Gods, and represents his hero as appealing to the same Gods for succour in times of distress while he carefully makes the Dutch characters swear like Christians"

Mr. M. is therefore wrong in stating that the author of Poothathampy Nadakam was a Christian ; and his inference that as a Christian he would have spared Andrado who was a co-religionist, is equally erroneous. On the contrary, there are reasons to believe that the author of the Nadakam would have heaped on Andrado all the obloquy and odium, he was capable of mustering. Baldaeus, in his account of the conspiracy, makes mention of a native of Mannar, who was the leader of it. This native of Mannar was of the same clan as the author of the Nadakam—perhaps one of his ancestors. Poothathampy was indicted, brought to trial and condemned to an ignominious death on the information furnished by Andrado. This affords the true explanation for the vindictive spleen which the author of the Nadakam has vented on Andrado, who was instrumental in implicating the author's compatriot.

In the second place it is not known when the author of Poothathampy Nadakam lived. No writer makes mention of that date. The author himself has not stated it. Mr. Brito who has made an elaborate study of a series of books and manuscripts for the purpose of compiling the appendix to his translation of the Vaipava-malai, with a view to illustrating the latter work, says of the author of the Nadakam that "he gives us neither the date of the work nor that of the events which he dramatises." We must therefore look up to internal evidence, to allusions to events contained in the Nadakam to help us to decide the date. Mr. Brito has given a satisfactory summary of the events of this Nadakam. This summary I have quoted. In it the reader will find that the author makes a reference to Kirthisinghan, King of Kandy. This King of Kandy came to the throne in 1747. It is thus clear that the author who makes reference to this king must have been a contemporary of, or have lived after, that king. A writer can only refer to persons or things that have preceded him or are contemporaneous with him. No writer can refer to persons or things of a period subsequent to the times in which he lived. The reader of Poothathampy Nadakam will find sufficient evidence in the work itself to show that it was composed several years after the death of Kirthi-Singhan. Now the Poothathampp—Andrado incident took place in 1658. Kirthisinghan, King of Kandy, died in 1780. Thus an interval of 122 years intervened between the occurence of the incident and the stringing together of the details of that incident into a dramatic work. How could Mr. M. be so bold, positive and deliberate in making the statement that the author of the Nadakam lived at a time near the occurrence of the incident relating to Poothathampy. Mr. M's statement is therefore clearly wrong.

It is curious that the only authority Mr. M. quotes in support of his version of this story is the author of the Nadakam, whom Mr. Brito characterises as a very ignorant man; and Mr. M's reason for quoting him is that as he lived not very long subsequent to the occurrence of the incidents, he must have ascertained their truth. It is needless to point out that Mr. M's inference is sophistical. Nevertheless one is tempted to ask why has Mr. M. not followed the same authority throughout the entire details of the story. Why has he omitted certain parts, changed others and inserted new matter? Regarding Sinne Ulanthes, the author of the Nadakam says that he committed suicide through fear. But Mr. M. says that if Sinne Ulanthes had known that his intimate friend Poothathampy was condemned to death, he would have saved him; and Andrado knowing this had him executed that night without allowing him any respite. Certainly, according to the showing of Mr. M., Andrado must have been an extraordinarily mighty being, able to carry out the penalty of the law even at dead of night, when no law allows it. It is also worthy of remark that Mr. M. makes no mention of the capture, by the Dutch, of Fort Hammenheil at Kayts. He only says that the Dutch took Kayts on the 16th April. This date is wrong as many of the dates and names, and facts and figures in his "Jaffna History," are.

Mr. M's version of the story is the most reckless of all the versions quoted above. It is full of gross misrepresentations and erroneous statements. Such indiscriminate writing is calculated to take away public confidence from a writer.

In a paper contributed to the 'Ceylon Antiquary' on the "Sinhalese Place Names in the Jaffna Peninsula," Mr. B. Horsburgh, G. A., N. P., whose attainments in Tamil are well-known, points out certain important statements in Mr. MootootambyPillay's "Jaffna History", for which no authority has been given.

Mr. M. is the author of several books in Tamil. Some of these are intended as contributions to the school literature of the island, that is forming under the influence of the Revised Code, and as such are used as text books in some vernacular schools. He is also a member of the local "Committee on Oriental Studies," formed at the instance of the Department of Puplic Instruction. New books in Tamil published for the use of schools are sent to him by the Department for inspection and perusal and his opinion is asked on those books. These considerations led us to expect from his pen an account of Jaffna and its people, fair and impartial, and acceptable to all communities. But the work under review is greatly disappointing and does not seem to redound to the prestige and credit of the author as a popular writer.

The book on its first appearance was unfavourably received by the press and condemned as a partial and one-sided account. One of the editors of a local newspaper, to whom the book was sent for review, remarked that the book even in the first pages was not free from faults and blemishes.

It is needless for the intelligent reader to be told of the fortune the book has had. A critical examination of the preface to the first edition, will show what value to attach to the work as an historical account.

Mr. M. says that he had long cherished the desire of writing a good history of Jaffna and he set to work about it. He hunted after works on local history and he found five old accounts extant. These are:—

1. Vaipava-Malai
2. Kailaya-Malai
3. Para-Raja-Sekaran Ula
4. Raja-Murai
5. Vai-iai-Padal

Of the above, Mr. M. says, he was not successful in getting copies of the last three. The only works therefore available for consultation and information were the Vaipava-Malai and Kailaya Malai. But these Mr. M. candidly admits, had become corrupted in the course of time. Of the latter Mr. Brito writes:

"This is a poetical composition of no mean ability and was evidently designed to celebrate the praises of Seka-rasa-Sekaran under the very thin disguise of celebrating the sanctity of the temple of Kayilaya Nathar of Nallur. The author was Muththurasan, son of Senthiyappan of Chola, who was no doubt a contemporary of the king".

And of the former Mr. M. further admits on page 46 of his Jaffna History, that having been kept in ola-books, it had undergone alterations and modifications in the course of transcriptions. Consequentiy it was not réliable.

Mr. M. therefore had to collect information for his work, in various ways, from a long time. It is amusing to hear of the manner in which this information was got together. In 1887 while residing at Madras Mr. M. learnt that at Conjeevaram, there was a *Thesigar*, by name Massillamany, who had in his possession an Erdu or ola book, containing notes about Jaffna. Anxious to have a look at these notes, Mr. M. travelled thither, saw the *Thesigar* and made known to him the object of his visit. The Thesigar demanded Rs. 50 for the privilege of seeing the document. Thinking this was too much for the privilege, Mr. M. retraced his steps back to Madras. Two years after, he started again on the same mission and this time he was fortunate in being allowed to see the Erdu gratis. On examination it was found to contain notes made by a Prohithan. With it there were twenty seven other erdus. All these contained notes, of an ancient date, made by a Prohitha Brahmin. Examining these, Mr. M. took notes of these notes and was able to get through them all in three days. These notes, Mr. M. assures the reader, were of great help to him in compiling his Jaffna History.

Now who was this Prohitha Brahmin and how came he to write notes about Jaffna. Could he be the same Prohitha Brahmin, who, along with a Manippay carpenter was admitted by the infamous queen Anoola to her bed and throne, as related in the Mahawanso (Pages 208, 209) and who perhaps migrated to the mainland after the death of the queen. If so, the information about Jaffna must have been imparted to him by the carpenter, when associated with him in his love intrigues.

Mr. M. does not enlighten us as to the nature and extent of these notes which he had come by under such peculiar and trying circumstances. As he acknowledges that they have been chiefly availed of in the compilation of his history, the reader expects to know what era they relate to, or what questions of local history they elucidate. Mr. M., however, has elected to keep dark on these points.

Erdus or ola books are made up mostly of Palmirah leaves written on with a style. The writing in many cases is indistinct. Reading them is not so easy or expeditious as reading printed books. To read and examine twenty-eight Erdus, taking notes carefully for the purpose of using them for a future important work, and get through them all, neck and crop, in three days, is a feat worthy of the admirable Crichton.

Mr. M. proceeds to tell the reader that he has been the happy recipient of a gift, from Mr. Maniaratnam of Achchankulam, in the shape of an Erdu in which he exults to have lighted upon much information on the distinctions of the caste system. But of the name of its author, the date of its composition, the merit of its contents, or the literary status of the donor, nothing is made known. What value can be attached to information gathered from such trash?

Mr. M. makes mention of three persons who have furnished him with special information for his work. The last, though not least, is Mr. Thampupillai who hailing from Paria Mathagal, was brought up at St. Joseph's Orphanage at Colombogam—an institution founded by the late Archbishop Christopher Bonjean of illustrious and happy memory, for housing, feeding, clothing, teaching and training orphan children of heathen parentage. He is better known in the town as V. Francis Thambo and he is now for several years the Tamil Editor of the J. C. Guardian. But we are not aware of his having made any permanent or valuable contribution to the historical literature of Jaffna or of his possessing any special claims to entitle him to be recognized as an authority on historical questions. Merely being the editor of a vernacular newspaper, all whose contributions are ephemeral, does not constitute a sufficient guarantee for literary competency, historical research or for accuracy and authoritativeness of information. Nevertheless it would have greatly interested the reader to be told of the nature of the information furnished by Mr. Thampupillai. But Mr. M. is provokingly silent on this point, disclosing nothing more than making the dry acknowledgment which, in strict literal rendering, runs thus:—Some (information) was asked from Mr. Thampupillai".

Had Mr. M. obtained his information from Mr. Velupillai of "The Jaffna Native Opinion," or the Rev. Father Gnanapragasar, both of whom are publicly credited with tolerable acquiantance with local history, he would have been spared the scathing criticism to which his book was exposed, and made it more acceptable to the general public. But beyond getting from the latter a well-known work on Ceylon—the receipt of which is acknowledged in a prominent foot-note on page 3 of the preface to the "Jaffna History"—and asking the former for the favour of a review of the book after its publication, he does not appear to have sought the aid or advice of either.

Mr. M. gives a list of the books, which he has consulted in the compilation of his work, and among which there appears the name of one, which savours of a hoax. This is "Brito's Jaffna History." It is well-known that Mr. Brito never wrote a history of Jaffna. He only translated the Vaipava-Malai and added an appendix to it. Even if he had written one, he would certainly not have given it the title of "Jaffna History."

Such are the chief materials out of which Mr. M. has composed his history; and it is for the reader to judge of the value and confidence that should be placed on such a work. I close this notice, imperfect as it is, with the following observations of Rollin, which are as just as they are eloquent—as apposite as they are complete:—

"It is History which fixes the seal of immortality upon actions truly great, and sets a mark of infamy on vices, which no after age can ever obliterate. It is by History that mistaken merit, and oppressed virtue, appeal to the incorruptible tribunal of posterity which renders them the justice their own age has sometimes refused them, and without respect of persons, and the fear of a power which subsists no more, condemns the unjust abuse of authority with inexorable rigour.... Thus History, when it is well taught, becomes a school of morality for all mankind. It condemns vice, throws off the mask from false virtues, lays open popular errors and prejudices, dispels the delusive charms of riches, and all the vain pomp which dazzles the imagination, and shews, by a thousand examples, that are more availing than all reasonings whatsoever, that nothing is great and commendable but honour and probity."

Chavakacheheri
25th July 1916

YALPANA VAIPAVA KUVMUTHY—1918

No. 9. This is a recent publication. The Author is Mr. K. Velupillai, the Manager of the Jaffna "Native Opinion." The work bears evidence of considerable and painstaking research and it contains much useful and interesting information. It is written in Tamil and though in some passages engaging, its style is deficient in ease and variety.

The correct version of the Andrado—Puthathamby story is given here. But it is marred with a singular addition. Mr. Velupillai, not to be outdone by previous writers, who had given out the story with their own figments and pigments, makes the peculiarly curious statement that Father Caldero came by a knowledge of the conspiracy through the secret of the confessional. No authority is however given for the statement.

Dr. Baldaeus, whom Mr. V. follows in his version of the story, says that "the lonely part he (Father Caldero) had taken in the shameful affair, was a letter written to him by the conspirators, in which they declared to him their purpose, addressing him Padre detuas almas (the father of their souls). On this letter only Mr. Velupillai seems to base his statement; he is wrong. Confession cannot be made through letters. What the Church of Rome teaches and practises in respect of the Sacrament of Penance is so definite and clear that it is needless to waste words on it. It is a pity that Fr. Gnanapragasar, from whom Mr. V. acknowledges to have received the greatest help in the compilation of his work, has not enlightened him on the point.

To make the confession, priest and penitent should meet together at the same time and place. Where were the conspirators? According to contemporary history, they were within the fort of Jaffna and they were prisoners of war. Where was Father Caldero? We are not told, nor are we sure of where he then was—At any rate it is certain, that the priest was not close by, to enable the conspirators to make their communication by word of mouth. Their writing to him the letter is proof positive of the fact that the priest was away at a distance. The matter, on which the conspirators were anxious to lay heads together with the priest, admitted of no delay, required the utmost caution and secrecy, and involved such serious risks that they would surely have preferred to have met and spoken to him, had he been within easy reach. But in the situation in which they were placed this was not practicable. Hence they wrote him the letter,

From the commencement of their occupation of Jaffna, the policy of the Dutch Rulers was characterised by religious intolerance of a violent nature. The Catholic Clergy were prohibited from performing Sacerdotal functions and the laity from following their religious avocations. Immediately on the surrendor of Jaffna to the Dutch, the Jesuit Missionaries working in Jaffna under the Portuguese were sent away, and Fr. Caldero, as Dr. Baldaeus says "was prevented through sickness and debility to take his departure with his brethren."

Being sick and weak it is doubtful if the priest (Father Caldero) was able to have attended to his duties even unnoticed or covertly. On the other hand, could we for a moment suppose that the Dutch Authorities with their known intolerance and bigotry would have permitted the conspirators, who were prisoners of war under their immediate charge, to follow their religious duties as they pleased.

Further there are sufficient grounds to infer that the priest was not within the fort. The College, the Hospital and Convents of the Portuguese Jesuit Missionaries of Jaffna were, according to Ribeiro, in the town, "outside the walls of the fort." The priest being an invalid must then have been an inmate of one of these institutions, most probably of the hospital. This accounts fully and clearly for the why and the wherefore of the necessity for the conspirators to have written to him the letter in question.

The reader would thus see that every writer who has written on this subject, has been giving out the story with his own additions and alterations, so that we have now a variety of versions of this silly story.

Mr. V. characterises the version of the story as given by Mr. Mootootamby Pillai in his "Jaffna History" as purely imaginative. But he shows a lamentable lack of judiciousness in quoting it "*in extenso*" after such condemnation.

Jaffna, 3rd Dec. 1920.

INDEX.

THE REFERENCES ARE TO NOTES.

A.

B.

C.

D.

E.

F.

G.

H.

I.

J.

K.

L.

M.

O.

P.

Q.

R.

S.

T.

U.

V.

W.

X.

Y.

Z.

The following contributions received towards the printing of this book are thankfully acknowledged:—

		Rs.	Cts.
Dr.	W. A. Chinniah	50	00
Mr.	L. P. Spencer, B. A.	20	00
"	A. B. Rajakarier, Town Udaiyar	10	00
"	D. A. Phillips	10	00
"	L. Muttukistna Pathther	25	00
"	J. A. J. Tisseverasinghe, Proctor	30	00
"	B. Joachimpillai, Notary Public	25	00
"	Joseph Machado, Merchant	25	00
"	P. Christopher, Proprietor, Premier Bakery	30	00
"	P. J. Rajah, Maniagar, Delft	50	00
"	Samuel F. Johnpulle, Chief Clerk, Loan Board	50	00
"	K. Kandaswamy, Retired Sergeant	5	00

	Rs.	Cts
Mrs. B. M. Selvatambo	150	00
Mr. V. Avurampillai	5	00
" M. J. Vytilingam	5	00
" John Edirveerasinghe, Post Master	10	00
J. G. Puvimanasinghe Mudlr.	10	00
Mr. H. Patrick, Minor Courts, Jaffna	5	00
" M. Jacob	10	00
" Philip Moses, J. P.	20	00